Economic, Educational, and Touristic Development in Asia

Bryan Christiansen
Global Training Group, Ltd, UK

Hakan Sezerel
Anadolu University, Turkey

A volume in the Advances in Hospitality, Tourism, and the Services Industry (AHTSI) Book Series

Published in the United States of America by
  IGI Global
  Business Science Reference (an imprint of IGI Global)
  701 E. Chocolate Avenue
  Hershey PA, USA 17033
  Tel: 717-533-8845
  Fax: 717-533-8661
  E-mail: cust@igi-global.com
  Web site: http://www.igi-global.com

Copyright © 2020 by IGI Global. All rights reserved. No part of this publication may be reproduced, stored or distributed in any form or by any means, electronic or mechanical, including photocopying, without written permission from the publisher.
Product or company names used in this set are for identification purposes only. Inclusion of the names of the products or companies does not indicate a claim of ownership by IGI Global of the trademark or registered trademark.

Library of Congress Cataloging-in-Publication Data

Names: Christiansen, Bryan, 1960- editor. | Sezerel, Hakan, 1981- editor.
Title: Economic, educational, and touristic development in Asia / Bryan
  Christiansen and Hakan Sezerel, editors.
Description: Hershey, PA : Business Science Reference, [2020] | Includes
  bibliographical references and index.
Identifiers: LCCN 2019037760 (print) | LCCN 2019037761 (ebook)
  | ISBN 9781799822394¬(hardcover) | ISBN 9781799831655¬(softcover)
  | ISBN 9781799822400¬(ebook)
Subjects: LCSH: Economic development--Asia, Central. | Tourism--Asia, Central.
Classification: LCC HC420.3 (ebook) | LCC HC420.3 .E2675 2020 (print) | DDC
  338.958--dc23
LC record available at https://lccn.loc.gov/2019037760

This book is published in the IGI Global book series Advances in Hospitality, Tourism, and the Services Industry (AHTSI) (ISSN: 2475-6547; eISSN: 2475-6555)

British Cataloguing in Publication Data
A Cataloguing in Publication record for this book is available from the British Library.

All work contributed to this book is new, previously-unpublished material.
The views expressed in this book are those of the authors, but not necessarily of the publisher.

For electronic access to this publication, please contact: eresources@igi-global.com.

Advances in Hospitality, Tourism, and the Services Industry (AHTSI) Book Series

ISSN:2475-6547
EISSN:2475-6555

Editor-in-Chief: Maximiliano Korstanje, University of Palermo, Argentina

MISSION

Globally, the hospitality, travel, tourism, and services industries generate a significant percentage of revenue and represent a large portion of the business world. Even in tough economic times, these industries thrive as individuals continue to spend on leisure and recreation activities as well as services.

The Advances in Hospitality, Tourism, and the Services Industry (AHTSI) book series offers diverse publications relating to the management, promotion, and profitability of the leisure, recreation, and services industries. Highlighting current research pertaining to various topics within the realm of hospitality, travel, tourism, and services management, the titles found within the AHTSI book series are pertinent to the research and professional needs of managers, business practitioners, researchers, and upper-level students studying in the field.

COVERAGE

- Hotel Management
- Leisure & Business Travel
- Service Management
- Travel Agency Management
- Food and Beverage Management
- Casino Management
- Customer Service Issues
- Tourism and the Environment
- Health and Wellness Tourism
- Destination Marketing and Management

IGI Global is currently accepting manuscripts for publication within this series. To submit a proposal for a volume in this series, please contact our Acquisition Editors at Acquisitions@igi-global.com or visit: http://www.igi-global.com/publish/.

The Advances in Hospitality, Tourism, and the Services Industry (AHTSI) Book Series (ISSN 2475-6547) is published by IGI Global, 701 E. Chocolate Avenue, Hershey, PA 17033-1240, USA, www.igi-global.com. This series is composed of titles available for purchase individually; each title is edited to be contextually exclusive from any other title within the series. For pricing and ordering information please visit http://www.igi-global.com/book-series/advances-hospitality-tourism-services-industry/121014. Postmaster: Send all address changes to above address. Copyright © 2020 IGI Global. All rights, including translation in other languages reserved by the publisher. No part of this series may be reproduced or used in any form or by any means – graphics, electronic, or mechanical, including photocopying, recording, taping, or information and retrieval systems – without written permission from the publisher, except for non commercial, educational use, including classroom teaching purposes. The views expressed in this series are those of the authors, but not necessarily of IGI Global.

Titles in this Series

For a list of additional titles in this series, please visit:
https://www.igi-global.com/book-series/advances-hospitality-tourism-services-industry/121014

Industrial and Managerial Solutions for Tourism Enterprises
Atilla Akbaba (Izmir Katip Çelebi University, Turkey) and Volkan Altıntaş (Izmir Katip Celebi University Turkey)
Business Science Reference • © 2020 • 300pp • H/C (ISBN: 9781799830306) • US $225.00

Handbook of Research on Smart Technology Applications in the Tourism Industry
Evrim Çeltek (Gaziosmanpasa University, Turkey)
Business Science Reference • © 2020 • 430pp • H/C (ISBN: 9781799819899) • US $295.00

Global Opportunities and Challenges for Rural and Mountain Tourism
Devkant Kala (University of Petroleum and Energy Studies, India) and Satish Chandra Bagri (Hemvati Nandan Bahuguna Garhwal University, India)
Business Science Reference • © 2020 • 354pp • H/C (ISBN: 9781799813026) • US $225.00

Organizational Behavior Challenges in the Tourism Industry
Şule Aydin (Nevsehir Haci Bektas Veli University, Turkey) Bekir Bora Dedeoglu (Nevsehir Haci Bektas Veli University, Turkey) and Ömer Çoban (Nevsehir Haci Bektas Veli University, Turkey)
Business Science Reference • © 2020 • 524pp • H/C (ISBN: 9781799814740) • US $225.00

Handbook of Research on Social Media Applications for the Tourism and Hospitality Sector
Célia M.Q. Ramos (University of Algarve, Portugal) Cláudia Ribeiro de Almeida (University of Algarve, Portugal) and Paula Odete Fernandes (Polytechnic Institute of Bragança, Portugal)
Business Science Reference • © 2020 • 477pp • H/C (ISBN: 9781799819479) • US $295.00

New Trends and Opportunities for Central and Eastern European Tourism
Puiu Nistoreanu (The Bucharest University of Economic Studies, Romania)
Business Science Reference • © 2020 • 338pp • H/C (ISBN: 9781799814238) • US $225.00

For an entire list of titles in this series, please visit:
https://www.igi-global.com/book-series/advances-hospitality-tourism-services-industry/121014

701 East Chocolate Avenue, Hershey, PA 17033, USA
Tel: 717-533-8845 x100 • Fax: 717-533-8661
E-Mail: cust@igi-global.com • www.igi-global.com

Editorial Advisory Board

Asmat Nizam Abdul Talib, *Universiti Ultara Malaysia, Malaysia*
Yakup Ari, *Yeditepe University, Turkey*
Neeta Baporikar, *Ministry of Higher Education, Oman*
Evangelina Cruz Barba, *University of Guadalajara, Mexico*
Rajat Deb, *Tripura University, India*
Onur Dirlik, *Osmangazi University, Turkey*
Michael Gardner, *Independent Researcher, Canada*
Gordana Pesakovic, *Argosy University, USA*
Duane Windsor, *Rice University, USA*

Table of Contents

Preface xii

Chapter 1
The Causality Relationship Between Natural Gas Consumption and
Economic Growth in Caucasus and Central Asian Economies With Natural
Gas Exporters 1
    Meryem Filiz Baştürk, Bursa Uludag University, Turkey

Chapter 2
Building a Diversified and Sustainable Economy in Kazakhstan: Towards the
Green Economy Through a Triple Helix Approach 18
    Cinzia Colapinto, Ca' Foscari University of Venice, Italy

Chapter 3
Corruption and Anti-Corruption Reform in Central Asia 39
    Duane Windsor, Rice University, USA

Chapter 4
The Impact of USD-TRY Forex Rate Volatility on Imports to Turkey from
Central Asia 70
    Yakup Ari, Alanya Alaaddin Keykubat University, Turkey

Chapter 5
Nation and Regional Branding of Central Asia: Kazakhstan, Kyrgyzstan, and
Uzbekistan 90
    *Gordana Pesakovic, Southern New Hampshire University, USA & OSCE
    Academy, Kyrgyzstan*

Chapter 6
Brand Consciousness and Brand Loyalty: A Study on Foreign Brand Beauty
and Skin Care Products 106
    Asmat Nizam Abdul-Talib, Universiti Utara Malaysia, Malaysia
    Nadia Japeri, Universiti Utara Malaysia, Malaysia

Chapter 7
The Context of the Tourism Market in Kazakhstan: State, Firms, Old and
New Practices 127
    Onur Dirlik, Eskişehir Osmangazi University, Turkey
    Janset Özen-Aytemur, Akdeniz University, Turkey
    Murat Atalay, Akdeniz University, Turkey

Chapter 8
A Temporal and Situational Approach in Tourism Education as a Mechanism
for Economic Growth and Development 151
    Evangelina Cruz Barba, University of Guadalajara, Mexico

Compilation of References 176

Related References 206

About the Contributors 237

Index 240

Detailed Table of Contents

Preface..xii

Chapter 1
The Causality Relationship Between Natural Gas Consumption and
Economic Growth in Caucasus and Central Asian Economies With Natural
Gas Exporters..1
Meryem Filiz Baştürk, Bursa Uludag University, Turkey

In this study, the causality relationship between natural gas consumption and economic
growth in the Caucasus and Central Asian economies (Azerbaijan, Kazakhstan,
Uzbekistan, and Turkmenistan) exporting natural gas was investigated using the
bootstrap panel Granger causality analysis developed by Kónya for the period
1993–2017. As a result of the analysis, a causality from natural gas consumption to
real GDP for Azerbaijan and a causality from real GDP to natural gas consumption in
Uzbekistan and Turkmenistan were found. For Kazakhstan, the authors concluded that
there was a bi-directional causality between natural gas consumption and real GDP.

Chapter 2
Building a Diversified and Sustainable Economy in Kazakhstan: Towards the
Green Economy Through a Triple Helix Approach...18
Cinzia Colapinto, Ca' Foscari University of Venice, Italy

Due to globalization, entrepreneurship has become fundamental for the competitiveness
of countries, and as shown by the Triple Helix Framework enterprises, universities
and governments must create synergies to their mutual advantage. In Kazakhstan,
a Post-Soviet transition economy, gross domestic product has doubled over the
past decade thanks to the extractive and heavy industries and on an intensive use
of electricity produced from coal. The authors present a goal programming model
for environmental policy analysis involving criteria such as economic development,
electricity consumption, greenhouse gas emissions, and the total number of employees
to determine the optimal labour allocation across different economic sectors. The
purpose is to provide empirical evidence and policy recommendations to decision

makers in developing the optimal strategy able to simultaneously satisfy energy demand, decrease GHG emissions, increase economic growth, and foster labour development by 2050. The analysis will allow to compare Kazakhstan with similar economies.

Chapter 3

Corruption and Anti-Corruption Reform in Central Asia 39
Duane Windsor, Rice University, USA

This chapter surveys information available in English from public sources concerning levels and composition of corruption in the five countries of Central Asia. Similarly, the chapter examines relevant information available in English from public sources concerning anti-corruption reform efforts in Central Asia. Focus is on the relationship between corruption and reform and economic, educational, and touristic development in the five countries. There is consideration of possible links to foreign direct investment and operations by multinational corporations. There is some comparison to neighboring countries. The chapter proceeds in the following phases. The first step is to assemble available information and studies concerning corruption and anti-corruption conditions in the five countries. The second step is to assess the determinants and consequences of both corruption and anti-corruption reform. The third step is to place information and assessment into regional context. The chapter provides a conceptual framework for interpreting detailed country information.

Chapter 4

The Impact of USD-TRY Forex Rate Volatility on Imports to Turkey from Central Asia 70
Yakup Ari, Alanya Alaaddin Keykubat University, Turkey

The purpose of this study is to put out the impact of volatility of the USD-TRY forex rate on imports to Turkey from Central Asia. The volatility of the USD/TRY exchange rate is analysed with a conditional variance model which is Generalised Autoregressive Conditional Heteroscedastic (GARCH) model and its extensions. The other section of the methodology is an application of Autoregressive Distributed Lag (ARDL) bounds test which is an efficient approach to determine the cointegration, long-term and short-term relations between macroeconomic variables. The exponential GARCH volatility of the exchange rate and the monthly trade data between the years 2005 and 2018 are used in the ARDL bounds test.

Chapter 5

Nation and Regional Branding of Central Asia: Kazakhstan, Kyrgyzstan, and Uzbekistan..90
Gordana Pesakovic, Southern New Hampshire University, USA & OSCE

Academy, Kyrgyzstan

Central Asia is defined by its history and geography, by its people and cultures, and by geopolitics and geo-economics. Therefore, analyzing a country in the region, past, present, and future should incorporate all these elements. The purpose of this chapter is to present the development of nation branding in three countries: Kazakhstan, Kyrgyzstan, and Uzbekistan. The chapter starts with the theory of nation branding. The particularity of the Central Asia as a region and three selected countries follow. Global ranking based on different indices is presented. In the fourth section, the nation branding of each country is addressed. The fifth section highlights lessons learned from the Borat case on nation branding in Kazakhstan but relevant for other countries in the region as well. The chapter ends with the section on branding the region as a whole.

Chapter 6
Brand Consciousness and Brand Loyalty: A Study on Foreign Brand Beauty and Skin Care Products 106
> *Asmat Nizam Abdul-Talib, Universiti Utara Malaysia, Malaysia*
> *Nadia Japeri, Universiti Utara Malaysia, Malaysia*

It is often argued that consumers become loyal to a particular brand based on their perception of the brand itself. This study investigates the relationship between brand consciousness and three key variables: perceived quality, emotional value, and brand involvement. It also examines the influence of these three variables on students' brand loyalty to foreign-brand beauty and skin care products. A total of 318 female students from a public university in Malaysia participated in the survey. Using multiple regression analysis, the study found that brand consciousness is positively related to perceived quality and emotional value, but not brand involvement. Perceived quality and emotional value positively influence loyalty toward foreign beauty and skin care products, while brand involvement negatively influences brand loyalty.

Chapter 7
The Context of the Tourism Market in Kazakhstan: State, Firms, Old and New Practices 127
> *Onur Dirlik, Eskişehir Osmangazi University, Turkey*
> *Janset Özen-Aytemur, Akdeniz University, Turkey*
> *Murat Atalay, Akdeniz University, Turkey*

This chapter is designed to reveal the development of the tourism sector in Kazakhstan as an example of the process of integrating Central Asia countries into the capitalist world economy at various levels in the post-Soviet period. The study aims to understand the effects of some contextual elements that affect the development process of the tourism sector in Kazakhstan. For this purpose, interviews were conducted with the managers of foreign tour operators operating in Kazakhstan. It is expected some context-based elements may be observed by the managers and to obtain some clues about the distinctive path of developing capitalist economy of the country. Following a brief literature review about the role of the state and tourism sector in Kazakhstan, the rest of the chapter includes the authors' findings on the characteristics of the institutional context of the tourism market in Kazakhstan.

Chapter 8
A Temporal and Situational Approach in Tourism Education as a Mechanism
for Economic Growth and Development 151
Evangelina Cruz Barba, University of Guadalajara, Mexico

The argument of this chapter is that tourism education can generate a positive impact on the economic growth of a country by fostering a link between education and work, including economic development. A review of the literature based on the use of bibliometric techniques is performed, but quantification of the work is not conducted; however, Web of Science and Scopus, among other databases, are consulted in relation to economic growth, economic development, human capital and tourism education. All this around the theoretical economic and sociological framework that sustains this work.

Compilation of References 176

Related References 206

About the Contributors 237

Index 240

Preface

The Asia region is currently the fastest growing in the world, and Central Asia in particular represents one of the unique regions of the world that remains relatively understudied in the extant literature. Therefore, the purpose of this book is to present some of the economic, educational, and touristic aspects of the region that are not normally covered in one volume.

Chapter 1 examines the causality relationship between natural gas consumption and economic growth in the Caucasus and Central Asian economies (Azerbaijan, Kazakhstan, Uzbekistan, and Turkmenistan) exporting natural gas was investigated using the bootstrap panel Granger causality analysis developed by Kónya for the period 1993 – 2017. As a result of the analysis, a causality from natural gas consumption to real GDP for Azerbaijan and a causality from real Gross Domestic Product (GDP) to natural gas consumption in Uzbekistan and Turkmenistan were found. For Kazakhstan, the author concluded there was a bi-directional causality between natural gas consumption and real GDP.

Chapter 2 provides empirical evidence and policy recommendations to decision makers in developing an optimal strategy able to simultaneously satisfy energy demand, decrease GHG emissions, increase economic growth, and foster labour development by 2050. The analysis will allow to compare Kazakhstan with similar economies. Due to globalization, entrepreneurship has become fundamental for the competitiveness of countries, and as shown by the Triple Helix Framework enterprises, universities and governments must create synergies to their mutual advantage. In Kazakhstan, a Post-Soviet transition economy, gross domestic product has doubled over the past decade, thanks to the extractive and heavy industries and on an intensive use of electricity produced from coal. The authors present a Goal Programming model for environmental policy analysis involving criteria such as economic development, electricity consumption, greenhouse gas emissions, and the total number of employees to determine the optimal labour allocation across different economic sectors.

Chapter 3 surveys information available in English from public sources concerning levels and composition of corruption in the five countries of Central

Preface

Asia. Similarly, the chapter examines relevant information available in English from public sources concerning anti-corruption reform efforts in Central Asia. Focus is on the relationship between corruption and reform and economic, educational, and touristic development in the five countries. There is consideration of possible links to foreign direct investment and operations by multinational corporations. There is some comparison to neighboring countries. Chapter development proceeds in the following phases. The first step is to assemble available information and studies concerning corruption and anti-corruption conditions in the five countries. The second step is to assess the determinants and consequences of both corruption and anti-corruption reform. The third step is to place information and assessment into regional context. The chapter provides a conceptual framework for interpreting detailed country information.

Chapter 4 highlights the impact of the exchange rate volatility on the international trade between Turkey and Central Asia countries. The volatility of the US Dollar / Turkish Lira (USD/TRY) exchange rate is analyzed with a conditional variance model that is Generalised Autoregressive Conditional Heteroscedastic (GARCH) model and its extensions. The other section of methodology is an application of Autoregressive Distributed Lag (ARDL) model which is an efficient model to determine the cointegration, long-term and short-term relations between macroeconomic variables. The monthly trade data period between the years 2005 and 2018 is used with the volatility in the ARDL approach.

Chapter 5 provides the development of nation branding in three countries: Kazakhstan, Kyrgyzstan, and Uzbekistan. The chapter starts with the theory of nation branding. The particularity of Central Asia as a region and three selected countries follow. Global ranking based on different indexes is presented. In the fourth section, the nation branding of each country is addressed. The fifth section highlights lessons learned from the Borat case on nation branding in Kazakhstan but relevant for other countries in the region as well. The chapter ends with the section on branding the region as a whole.

Chapter 6 investigates the relationship between brand consciousness and three key variables: perceived quality, emotional value, and brand involvement. It also examines the influence of these three variables on students' brand loyalty to foreign-brand beauty and skin care products. A total of 318 female students from a public university in Malaysia participated in the survey. Using multiple regression analysis, the study found that brand consciousness is positively related to perceived quality and emotional value, but not brand involvement. Perceived quality and emotional value positively influence loyalty toward foreign beauty and skin care products, while brand involvement negatively influences brand loyalty.

Chapter 7 reveals the development of the tourism sector in Kazakhstan as an example of the process of integrating Central Asia countries into the capitalist world economy at various levels in the post-Soviet period. The study aims to understand the effects of some contextual elements that affect the development process of the tourism sector in Kazakhstan. For this purpose, interviews were conducted with the managers of foreign tour operators operating in Kazakhstan. It is expected some context-based elements may be observed by the managers and to obtain some clues about the distinctive path of developing capitalist economy of the country. Following a brief literature review about the role of the state and tourism sector in Kazakhstan, the rest of the chapter includes the authors' findings on the characteristics of the institutional context of the tourism market in Kazakhstan.

Chapter 8 argues that tourism education can generate a positive impact on the economic growth of a country by fostering a link between education and work, including economic development. A review of the literature based on the use of bibliometric techniques is performed, quantification of the work is not conducted, but Web of Science and Scopus, among other databases, in relation to economic growth; economic development; human capital and tourism education. All this around the theoretical economic and sociological framework that sustains this work.

We trust the reader will find this work interesting and informative with lessons for other regions of the world beyond Asia. We are very thankful for the many hours chapter authors and editorial board members alike put into the development of this book.

Bryan Christiansen
Global Training Group, Ltd., UK

Hakan Sezerel
Anadolu University, Turkey

Chapter 1

The Causality Relationship Between Natural Gas Consumption and Economic Growth in Caucasus and Central Asian Economies With Natural Gas Exporters

Meryem Filiz Baştürk
Bursa Uludag University, Turkey

ABSTRACT

In this study, the causality relationship between natural gas consumption and economic growth in the Caucasus and Central Asian economies (Azerbaijan, Kazakhstan, Uzbekistan, and Turkmenistan) exporting natural gas was investigated using the bootstrap panel Granger causality analysis developed by Kónya for the period 1993–2017. As a result of the analysis, a causality from natural gas consumption to real GDP for Azerbaijan and a causality from real GDP to natural gas consumption in Uzbekistan and Turkmenistan were found. For Kazakhstan, the authors concluded that there was a bi-directional causality between natural gas consumption and real GDP.

DOI: 10.4018/978-1-7998-2239-4.ch001

Copyright © 2020, IGI Global. Copying or distributing in print or electronic forms without written permission of IGI Global is prohibited.

INTRODUCTION

Energy is important for economies because it has a huge share in achieving the sustainable growth targets of the economies. However, the environmental destruction caused by the solid/fossil fuels from sources such as oil and coal is at the top of the problems that the sustainability policies of economies have focused on in recent years. The climate change instigated by environmental destruction caused by the consumption of solid/fossil fuels has also brought up some precautions on a global scale. In this context, the Paris climate change agreement (COP21) was signed in December, 2015 (REN21, 2016: 110). The countries have now begun to turn to alternatives that are less harmful or harmless to the environment, instead of solid/fossil fuels such as oil and coal that damage the environment, in order to achieve their sustainable growth targets. In this sense, natural gas, which is less harmful to the environment than petroleum and coal, and renewable energy that does not damage the environment have become increasingly important for the economies.

In the literature, four hypothesis have been developed for explaining the relationship between energy consumption and economic growth. One of these is the *growth hypothesis*. In this hypothesis, there is causality from energy consumption towards economic growth. The second one is the *feedback hypothesis*. In this hypothesis, there is a bi-directional causality between economic growth and energy consumption. The third one is the *conservation hypothesis*, with which there is causality from economic growth towards energy consumption. The fourth one is the *neutrality hypothesis*. Here, there is no causality between energy consumption and economic growth (Ozturk, 2010: 340-341; Nazlioglu, et al. 2011: 6616).

The relationship between natural gas consumption and economic growth has not been studied in the relevant literature as much as the relationship between energy consumption and economic growth. Furthermore, no study was encountered in the relevant literature investigating the causality relationship between natural gas consumption and economic growth in the Caucasus and Central Asian economies exporting natural gas (Azerbaijan, Kazakhstan, Uzbekistan, and Turkmenistan).[1] In this context, the present study is believed to make a contribution to the relevant literature.

This study firstly emphasizes the role natural gas plays in the Caucasus and Central Asian economies (Azerbaijan, Kazakhstan, Uzbekistan, and Turkmenistan). Secondly, this study reviews the literature relevant to this topic. Thirdly, the data set are introduced. Fourthly, the methodology is emphasized, then the results of the study are included and a general evaluation is carried out.

THE RESERVES, PRODUCTION AND CONSUMPTION OF NATURAL GAS IN THE CAUCASUS AND CENTRAL ASIAN COUNTRIES EXPORTING NATURAL GAS

The Caucasus countries of Azerbaijan, Georgia, and Armenia and the Central Asian countries of Kazakhstan, Uzbekistan, Turkmenistan, Tajikistan, and Kyrgyzstan, are divided into two among themselves, with some countries exporting natural gas (Azerbaijan, Kazakhstan, Uzbekistan, and Turkmenistan) and some importing it (Armenia, Georgia, Tajikistan, and Kyrgyzstan). These economies achieved high growth rates in the period of 1996 – 2011. The oil and natural gas exporters achieved a growth of 7.7%, and the importers achieved 6.4%. However, the fact that the main determinant of growth is the energy sources, especially in the oil and gas exporting countries, makes the growth unstable due to fluctuations in the energy prices. The achievement of these economies to reach stable and sustainable growth rates depends on the structural reforms they will apply, strengthening and diversifying the production infrastructure (IMF, 2014: 2-5). In a sense, these economies need to change the growth model that has been effective up to the present time. Actually, the weakening observed in the growth of these economies due to external shocks, such as a fall in the commodity prices during the period of 2014 – 2016 and a decrease in the growth rates of their main trading partners (Russia and China), reveal this fact. In this context, finding new sources of growth is of great importance for these economies. The diversification of resources, increasing the foreign trade and investments, the elimination of obstacles blocking the private sector from funneling the oil and natural gas exports through different routes to Europe, and the private sector – based growth need to be supported (IMF, 2018: 1-32).

Even though these economies have adopted some policies, such as new fiscal frameworks, in order to strengthen their macroeconomic structures, the incomplete institutional and structural reforms remain the biggest obstacle for investments. Moreover, this situation eventually causes the growth rates of the countries to remain below their long-term growth potential. In fact, in 2018, the Caucasus and Central Asian countries (CCA countries) achieved a 4.2% stable growth rate. The oil and gas exporters grew by 4.1% (IMF, 2019: 2-5). Table_1 illustrates the real GDP growth rates of oil and gas exporting economies realized on the basis of countries during the years 2014 – 2018.

The countries of Azerbaijan, Kazakhstan, Uzbekistan, and Turkmenistan in the Caucasus and Central Asian economies are rich in oil and natural gas resources. However, it is not possible to say the same for the other two Central Asian countries (Kyrgyzstan and Tajikistan).[2] Considering the dependence of many countries on foreign sources, especially in terms of energy resources, the importance of the energy resources owned by Azerbaijan, Kazakhstan, Uzbekistan, and Turkmenistan

Table 1. Real GDP growth (percent)

Countries	2014	2015	2016	2017	2018
Azerbaijan	2.8	1.0	-3.1	0.1	1.4
Kazakhstan	4.2	1.2	1.1	4.1	4.1
Uzbekistan	8.0	7.8	9.0	8.9	5.0
Turkmenistan	10.3	6.4	6.2	6.5	6.2

Source: IMF DATA Access to Macroeonomic Financial Data

is increasing. Among these energy resources, natural gas plays as an important a role as oil in these economies. Especially with the natural gas reserves it owns, Turkmenistan is of increasing importance for the economies whose natural gas demand is constantly increasing (Yazar, 2011: 21 - 43). Moreover, natural gas in Turkmenistan is one of the main export items of the country (Syzdykova, 2018: 89).

Natural gas production, consumption, and export are still the dominant trigger of economic growth. Natural gas exports are seen as an important item in foreign trade revenue. On the other hand, the role of natural gas consumption as internal (endogenous) means should not be underestimated, in regards to strengthening the existing production potential. The policies that will activate the production resources of the mentioned country group will benefit from the potential that the natural gas reserve will provide. Therefore, it becomes all the more important to determine the growth potential that natural gas consumption will create for the countries in this group.

Table_2 illustrates the proven natural gas reserves, natural gas production, and natural gas consumption of Azerbaijan, Kazakhstan, Uzbekistan, and Turkmenistan as of the end of 2018. It is seen that Turkmenistan ranks first in terms of proven natural gas reserves. Azerbaijan, Uzbekistan, and Kazakhstan follow Turkmenistan. When the natural gas production data are analyzed, Turkmenistan ranks first again. Uzbekistan, Kazakhstan, and Azerbaijan come after Turkmenistan in natural gas production. In addition, Uzbekistan ranks first in natural gas consumption. Uzbekistan is followed by Turkmenistan, Kazakhstan, and Azerbaijan.

Table_3 illustrates the share of natural gas in primary energy consumption in Azerbaijan, Kazakhstan, Uzbekistan, and Turkmenistan. The share of natural gas in primary energy consumption is 83.3% in Uzbekistan, 77.4% in Turkmenistan, 64.5% in Azerbaijan, and 21.8% in Kazakhstan. These shares clearly demonstrate the role that natural gas plays for these economies.

Table 2. Natural gas reserve status, natural gas production, and natural gas consumption as of the end of 2018

Countries	Proven Natural Gas Reserves (Trillion m^3)	Natural Gas Production (Million tonnes oil equivalent)	Natural Gas Consumption (Million tonnes oil equivalent)
Azerbaijan	2,1	16,1	9,3
Kazakhstan	1,0	21,0	16,7
Uzbekistan	1,2	48,7	36,6
Turkmenistan	19,5	52,9	24,4

Source: BP Statistical Review of World Energy, 2019

Table 3. The share of natural gas in primary energy consumption as of 2018

Countries	The Share of Natural Gas in Primary Energy Consumption (%)
Azerbaijan	% 64,5
Kazakhstan	% 21,8
Uzbekistan	%83,3
Turkmenistan	%77,4

Source: BP Statistical Review of World Energy, 2019

LITERATURE REVIEW

In the literature, the studies examining the relationship between natural gas consumption and economic growth have assessed this relationship either on the basis of a group of countries, or in the context of a single country, or considering natural gas consumption as well as oil and coal consumption. It is difficult to say that the studies have been clearly conclusive. That the countries, periods and the methods used which have been examined are different. Furthermore, the fact that the number of studies examining the relationship between natural gas consumption and economic growth is not high makes it difficult to reach a general conclusion. In this study, firstly the studies that examine the country groups were emphasized, and then the studies explaining the individual country examples were revealed.[3] Finally, the studies handling the relationship between oil and coal consumption with economic growth, besides the natural gas consumption, were discussed.

Solarin and Ozturk (2016) analyzed the causality relationship between natural gas consumption and economic growth. Twelve OPEC countries between 1980 and 2012 were examined. A bi-directional relationship was found between natural gas consumption and real GDP per capita for the panel. In the study, findings supporting all of the four hypotheses that are valid in the energy literature (feedback hypothesis, growth hypothesis, conservation hypothesis, and neutrality hypothesis) were reached. In the countries examined in this context, a bi-directional relationship was encountered for Ecuador, and a uni-directional causality relationship from natural gas consumption to economic growth was encountered in Libya, Iraq, Nigeria, Kuwait, and Saudi Arabia. A causality relationship was encountered from real GDP to natural gas consumption in the United Arab Emirates, Venezuela, Algeria, and Iran.

No causality was found in Qatar and Angola. Furuoka (2016) analyzed the same relationship for Japan and China in the 1980 – 2012 period. For China, a uni-directional causality from natural gas consumption to economic growth was found; for Japan, a bi-directional causality relationship was found between the two variables. The study was also extended in such a way to cover Bangladesh, India, South Korea, Malaysia, Thailand, Pakistan, and Singapore. According to the results of the extended analysis, in Japan, India, and Pakistan, the feedback hypothesis is valid. In South Korea, the neutrality hypothesis is valid. In China and Thailand the growth hypothesis is valid. In Bangladesh and Singapore, the conservation hypothesis is valid. In a study conducted by Apergis and Payne (2010) natural gas consumption and economic growth relationship for 67 countries was investigated during the period of 1992 – 2005. A bi-directional causality relationship between natural gas consumption and economic growth in both the short and long run was found. They emphasized that this result supports the feedback hypothesis. Kum et al. (2012) analyzed the causality relationship between natural gas consumption and economic growth for G-7 countries.

In the study where the period of 1970 – 2008 was examined, it was stated that for Japan and Canada, the neutrality hypothesis is valid. There is a bi-directional causality for Germany, France, and the U.S., and the feedback hypothesis is valid. In England, the conservation hypothesis is valid. For Italy, the growth hypothesis is valid. Chang et al. (2016) also investigated the same relationship in G-7 countries; however, unlike the study of Kum et al. (2012) the 1965 – 2011 period was examined. No causality between natural gas consumption and economic growth was found for the panel. When the country results were examined, results different from those of the study conducted by Kum et al. (2012) were found. Only for England was a causality relationship from real GDP to natural gas consumption found; no causality between the two variables was encountered in the other countries. In this context, it was stated that the neutrality hypothesis is valid for both the panel and the countries where a causality relationship does not exist. Uzgören and Aslan (2019) analyzed natural gas consumption and economic growth relationship in the eight MENA countries (Turkey, Pakistan, Iran, Egypt, Algeria, Israel, UAE, and Saudi Arabia). In the study, covering the 1989 – 2014 period, it was stated that there is a co-integration relationship between natural gas consumption and economic growth. Furthemore, according to the causality results for the panel, a finding was encountered that a bi-directional relationship exists between the variables.

Lim and Yoo (2012) carried out a study during the period of 1991 – 2008 for Korea, and they found short- and long- run causality relationships between natural gas consumption and economic growth. In the short run, causality from natural gas to real GDP was found; in the long run, bi-directional causality was found between them. Işik (2010) analyzed the impact of natural gas consumption on economic growth in Turkey for the 1977 – 2008 period, and a long-run relationship between the two variables was found. Heidari et al. (2013) explored the 1972 – 2007 period for Iran. A bi-directional relationship was found between the variables in both the short and long run. Das et al. (2013) analyzed the causality relationship within economic growth and natural gas consumption for the period of 1980 – 2010 in Bangladesh, and a uni-directional causality from real GDP to natural gas consumption was reached. The study emphasized that the conservation hypothesis is valid in Bangladesh.

Payne (2011) addresses, in addition to natural gas consumption, the relationship between oil and coal consumption and economic growth for the U.S. He analyzed the period 1949 – 2006, and a uni-directional causality relationship from real GDP to natural gas consumption and a uni-directional causality relationship from oil consumption to real GDP was found. He stated that there is no causality relationship between coal consumption and real GDP. Bildirici and Bakirtas (2014) analyzed the causality relationship between natural gas, coal, and oil, and economic growth, for the BRICTS countries. The study covered the period of 1980 – 2011. However, natural gas consumption and economic growth data in Turkey only included the period of 1987 – 2011. Long-term causality results reveal that there is a bi-directional relationship between natural gas consumption and economic growth in Turkey, Brazil, and Russia; a bi-directional relationship between oil consumption and economic growth for all countries; and a bi-directional relationship between coal consumption and economic growth in China and India. Zamani (2007) carried out a study on the causality relationship between different energy types and economic growth in Iran for the 1967 – 2003 period. In the long run, a bi-directional causality relationship was found between natural gas consumption and economic growth, and between oil consumption and economic growth.

DATA SET

In this study, the causality relationship between natural gas consumption and economic growth was examined in the Caucasus and Central Asian economies (Azerbaijan, Kazakhstan, Uzbekistan, and Turkmenistan)[4] exporting natural gas for the period 1993 – 2017 using annual data. The variables that were used in this study, their

Table 4. The variables used in the analysis and their sources.

Variable	Definition	Source
Natural gas consumption (million tones oil equivalent)	lnNGC	BP Statistical Review of World Energy- all data, 1965 – 2018
Real GDP (Millions of 2011 U.S. Dollars)	lnGDP	FRED (Federal Reserve Bank St. Louis Economic Research)
Population		FRED (Federal Reserve Bank St. Louis Economic Research)

abbreviations, and their sources are shown in Table_4. The natural gas consumption per capita and real GDP per capita variables were obtained by dividing the natural gas consumption and real GDP variables by the population variable. The natural logarithm of both variables was used in the analysis.

METHODOLOGY

Two factors should be taken into consideration when examining the causality relationship between variables in the panel data. The first is whether or not there is a cross-sectional dependency. Because a shock that can happen in one of the countries within the panel can affect others, due to factors such as globalization and international trade (Menyah et al., 2014: 389; Nazlioglu et al., 2011: 6618). The second one is to consider heterogeneity within the predicted parameters (Kar et al., 2011: 688).

Cross-Sectional Dependence

One of the tests developed to test the cross-sectional dependence is the LM test developed by Breusch and Pagan (1980). Here, the H_0 hypothesis, stating that there is no cross-section dependency, is tested against the H_1 hypothesis, stating that there is cross-section dependency.

$$H_0 = \text{Cov}(\varepsilon_{it}\varepsilon_{jt}) = 0 \text{ for all t and i } ^1 \text{ j;}$$

$$H_1 = \text{Cov}(\varepsilon_{it}\varepsilon_{jt}) ^1 0 \text{ for all least one pair of i } ^1 \text{ j.}$$

The LM test that is valid in the cases where N is quite small and T is large enough is calculated as follows.

The Causality Relationship Between Natural Gas Consumption and Economic Growth

$$LM = T \sum_{i=1}^{N-1} \sum_{j=i+1}^{N} \hat{\rho}_{ij}^2$$

However, Pesaran (2004) stated that in cases where N is large enough, the LM test is not applicable, and other approaches should be considered. In this context, the CD_{lm} test was developed by Pesaran (2004), which is a scaled version of the LM test. This test is valid for N> T. CD_{lm} is calculated as follows.

$$CD_{lm} = \sqrt{\frac{1}{N(N-1)}} \sum_{i=1}^{N-1} \sum_{j=i+1}^{N} \left(T\hat{\rho}_{ij}^2 - 1 \right)$$

However, this test can cause size distortions in cases where N is large and T is small. In this context, the CD test was developed by Pesaran (2004), which is valid for T ® ¥, N ® ¥ cases.

$$CD = \sqrt{\frac{2T}{N(N-1)}} \left(\sum_{i=1}^{N-1} \sum_{j=i+1}^{N} \hat{\rho}_{ij} \right)$$

The LM_{adj}, which is the bias-adjusted version of the LM test developed by Pesaran et al. (2008), is calculated as follows.

$$LM_{adj} = \sqrt{\frac{2}{N(N-1)}} \sum_{i=1}^{N-1} \sum_{j=i+1}^{N} \frac{(T-k)\hat{\rho}_{ij}^2 - \mu_{Tij}}{v_{Tij}}$$

Slope Homogeneity Tests

The delta ($\tilde{\Delta}$) test developed by Pesaran and Yamagata (2008) was used to test the homogeneity. Here, the H_0 slope homogeneity hypothesis is tested against the alternative H_1 slope heterogeneity hypothesis.

$H_0 = \beta_i = \beta$ for all i;

$H_1 = \beta_i{}^1\beta_j$ for a non-zero fraction of pair-wise slopes for i ¹ j.

The homogeneity test developed by Swamy (1970) was enhanced for the panels where N is relatively small compared to T, like the F test. The F test and its extended version of the Swamy test is valid for the cases where N is small and T is large. The standardized version of the Swamy test has been developed for the large panels by Pesaran and Yamagata (2008).

Panel Causality Test

In this study, a bootstrap panel causality test developed by Kónya (2006) was used. This approach has two advantages. Firstly, it does not assume that the panel is homogeneous. Secondly, there is no need to investigate the relationship between the unit root and co-integration in this approach (Kónya, 2006: 990-91). According to Kónya (2006), the two equations can be expressed as follows.

$$y_{1,t} = \alpha_{1,1} + \sum_{l=1}^{mly_1} \beta_{1,1,l} y_{1,t-1} + \sum_{l=1}^{mlx_1} \gamma_{1,1,l} x_{1,t-1} + \varepsilon_{1,1,t}$$

$$y_{2,t} = \alpha_{1,2} + \sum_{l=1}^{mly_1} \beta_{1,2,l} y_{2,t-1} + \sum_{l=1}^{mlx_1} \gamma_{1,2,l} x_{2,t-1} + \varepsilon_{1,2,t} \tag{1}$$

$$y_{N,t} = \alpha_{1,N} + \sum_{l=1}^{mly_1} \beta_{1,N,l} y_{N,t-1} + \sum_{l=1}^{mlx_1} \gamma_{1,N,l} x_{N,t-1} + \varepsilon_{1,N,t}$$

and

$$x_{1,t} = \alpha_{2,1} + \sum_{l=1}^{mly_2} \beta_{2,1,l} y_{1,t-1} + \sum_{l=1}^{mlx_2} \gamma_{2,1,l} x_{1,t-1} + \varepsilon_{2,1,t}$$

$$x_{2,t} = \alpha_{2,2} + \sum_{l=1}^{mly_2} \beta_{2,2,l} y_{2,t-1} + \sum_{l=1}^{mlx_2} \gamma_{2,2,l} x_{2,t-1} + \varepsilon_{2,2,t} \tag{2}$$

$$x_{N,t} = \alpha_{2,N} + \sum_{l=1}^{mly_2} \beta_{2,N,l} y_{N,t-1} + \sum_{l=1}^{mlx_2} \gamma_{2,N,l} x_{N,t-1} + \varepsilon_{2,N,t}$$

First of all, these two equations are dependent on the SUR system. Secondly, there is no need for the variables to be stationary. The country-specific bootstrap critical values are used here. According to this SUR system, there are four cases. First of all, if all $\gamma_{1,i}$ in equation 1 are not equal to zero and all $\beta_{2,i}$ in equation 2

The Causality Relationship Between Natural Gas Consumption and Economic Growth

are equal to zero, there is causality from X to Y. Secondly, if all $\gamma_{1,i}$ in equation 1 are equal to zero and all $\beta_{2,i}$ in equation 2 are not equal to zero, there is causality from Y to X. Thirdly, if both all $\gamma_{1,i}$ and all $\beta_{2,i}$ are not equal to zero, there is a bi-directional causality between X and Y. Fourthly, if all $\gamma_{1,i}$ and all $\beta_{2,i}$ are equal to zero, there is no causality between X and Y (Kónya, 2006: 981).

EMPIRICAL FINDINGS

LM, CD_{lm}, CD, and LM_{asj} tests were applied in order to test the cross-sectional dependence. When the results of each test in Table_5 are examined, it is seen that the H_0 hypothesis, which states that there is no cross-section dependence, is rejected at a 1% significance level and there is a cross-section dependency among the variables.

When the homogeneity test results are examined in Table_5, it is also seen that the H_0 hypothesis, which states that the variables are homogeneous, is rejected at a 1% significance level, and the variables are heterogeneous.

According to the bootstrap panel causality test developed by Kónya (2006), there is a causality from natural gas consumption to real GDP in Azerbaijan, and the growth hypothesis is valid. In this case, an increase in natural gas consumption for Azerbaijan raises the real GDP. A similar result was found in the study conducted by Solarin and Ozturk (2016), for Libya, Iraq, Nigeria, Kuwait, and Saudi Arabia, in the 12 OPEC countries. In the study conducted by Furuoka (2016), a uni-directional causality from natural gas consumption to economic growth was found in China. Kum et al. (2012) was found for Italy the mentioned relationship.

Table 5. Cross-sectional dependence and homogenous tests results

	lnGDP	*lnNGC*
Cross-sectional dependence		
LM	19.876***	22.577***
CDlm	4.006***	4.785***
CD	-3.099***	-3.150***
LM_{adj}	8.947***	8.434***
Homogeneity		
$\tilde{\Delta}$	3.116***	2.847***
$\tilde{\Delta}_{adj}$	3.322***	3.035***

Note: *** indicates significance at the 1% level, respectively

In Uzbekistan and Turkmenistan, there is a causality from real GDP to natural gas consumption, and the conservation hypothesis is valid. This result was encountered for the United Arab Emirates, Venezuela, Algeria, and Iran in the study conducted by Solarin and Ozturk (2016). Kum et al. (2012) encountered the conservation hypothesis for England. In the study conducted by Chang et al. (2016), the G-7 countries were also examined and a causality relationship from real GDP to natural gas consumption was observed only for England. In the study conducted by Das et al. (2013), it was emphasized that the conservation hypothesis is valid in Bangladesh. Payne (2011) found a uni-directional causality from real GDP to natural gas consumption for the U.S.

For Kazakhstan, on the other hand, there is a causality both from natural gas consumption to real GDP, and from real GDP to natural gas consumption. The feedback hypothesis is valid here. A similar result was found for Ecuador by Solarin and Ozturk (2016). In a study conducted by Furuoka (2016), a bi-directional causality relationship was found for Japan. Kum et al. (2012), found a bi-directional causality relationship for Germany, France, and the U.S. In a study by Bildirici and Bakirtas (2014), conducted for the BRICTS countries, a bi-directional causality relationship was found between the economic growth and the consumption of natural gas in Turkey, Brazil, and Russia in the long term. Also, in the study conducted by Zamani (2007) in Iran, a bi-directional causality relationship was found between natural gas consumption and economic growth in the long term.

CONCLUSION

In this study, the causality relationship between natural gas consumption and economic growth in Azerbaijan, Kazakhstan, Uzbekistan, and Turkmenistan, which are included in the Caucasus and Central Asian economies, was examined. The reason for preferring these economies is that they are rich in oil and gas resources compared to the other Caucasus and Central Asian economies. Because of the fact that many countries are dependent on foreign sources in terms of energy resources, the importance of energy resources of these economies is increasing. Natural gas plays as important of a role as oil among these energy resources. The effect of natural gas reserves on growth can be considered to have effects in two directions. First of all, the natural gas and the derivative products have a significant share in the export of this mentioned country group. Therefore, it contributes to the formation of the current balance as well as acquisition of trade income.

Secondly, the rich reserves are a factor facilitating, especially, the increase of industrial production levels of these countries. The fact that industrial production units do not need to import extra energy for their energy needs creates effects

The Causality Relationship Between Natural Gas Consumption and Economic Growth

Table 6. Panel Granger causality test results

		Bootstrap critical values		
Ho: Natural gas consumption does not cause GDP				
Country	**Wald Stat**	**%1**	**%5**	**%10**
Azerbaijan	3.096***	2.032	1.030	0.715
Kazakhstan	21.503***	3.281	2.096	1.605
Uzbekistan	0.518	1.847	1.182	0.893
Turkmenistan	0.254	3.340	2.027	1.499

Note: ***, ** indicates significance at the 1%, 5% level, respectively. The critical values were obtained with 10,000 bootstraps.

Table 7. Panel Granger causality test results

		Bootstrap critical values		
Ho: GDP does not cause natural gas consumption				
Country	**Wald Stat**	**%1**	**%5**	**%10**
Azerbaijan	4.501	14.263	7.453	5.259
Kazakhstan	12.511**	16.189	8.731	6.097
Uzbekistan	10.009**	14.717	8.586	6.175
Turkmenistan	23.642***	13.764	8.077	5.784

Note: ***, ** indicates significance at the 1%, 5% level, respectively. The critical values were obtained with 10,000 bootstraps.

towards increasing investment and productivity rates. Among the previous studies, no research was encountered that examines the mentioned relationship in the context of this country group. On the other hand, the studies are mainly based on the comparison of different country groups, individual country examples, and on the investigation of the relationship between different energy types and economic growth. In the literature, it is difficult to say that there has been a conclusive result in the studies examining the mentioned relationship. Findings supporting all of the four hypothesis (growth hypothesis; conservation hypothesis; feedback hypothesis; neutrality hypothesis) that are valid in the energy literature have been encountered. However, in this study, findings supporting the other hypothesis except the neutrality hypothesis, were obtained.

The results found through this study used the bootstrap panel causality test developed by Kónya (2006). The results showed a causality for Azerbaijan from natural gas consumption to real GDP; for Uzbekistan and Turkmenistan, there was a causality from real GDP to natural gas consumption; for Kazakhstan, on the other hand, there was a causality both from natural gas consumption to real GDP; and from real GDP to natural gas consumption. According to these results, the growth hypothesis in Azerbaijan, the conservation hypothesis in Uzbekistan and Turkmenistan, and the feedback hypothesis in Kazakhstan are valid. When all of the results obtained in this context are evaluated, it can be stated that the implementation of a policy of reducing natural gas consumption for Azerbaijan and Kazakhstan will adversely affect economic growth.

REFERENCES

Apergis, N., & Payne, J. E. (2010). Natural gas consumption and economic growth : A panel investigation of 67 countries. *Applied Energy*, *87*(8), 2759–2763. doi:10.1016/j.apenergy.2010.01.002

Bildirici, M. E., & Bakirtas, T. (2014). The relationship among oil, natural gas and coal consumption and economic growth in BRICTS (Brazil, Russian, India, China, Turkey and South Africa) countries. *Energy*, *65*, 134–144. doi:10.1016/j.energy.2013.12.006

Bildirici, M. E., & Kayıkçı, F. (2013). Effects of oil production on economic growth in Eurasian Countries: Panel ARDL Approach. *Energy*, *49*, 156–161. doi:10.1016/j.energy.2012.10.047

BP. (2019). *Statistical Review of World Energy*. Author.

Breusch, T. S., & Pagan, A. R. (1980). The lagrange multipler test and its applications to model specification in econometrics. *The Review of Economic Studies*, *47*(1), 239–253. doi:10.2307/2297111

Chang, T., Gupta, R., Inglesi-Lotz, R., Masabala, L. S., Simo-Kengne, B. D., & Weideman, J. P. (2016). The causal relationship between natural gas consumption and economic growth : Evidence from the G7 countries. *Applied Economics Letters*, *23*(1), 38–46. doi:10.1080/13504851.2015.1047085

Das, A., McFarlane, A. A., & Chowdhury, M. (2013). The dynamics of natural gas consumption and GDP in Bangladesh. *Renewable & Sustainable Energy Reviews*, *22*, 269–274. doi:10.1016/j.rser.2013.01.053

Furuoka, F. (2016). Natural gas consumption and economic development in China and Japan : An empirical examination of the Asian context. *Renewable & Sustainable Energy Reviews*, *56*, 100–115. doi:10.1016/j.rser.2015.11.038

Heidari, H., Katircioglu, S. T., & Saeidpour, L. (2013). Natural gas consumption and economic growth : Are we ready to natural gas price liberalization in Iran? *Energy Policy, 63,* 638–645. doi:10.1016/j.enpol.2013.09.001

International Monetary Fund (IMF). (2014). The Caucasus and Central Asia: Transitioning to Emerging Markets. Washington, DC: IMF.

International Monetary Fund (IMF). (2018). Opening Up in the Caucasus and Central Asia: Policy Frameworks to Support Regional and Global Integration. IMF Departmental Paper, 18/07. Washington, DC: IMF.

International Monetary Fund (IMF). (2019). *Regional Economic Outlook Update Caucasus and Central Asia.* Washington, DC: IMF.

Işik, C. (2010). Natural gas consumption and economic growth in Turkey : A bound test approach. *Energy Syst, 1*(4), 441–456. doi:10.100712667-010-0018-1

Kar, M., Nazlıoğlu, Ş., & Ağır, H. (2011). Financial development and economic growth nexus in the MENA countries : Bootstrap panel granger causality analysis. *Economic Modelling, 28*(1-2), 685–693. doi:10.1016/j.econmod.2010.05.015

Koç, S., & Saidmurodov, S. (2018). Orta Asya Ülkelerinde elektrik enerjisi, doğrudan yabancı yatırımı ve ekonomik büyüme ilişkisi. *Ege Akademik Bakış, 18*(2), 321–328.

Kónya, L. (2006). Exports and growth: Granger causality analysis on OECD countries with a panel data approach. *Economic Modelling, 23*(6), 978–992. doi:10.1016/j.econmod.2006.04.008

Kum, H., Ocal, O., & Aslan, A. (2012). The relationship among natural gas energy consumption, capital and economic growth : Bootstrap-corrected causality tests from G-7 countries. *Renewable & Sustainable Energy Reviews, 16*(5), 2361–2365. doi:10.1016/j.rser.2012.01.041

Lim, H., & Yoo, S. (2012). Natural gas consumption and economic growth in Korea : A causality analysis. *Energy Sources. Part B, Economics, Planning, and Policy, 7*(2), 169–176. doi:10.1080/15567240902882864

Menyah, K., Nazlioglu, S., & Wolde-Rufael, Y. (2014). Financial development, trade openness and economic growth in African countries : New insights from a panel causality approach. *Economic Modelling, 37,* 386–394. doi:10.1016/j.econmod.2013.11.044

Nazlioglu, S., Lebe, F., & Kayhan, S. (2011). Nuclear energy consumption and economic growth in OECD countries: Cross-sectionally dependent heterogeneous panel causality analysis. *Energy Policy*, *39*(10), 6615–6621. doi:10.1016/j.enpol.2011.08.007

Ozturk, I. (2010). A literature survey on energy-growth nexus. *Energy Policy*, *38*(1), 340–349. doi:10.1016/j.enpol.2009.09.024

Payne, J. E. (2011). US disaggregate fossil fuel consumption and Real GDP : An Empirical Note. *Energy Sources. Part B, Economics, Planning, and Policy*, *6*(1), 63–68. doi:10.1080/15567240902839278

Pesaran, M. H. (2004). *General diagnostic tests for cross section dependence in panels*. CESifo Working Paper Series, No. 1229; IZA Discussion Paper No. 1240. Available at SSRN: https://ssrn.com/abstract=572504

Pesaran, M. H., Ullah, A., & Yamagata, T. (2008). A bias-adjusted LM test of error cross-section independence. *The Econometrics Journal*, *11*(1), 105–127. doi:10.1111/j.1368-423X.2007.00227.x

Pesaran, M. H., & Yamagata, T. (2008). Testing slope homogeneity in large panels. *Journal of Econometrics*, *142*(1), 50–93. doi:10.1016/j.jeconom.2007.05.010

REN-21. (2016). *Renewables – Global Status Report: 2016*. Retrieved on June 4, 2017, from: http://www.ren21.net/wp-content/uploads/2016/05/GSR_2016_Full_Report_lowres.pdf

Solarin, A. S., & Ozturk, I. (2016). The relationship between natural gas consumption and economic growth in OPEC members. *Renewable & Sustainable Energy Reviews*, *58*, 1348–1356. doi:10.1016/j.rser.2015.12.278

Swamy, P. A. V. B. (1970). Efficient inference in a random coefficient regression model. *Econometrica*, *38*(2), 311–323. doi:10.2307/1913012

Syzdykova, A. (2018). Orta Asya Ülkelerinde enerji tüketimi ve ekonomik büyüme ilişkisi: Panel veri analizi. *AKÜ İktisadi ve İdari Bilimler Fakültesi Dergisi*, *20*(1), 87–99. doi:10.5578/jeas.67162

Uzgören, E., & Aslan, V. (2019). Seçili MENA Ülkelerinde doğalgaz tüketimi ile iktisadi büyüme arasındaki ilişki. *Dumlupınar Üniversitesi Sosyal Bilimler Dergisi*, *59*, 13–20.

Yazar, Y. (2011). *Enerji İlişkileri Bağlamında Türkiye ve Orta Asya Ülkeleri*. Ahmet Yesevi Üniversitesi. Retrieved on April 15, 2019, from: http://www.ayu.edu.tr/static/kitaplar/enerji_raporu.pdf

Zamani, M. (2007). Energy consumption and economic activities in Iran. *Energy Economics*, *29*(6), 1135–1140. doi:10.1016/j.eneco.2006.04.008

KEY TERMS AND DEFINITIONS

Caucasus Economies: The Caucasus economies consisting of Azerbaijan, Georgia, and Armenia.

Central Asian Countries: The Central Asian countries consisting of Kazakhstan, Uzbekistan, Turkmenistan, Tajikistan, and Kyrgyzstan.

Climate Change: This refers to environmental destruction caused by solid/fossil fuel waste.

Economic Growth: Economic growth refers to an increase in real GDP.

Natural Gas Exporters: The countries in the Caucasus and Central Asian that have natural gas reserves and export natural gas, which include Azerbaijan, Kazakhstan, Uzbekistan, and Turkmenistan.

Natural Gas Importers: The countries in the Caucasus and Central Asian that import natural gas, which include Armenia, Georgia, Tajikistan, and Kyrgyzstan.

Paris Climate Change Agreement (COP21): An agreement that the signatory countries would decrease the global temperature below 2 degrees Celcius.

ENDNOTES

[1]   In the study carried out by Syzdykova (2018), the relationship between energy consumption and economic growth in Central Asian countries has been analyzed. The relationship between oil production and economic growth in Azerbaijan, Kazakhstan, Turkmenistan, and Russia has been analyzed by Bildici and Kayıkçı (2013).

[2]   Kyrgyzstan and Tajikistan have hydroelectric reserves. Tajikistan ranks first in hydroelectric reserves (Koc and Saidmurodov, 2018).

[3]   A similar classification was made by Solarin and Ozturk (2016) as well. Moreover, country groups-single country examples were also made by Ozturk (2010) in his study examining the energy consumption-economic growth literature. However, in this study, different from the studies of Solarin and Ozturk (2016) and Ozturk (2010), a triple categorization was made.

[4]   The reason that the other Central Asian countries (Kyrgyzstan and Tajikistan) have not been included in the analysis is that they do not have sufficient natural gas reserves.

Chapter 2

Building a Diversified and Sustainable Economy in Kazakhstan:
Towards the Green Economy Through a Triple Helix Approach

Cinzia Colapinto

iD https://orcid.org/0000-0003-1211-8033
Ca' Foscari University of Venice, Italy

ABSTRACT

Due to globalization, entrepreneurship has become fundamental for the competitiveness of countries, and as shown by the Triple Helix Framework enterprises, universities and governments must create synergies to their mutual advantage. In Kazakhstan, a Post-Soviet transition economy, gross domestic product has doubled over the past decade thanks to the extractive and heavy industries and on an intensive use of electricity produced from coal. The authors present a goal programming model for environmental policy analysis involving criteria such as economic development, electricity consumption, greenhouse gas emissions, and the total number of employees to determine the optimal labour allocation across different economic sectors. The purpose is to provide empirical evidence and policy recommendations to decision makers in developing the optimal strategy able to simultaneously satisfy energy demand, decrease GHG emissions, increase economic growth, and foster labour development by 2050. The analysis will allow to compare Kazakhstan with similar economies.

DOI: 10.4018/978-1-7998-2239-4.ch002

Copyright © 2020, IGI Global. Copying or distributing in print or electronic forms without written permission of IGI Global is prohibited.

INTRODUCTION

Due to globalization, entrepreneurship has become fundamental for the economic growth of territories and countries, and for policy management. In order to support the local economy, interactions and alliances with universities and governments is a must to emerge. As shown by the Triple Helix Framework (Etzkowitz & Leydesdorff, 2000) and its variants, enterprises, universities and governments have to create synergies and spill-overs to their mutual advantage. In Kazakhstan, a Post-Soviet transition economy, the stimulation of private-sector entrepreneurship has been a key public policy objective for at least a decade. The country's gross domestic product (GDP) has doubled over the past decade; however, much of this growth has depended on the extractive and heavy industries and on an intensive use of electricity produced from coal (IEA, 2016).

Kazakh energy intensity has not improved and the country is still one of the most energy-intensive countries in the world. The environmental damage and high pollution pose serious challenges to the policy-makers. The steps towards a more sustainable model of development are presented in two main documents: The 2012 "Kazakhstan 2050 strategy" and the 2013 "Green economy concept" (GEC). The 2012 "Kazakhstan 2050 strategy" aims at developing a sustainable growth in the long-run in Kazakhstan. This strategy relies on the use of electricity generated by renewable and alternative sources to create the "Green Economy", decreasing greenhouse gas emissions. This process will concern the development of agricultural and waste management sectors along with the economic growth of Kazakhstan. The GEC outlines the path to ensure long-term growth based on climate-friendly technologies, energy efficiency measures, and a wise management of natural resources.

In the last decade, researchers (e.g., André, 2009; San Cristóbal, 2012) have focused on the development of adequate quantitative models for environmental policy analysis, to understand the effects of environmental policies and the roles of all different players/actors. This chapter presents a Goal Programming (GP) model involving criteria such as economic development (GDP), electricity consumption, greenhouse gas emissions, and the total number of employees to determine the optimal labour allocation across different economic sectors. The purpose is to provide empirical evidence and policy recommendations to decision makers in developing the optimal strategy that will allow to simultaneously satisfy energy demand, decrease greenhouse gas emissions, increase economic growth, and foster labour development by 2050. The analysis will allow to compare Kazakhstan with similar economies, i.e. the United Arab Emirates.

This chapter is structured as follows. In the next paragraph we better explain the multi-criteria nature of a sustainable growth and present a literature review of previous works dealing with long-run sustainable growth in different countries or regions. Then we present a literature review about the Goal Programming approach, thus the reader can better understand our model. We describe how the data has been collected, and the following section illustrates the results. After discussing about possible future research directions, in the concluding paragraph we illustrate policy implications.

BACKGROUND: MOVING TOWARDS GREEN ECONOMY: A MULTI-CRITERIA CHALLENGE

Since Schumpeter's (1943) seminal contribution, researchers have found that entrepreneurship is associated with varying levels of economic development (Carree, Van Stel, Thurik, & Wennekers, 2007; Wennekers, Van Wennekers, Thurik, & Reynolds, 2005), economic growth (Audretsch, Keilbach, & Lehmann, 2006; Carree & Thurik, 2003; Koellinger & Roy Thurik, 2012) and national economic competitiveness (Porter, 1990). The economic growth model developed by Schumpeter argues competition through innovation and the importance of education in ensuring economic growth, these assumptions are also supported by empirical studies (Aghion et al., 2005). Given the positive link between entrepreneurship and national economic outcomes, policymakers in the last two decades have prioritized supporting business start-ups as a means to generate innovation, employment and transform their economies and fostering collaborations between different actors (Audretsch et al., 2006, pp. 1 - 11; Shane, 2009).

Three decades later, Meadows et al. (1972) looked at the interactions between the earth and human systems taking into account five variables, namely population, food production, industrialization, pollution, and consumption of non-renewable natural resources. The authors explored the system's behavioral tendencies and presented three possible scenarios: two scenarios saw "overshoot and collapse" of the global system by the mid/latter-part of the 21st century, while a third one resulted in a "stabilized world". What is relevant to the current discussion is the interplay between different spheres and the attention to the consequences of the interactions between economic policy goals and decisions.

Nordhaus has included the environmental and climatic variable in growth models and has shown that growth prospects can be very different from those designed by traditional economics when we consider this variable. Indeed, Nordhaus (1991) pointed out the relation between environment and economic growth maintaining that the reduction of emissions would ensure greater economic growth in the long term. His economic growth model (the so-called DICE model) firstly took into account both the benefits and the consequences of greenhouse emissions, as well as the costs of their reduction. According to Nordhaus (2008) the benefits of climate policy are

Building a Diversified and Sustainable Economy in Kazakhstan

the damages avoided, but there are also costs. The less warming a country wants to accept, the higher these costs will be. This explains why the cost-benefit analysis has come to dominate a large part of climate politics.

This chapter joins the discussion that has populated the last two decades. Indeed, a key topic for the academic community has been modelling relationships between environmental sustainability, economic growth, and human welfare. As policymakers have to reconcile economic, social, and environmental objectives, tackling varied and often competing objectives, many researchers have relied on multi-criteria decision analysis (MCDA) as a quantitative methodology based on available technical information to balance stakeholders' values and promote solutions able to foster environmental sustainability.

If we borrow theories and frameworks from the innovation management field literature, it is well known that nowadays innovation benefits from evolving and overlapping relationships between different players. Indeed, the (second) academic revolution has transformed the traditional Teaching and Research University into an Entrepreneurial University, adding a third mission for economic and social development. A major catalyst for the entrepreneurial model has been the emergence and development of an interdependent relationship between science, industrial innovation and government policy (Etkzowitz et al., 2000). This approach can be found in the so-called Triple Helix model (THM), a development strategy based on collaborations among university, industry and government, where the university has the leading role in innovation. The trilateral interactions described by the THM are taking their role in the technological universities since the 1950s in the western world, but nowadays the change is relevant in many other fields, and globally.

Moving away from the isolation, universities cannot rely anymore on the mere possession of potentially valuable knowledge assets, they have to foster knowledge transfer in the current competitive scenario. Industry is continuously evolving, reflecting changes in society, and the relationship between university, industry, and government grows stronger, shifting the focus on technology transfer processes from university to industry, at local, regional and national levels. Etzkowitz and Zhou (2006) has extended the model talking about twins concepts: the Triple Helix of innovation (University – Industry – Government) and the Triple Helix of sustainability (University – Public - Government). The latter serves as a balance wheel to insure that innovation and growth take place in ways that will not be harmful to the environment and health. The shift towards a sustainable growth is evident.

It is clear that in such a complex scenario, it is crucial for decision makers to consider several aspects when taking decisions about investments. Previous works suggested that policy makers can use various sustainability assessment methods and multi-dimensional frameworks based on the interactions and trade-offs between economic, energy, and environmental indicators (the so-called E3). Moreover,

21

energy economics researchers have been studying the relationships between energy consumption, economic growth and the environment, with inconsistent or conflicting results. For instance, if we focus on MCDA applications, the paper by Oliveir and Antunes (2010) assesses the trade-offs between maximizing of GDP and employment levels, and minimizing of energy imports and environmental impact. Henriques and Antunes (2012) use a multi-objective linear programming model based on input-output analysis to discuss the influence of the measures adopted by the Portuguese government on economic growth, social wellbeing, and energy consumption, and their impact on the environment.

San Cristóbal (2012) develops a GP model based on an environmental/input-output linear programming model, and applies it to the Spanish economy. Jayaraman et al. (2015) propose a weighted GP model that integrates efficient resource allocation to achieve simultaneously sustainability related goals for GDP growth, electricity consumption, and GHG emissions in the United Arab Emirates. Expanding the scope of their research, Jayaraman et al. (2017a) develop a weighted GP model for sustainability planning for Gulf Cooperation Countries. These authors (2017b) study a fuzzy GP (FGP) application for efficient resource allocation to achieve sustainability related goals and (2017c) present a scenario based stochastic GP model for sustainability planning. They apply both fuzzy and stochastic variants of the models to the United Arab Emirates.

More recently, Tan et al. (2017) point out that fuzzy logic theory has been widely used for sustainability assessment. They introduce the adaptive neuro-fuzzy inference system (ANFIS) approach for country level sustainability assessment. These membership functions and fuzzy rules are generated from 128 training samples. Of the three different types of non-linear membership functions employed, they maintain that the Gaussian membership function is the best for country sustainability assessment. As policies often rely on imprecise information on data and goals, fuzzy goal programming modelling is a relevant choice to evaluate multi-criteria sustainability. This technique is suitable for the analysis of the Europe 2020 strategy plan dealing with several possibly conflicting objectives in economy, environment, energy and employment. Vié et al. (2019) present a FGP model for sustainable implementations for all European Union (EU) countries with respect to Europe 2020 policy goals and provide insights for decision makers to better satisfy conflicting criteria by suggesting optimal allocations of workers in several economic sectors.

GOAL PROGRAMMING: A BRIEF LITERATURE REVIEW

As previously mentioned, MCDA usually deals with decision-making with multiple and conflictual criteria, objectives or attributes, and considers decision makers' preferences to determine the best compromise among optimal solutions. The Goal Programming (GP) model is a well-known aggregating methodology for solving multi-objective programming decision aid processes. GP model takes into account simultaneously several conflicting objectives and its solution represents the best compromise that can be made by the decision maker (DM). The GP model is indeed based on a satisfying philosophy, and is a distance function where the deviation, between the achievement and aspiration levels, is to be minimized. Indeed, both positive and negative deviations are unwanted by DMs. The first formulation of a GP model was presented by Charnes et al. (1955), Charnes and Cooper (1952, 1959, 1961). GP model is widely applied in several fields such as: accounting and financial aspect of stock management, marketing, quality control, human resources, production and operations management (Romero, 1991).

Goal programming models are quite popular due to their simplicity, tractability, and diversity of applications. Moreover, the GP formulation can be solved through some powerful mathematical programming software such as Lindo and CPLEX. The central idea of the GP method is to determine the aspiration levels of an objective function and minimize any (positive or negative) deviations from these levels. When the decision maker strives to optimize simultaneously "p" different conflicting criteria F_i, $i \in I = \{1, 2, ..., p\}$, the GP model enables to obtain the best achievable compromise by the DM. The DM's preferences can be represented assigning weights and calculate the sum of the deviation variables multiplied by their individual weights, as in the Weighted GP (WGP). Given a set of n linear criteria

$$F_i\left(X_1, X_2, ..., X_n\right) = \sum_{j=1}^{n} A_{ij} X_i \text{ . and a set of goals } G_i \text{ the WGP model reads as:}$$

$$\min_{X_j, D_i^+, D_i^-} \sum_{i=1}^{p} \alpha_i^+ D_i^+ + \alpha_i^- D_i^- \text{ .}$$

Subject to:

$$D_i^-, D_i^+ \geq 0, i = 1...p \text{ .}$$

where Ω is a feasible set, and are weights associated with positive and negative deviations (D_i^+ and D_i^-) of each goal, X_j are the input variables, the coefficient A_{ij} states the contribution of the jth variable to the achievement of the ith criterion, and D_i^- and D_i^+ are the positive and negative deviations with respect to the aspirational goal levels G_i, $i = 1...n$, respectively.

The Model

Previous researchers (e.g., Andre' et al., 2009; San Cristóbal, 2012; Jayaraman et al., 2017a, 2017b) have shown how the government can determine its optimal policy according to different criteria using the GP approach. Considering the "Kazakhstan 2050" objectives established by the Kazakh Government in 2012, we formulate a macroeconomic model that simultaneously considers the following four criteria with their respective units:

a) F_1 is the economic output (in million US$)
b) F_2 is the GHG emissions (in Gg of CO_2 equivalent kilo tonnes)
c) F_3 is the electric consumption (in thousand tonnes of oil equivalent)
d) F_4 is the number of employees (in thousands)

The output variables (F_1, F_2, F_3 and F_4) aim to represent economic, social, environmental, and energy characteristics of the Kazakh economy. The decision variables (X_1, ..., X_6) in the GP model are related to all relevant economic sectors (https://stat.gov.kz/) and they represent the amount of skilled labour employed in each sector (they are equivalent to the main activities identified by NACE Rev. 2 classification):

- **X_1**: Agriculture, Forestry, and Fisheries
- X_2: Industry
- **X_3**: Construction
- **X_4**: Trade, Transportation
- **X_5**: Manufacturing, Mining, Oil
- **X_6**: General services: Education, Health, Social Services

Such a classification is complete, aiming to describe efficiently whole economic patterns. Our choice of categories is restricted either to specific global categories, such as agriculture combined with fishing and forestry, either to an aggregate category as general services, which includes both education, health and social services.

Each criterion F_i is linear with respect to the decision variable X_j and takes the form:

$$F_1(X_1, X_2, ..., X_6) = A_{11}X_1 + A_{12}X_2 + ... + A_{16}X_6$$

$$F_2(X_1, X_2, ..., X_6) = A_{21}X_1 + A_{22}X_2 + ... + A_{26}X_6$$

$$F_3(X_1, X_2, ..., X_6) = A_{31}X_1 + A_{32}X_2 + ... + A_{36}X_6$$

Building a Diversified and Sustainable Economy in Kazakhstan

$$F_4(X_1, X_2, ..., X_6) = A_{41}X_1 + A_{42}X_2 + ... + A_{46}X_6$$

The GP problem we intend to solve can then be written in the following form:

$$\min_{X_j, D_i^-, D_i^+} (\alpha_1^+ D_1^+ + \alpha_1^- D_1^-) + (\alpha_2^+ D_2^+ + \alpha_2^- D_2^-) + (\alpha_3^+ D_3^+ + \alpha_3^- D_3^-) + (\alpha_4^+ D_4^+ + \alpha_4^- D_4^-).$$

Subject to:

$$A_{11}X_1 + A_{12}X_2 + ... + A_{16}X_6 - D_1^+ + D_1^- = G_1$$

$$. A_{21}X_1 + A_{22}X_2 + ... + A_{26}X_6 - D_2^+ + D_2^- = G_2.$$

$$A_{31}X_1 + A_{32}X_2 + ... + A_{36}X_6 - D_3^+ + D_3^- = G_3.$$

$$X_1 + X_2 + ... + X_7 - D_4^+ + D_4^- = G_4.$$

$$X_1 \geq \Omega_1, X_2 \geq \Omega_2, X_3 \geq \Omega_3, X_4 \geq \Omega_4, X_5 \geq \Omega_5, X_6 \geq \Omega_6.$$

$$X_j, j = 1, 2, ... 6 \text{ are positive and integer}.$$

$$D_i^+, D_i^- \geq 0, i = 1, 2, 3, 4$$

The variables D_i^+, D_i^- describe the positive and the negative deviations. The input variables X_j take integer values and must be at least equal to the positive number Ω_j which is the number of current employees in each sector of our analysis. A_{1j} is the economic output per capita (worker) for the jth economic sector. A_{2j} describes the GHG emission per capita (worker) for the jth economic sector. A_{3j} models the energy consumption per capita (worker) for the jth economic sector.

The above formulation takes the form of a Mixed Integer Linear Programming (MILP) model. We have implemented it using LINGO and assumed equal weights normalized to one for each objective. Our choice is motivated by the fact that the Kazakh agenda does not provide any priority or ranking among the objectives and all of them must be jointly met. However, these weights might be modified at the regional level when the national preferences and the local economic situation of each regions have to be taken into account.

25

THE CASE OF KAZAKHSTAN

After the dissolution of the Soviet Union in the eve of the 1990s, Kazakhstan had to cope with the resulting power vacuum and the difficult transition from a centrally planned state economy towards free market structures. However, Kazakhstan's vast hydrocarbon and mineral reserves (i.e., in the Caspian Basin) formed the backbone of its economy. Indeed, it is the world's largest producer of uranium and also has a large agricultural sector (i.e. livestock and grain). Unfortunately, Kazakhstan's economic expansion since 2000 relied on high rates of energy use and generated significant pollution. Kazakh poor environmental performance is also in part a consequence of outdated infrastructure, technologies, standards, and practices inherited from the Soviet past. Even if Kazakhstan is one of the most energy-intensive economies in the world, it has committed to national and international action to achieve ambitious environmental targets on a path to sustainable growth and diversified economy.

On one hand, these ambitious goals have been requiring an enormous investment in education. In the last decade many Small- and Medium-sized Enterprises (SMEs) and entrepreneurship development programmes has been established but with limited impact on skills development and innovation (OECD, 2018). Indeed skills and education levels remain weak and inadequately educated workforce is a main obstacle in the business environment. Moreover, employers in Kazakhstan rarely invest in the training of their employees: in 2013, only 28.3% of firms offered formal training to their employees, compared with an OECD average of 44.6% and the average for Eastern Europe and Central Asian countries of 32.8% (World Bank Enterprise Survey).

The demand of skilled labour has been partly fulfilled by the Nazarbayev university project and entrepreneurial skills trainings for small and medium sized enterprises (SMEs) as part of its Business Roadmap 2020 programme (Government of Kazakhstan, 2016). Since 2011, in collaboration with Duke University Corporate Education and the Nazarbayev University Graduate School of Business (NUGSB), the government of Kazakhstan, represented by Committee of Entrepreneurship Development of the Ministry of Regional Development and the Kazakhstan Entrepreneurship Development Fund (DAMU), has sponsored entrepreneurship workshops for entrepreneurs across the country: more than 2,900 participants from all industries have been trained at the SME Top Management Training programme in the last nine years. Since 2015 in partnership with the government, the World Bank developed a $137 million Skills and Jobs Project to improve employment outcomes and skills by providing relevant workforce training to the unemployed, self-employed, and employed (World Bank, 2015).

On the other hand, sustainability focuses on the energy sector per se. As said above, "Kazakhstan 2050" is a strategy developed on the sustainability and the long-run growth of Kazakh economy. One of the aims of this strategy is to use electricity generated by renewable and alternative sources to create the "Green Economy", and respectively to decrease greenhouse gas emissions. It also concentrates on the development of agricultural and waste management sectors, as well as on the total economic growth of Kazakhstan.

In this chapter, we use Weighted Goal Programming model involving criteria such as economic development (GDP), the electricity consumption, the greenhouse gas emissions, and the total number of employees to determine the optimal labour allocation across different economic sectors. The purpose of this chapter is to give the concept and empirical evidence to decision makers and specialists in developing the optimal strategy that will allow to simultaneously reach the goals of the strategy "Kazakhstan 2050" in terms of satisfying energy demand, decreasing greenhouse gas emissions, economic growth, and labour development by 2050.

In Table 1, the third column lists the economic output per capita (reference year 2014) for each economic sector. In a similar way the fourth, fifth and sixth columns, describe the electricity consumption per capita (in GWh, reference year 2014), the GHG emissions per capita (kt of CO2 equivalent. reference year 2012) and the number of employees (reference year 2014) per economic sector, respectively.

We collected the data presented in table 1 from different sources. The economic output per capita A_{1i}, expressed in thousands of US\$ per capita, for a given sector i is obtained from the Ministry of National Economy of the Republic of Kazakhstan Statistics committee[4]. The GHG emission per capita A_{2i} is expressed in tonnes of CO_2 equivalent per capita, for a given sector i.[5] The energy consumption per capita A_{i3} is expressed in tonnes of oil equivalent per capita, for a given sector i looking

Table 1. Output per capita (per worker) for each economic sector

Variables	Sector	GDP per capita (only work force)	Electricity consumption per capita[1]	GHG emissions per capita[2]	Amount of work force[3] (thousands)
X_1	Agriculture, Fishing, Forestry	4,280	0.00023	0.0268	1,605
X_2	Industry	40,020	0.0208	0.0161	1,090
X_3	Construction	15,480	0.0221	0.0546	1,650
X_4	Trade	20,170	0.0070	0.0066	1,833
X_5	Manufacturing, Mining, Oil,	49,130	0.0139	0.0431	879
X_6	Education, Health, Social Services	28,000	0.005	0.0155	1,948

Source GDP per capita (reference year 2014), electricity consumption per capita (in GWh, reference year 2014), GHG emissions per capita (Kt of CO2 equivalent. reference year 2012) and the number of employees (reference year 2014) per economic sector.

at the data from the International Energy Agency[6]. The employment constraint is simple and refer to the desired employment level[7].

The four goals, namely the economic output, the GHG emissions level, the electric consumption and the number of employees (see table 2) are forecasted according to actual Kazakh trends and the directions indicated by of the national strategic planning.

We run the selected model using Lingo 14®

```
MIN = D11+D21+D22+D31+D32+D41+D42;
4.28*X1 + 40.02*X2+ 15.48*X3+20.17*X4+49.13*X5+28*X6 +D11 =
1346820000;
1000*(0.00023*X1+0.0208*X2+ 0.0221*X3+0.007*X4+0.0139*X5 +
0.005*X6) + D21 - D22 = 151000000;
1000*(0.0268*X1+0.0161*X2+0.0546*X3+0.0066*X4+0.0431*X5+0.0155
*X6) + D33 - D32 = 190000000;
X1 + X2 + X3 + X4 + X5 + X6 + D41 = 22447000;
X1>=1605000;
X2>=1090000;
X3>=1650000;
X4>=1833300;
X5>=879000;
X6>=1948000;
END
```

We assumed that the need for skilled labour is satisfied, without differentiating if the labour is formed internally or externally (imported knowledge). Moreover, in the recent years many relevant investments have been done as international scholarship

Table 2. Goals to be achieved in 2050, in Kazakhstan

Goals	Criteria	Year 2050 goals values [5]
G_1	GDP	1,346,820,000,000 US dollars
G_2	Electricity consumption	151,000 GWh
G_3	GHG emissions	190,000 Kt (75% of 252400 Kt in 1992)
G_4	Labour	22,447,000

Source: http://scholar.dickinson.edu/cgi/viewcontent.cgi?article=1194&context=student_honors, http://www.nationalbank.kz/cont/publish488539_24140.pdf

Building a Diversified and Sustainable Economy in Kazakhstan

Table 3. Results of our GP model

Global optimal solution found.		
Objective value	0.1019396E+10	
Infeasibilities	0.000000	
Total solver iterations:	3	
Elapsed runtime seconds:	0.11	
Model Class: LP		
Total variables: 14		
Nonlinear variables: 0		
Integer variables: 0		
Total constraints: 11		
Nonlinear constraints: 0		
Total nonzeros: 43		
Nonlinear nonzeros: 0		
Variable	**Value**	**Reduced Cost**
D11	0.7597123E+09	0.000000
D21	0.000000	2.000000
D22	0.1050585E+08	0.000000
D31	0.000000	1.000000
D32	0.2491780E+09	0. 000000
D41	0.000000	8.500000
D42	0.000000	1.000000
X_1	1605000.	0.000000
X_2	1090000.	0.000000
X_3	1650000.	0.000000
X_4	1833300.	0.000000
X_5	879000.0	0.000000
X_6	0.1538970E+08	0.000000
D_{33}	0.000000	1.000000
Row	**Slack or Surplus**	**Dual Price**
1	0.1019396E+10	-1.000000
2	0.000000	-1.000000
3	0.000000	1.000000
4	0.000000	1.000000
5	0.000000	7.500000
6	0.000000	-30.25000
7	0.000000	-4.380000
8	0.000000	-68.72000
9 -	0.000000	-0.9300000
10	0.000000	-15.37000
11	0.1344170E+08	0.000000

or the settlement of Nazarbayev University whose mission implies to educate and stimulate the other local universities as well.

The above Figure 1 shows the associated sensitivity analysis and the ranges in which the solutions remain optimal. All scenarios out of these ranges imply a rerun of the model.

FUTURE RESEARCH DIRECTIONS

In Kazakhstan, there are a lot of constraining factors for the development of a Triple helix model. We can refer to institutional and social factors and think about the culture of business, unfair competition, low trust of economic agents, still limited development of chambers of commerce, and industrial associations. This open innovation model is realized in a limited scale, and to expand it is necessary to focus not only on science but also on industry which should play the central role in the innovation process.

We have discussed how the Triple Helix model has been extended and enriched to better fit more and more complex scenarios. In the last decade, the THM model has been developed and extended to further depict the more and more complex innovation and economic growth patterns. Financing is one of the main assets of the innovation process. Some technology clusters (e.g. Silicon Valley and Route 128 in the U.S. and Waterloo Region in Canada) have shown the role of Venture Capital (VC) companies (Colapinto, 2007). VC represents an alternative to raising funds via public equity or debt markets, especially if uncertainty or simply a long time horizon associated with the investment deter debt providers from funding these endeavours.

Moving forward from the THM, a "Quadruple Helix" model involves different actors such as financing organizations (Carayannis and Campbell, 2006; Colapinto and Porlezza, 2012). In this setting innovation is sustained by free interaction of information, human resources, financial capital and institutions. The Quintuple Helix model describes the necessary socio-ecological transition of society and economy in the twenty-first century and, therefore, it is ecologically sensitive. As highlighted by Carayannis and others (2012), it cannot be denied that nowadays the natural environments of society and the economy are seen as drivers for knowledge production and innovation and they define opportunities for the knowledge economy.

The Quintuple Helix approach combines knowledge, know-how, and the natural-environment-system together into one 'interdisciplinary' and 'transdisciplinary' framework. It provides a "step-by-step model to comprehend the quality-based management of effective development, recover a balance with nature, and allow future generations a life of plurality and diversity on earth" (Carayannis et al.,

Building a Diversified and Sustainable Economy in Kazakhstan

Figure 1. Sensitivity analysis

Ranges in which the basis is unchanged:
Objective Coefficient Ranges:

Variable	Current Coefficient	Allowable Increase	Allowable Decrease
D11	1.000000	0.3643927	0.1187739
D21	1.000000	INFINITY	2.000000
D22	1.000000	1.700000	0.2772152
D31	1.000000	INFINITY	1.000000
D32	1.000000	0.1044944	0.5568841
D41	1.000000	INFINITY	8.500000
D42	1.000000	INFINITY	1.000000
X1	0.000000	INFINITY	30.25000
X2	0.000000	INFINITY	4.380000
X3	0.000000	INFINITY	68.72000
X4	0.000000	INFINITY	0.9300000
X5	0.000000	INFINITY	15.37000
X6	0.000000	0.9300000	INFINITY
D33	0.000000	INFINITY	1.000000

Righthand Side Ranges:

Row	Current RHS	Allowable Increase	Allowable Decrease
2	0.1346820E+10	INFINITY	0.7597123E+09
3	0.1510000E+09	0.1050585E+08	INFINITY
4	0.1900000E+09	0.2491780E+09	INFINITY
5	0.2244700E+08	0.2713258E+08	2101170.
6	1605000.	2202484.	1605000.
7	1090000.	0.1344170E+08	664927.2
8	1650000.	0.1344170E+08	614377.2
9	1833300.	0.1344170E+08	1833300.
10	879000.0	0.1344170E+08	879000.0
11	1948000.	0.1344170E+08	INFINITY

2012: 1). All these variants could be studied and empirically tested in the context of emerging economies, such as Kazakhstan.

CONCLUSIONS, ENTREPRENEURIAL AND POLICY IMPLICATIONS

Kazakhstan has already undertaken actions to move towards a more sustainable development growth and a diversified economy as shown in the 2010s strategic documents. However, their implementation faces serious challenges. We imposed a null deviation of D_4 implies that the requirement of skilled workforce is matched. From the results of the WGP model shown in Table (3) the following conclusions can be made: A positive D11 means that the country cannot achieve the economic goal that appears to be very unrealistic; a positive deviation of $D2_2$ means that the electricity consumption is supposed to rise further; a positive deviation of $D2_3$ means that GHG emissions in Kazakhstan are expected to grow beyond the current trends;. To sum up, Kazakhstan should invest more in developing sustainable energy sources to face the current electricity consumption demand and reduce the GHG emission in the future.

Reading these results through the theoretical THM (and relative extensions) framework, allows us to observe that all actors have to participate and to point out the strategical role of the industry and *education system*. Indeed, the 'higher education systems' have to form the necessary human capital, such as students, teachers, scientists/researchers, and academic entrepreneurs, by diffusion and research of knowledge. We have reported that a series of 'green-oriented' trainings for top managers and governmental officials have being set since 2015 in preparation for Expo-2017. The change in the mindset and the new sustainable approach are crucial for achieving the desired goals, and they rely on the capacity of strengthening the science–policy–industry interface to effectively co-create knowledge and solutions for sustainability.

What is evident is that the 'triple helix' is a relevant model for sustainability that pose the conditions for knowledge co-creation and effective *university*–government/*policy–industry* collaboration. This observation is in line with the findings by Saad et al. (2008), who pointed out that the policy shift in developing countries (such as Malaysia and Algeria), which gives gradually to universities the role of being the sustainable basis for innovation and technological progress, is critical. They sustain that universities in developing countries should act as agents of innovation and sustainable development.

Drawing a comparison with similar contexts such as the United Arab Emirates and Saudi Arabia, all countries have to promote renewable energies and technology

Building a Diversified and Sustainable Economy in Kazakhstan

clusters to pursue a long-term economic diversification strategy. We should mention Astana Expo in 2017 as an attempt to cultivate an "environmentally progressive image" as Reiche (2010) suggested for the United Arab Emirates. In details, Jayaraman et al. (2015, 2017a) show that the UAE will struggle to achieve the goal for electricity consumption, whilst Saudi Arabia will not achieve the GHG emission goal.

In the comparison, we can argue that Kazakh goals appear to be too ambitious and require intensive investments in many directions: to achieve a more sustainable development path, Kazakhstan has to pursue strategic energy options beyond hydrocarbons by refocusing its investments on: energy efficiency, conservation and incrementing the share of renewable, non-emitting sources of energy production in order to achieve sustainable; and pollution abatement activities financing technology progress, innovation, and acquisition of skilled labour. According to the "Kazakhstan 2050" vision (2012), Kazakhstan aims to generate up to 50 per cent of the entire consumed energy by using alternative energy sources. Our results are in line with the findings in the OECD report Building Inclusive Labour Markets in Kazakhstan (OECD, 2017) that point out investing in skills and human capital is crucial to tackle Kazakhstan's strong dependence on natural resources and embark on a path of economic diversification. All actors have to align and equip the workforce with the right types of skills able to help the country adapt to the megatrends (globalisation, technological progress and sustainability).

REFERENCES

Aghion, P., Bloom, N., Blundell, R., Griffith, R., & Howitt, P. (2005). Competion and innovation: An inverted U relationship. *The Quarterly Journal of Economics*, *120*(2), 701–728.

André, F. J., Cardenete, M. A., & Romero, C. (2009). A goal programming approach for a joint design of macroeconomic and environmental policies: A methodological proposal and an application to the Spanish economy. *Environmental Management*, *43*(5), 888–898. doi:10.100700267-009-9276-x PMID:19224273

Audretsch, D. B., Keilbach, M. C., & Lehmann, E. E. (2006). *Entrepreneurship and economic growth*. New York: Oxford University Press. doi:10.1093/acprof:o so/9780195183511.001.0001

Carayannis, E. G., Barth, T. D., & Campbell, D. F. J. (2012). The Quintuple Helix innovation model: Global warming as a challenge and driver for innovation. *Journal of Innovation and Entrepreneurship*, *1*, 1–12. doi:10.1186/2192-5372-1-1

Carayannis, E. G., & Campbell, D. F. (2006). *Knowledge creation, diffusion, and use in innovation networks and knowledge clusters. A comparative systems approach across the United States, Europe, and Asia.* London: Praeger.

Carree, M. A., & Thurik, A. R. (2003). The impact of entrepreneurship on economic growth. In J. Acs & D. B. Audretsch (Eds.), *Handbook of entrepreneurship research* (pp. 437–471). Boston: Kluwer Academic.

Carree, M. A., Van Stel, A., Thurik, R., & Wennekers, S. (2007). The relationship between economic development and business ownership revisited. *Entrepreneurship and Regional Development, 19*(3), 281–291. doi:10.1080/08985620701296318

Charnes, A., & Cooper, W. W. (1952). Chance constraints and normal deviates. *Journal of the American Statistical Association, 57*(297), 134–148. doi:10.1080/0 1621459.1962.10482155

Charnes, A., & Cooper, W. W. (1959). Chance-constrained programming. *Management Science, 6*(1), 73–80. doi:10.1287/mnsc.6.1.73

Charnes, A., & Cooper, W. W. (1961). *Management models and industrial applications of linear programming.* New York: Wiley.

Charnes, A., Cooper, W. W., & Ferguson, R. (1955). Optimal estimation of executive compensation by linear programming. *Management Science, 1*(2), 138–151. doi:10.1287/mnsc.1.2.138

Colapinto, C. (2007). A way to foster innovation: A venture capital district from Silicon Valley and route 128 to Waterloo Region. *International Review of Economics, 54*(3), 319–343. doi:10.100712232-007-0018-1

Colapinto, C., & Porlezza, C. (2012). Innovation in creative industries: From the quadruple-helix model to the systems theory. *Journal of the Knowledge Economy, 3*(4), 343–353. doi:10.100713132-011-0051-x

Etkzowitz, H., Webster, A., Gebhardt, C., & Cantisano Terra, B. R. (2000). The future of the university and the university of the future: Evolution of ivory tower to entrepreneurial paradigm. *Research Policy, 29*(2), 313–331. doi:10.1016/S0048-7333(99)00069-4

Etzkowitz, H., & Leydesdorff, L. (2000). The Dynamics of Innovation: From National Systems and 'Mode 2' to a Triple Helix of University-Industry-Government Relations. *Research Policy, 29*(2), 109–123. doi:10.1016/S0048-7333(99)00055-4

Etzkowitz, H., & Zhou, C. (2006). Triple Helix twins: Innovation and sustainability. *Science & Public Policy, 33*(1), 77–83.

Government of Kazakhstan. (2016). *About Joint Business support and development Program "Business Roadmap - 2020"*. Retrieved on June 2, 2017, from: http://egov.kz/cms/en/articles/road_business_map

Henriques, C. O., & Antunes, C. H. (2012). Interactions of economic growth, energy consumption and the environment in the context of the crisis - A study with uncertain data. *Energy, 48*(1), 415–422. doi:10.1016/j.energy.2012.04.009

IEA, 2016

Jayaraman, R., Colapinto, C., La Torre, D., & Malik, T. (2015). Multi-criteria model for sustainable development using goal programming applied to the United Arab Emirates. *Energy Policy, 87*, 447–454. doi:10.1016/j.enpol.2015.09.027

Jayaraman, R., Colapinto, C., La Torre, D., & Malik, T. (2017a). A Weighted Goal Programming model for planning sustainable development applied to Gulf Cooperation Council Countries. *Applied Energy, 185*(Part 2, 1), 1931-1939.

Jayaraman, R., Colapinto, C., Liuzzi, D., & La Torre, D. (2017c). Planning sustainable development through a scenario-based stochastic goal programming model. *Operations Research, 17*(3), 789–805. doi:10.100712351-016-0239-8

Jayaraman, R., Liuzzi, D., Colapinto, C., & Malik, T. (2017b). A fuzzy goal programming model to analyse energy, environmental and sustainability goals of the United Arab Emirates. *Annals of Operations Research, 251*(1–2), 255–270. doi:10.100710479-015-1825-5

Koellinger, P. D., & Roy Thurik, A. (2012). Entrepreneurship and the business cycle. *The Review of Economics and Statistics, 94*(4), 1143–1156. doi:10.1162/REST_a_00224

Meadows, D. H., Meadows, D. L., Randers, J., & Behrens, W. W. III. (1972). *The Limits to Growth. A Report for the Club of Rome's Project on the Predicament of Mankind*. New York: Universe Books.

Nazarbayev, N. (2012). *Strategy Kazakhstan-2050: New political course of the established state*. Retrieved on November 11, 2014, from: https://strategy2050.kz/en/multilanguage/

Nordhaus, W. (1991). To Slow or Not to Slow: The Economics of the Greenhouse Effect. *Economic Journal (London), 101*(407), 920–937. doi:10.2307/2233864

Nordhaus, W. (2008). *A Question of Balance: Weighing the Options on Global Warming Policies*. New Haven, CT: Yale University Press.

OECD. (2017). *Building inclusive labour markets in Kazakhstan: a focus on youth, older workers, and people with disabilities*. Paris: OECD Publishing.

OECD. (2018). *SME and Entrepreneurship Policy in Kazakhstan 2018, OECD Studies on SMEs and Entrepreneurship*. Paris: OECD Publishing.

Oliveira, C., & Antunes, C. H. (2010). A macro-level multi-objective model with uncertain data for sustainability studies. *Proceedings of the 23rd International Conference on Efficiency, Cost, Optimization, Simulation, and Environmental Impact of Energy Systems. Ecos, 2010*, 329–336.

Reiche, D. (2010). Renewable energy policies in the Gulf countries – a case study of the carbon-neutral "Masdar City" in Abu Dhabi. *Energy Policy, 38*(1), 378–382. doi:10.1016/j.enpol.2009.09.028

Romero, C. (1991). *Handbook of Critical Issues in Goal Programming*. Oxford, UK: Pergamon Press.

Saad, M., Zawdie, G., & Malairaja, C. (2008). The triple helix strategy for universities in developing countries: The experiences in Malaysia and Algeria. *Science & Public Policy, 35*(6), 431–443. doi:10.3152/030234208X323316

San Cristóbal, J. R. (2012). A goal programming model for environmental policy analysis: Application to Spain. *Energy Policy, 43*, 303–307. doi:10.1016/j.enpol.2012.01.007

Schumpeter, J. A. (1943). *Capitalism, socialism and democracy*. New York: Routledge.

Shane, S. (2009). Why encouraging more people to become entrepreneurs is bad public policy. *Small Business Economics, 33*(2), 141–149. doi:10.100711187-009-9215-5

Tan, Y., Shuai, C., Jiao, L., & Shen, L. (2017). An adaptive neuro-fuzzy inference system (ANFIS) approach for measuring country sustainability performance. *Environmental Impact Assessment Review, 65*, 29–40. doi:10.1016/j.eiar.2017.04.004

Vié, A., Liuzzi, D., Colapinto, C., & La Torre, D. (2019). The long-run sustainability of the European Union countries: Assessing the Europe 2020 strategy through a fuzzy goal programming model. *Management Decision, 57*(2), 523–542. doi:10.1108/MD-05-2018-0518

Wennekers, S., Van Wennekers, A., Thurik, R., & Reynolds, P. D. (2005). Nascent entrepreneurship and the level of economic development. *Small Business Economics, 24*(3), 293–309. doi:10.100711187-005-1994-8

World Bank. (2015). *KZ Skills and Jobs Project*. Retrieved on December 2, 2017, from: https://projects.worldbank.org/P150183?lang=en

ADDITIONAL READING

Colapinto, C., Jayaraman, R., & Marsiglio, S. (2017). Multi-criteria decision analysis with goal programming in engineering, management and social sciences: A state-of-the art review. *Annals of Operations Research, 251*(1-2), 7–40. doi:10.100710479-015-1829-1

La Torre, D., Liuzzi, D., & Marsiglio, S. (2019). Population and geography do matter for sustainable development. *Environment and Development Economics, 24*(2), 201–223. doi:10.1017/S1355770X18000475

Marsiglio, S., & La Torre, D. (2018). Economic growth and abatement activities in a stochastic environment: A multi-objective. *Annals of Operations Research, 267*(1-2), 321–334. doi:10.100710479-016-2357-3

OECD. (2018). *SME and Entrepreneurship Policy in Kazakhstan 2018, OECD Studies on SMEs and Entrepreneurship*. Paris: OECD Publishing.

KEY TERMS AND DEFINITIONS

Economic Growth: An increase in the total amount of goods and services produced per head of the population of a specific country over a year, it can be measured in terms of Gross Domestic Product (GDP).

Goal Programming: It is an optimization model to balance conflicting criteria. Its major strength is its simplicity and ease of use.

Human Capital: The stock of skills, attributes, and experiences gained by an individual viewed in terms of their value to an organization and/or country.

Kazakhstan: This Post-Soviet transition economy is the largest economy in Central Asia. It possesses oil reserves as well as minerals and metals. It also has considerable agricultural potential. The population is around 18 million.

Multi-Criteria: In many real-world decisions, we need to take into account simultaneously different conflicting criteria.

Sustainability: The capability to preserve natural resources in order to maintain an ecological and economic balance without adversely affecting the needs of future generations.

Triple Helix Model: This model of innovation refers to a set of interactions between academia, governments and industry to foster economic and/or social development. It has been extended to include other relevant actors (i.e., media, financial actors).

ENDNOTES

[1] Electricity consumption data source: https://www.iea.org/statistics/statisticssearch/report/?year=2014&country=KAZAKHSTAN&product=ElectricityandHeat

[2] GHG emission data sources: http://www.tradingeconomics.com/kazakhstan/total-greenhouse-gas-emissions-kt-of-co2-equivalent-wb-data.html, http://stat.gov.kz/faces/wcnav_externalId/ecolog-B-6;jsessionid=1nRwZpMGFgNj73kVCHMGzvzxfvbfsyLSycsmS4hJWYvx2RLkL0KM!-627311938!1518861454?lang=ru&_afrLoop=24361420237447530#%40%3F_afrLoop%3D24361420237447530%26lang%3Dru%26_adf.ctrl-state%3Djm17iubr7_4,https://unfccc.int/files/ghg_data/ghg_data_unfccc/ghg_profiles/application/pdf/kaz_ghg_profile.pdf

[3] Employment data source: http://www.stat.gov.kz/faces/wcnav_externalId/publicationsMonitoring?_afrLoop=4644604121093692#%40%3F_afrLoop%3D4644604121093692%26_adf.ctrl-state%3Dmwk4bqmtw_29

[4] Data from retrieved in January 2019 from http://www.stat.gov.kz/faces/wcnav_externalId/publicationsMonitoring?_afrLoop=4644604121093692#%40%3F_afrLoop%3D4644604121093692%26_adf.ctrl-state%3Dmwk4bqmtw_29.

[5] GHG emission data sources are: http://www.tradingeconomics.com/kazakhstan/total-greenhouse-gas-emissions-kt-of-co2-equivalent-wb-data.html, http://stat.gov.kz/faces/wcnav_externalId/ecolog-B6;jsessionid=1nRwZpMGFgNj73kVCHMGzvzxfvbfsyLSycsmS4hJWYvx2RLkL0KM!-627311938!1518861454?lang=ru&_afrLoop=24361420237447530#%40%3F_afrLoop%3D24361420237447530%26lang%3Dru%26_adf.ctrl-state%3Djm17iubr7_4, https://unfccc.int/files/ghg_data/ghg_data_unfccc/ghg_profiles/application/pdf/kaz_ghg_profile.pdf.

[6] Electricity consumption data source is: https://www.iea.org/statistics/statisticssearch/report/?year=2014&country=KAZAKHSTAN&product=ElectricityandHea

[7] We retrieve our data from http://www.stat.gov.kz/faces/wcnav_externalId/publicationsMonitoring?_afrLoop=4644604121093692#%40%3F_afrLoop%3D4644604121093692%26_adf.ctrl-state%3Dmwk4bqmtw_29

Chapter 3
Corruption and Anti-Corruption Reform in Central Asia

Duane Windsor
https://orcid.org/0000-0003-0406-1030
Rice University, USA

ABSTRACT

This chapter surveys information available in English from public sources concerning levels and composition of corruption in the five countries of Central Asia. Similarly, the chapter examines relevant information available in English from public sources concerning anti-corruption reform efforts in Central Asia. Focus is on the relationship between corruption and reform and economic, educational, and touristic development in the five countries. There is consideration of possible links to foreign direct investment and operations by multinational corporations. There is some comparison to neighboring countries. The chapter proceeds in the following phases. The first step is to assemble available information and studies concerning corruption and anti-corruption conditions in the five countries. The second step is to assess the determinants and consequences of both corruption and anti-corruption reform. The third step is to place information and assessment into regional context. The chapter provides a conceptual framework for interpreting detailed country information.

DOI: 10.4018/978-1-7998-2239-4.ch003

Copyright © 2020, IGI Global. Copying or distributing in print or electronic forms without written permission of IGI Global is prohibited.

INTRODUCTION

The research problem addressed in this chapter is how to study the relationship of corruption conditions and anti-corruption reform efforts to economic development, educational development, and touristic development in the five countries of Central Asia. Recent empirical scholarship finds that the relationship of corruption to development dimensions and to effectiveness of anti-corruption reform efforts is ambiguous, non-linear, and context dependent.

Corruption is pervasive across Central Asia. Anti-corruption reforms seem tepid. The political regimes are authoritarian. In the 2018 Corruption Perceptions Index (CPI) measures for 180 countries and territories (Transparency International, 2019a), three Central Asian countries rank in the bottom quartile (152nd or below) and two other countries rank in the bottom half (132nd and 124th). Regionally, only Africa averages as more corrupt than Eastern Europe and Central Asia (Transparency International, 2019b, Paragraph 4).

The methodological issue is how to study corruption and anti-corruption reform in specific countries. Given the latest scholarship findings suggesting complexity of corruption and anti-corruption, detailed country-level information is essential for understanding and research about Central Asia. The chapter provides a conceptual framework for helping to interpret detailed information about Central Asia. The general perspective of the chapter is a study of publicly available key information in English on corruption and anti-corruption reform. The methodology is a survey and analytical interpretation of that information. This survey is not a complete and exhaustive study of all publicly available information. Instead the inquiry is focused on essential aspects of the research problem to develop a general picture.

The importance of Central Asia is due in part to its unique geographical location. The five countries are adjacent (on different frontiers) to Afghanistan, China, Iran, Pakistan, and Russia. All these neighbors are corrupt. Afghanistan is an active war zone. Central Asia is a useful setting for studying possible regional cooperation and influence of adjacent corruption conditions and anti-corruption efforts. For purposes of assessing anti-corruption campaigns, India (adjacent to Pakistan and China) and China are highly relevant.

The objectives of the chapter are as follows. The first is to examine available key information on corruption in Central Asia. The second investigates such information on anti-corruption reform efforts. The third is to relate corruption and anti-corruption reform to the evolution of the political regimes in Central Asia. The chapter then considers solutions, recommendations, and future research directions. A further purpose is to provide the general reader with references and additional readings that should prove useful in the further study of Central Asia.

BACKGROUND

Conceptual Framework for Interpreting Country Information

Recent empirical studies argue there are both negative and positive effects of corruption. Assessing corruption, occurring in multiple forms (Knack, 2007), and anti-corruption recommendations is difficult and context specific. Empirical reality concerning corruption (including definitions, kinds, causes, and effects) may prove to be multi-dimensional (Pertiwi, 2018). Implementation and study of anti-corruption efforts and measures occur in this possibly quite complicated setting (Gephart, 2015). If so then causes, perceptions, behaviors, and consequences in one country (or even within-country) may or may not occur in similar combinations in another country.

For economic development, Huang (2015) finds (using bootstrap panel Granger causality methodology for 1997-2013 data) corruption promoting growth in South Korea (so that "grease" for wheels is good), while growth promotes corruption in China (so that "sand" is generated for wheels), and no causal relationship in eleven other Asia-Pacific countries. The implication is that anti-corruption efforts may not be effective in most of these countries, if any (Huang, 2015). A panel data analysis of 88 countries (1984-2011) reports that beyond an optimal threshold both low and high corruption levels reduce growth, while below that threshold a moderate level of corruption promotes growth (Trabelsi & Trabelsi, 2014). El Bahnasawy and Revier (2012) conclude that rule of law, common in rich countries, strongly correlates with reduced corruption. They find further that "natural resource abundance, country population size, country's dominant religious tradition, ethnic fractionalization, and political stability are unimportant determinants of corruption" contrary to some previous research (El Bahnasawy & Revier, 2012: 311).

For educational development, some recent literature continues to confirm that corruption in education reduces human capital formation and long-run productivity. For 88 developing countries, Duerrenberger and Warning (2018) find that corruption reduces expected years of schooling. In low corruption countries the fraction of public higher education enrollment decreases corruption while in high corruption countries that fraction increases corruption. However, economic growth may not reduce educational corruption in the short run, based on a study in Russia (Osipian, 2012). Educational development may encompass both human capital formation and also fostering of moral and professional standards for conduct (Osipian, 2012). Morality and human capital appear to be important to economic growth (Balan & Knack, 2012).

For touristic development, there may be a complicated relationship (Poprawe, 2015). Corruption seems to reduce touristic demand and more so for developing than developed countries (Das & Dirienzo, 2010, for 119 countries), but the effect may be dampened by desirability of the tourism site as with the threats of crime and fraud and also by the tourist's tolerance for risk relative to desirability of the tourism site (Yap & Saha, 2013). Saha and Yap (2015), using 1999-2009 data, report a non-linear relationship in which up to a threshold corruption increases tourism and then beyond that threshold reduces tourism. Tourism to Central Asia may thus be a function of accessibility, desirability, and the negative effect of corruption.

Knack (2007) highlights that there are potentially numerous definitions of corruption. Knack suggests classification according to level of political system (such as national versus local governments), purpose of corruption (such as state capture versus administrative corruption), kinds of actors involved (such as firms, households, and public officials), characteristics of actors involved (such as large versus small firms, or rich versus poor households), administrative agency or service involved (such as courts or customs officials), and incidence or magnitude of bribes or uncertainty involved for businesses or households. Knack's classification proposal is one and likely not fully exhaustive decomposition of the notion of corruption. There may also on the same logic be various forms of corruption (such as bribery, extortion, cash, favoritism, contracts, nepotism, and so on) interacting with the dimensions of Knack's classification scheme.

The resulting problem in Central Asia is how to study corruption and anti-corruption reform. The fine-grained micro-information required to study corruption in detail in corruption could be both complicated and difficult to obtain. A simple conceptual framework may be of help in interpreting descriptive and perceptual information about corruption and anti-corruption reform in the five countries of Central Asia. This conceptualization is not a formal model in any sense, but it can be linked to specification of some general hypotheses. The available information for Central Asia is not suitable for trying to test specific hypotheses directly, but specifying the hypotheses in general form may prove useful in interpretation.

The conceptual framework draws on two distinctions: "bad corruption" forms versus "good corruption" forms; "weakly functioning institutions" versus "well functioning institutions." The basic distinction is that contingently for "sand" for the wheels has (or can have) negative effects and "grease" for the wheels has (or can have) positive effects. Nur-tegin and Jakee (in press) conclude that overall "sand" outweighs "grease" although some types of the latter can have beneficial effects. The effects for either sand or grease likely are greater with weakly functioning institutions.

The three consequences of the interactions of corruption forms and institutions are, for purposes of this handbook, economic development, educational development, and touristic development. In general terms, if institutions are well functioning, then one would expect the influence of all forms of corruption to be essentially zero. That expectation does not mean that no one undertakes to practice bribery or extortion, or other forms of corruption. Rather, in general, there is no particular influence overall on economic, educational, and touristic development. Any hypotheses linking corruption (bad or good) to the three outcomes would specify close to zero influence. The anti-corruption problem is to defend the institutions through constant vigilance against specific instances of corruption.

The attention is then on weakly functioning institutions. In that condition, bad corruption forms might have negative effects on the three outcomes; good corruption forms might have positive effects on the three outcomes. Hypotheses linking bad or good corruption to the three outcomes would specify and test for negative or positive influences accordingly. Anti-corruption efforts arguably have two different tasks. One task is detection and deterrence of specific instances of corruption. The other task is improving the institutions toward the desirable ideal standard of well functioning. Institutions can take a broad definition: democracy, rule of law, official honesty, citizen support for anti-corruption, and so forth.

Unique Characteristics of Central Asia

Central Asia forms a distinct geographical region. The five countries are culturally and ethnically diverse, although the dominant religion in all five countries is Islam (mostly Sunni) as in Afghanistan and Pakistan. The country name in Central Asia reflects the historically dominant ethnic group. The five countries are developing economies highly dependent on agriculture and minerals including oil and gas, mainly in Kazakhstan, Turkmenistan, and Uzbekistan (Raimondi, 2019).

The history of Central Asia is important. During August to December 1991, the Union of Soviet Socialist Republics (USSR) disintegrated into 15 independent countries, including the five Central Asia countries. All 15 previously had been Soviet "soviet socialist" (i.e., communist) republics. Research questions concern whether corruption patterns in Central Asia reflect the Soviet and communist party heritage or local culture in some way. Corruption and authoritarianism have been persistent in transition societies including Central Asia (Swartz, Wadsworth, & Wheat, 2011) formerly part of or dominated in Eastern Europe by the USSR, other than the Baltic republics to date (Sandholtz & Taagepera, 2005; Walker, 2011). Political leadership emerged from the SSR communist parties in each country. Authoritarianism is the political pattern. Local culture is a complicated issue to diagnose, both because "culture" is arguably an awkward social scientific construct and because the five countries are highly diverse.

Russia and China (a communist party-state) are authoritarian regimes with power expansion ambitions. China and Russia both compete and cooperate in Central Asia (Kirişci & Le Corre, 2018; Marantidou & Cossa, 2014; Rumer, Sokolsy, & Stronski, 2016). The northwest area of China bordering on Central Asia (Uyghur Autonomous Region of Xinjiang) has a large Uighur (Uyghur) Muslim population, reportedly

43

INFORMATION ON THE COUNTRIES OF CENTRAL ASIA

Given conflicting empirical results about corruption, institutions, and effects on economic, educational, and touristic development, a review of detailed country-level information is essential for understanding and future research. This section provides four kinds of information about corruption from several sources comparing expert perceptions, citizen reports, and enterprise reports; anti-corruption reform; cultural and ethnic diversity; and executive and political change. The section draws on information assembled in five tables. GAN Integrity Business Anti-Corruption Portal (2016a, 2016b, 2016c, 2016d, 2017) provides detailed reports for each of the five countries.

The basic findings are as follows. Corruption is pervasive, with variations by country, and anti-corruption reforms are tepid across Central Asia. Neighboring countries are also generally corrupt. There are active anti-corruption campaigns underway in China and India. There is considerable ethnic and religious diversity across Central Asia. Whether cultural and historical features promote corruption and deter anti-corruption reform is unknown. Authoritarianism is the prevailing political model. Top leadership is generally corrupt. Whether external influences including foreign direct investment (FDI) into minerals extraction will help improve the situation is debatable, in light of scholarly findings rejected earlier views of the corruption effect of natural resource abundance noted earlier.

Corruption Information

Table 1 provides Transparency International's CPI data for the years 2018 through 2012 (columns 1 through 7), 2019 Freedom House Index (column 8), and 2014 Worldwide Governance Indicators (WGI) Control of Corruption Index (column 9) for the five Central Asian countries and neighboring countries including Mongolia. The states appear ordered from relatively best to relatively worst CPI score for 2018 (column 1). CPI scores are based on variable numbers of surveys of experts. Transparency International aggregates the polls into a summary estimate (for which Transparency International) also provides ranges and confidence estimates. CPI scores for each country seem reasonably consistent across 2012 to 2018.

CPI reports subjective information dependent on the unbiased knowledge of the experts surveyed. For each country, the first row under CPI is the score, the second

Corruption and Anti-Corruption Reform in Central Asia

Table 1. Corruption perceptions index (CPI) data for five Central Asian countries and neighboring countries (2012-2018 comparable years) and related data for freedom and control of corruption

Transparency International Corruption Perceptions Index (CPI) cross-year comparable data listed from relatively highest to relatively worst score (Central Asian countries noted in *italics*)*								Freedom House Index**	WGI Control of Corruption Index+
Column	1	2	3	4	5	6	7	8	9
Country	2018	2017	2016	2015	2014	2013	2012	2019	2014
China	39	41	40	37	36	40	39	11	-0.34
rank	87	77	79	83	100	80	80	not free	category 3
percent	0.483	0.428	0.449	0.494	0.571	0.452	0.455		
Mongolia	37	36	38	39	39	38	36	85	-0.47
	93	103	87	72	80	83	94	free	category 2
	0.517	0.572	0.494	0.429	0.457	0.469	0.534		
Pakistan	33	32	32	30	29	28	27	39	-0.83
	117	117	116	117	126	127	139	partly free	category 2
	0.650	0.650	0.659	0.696	0.720	0.718	0.790		
Kazakhstan	31	31	29	28	29	26	28	22	-0.83
	124	122	131	123	126	140	133	not free	category 2
	0.689	0.678	0.744	0.732	0.720	0.791	0.756		
Kyrgyzstan	29	29	28	28	27	24	24	38	-1.13
	132	135	136	123	136	150	154	partly free	category 1
	0.733	0.750	0.773	0.732	0.777	0.847	0.875		
Russia	28	29	29	29	27	28	28	20	-0.92
	138	135	131	119	136	127	133	not free	category 1
	0.767	0.750	0.744	0.708	0.777	0.718	0.756		
Iran	28	30	29	27	27	25	28	18	-0.62
	138	130	131	130	136	144	133	not free	category 2
	0.767	0.722	0.744	0.774	0.777	0.814	0.756		
Tajikistan	25	21	25	26	23	22	22	9	-1.13
	152	161	151	136	152	154	157	not free	category 1
	0.844	0.894	0.858	0.810	0.869	0.870	0.892		
Uzbekistan	23	22	21	19	18	17	17	9	-1.19
	158	157	156	153	166	168	170	not free	category 1
	0.878	0.872	0.886	0.911	0.949	0.949	0.966		
Turkmenistan	20	19	22	18	17	17	17	2	-1.31
	161	167	154	154	169	168	170	not free	category 1
	0.894	0.928	0.875	0.917	0.966	0.949	0.966		
Afghanistan	16	15	15	11	12	8	8	27	-1.35
	172	177	169	166	172	175	174	not free	category 1
	0.956	0.983	0.960	0.988	0.983	0.989	0.989		
Count of Countries & Territories	180	180	176	168	175	177	176	209	215

Sources: (CPI, Transparency International, https://www.transparency.org/research/cpi/overview); (Freedom House, 2019); (Worldwide Governance Indicator for Control of Corruption Index, World Bank, n.d.) Readers should note that Transparency International may issue periodic corrections of errors affecting scores and rankings, although these corrections tend to be relatively minor. Readers should always check original sources for accuracy of tables in this chapter.

*For CPI data, first row for each country is the reported CPI score (0 to 100). The closer to 0, the cleaner the country is. Second row for each country is the reported ranking of a varying number of countries and territories reported each year. The closer to 1, the cleaner the country is. Third row for each country is a percent computed here: the ratio of country rank over count of total number of countries and jurisdictions for each year. The closer to 1.00, the dirtier the country is. "In 2012, Transparency International revised the methodology used to construct the index to allow for comparison of scores from one year to the next." (TI 2018)

**Freedom House Index draws on 25 indicators. The closer to 100, the freer the country is; the closer to 0, the less free the country is.

+World Governance Indicator (WGI) for Control of Corruption reflects a normalized curve from about -2.5 (lowest control) to about +2.5 (highest control). Negative is a bad score, worsening as the score moves toward 2.5 lowest score. The lowest category (here category 1) is below -0.89; the second lowest category (here category 2) is below -0.44; the third lowest category (here category 3) is below +0.14.

row is the rank (among the number of countries and territories reported), and the third row is an author-computed percent. China is the relatively least corrupt country in Table 1 at about 48.3% in 2018, followed by Mongolia and Pakistan. Kazakhstan and Kyrgyzstan are also less corrupt than Russia and Iran. Tajikistan (about 84%), Uzbekistan (about 88%), and Turkmenistan (about 89%) are relatively the most corrupt of the Central Asian countries. Afghanistan (about 96%) is a war zone. WGI Control of Corruption Index information appears reasonably consistent with CPI information for the countries in Table 1.

Freedom House classifies Mongolia as free, and Pakistan and Kyrgyzstan as partly free; all other countries in Table 1 as not free. Freedom House (2018) in a country report classifies Turkmenistan as a "consolidated authoritarian regime" rated 6.96 of 7 on the "democracy score" in which 7 is the least democratic regime. Corruption perceptions data are subject to continuing and reasonable criticism on several grounds (Andersson & Heywood, 2009; Ko & Samajdar, 2010). Wilhelm (2002) argues that CPI has sufficient validity for careful use; and I follow this line of reasoning. Rusch (2019, Paragraph 4) explains that there are methods for measuring critical, if not all, dimensions of corruption; and that it is not necessary to agree on a comprehensive definition covering all kinds of corruption to practice measurement.

CPI and similar information provide a general idea of corruption by country. However, there are two key lessons to take from the critical literature. First, we may not know enough from such information to craft effective anti-corruption measures. Policy design is a very different problem. Second, as Andersson and Heywood (2009) emphasize that the CPI approach may risk a "corruption trap" in which deeply corrupt countries are denied international development aid unless they adopt anti-corruption reforms that are dependent on such assistance.

Transparency International (2015) reported that six of the ten most corrupt countries were conflict areas ("least peaceful"). From the bottom up, the list was Somalia, North Korea, Afghanistan, Sudan, South Sudan, Angola, Libya, Iraq, Venezuela, Guinea-Bissau, Haiti, and Yemen. The next country up in the list was Turkmenistan; and Uzbekistan was close by, separated from Turkmenistan by Syria and then Eritrea.

There are two other approaches to studying corruption at the country level that may partially help offset difficulties in CPI and similar sources. One method is to survey citizens directly. Another technique is to address businesses directly. Charron (2016) examines the differences between corruption information from citizens and experts.

Transparency International has produced five regional Global Barometer Surveys reports in recent years for the following regions as defined by that organization: "Asia Pacific" (Transparency International, 2017a); "Eastern Europe and Central Asia;" "Latin America and the Caribbean," "Middle East and North Africa;" and

Corruption and Anti-Corruption Reform in Central Asia

Table 2. Transparency International Global Barometer Surveys (2016, 2017)

Country (Central Asia in italics)	Corruption One of 3 Biggest Problems	Bribery Paid in Past 12 Months	Government Anti-Corruption Going Badly	Corruption Has Increased	Year of Regional Survey	Regional Survey
China		26%	[60% in Hong Kong]	73%	2017	Asia Pacific
Mongolia		20%	61%		2017	Asia Pacific
Pakistan		40%	55%	35%	2017	Asia Pacific
Kazakhstan	37%	20%	46%		2016	Europe & Central Asia
Kyrgyzstan	47%	38%	57%		2016	Europe & Central Asia
Russia	39%	34%	62%		2016	Europe & Central Asia
Tajikistan	18%	50%			2016	Europe & Central Asia
Uzbekistan	23%	18%			2016	Europe & Central Asia
Afghanistan, Iran, Pakistan, and *Turkmenistan* were not surveyed. Europe and Central Asia 2016 survey involved nearly 60,000 respondents across 42 countries. Asia Pacific 2015-17 survey involved nearly 22,000 people across 16 countries and territories.						

Sources: (Transparency International, 2016, 2017a)

"Sub-Saharan Africa." Some countries in this chapter's study area had surveys in 2016 or 2017. However, these data are relatively incomplete due to variations in methodology. Table 2 assembles some available information.

The consolidated version of Transparency International's Global Corruption Barometer uses data from the five regional reports (Transparency International, 2017b). Globally, nearly 25% of 162,136 respondents surveyed from March 2014 until January 2017 reported paying a bribe to public officials over a twelve-month period. The most corrupt institution varied considerably by region: police in the Asia Pacific and Sub-Saharan Africa regions; elected representatives in the Europe and Central Asia region; police and elected representatives in the Americas; elected representatives, tax officials, and government officials in the Middle East and North Africa region.

Corruption and Anti-Corruption Reform in Central Asia

World Bank surveys of businesses by country (more than 135,000 businesses in 139 countries, occurring in different years) find high business perceptions of corruption in Kyrgyzstan, Afghanistan, Tajikistan, Mongolia, and Pakistan from highest to lowest. Kazakhstan fared better. China and, somewhat surprisingly, Uzbekistan had the most moderate business perceptions of corruption. Table 3 includes India for comparison. (Turkmenistan does not appear in the survey results.) Over the years, the World Bank has surveyed more than 135,000 businesses in 139

Table 3. World Bank Group enterprise surveys on dimensions of bribery by country (listed alphabetically)

Country (Central Asia countries shown in italics)	Bribery incidence (% of firms experiencing at least one bribe payment request)	Bribery depth (% of public transactions where a gift or informal payment was requested)	Percent of firms expected to give gifts in meetings with tax officials	Percent of firms expected to give gifts to secure government contract	Value of gift expected to secure a government contract (% of contract value)	Percent of firms expected to give gifts to get an operating license
Afghanistan 2014 +	46.8	34.6	34.0	46.9	4.4	31.6
China 2012 **	11.6	9.9	10.9	42.2	0.2	7.8
India 2014 +	22.7	19.6	15.3	39.8	0.1	25.8
Kazakhstan 2012 *	26.7	22.0	22.3	19.1	0.8	15.8
Kyrgyzstan 2012 *	59.8	53.6	54.8	55.1	2.4	59.6
Mongolia 2013 **	33.4	25.8	19.5	25.9	1.5	29.7
Pakistan 2013 +	30.8	28.5	28.8	88.2	8.2	31.0
Russia 2012 *	14.2	9.7	7.3	30.9	2.6	12.6
Tajikistan 2013 *	36.3	29.6	31.9	33.6	2.0	28.7
Uzbekistan 2013 *	7.0	4.6	2.4	8.0	0	11.3
Europe & Central Asia (average) *	13.1	10.2	9.7	22.4	1.6	11.1
East Asia & Pacific (average) **	31.2	24.9	22.0	40.7	2.4	25.2
South Asia (average) +	24.8	21.0	19.6	45.5	2.9	25.3

Turkmenistan not reported by World Bank Group. South Asia average includes India. * Countries in Europe & Central Asia. ** Countries in East Asia & Pacific. + Countries in South Asia. Country data and regional averages are as available at time of chapter preparation. In 2019, the website updated estimates for Kazakhstan, Kyrgyzstan, Mongolia, Russia, Tajikistan, and Uzbekistan. There were also 2019 updates for Europe & Central Asia and East Asia & Pacific but not for South Asia. Readers can see the 2019 updated information at the World Bank Group website.

Source: (World Bank Group, n.d.)

48

Anti-Corruption Reform Information

China and India, like Brazil, have active anti-corruption efforts. In Table 1, WGI places Kyrgyzstan, Tajikistan, Uzbekistan, Turkmenistan, and Afghanistan in the lowest category of control of corruption (group 1) with Russia. Mongolia, Pakistan, Kazakhstan, and Iran are in division 2. Only China places in set 3; this placement corresponds to China having the relatively best CPI score in Table 1. There is some evidence of anti-corruption progress in Kazakhstan (Omirgazy, 2016).

A significant dimension of anti-corruption and democratic reform is the rule of law. The World Justice Project (2019) draws on 120,000 household respondents and 3,800 expert respondents across 125 countries and jurisdiction to construct an index based on eight factors (including the absence of corruption). The justice index score is from 0 (worst) to 1 (best); and each country has a ranking out of 126. (Tajikistan and Turkmenistan do not appear in the project report.) Australia is scored 0.80 and 11th out of 126. In the chapter study area, Afghanistan is worst at 0.35 (123 of 126). Mongolia is best at 0.55 (53) followed by Kazakhstan (0.52, 65), India (0.51, 68), China (0.49, 82), Kyrgyzstan (0.48, 85), Russia (0.47, 88), Uzbekistan (0.46, 94), and Iran (0.45, 102). Pakistan (0.39, 117) is closer to Afghanistan. World Bank (2018) provides country information on business regulations.

The Central Asian countries are members of the Istanbul Anti-corruption Action Plan, initiated in 2003 by the Organisation for Economic Co-operation and Development (OECD), within its Anti-Corruption Network (Organisation for Economic Co-operation and Development, n.d.). This program undertakes monitoring rounds as a basis for making recommendations for anti-corruption efforts. The previous three rounds for 2004-2007, 2008-2012, and 2013-2015 all resulted in reports (see especially Organisation for Economic Co-operation and Development, 2008, 2016). The current series of monitoring launched in 2016 (Organisation for Economic Co-operation and Development, 2018). The nine countries involved are Armenia, Azerbaijan, Georgia, Kazakhstan, Kyrgyzstan, Mongolia, Tajikistan, Ukraine, and Uzbekistan. The initiative combines the Caucasus and Central Asia with Mongolia and Ukraine.

The least corrupt countries in Asia are the wealthiest countries: Japan, Singapore, South Korea, and Taiwan (Warf, 2019, p. 143). In contrast, "severely corrupt states" include "North Korea, Bangladesh, Central Asia ..." (Warf, 2019, p. 143). Warf emphasizes, "... that while Asian anti-corruption campaigns have had mixed

Cultural and Ethnic Diversity across Central Asia

Table 4 reveals the cultural, ethnic, and religious diversity of the Central Asian countries (see Nichol, 2014; Schenkkan, 2016; World Bank, 2017). Four of the countries employ Turkic languages. Tajikistan is a Persian-speaking country. Physically, Central Asia (four million square kilometers) is almost as large as the EU. The total population of the region is nearly 70 million, Uzbekistan being about 30 million and Kazakhstan about 18.7 million. Each country has a dominant ethnic group: Kazakhs, Kyrgyz, Tajiks, Turkmen, and Uzbeks. Kazakhstan, bordering on Russia to the north, has the most substantial proportion of Russians (nearly 24%). Russian is an official language in Kazakhstan and also is in widespread use in Tajikistan. The other four countries have relatively small proportions of Russians. Uzbeks are a significant proportion of the Afghanistan population and in the other Central Asian nations except for Kazakhstan. Islam is the dominant religion in all five countries.

One interpretation of "culture" is that it reflects some "embedded normative system" patterning daily behavior of a population (Kassab & Rosen, 2019). Kassab and Rosen argue that "Culture plays an important role in the spread of corruption …" in the Middle East and Central Asia including through narcotics trafficking out of Afghanistan; "…the embedded normative system of the region" makes "dealing with corruption" more complex (2019, p. 65). McMann (2014) based on research in Kazakhstan and Kyrgyzstan, argues that citizens engage in corruption as a "last resort" to obtain "essential goods and services" when not provided by other institutions (public and private). The causation is not "bureaucrats, poverty, and culture" but institutional failures. McMann argues that market-oriented reform has generated "resource scarcity" (Prasad, da Silva, & Nickow, 2019), resulting in what I shall characterize as demand-side corruption (see Dixit, 2016). Prasad et al., drawing on McMann and studies in other countries, suggest that the anti-corruption policy solution may be to supply citizens with viable alternatives to corruption. Urinboyev (2018, 2019) provides information on daily corruption and social norms in Uzbekistan. Hornberger (2018) reports on bribe demands in driver licensing in South Africa. Road police are reportedly corrupt in at least Kazakhstan, Kyrgyzstan, and especially Tajikistan (Transparency International, 2016, p. 22).

Corruption and Anti-Corruption Reform in Central Asia

Authoritarianism in Central Asia

Effective anti-corruption reform depends on political will at the top of regimes. Gründler and Potrafke (in press) report that the negative effect of corruption on economic growth is strongest in autocratic regimes. This negative effect on growth occurs through decreased FDI and increased inflation. Corruption tends to deter FDI (Zakharov, 2019). Non-stable democracies tend to be less corrupt than stable dictatorships (Nur-tegin & Czap, 2012). Rahmon, president of Tajikistan since 1992, arguably squeezes out rivals and consolidates family control over assets to secure power (Rumer et al., 2016). A consequence is that any succession struggle could destroy quite "fragile" political institutions (Rumer et al., 2016). The stability is arguably an appearance dependent on Rahmon personally.

Reportedly Turkmenistan is authoritarian and Uzbekistan is highly authoritarian (Central Intelligence Agency, n.d.). However, only Kyrgyzstan can be said to have had much leadership turnover due to the two Tulip Revolutions. Leadership in the five newly independent countries emerged out of the SSR communist parties, which remained in power in democratic guise: "communists-turned-nationalists" deflected democratic reforms (Kudaibergenova & Shin, 2018).

Table 5 provides more detailed information. In Kazakhstan, Nazarbayev ruled from 1990 (SSR) to March 2019 resignation to First President status. In Tajikistan, Rahmon has been in power since 1992. In Turkmenistan, Niyazov ruled from 1985 (SSR) to his death in 2006, being declared President for Life in 1999. In Uzbekistan, Karimov ruled from 1989 (SSR) to his death in 2016.

In Central Asia, top leadership is corrupt, and this corruption arguably causes rot downward (Holmes, 2018). One study characterizes Kyrgyzstan as "the region's one nominal democracy" and "perennially unstable" (Rumer et al., 2016). These characterizations suggest a kind of continuum from highly authoritarian (Uzbekistan) through authoritarian (Turkmenistan) to nominal democracy (Kyrgyzstan), with Kazakhstan and Tajikistan in between. Instability has associated with presidential turnover, but stability is not an accepted justification for corruption and other abuses of power (Kendzior, 2013).

Kyrgyzstan is the one variation on the theme of single president domination in Central Asia. There has been considerable turnover in the Kyrgyz presidency. The Tulip Revolutions, or First (2005) and Second (2010) Kyrgyz Revolutions, did result in changes of the president. (The tulip is the national flower.) However, the increased competition may be among corrupt rivals.

A new constitution enacted on the heels of an anticorruption revolution in 2010 has increased the degree of competition among rival corrupt networks in Kyrgyzstan. (Chayes, 2016, p. 1)

Corruption and Anti-Corruption Reform in Central Asia

Table 4. Basic demographic information about the five Central Asian countries

	Kazakh (stan)	Kyrgyz (stan)	Tajik (istan)	Turkmen (istan)	Uzbek (istan)
Meaning	"Land of the Wanderers"	"Land of the Forty Tribes"	"Land of the Tajik"	"Land of the Turkmen"	"Land of the Free"
Official title (in English)	Republic of Kazakhstan	Kyrgyz Republic	Republic of Tajikistan	Turkmenistan	Republic of Uzbekistan **
Population (July 2018)	18,744,548	5,849,296	8,604,882	5,411,012	30,023,709
Dominant ethnicities (2009)	Kazakh 63.1%	Kyrgyz 73.5% Uzbek 14.7%	Tajik 84.3% * Uzbek 13.8%	Turkmen 85% Uzbek 5%	Uzbek 83.8% Tajik 4.8% Kazakh 2.5%
Russians	23.7% plus Ukrainians 2.1%	5.5%	below 2%	4%	2.3%
Languages (official)	Kazakh (Qazaq) 74% Russian 94.4%	Kyrgyz 71%	Tajik 84.4%	Turkmen 72%	Uzbek 74.3%
Languages (other significant)		Russian 9% Uzbek 14.4%	Russian widely used Uzbek 11.9%	Russian 12% Uzbek 9%	Russian 14.2% Tajik 4.4%
Muslim religions	70.2% (majority Sunni) 2009	90% (majority Sunni) 2017	98% (Sunni 95%)	89%	88% (mostly Sunni)
Christian religions	26.2%	7%	negligible	Eastern Orthodox 9%	Eastern Orthodox 9%
Urban population (2018)	54.7%	36.4%	27.1%	51.6%	50.5%
Etymology	Turkic "kaz" ("to wander")	Turkic "kyrg" (forty) and "yz" (tribes)	Persian-dialects speaking populations +	Literal (Turkmen)	Turkic "uz" (self) and "bek" (master) meaning "free"

Source: (Central Intelligence Agency, n.d.) The CIA website updates periodically, so readers should consult the original source for updates and corrections. The CIA website updated population estimates at July 2020, for instance.

* Includes Pamiri and Yagnobi.

** Uzbekistan includes an autonomous Karakalpakstan Republic in which Karakalpak and Uzbek languages are official. Karakalpak are 2.2% of the country's population.

+ Tajik may mean roughly "Arab" or "Persian" as a term applied by Turks of Central Asia to Muslim invaders from Iran: J. Perry, "Tajik," Encyclopedia Iranica (July 20, 2009), retrieved June 15, 2019, from http://www.iranicaonline.org/articles/tajik-i-the-ethnonym-origins-and-application

52

Corruption and Anti-Corruption Reform in Central Asia

Table 5. Executive and political transitions in Central Asia

KAZAKHSTAN

CIA classifies Kazakhstan as a "presidential republic."* Ruling party is the Nur Otan Democratic People's Party (Nur Otan). Nursultan Nazarbayev was in power 1990 to resignation in March 2019.

● Nursultan Nazarbayev, a Doctor of Economics, first president of Kazakh SSR in April 1990 and first president of the Republic of Kazakhstan in December 1991, had been First Secretary of the Communist Party (1989-91) and then concurrently Chairman of the Supreme Council of the SSR (February-April 1990). There was essentially no effective opposition during any sequence of elections or referenda through 2015 confirming Nazarbayev in power until 2020.
● In March 2019, Nazarbayev resigned retaining title of First President with powers. Name of the capital city changed from Astana to Nur-Sultan in honor of the resigned First President.
● From March 2019, Kassym-Jomart Tokayev, a diplomat and Chairman of the Senate, of the same political party became interim president.
● Tokayev won the June 9, 2019 election with about 70% of the vote, based on exit polls. Protests and arrests were reported.

Sources: ("The First President of the Republic of Kazakhstan – Elbasy," retrieved June 7, 2019, from http://www.akorda.kz/en/republic_ of_kazakhstan/elbasy; "The President of the Republic of Kazakhstan," retrieved June 7, 2019, from http://www.akorda.kz/en/republic_of_ kazakhstan/president; Reuters (2019), Nazarbayev ally set to win Kazakh vote as hundreds protest. Retrieved June 15, 2019, from https://www. reuters.com/article/us-kazakhstan-election-idUSKCN1T90NY)

KYRGYZSTAN

CIA classifies Kyrgyzstan as a "parliamentary republic"*. President as head of state appoints prime minister. Ruling party since 2010 has been the Social Democratic Party of Kyrgyzstan.

● Askar Akayev served as president from October 1990 to March 2005.
● The July 2005 first Tulip (Kyrgyz) Revolution elected Kurmanbek Bakiyev, reelected 2009.
● The April 2010 second Tulip (Kyrgyz) Revolution drove Bakivev into exile, replaced by Roza Otunbayeva as interim president.
● The 2011 election selected Almazbek Atambayev.
● The October 2017 election selected Sooronbay Jeenbekov, former prime minister.

Source: (https://www.worldatlas.com/articles/presidents-of-kyrgyzstan-since-1991.html, retrieved June 15, 2019, from https://www.worldatlas. com/articles/presidents-of-kyrgyzstan-since-1991.html)

TAJIKISTAN

CIA classifies Tajikistan as a "presidential republic"*. Ruling party since 1994 is the People's Democratic Party of Tajikistan (PDP). Emomali Rahmon has been in power since 1992.

● From April 1990, a number of individuals served as Chairman of the Supreme Soviet or president (Communist Party).
● From January 1992, the incumbent Emomali Rahmon was in power initially as an "independent" (1992-94) and then for the PDP. There were elections in 1994, 1999, 2005, and 2013.

Source: (Presidents Of Tajikistan Since The Fall Of The Soviet Union, retrieved June 15, 2019, from https://www.worldatlas.com/articles/ presidents-of-tajikistan-since-the-fall-of-the-soviet-union.html)

TURKMENISTAN

CIA classifies Turkmenistan as an authoritarian "presidential republic"*.Ruling party has been the Democratic Party of Turkmenistan, but the incumbent president Gurbanguly Berdimuhamedow is an "independent."

● Saparmura Niyazov was in control from 1985 to 2006 when he died. During 1985-1991, he was First Secretary of the Communist Party. In 1999, the Assembly declared him President for Life.
● Constitutionally, Öwezgeldi Ataýew, Chairman of the Assembly, became president. He was arrested in December 2006.
● The Deputy Prime Minister became acting president.
● The February 2007 election selected the incumbent Gurbanguly Berdimuhamedow, who won two subsequent elections and became an independent.

Source: (List of Presidents of Turkmenistan, retrieved June 15, 2019, from https://www.worldatlas.com/articles/presidents-of-turkmenistan-since- the-collapse-of-the-soviet-union.html)

UZBEKISTAN

CIA classifies Uzbekistan as a highly authoritarian "presidential republic"*. Ruling party is the Uzbekistan Liberal Democratic Party, replacing the Uzbekistan National Revival Democratic Party and sponsoring the incumbent president.

● Islam Karimov, a mechanical engineer and Doctor of Economics, was a member of the Council of Ministers and Chairman of the State Planning Committee. In June 1989, he became First Secretary of the Communist Party. In March 1990, he was elected President of the SSR by the Supreme Council. In December 1991, he was elected President of the Republic, being reelected in subsequent elections. He died in September 2016 from a stroke.
● The successor Shavkat Mirzivoyev, prime minister since 2003, assumed office as interim president in September 2016 and was elected in December 2016. Nigmatilla Yuldashev, Chairman of the Senate since 2015, constitutionally was briefly for a few days interim president immediately following Karimov's death; but deferred to Mirzivoyev.

Sources: (President of Uzbekistan, retrieved June 7, 2019, from https://www.tashkent.org/uzland/pres.html; Uzbekistan elects Shavkat Mirziyoyev as president,
retrieved June 7, 2019, from
https://www.theguardian.com/world/2016/dec/05/uzbekistan-elects-shavkat-mirziyoyev-president-islam-karimov)

* Source: (Central Intelligence Agency, n.d.) The CIA website updates and corrects information periodically. Readers should consult the original source for latest information or to check errors including names and political parties in this table, which attempts only to provide a basic summary of key information.

53

Corruption and Anti-Corruption Reform in Central Asia

Another study concludes of the Rose Revolution in Georgia (2003), the Orange Revolution in Ukraine (2004), and the Tulip Revolution (2005):

… civil society's weakness seriously affected the three revolutionary processes. These were in fact initiated, led, controlled, and finally subordinated by former members of the authoritarian regimes' political elite. Finally, the supposedly democratic revolutions proved to be little more than a limited rotation of ruling elites within undemocratic political systems. (Tudoroiu, 2007, p. 315)

The situations in Kazakhstan and Uzbekistan under Nazarbayev and Karimov, respectively, depended on "the force of their personalities, patronage, and political skills" (Rumer et al., 2016). A similar situation was discussed earlier concerning Rahmon in Tajikistan (Rumer et al., 2016). There have been now relatively smooth transitions of power in all Central Asian countries other than Kyrgyzstan. In October 2018, for example, Russia detained Ikramjan Ilmiyanov, once an adviser to former president Atambayev, at Kyrgyz request on bribery charges and transferred him to Kyrgyz custody (Putz, 2018). In October 2018, the Kyrgyz Supreme Court determined that immunity of former presidents is not constitutional (Putz, 2018).

Junisbai and Junisbai (2019) report little attitudinal difference between populations of Kazakhstan and Kyrgyzstan concerning democratic practices. The point of the study is that Kazakhstan has been a "consolidated authoritarian" regime and Kyrgyzstan more competitive for top political leadership. The authors argue that both countries feature "patronal," or "patronage-based," politics. Public attitudes align with this patronal politics and not with any difference in regime type. Constitutional reform in 2010 in Kyrgyzstan has proven mostly irrelevant in practice according to these authors.

Another study argues that Eurasian polities are "hybrid regimes" that innovatively combine elements of democracy (especially contested elections) and autocracy (especially "pervasive political clientelism"). These countries are neither democracies nor dictatorships conventionally defined, but rather a transition illustrated in Russia from "competing pyramids" to "single-pyramid" political machines: "… in single-pyramid systems that preserve contested elections, as does Russia, public opinion matters more than in typical authoritarian regimes" (Hale, 2010, p. 33). That study also argues that cross-country comparisons provide more insight than single-country studies. North Korea is an autocracy. The present chapter draws attention to a cross-country comparison methodology.

Political developments in these countries can thus be usefully understood as machine politics, and the development of political systems can be understood as processes of rearranging the components of the machines in different ways. (Hale, 2010, p. 33)

SOLUTIONS AND RECOMMENDATIONS

The corruption and authoritarian problems in Central Asia may prove stubbornly intractable (Windsor, 2018a, 2018b). Anti-corruption and democratic reforms may prove difficult in Central Asia (Know, 2019; Pannier, 2016; Persson, Rothstein, & Teorell, 2013; World Bank, 2017). Legislative corruption is especially troubling, as legislatures may in reality simply determine what is legal or illegal according to political convenience (Kaufmann & Vicente, 2011; Kotchegura, 2018).

Prasad et al. (2019) emphasize three challenges to anti-corruption reform. (1) The "resource challenge" is that citizens must engage in corruption for survival (see McMann, 2014). (2) The uncertainty challenge involves confusion over gift versus bribe and private versus public. (3) The normative challenge involves competing moral criteria for defining right and wrong. The "Normative Power Europe" (Ahrens & Hoen, 2019) approach is not at work in Central Asia. The essential idea of "Normative Power Europe" is that Europe diffuses its moral norms within the international system. In contrast, political realism and accompanying cynicism and self-interest seems to be at work in Central Asia (Hyde-Price, 2006).

Looking for Anti-Corruption Models from Other Countries

The Central Asian countries can look to strong models of anti-corruption reform for guidance (Rubasundram & Rasiah, 2019). Two notable instances for study are Hong Kong (Scott & Gong, 2015) and Singapore (Badawi & AlQudah, 2019). China and India are operating anti-corruption campaigns. Lessons might be learned as well from nearby countries also struggling with corruption such as South Korea.

The available information suggests marked weakness of the civil society expected typically to help lead in anti-corruption efforts. There are no Transparency International affiliates listed at June 12, 2019, for Afghanistan, Iran, Kyrgyzstan, Tajikistan, Turkmenistan, and Uzbekistan – or India. There are affiliates listed for China, Kazakhstan, Mongolia, and Pakistan.

Transparency International (2015) noted that clean at home (the five top countries were Denmark, New Zealand, Finland, Sweden, and Norway) may still involve "dodgy records overseas" illustrated by TeliaSonera (a Swedish-Finnish merger) in Uzbekistan (Pollack & Allern, 2018). Danske Bank (Denmark) and Swedbank (Sweden) have been implicated recently in Russian money laundering schemes operating through the Baltics.

Multinational Enterprises and FDI

Thus a key question concerns what multinational corporations and other countries can do effectively to encourage anti-corruption reform in Central Asia. Multinationals are both a source of corruption and a possible solution for corruption (Windsor, 2017, 2019). Multinationals from corrupt countries most likely will operate corruptly in other corrupt countries (Zyglidopoulos, Dieleman, & Hirsch, in press). The Bribe Payers Index 2011 (Transparency International, 2011) places China (27th) and then Russia (28th) at the very bottom, and at a noticeable distance behind Mexico (26th) of the list of 28 major economies as assessed by business executives for the likelihood of paying bribes abroad. This information is significant, given the possibility of Chinese and Russian multinationals operating in Central Asia. The World Bank debars specific companies from projects based on evidence of misconduct in various forms. Several Chinese companies have received recent debarments.

FDI from reasonably clean countries and the World Bank might help open up Central Asia to anti-corruption and democratic reforms. A recent report prepared by Boston Consulting Group (BCG) estimates an FDI potential of $170 billion across Central Asia for the next decade (Abdimomunova et al., 2018; Consultancy.asia, 2019). However, much of this potential associates with extractive and construction sectors, which historically have corruption difficulties. Only up to $70 billion would be in non-extractive industries. The BCG report estimates a Central Asia gross domestic product (GDP) of about $265 billion in 2017 or 0.3% of world GDP and roughly comparable to Central America (at $255 billion) or Finland (at $252 billion). The FDI potential might require regional cooperation on infrastructure, free trade, and regulations.

The U.S. Department of Justice reported indictments of two Uzbek citizens concerning the telecom industry in Uzbekistan. (Cassin, 2019, provides the information in this paragraph.) The charges accused the daughter of deceased president Karimov, Gulnara Karimova (once Uzbek ambassador to the United Nations), of conspiracy to commit money laundering through U.S. banks and Bekhzod Akhmedov (former head of MTS Uzbek subsidiary Uzdunrobita) of the same charge and also violations of the FCPA. Allegedly, Akhmedov had arranged payments of $866 million to Gulnara Karimova from MTS (Russia), Telia (Sweden), and Vimpelcom (Netherlands) as bribes to obtain telecom licenses in Uzbekistan. All three companies had previously settled charges and admitted the bribery. G. Karimova was under house arrest from 2014; in 2015, DOJ asked several European countries to freeze about $1 billion in G. Karimova assets. Telia was formerly TeliaSonera, which was a Swedish-Finnish firm reportedly owned 37% by the Swedish government (Transparency International, 2015).

FUTURE RESEARCH DIRECTIONS

Several research directions appear fruitful to understanding the corruption situations in Central Asia and the effectiveness or ineffectiveness of possible solutions and recommendations for anti-corruption and democratic reforms. Democratization and anti-corruption may require considerable time and effort into the future.

Does the Natural Resource Curse Operate in Central Asia?

As minerals extraction increases and FDI comes into Central Asia (Furstenberg, 2018), there may be an increasing impact of the so-called "resource curse." This hypothesis argues that natural resources tend to be associated with lower development outcomes, partly due to corruption effects. A study attempted to disentangle the direct and indirect effects of natural resource abundance (Papyrakis & Gerlagh, 2004). That study concluded that natural resources in isolation negatively impact economic growth, but have a positive direct impact after considering multiple explanatory variables, including corruption. The study's model calculates indirect effects for various transmission channels. Those authors conclude that negative indirect effects significantly outweigh the positive direct effect.

Country-Specific Contexts

Central Asia involves a constellation (d'Agostino & Pieroni, 2019; Windsor, 2019) of factors including post-Soviet, post-communist heritage including both authoritarianism and corruption, culture in each country, and demand and supply forces contributing to corruption. Culture is an awkward concept in that it implies something wrong in local attitudes and behaviors. A possible alternative interpretation may be there is a culture of corruption in which there is silent acceptance of the need for corruption in both government and daily life and a belief that anti-corruption reform efforts are ineffective. However, Kyrgyzstan illustrates that there can be anti-corruption efforts (the Tulip Revolutions of 2005 and 2010) – but without apparent effect on the continuation of authoritarianism or corruption carried out behind secretly. Detailed research into this constellation of factors – causes, processes, and outcomes – and the impact of this constellation on anti-corruption reforms and vice versa is certainly desirable. It is essential to study how corruption demand and supply affect foreign and domestic businesses in each country (Ashyrov & Masso, 2019). There are possibly multiple variations in how authoritarianism and corruption can and do operate.

Prospects for Increasing Democratic Governance

How government and corruption work in each country of Central Asia is also a desirable research direction. At best, the regimes are only nominally democratic. Turkmenistan and Uzbekistan are markedly authoritarian. The "hybrid regime" explanation is worth developing in detail for each country. A confounding difficulty for Central Asia is that Afghanistan, China, Iran, and Russia surround the region. These bordering countries are themselves corrupt – Afghanistan is a war zone, and the other surrounding countries are aggressively expanding power-oriented states. Mongolia points to a better situation, although it borders Russia and China. Comparative cross-country investigation is an important research direction. Something seems to be working in Mongolia that is missing in Central Asia.

CONCLUSION

This chapter addresses corruption and anti-corruption reform in the five countries of Central Asia. The study draws on publicly available literature and data in English. The primary purpose is a broad survey of the situation in the region relevant to the general interests of this volume. No original research in the field is involved. The methodology is assembly and reading of English-language literature, including several sources on corruption information.

In general terms, the problems in Central Asia presently look intractable. Corruption may be increasing in Eastern Europe and Central Asia (Anti-Corruption Digest, 2019). All the regimes are, at best, only nominally democratic. Corruption is pervasive in the region, although Turkmenistan and Uzbekistan seem to be considerably worse than the other three countries. Kazakhstan may be showing signs of improvement. In Kyrgyzstan, there is citizen opposition to authoritarianism and corruption. Most of the assembled information about Central Asia seems reasonably consistent for the region and for each country.

ACKNOWLEDGMENT

This research received no specific grant from any funding agency in the public, commercial, or not-for-profit sectors.

REFERENCES

Abdimomunova, L., Boutenko, V., Chin, V., Nuriyev, R., Perapechka, S., Raji, M., . . . Türpitz, A. (2018, December 23). *Investing in Central Asia: One region, many opportunities.* Retrieved on June 8, 2019, from: https://www.bcg.com/en-ru/perspectives/205272

Ahrens, J., & Hoen, H. W. (2019). The emergence of state capitalism in Central Asia: The absence of Normative Power Europe. In M. Neuman (Ed.), *Democracy promotion and the Normative Power Europe framework: The European Union in South Eastern Europe, Eastern Europe, and Central Asia* (pp. 81–97). Cham, Switzerland: Springer. doi:10.1007/978-3-319-92690-2_5

Andersson, S., & Heywood, P. M. (2009). The politics of perception: Use and abuse of Transparency International's approach to measuring corruption. *Political Studies, 57*(4), 746–767. doi:10.1111/j.1467-9248.2008.00758.x

Anti-Corruption Digest. (2019, February 5). *Corruption in Eastern Europe & Central Asia is on the rise.* Retrieved on May 31, 2019, from: https://anticorruptiondigest.com/2019/02/05/corruption-in-eastern-europe-central-asia-is-on-the-rise/#axzz5pVaWYDXg

Ashyrov, G., & Masso, J. (2019, February 5). *Does corruption affect local and foreign owned companies differently? Evidence from the BEEPS survey.* The University of Tartu FEBA Working Papers. doi:10.2139srn.3329236

Badawi, A., & AlQudah, A. (2019). The impact of anti-corruption policies on the profitability and growth of firms listed in the stock market: Application on Singapore with a panel data analysis. *Journal of Developing Areas, 53*(1), 179–204. doi:10.1353/jda.2019.0011

Balan, D. J., & Knack, S. (2012). The correlation between human capital and morality and its effect on economic performance: Theory and evidence. *Journal of Comparative Economics, 40*(3), 457–475. doi:10.1016/j.jce.2011.12.005

Cassin, H. (2019, March 7). *DOJ indicts [Gulnara] Karimova for taking $866 million in bribes.* Retrieved on May 31, 2019, from: http://www.fcpablog.com/blog/2019/3/7/doj-indicts-karimova-for-taking-866-million-in-bribes.html

Central Intelligence Agency. (n.d.). *The world factbook.* Retrieved on June 13, 2019, from: https://www.cia.gov/library/publications/the-world-factbook/

Charron, N. (2016). Do corruption measures have a perception problem? Assessing the relationship between experiences and perceptions of corruption among citizens and experts. *European Political Science Review*, *8*(1), 147–171. doi:10.1017/S1755773914000447

Chayes, S. (2016). *The structure of corruption in Kyrgyzstan*. Retrieved on May 31, 2019, from: https://carnegieendowment.org/files/9_Kyrgyzstan_Full_Web1.pdf

Consultancy.asia. (2019, March 19). *BCG outlines $170 billion FDI potential for Central Asia over next decade*. Retrieved on June 7, 2019, from: https://www.consultancy.asia/news/2078/bcg-outlines-170-billion-fdi-potential-for-central-asia-over-next-decade

d'Agostino, G., & Pieroni, L. (2019). Modelling corruption perceptions: Evidence from Eastern Europe and Central Asian countries. *Social Indicators Research*, *142*(1), 311–341. doi:10.100711205-018-1886-3

Das, J., & Dirienzo, C. E. (2010). Tourism competitiveness and corruption: A cross-country analysis. *Tourism Economics*, *16*(3), 477–492. doi:10.5367/000000010792278392

Dixit, A. K. (2016). Corruption: Supply-side and demand-side solutions. In S. M. Dev & P. G. Babu (Eds.), *Development in India: Micro and macro perspectives* (pp. 57–68). New Delhi: Springer India. doi:10.1007/978-81-322-2541-6_4

Duerrenberger, N., & Warning, S. (2018). Corruption and education in developing countries: The role of public vs. private funding of higher education. *International Journal of Educational Development*, *62*, 217–225. doi:10.1016/j.ijedudev.2018.05.002

El Bahnasawy, N. G., & Revier, C. F. (2012). The determinants of corruption: Cross-country-panel-data analysis. *The Developing Economies*, *50*(4), 311–333. doi:10.1111/j.1746-1049.2012.00177.x

Freedom House. (2018). *Turkmenistan*. Retrieved on May 31, 2019, from: https://freedomhouse.org/report/nations-transit/2018/turkmenistan

Freedom House. (2019). *Freedom in the World 2019*. Retrieved on June 4, 2019, from: https://freedomhouse.org/report/freedom-world/freedom-world-2019

Furstenberg, S. (2018). State responses to reputational concerns: The case of the Extractive Industries Transparency Initiative in Kazakhstan. *Central Asian Survey*, *37*(2), 286–304. doi:10.1080/02634937.2018.1428789

Gephart, M. (2015). Contested meanings in the anti-corruption discourse: International and local narratives in the case of Paraguay. *Critical Policy Studies*, *9*(2), 119–138. doi:10.1080/19460171.2014.951668

Gründler, K., & Potrafke, N. (2019). Corruption and economic growth: New empirical evidence. *European Journal of Political Economy*. doi:10.1016/j.ejpoleco.2019.08.001

Hale, H. E. (2010). Eurasian polities as hybrid regimes: The case of Putin's Russia. *Journal of Eurasian Studies*, *1*(1), 33–41. doi:10.1016/j.euras.2009.11.001

Holmes, L. (2018). A fish rots from the head: corruption scandals in post-Communist Russia. In O. E. Hawthorne & S. Magu (Eds.), *Corruption scandals and their global impacts* (pp. 57–76). London: Routledge. doi:10.4324/9781315142722-4

Hornberger, J. (2018). A ritual of corruption: How young middle-class South Africans get their driver's licenses. *Current Anthropology*, *59*(S18), S138–S148. doi:10.1086/696099

Huang, C.-J. (2016). Is corruption bad for economic growth? Evidence from Asia-Pacific countries. *The North American Journal of Economics and Finance*, *35*, 247–256. doi:10.1016/j.najef.2015.10.013

Hyde-Price, A. (2005). 'Normative' power Europe: A realist critique. *Journal of European Public Policy*, *13*(2), 217–234. doi:10.1080/13501760500451634

Integrity Business Anti-Corruption Portal, G. A. N. (2016a, May). *Turkmenistan Corruption Report*. Retrieved on May 31, 2019, from: https://www.business-anti-corruption.com/country-profiles/turkmenistan/

Integrity Business Anti-Corruption Portal, G. A. N. (2016b, July). *Kazakhstan Corruption Report*. Retrieved on May 31, 2019, from: https://www.business-anti-corruption.com/country-profiles/kazakhstan/

Integrity Business Anti-Corruption Portal, G. A. N. (2016c, July). *Kyrgyzstan Corruption Report*. Retrieved on May 31, 2019, from: https://www.business-anti-corruption.com/country-profiles/kyrgyzstan/

Integrity Business Anti-Corruption Portal, G. A. N. (2016d, August). *Tajikistan Corruption Report*. Retrieved on May 31, 2019, from: https://www.business-anti-corruption.com/country-profiles/tajikistan/

Integrity Business Anti-Corruption Portal, G. A. N. (2017, June). *Uzbekistan Corruption Report*. Retrieved on May 31, 2019, from: https://www.business-anti-corruption.com/country-profiles/uzbekistan/

Junisbai, B., & Junisbai, A. (2019). Regime type versus patronal politics: A comparison of "ardent democrats" in Kazakhstan and Kyrgyzstan. *Post-Soviet Affairs, 35*(3), 240–257. doi:10.1080/1060586X.2019.1568144

Kalyuzhnova, Y., & Belitski, M. (2019). The impact of corruption and local content policy in on firm performance: Evidence from Kazakhstan. *Resources Policy, 61*, 67–76. doi:10.1016/j.resourpol.2019.01.016

Kassab, H. S., & Rosen, J. D. (2019). Central Asia and Middle East. In *Corruption, institutions, and fragile states* (pp. 65–84). Cham, Switzerland: Palgrave Macmillan. doi:10.1007/978-3-030-04312-4_4

Kaufmann, D., & Vicente, P. C. (2011). Legal corruption. *Economics and Politics, 23*(2), 195–219. doi:10.1111/j.1468-0343.2010.00377.x

Kendzior, S. (2013, February 19). *The curse of stability in Central Asia: The autocrats of Central Asia like to tout the virtues of stability. But they're really making excuses for decay.* Retrieved on June 3, 2019, from: https://foreignpolicy.com/2013/02/19/the-curse-of-stability-in-central-asia/

Kirişci, K., & Le Corre, P. (2018, January 2). *The new geopolitics of Central Asia: China vies for influence in Russia's backyard: What will it mean for Kazakhstan?* Retrieved on May 14, 2019, from: https://www.brookings.edu/blog/order-from-chaos/2018/01/02/the-new-geopolitics-of-central-asia-china-vies-for-influence-in-russias-backyard/

Knack, S. (2007). Measuring corruption: A critique of indicators in Eastern Europe and Central Asia. *Journal of Public Policy, 27*(3), 255–291. doi:10.1017/S0143814X07000748

Ko, K., & Samajdar, A. (2010). Evaluation of international corruption indexes: Should we believe them or not? *The Social Science Journal, 47*(3), 508–540. doi:10.1016/j.soscij.2010.03.001

Kotchegura, A. (2018). Preventing corruption risk in legislation: Evidence from Russia, Moldova, and Kazakhstan. *International Journal of Public Administration, 41*(5-6), 377–387. doi:10.1080/01900692.2018.1426011

Kudaibergenova, D. T., & Shin, B. (2018). Authors and authoritarianism in Central Asia: Failed agency and nationalising authoritarianism in Uzbekistan and Kazakhstan. *Asian Studies Review, 42*(2), 304–322. doi:10.1080/10357823.2018.1447549

Marantidou, V., & Cossa, R. A. (2014, October 1). *China and Russia's Great Game in Central Asia: "The real problem is that wherever Russia turns it encounters China and vice-versa."* Retrieved on May 14, 2019, from: https://nationalinterest. org/blog/the-buzz/china-russias-great-game-central-asia-11385

McMann, K. M. (2014). *Corruption as a last resort: Adapting to the market in Central Asia.* Ithaca, NY: Cornell University Press.

Nichol, J. (2014, March 21). *Central Asia: Regional developments and implications for U.S. interests.* Congressional Research Service. Retrieved on May 31, 2019, from: https://fas.org/sgp/crs/row/RL33458.pdf

Nur-tegin, K., & Czap, H. J. (2012). Corruption: Democracy, autocracy, and political stability. *Economic Analysis and Policy, 42*(1), 51–66. doi:10.1016/S0313-5926(12)50004-4

Nur-tegin, K., & Jakee, K. (2019). Does corruption grease or sand the wheels of development? New results based on disaggregated data. *Quarterly Review of Economics and Finance.* doi:10.1016/j.qref.2019.02.001

Omirgazy, D. (2016, November 30). *More Kazakh citizens see progress in fight against corruption, according to Global Corruption Barometer.* Retrieved on June 12, 2019, from: https://astanatimes.com/2016/11/more-kazakh-citizens-see-progress-in-fight-against-corruption-according-to-global-corruption-barometer/

Organisation for Economic Co-operation and Development. (2008). *The Istanbul Anti-Corruption Action Plan: Progress and Challenges.* Retrieved on June 12, 2019, from: http://www.oecd.org/daf/anti-bribery/42740427.pdf

Organisation for Economic Co-operation and Development. (2016). *Anti-corruption Reforms in Eastern Europe and Central Asia: Progress and Challenges, 2013-2015.* Retrieved on June 12, 2019, from: http://www.oecd.org/corruption/acn/Anti-Corruption-Reforms-Eastern-Europe-Central-Asia-2013-2015-ENG.pdf

Organisation for Economic Co-operation and Development. (2018). *Anti-corruption reforms in Kyrgyzstan 4th round of monitoring of the Istanbul Anti-Corruption Action Plan.* Retrieved on May 31, 2019, from: https://www.oecd.org/corruption/acn/OECD-ACN-Kyrgyzstan-4th-Round-Monitoring-Report-2018-ENG.pdf

Organisation for Economic Co-operation and Development. (n.d.). *Anti-Corruption Network › Istanbul Action Plan.* Retrieved on June 12, 2019, from: http://www.oecd.org/corruption/acn/istanbulactionplan/

Osipian, A. L. (2012). Education corruption, reform, and growth: Case of Post-Soviet Russia. *Journal of Eurasian Studies*, *3*(1), 20–29. doi:10.1016/j.euras.2011.10.003

Pannier, B. (2016, June 4). The perfect storm of corruption in Central Asia. *RadioFreeEuropeRadioLiberty*. Retrieved on May 31, 2019, from: https://www.rferl.org/a/corruption-central-asia/27779246.html

Papyrakis, E., & Gerlagh, R. (2004). The resource curse hypothesis and its transmission channels. *Journal of Comparative Economics*, *32*(1), 181–193. doi:10.1016/j.jce.2003.11.002

Persson, A., Rothstein, B., & Teorell, J. (2013). Why anticorruption reforms fail—Systemic corruption as a collective action problem. *Governance: An International Journal of Policy, Administration and Institutions*, *26*(3), 449–471. doi:10.1111/j.1468-0491.2012.01604.x

Pertiwi, K. (2018). Contextualizing corruption: A cross-disciplinary approach to studying corruption in organizations. *Administrative Sciences, 8*(2), 12. doi:10.3390/admsci8020012

Pollack, E., & Allern, S. (2018). Disclosure of Scandinavian telecom companies' corruption in Uzbekistan: The role of investigative journalists. *European Journal of Communication*, *33*(1), 73–88. doi:10.1177/0267323117750697

Poprawe, M. (2015). A panel data analysis of the effect of corruption on tourism. *Applied Economics*, *47*(23), 2399–2412. doi:10.1080/00036846.2015.1005874

Prasad, M., da Silva, M. B. M., & Nickow, A. (2019). Approaches to corruption: A synthesis of the scholarship. *Studies in Comparative International Development*, *54*(1), 96–132. doi:10.100712116-018-9275-0

Putz, C. (2018, October 29). *Another Atambayev ally faces corruption charges in Kyrgyzstan: Ikramjan Ilmiyanov, a former adviser to previous Kyrgyz President Almazbek Atambayev, faces corruption charges*. Retrieved on May 31, 2019, from: https://thediplomat.com/tag/corruption-in-central-asia/

Raimondi, P. P. (2019, May 13). *Central Asia oil and gas industry – The external powers' energy interests in Kazakhstan, Turkmenistan and Uzbekistan*. Fondazione Eni Enrico Mattei Working Papers 1265. Retrieved on May 31, 2019, from: https://services.bepress.com/feem/paper1265/

Rodríguez-Merino, P. A. (2019). Old "counter-revolution", new "terrorism": Historicizing the framing of violence in Xinjiang by the Chinese state. *Central Asian Survey*, *38*(1), 27–45. doi:10.1080/02634937.2018.1496066

Rubasundram, G. A., & Rasiah, R. (2019). Corruption and good governance: An analysis of ASEAN's E-Governance experience. *Journal of Southeast Asian Economies*, *36*(1), 57–70. https://www.muse.jhu.edu/article/722710. doi:10.1355/ae36-1f

Rumer, E., Sokolsy, R., & Stronski, P. (2016, January 25). *U.S. policy toward Central Asia 3.0.* Retrieved on June 3, 2019, from: https://carnegieendowment.org/2016/01/25/u.s.-policy-toward-central-asia-3.0-pub-62556

Rusch, J. J. (2019, February 7). *Sorry, but corruption can be measured.* Retrieved on June 1, 2019, from: http://www.fcpablog.com/blog/2019/2/7/sorry-but-corruption-can-be-measured.html

Saha, S., & Yap, G. (2015). Corruption and tourism: An empirical investigation in a non-linear framework. *International Journal of Tourism Research*, *17*(3), 272–281. doi:10.1002/jtr.1985

Sandholtz, W., & Taagepera, R. (2005). Corruption, culture, and communism. *International Review of Sociology*, *15*(1), 109–131. doi:10.1080/03906700500038678

Schenkkan, N. (2016, January 22). *A perfect storm in Central Asia: For years, the five ex-Soviet republics have enjoyed surprising stability. But Russia's economic crisis is shaking their foundations.* Retrieved on May 31, 2019, from: https://foreignpolicy.com/2016/01/22/a-perfect-storm-in-central-asia/

Sciutto, J. (2019). *The shadow war: Inside Russia's and China's secret operations to defeat America.* New York: Harper.

Scott, I., & Gong, T. (2015). Evidence-based policy-making for corruption prevention in Hong Kong: A bottom-up approach. *Asia Pacific Journal of Public Administration*, *37*(2), 87–101. doi:10.1080/23276665.2015.1041222

Swartz, B., Wadsworth, F., & Wheat, J. (2011). Perceptions of corruption in Central Asian countries. *International Business & Economics Research Journal*, *7*(3), 71–78. doi:10.19030/iber.v7i3.3235

Trabelsi, M. A., & Trabelsi, H. (2014). *At what level of corruption does economic growth decrease?* Retrieved from https://mpra.ub.uni-muenchen.de/81279/

Transparency International. (2011, November 2). *Bribe Payers Index 2011.* Retrieved on June 12, 2019, from: https://www.transparency.org/whatwedo/publication/bpi_2011

Transparency International. (2015). *Corruption Perceptions Index 2015.* Retrieved on June 12, 2019, from: https://www.transparency.org/cpi2015

Transparency International. (2016, November 16). *People and corruption: Europe and Central Asia 2016*. Retrieved on June 11, 2019, from: https://www.transparency.org/whatwedo/publication/people_and_corruption_europe_and_central_asia_2016

Transparency International. (2017a, March 7). *People and corruption: Asia Pacific – Global Corruption Barometer*. Retrieved on June 11, 2019, from: https://www.transparency.org/whatwedo/publication/people_and_corruption_asia_pacific_global_corruption_barometer

Transparency International. (2017b, November 14). *People and corruption: Citizen's voices from around the world*. Retrieved on June 11, 2019, from: https://www.transparency.org/whatwedo/publication/people_and_corruption_citizens_voices_from_around_the_world

Transparency International. (2019a, January). *Corruption Perceptions Index*. Retrieved on June 5, 2019, from: https://www.transparency.org/research/cpi/overview

Transparency International. (2019b, January 29). *Eastern Europe & Central Asia: Weak checks and balances threat anti-corruption efforts: Corruption flourishing across the region while the quality of democracy continues to falter or stagnate*. Retrieved on May 31, 2019, from: https://www.transparency.org/news/feature/weak_checks_and_balances_threaten_anti_corruption_efforts_across_eastern_eu

Tudoroiu, T. (2007). Rose, Orange, and Tulip: The failed post-Soviet revolutions. *Communist and Post-Communist Studies*, *40*(3), 315–342. doi:10.1016/j.postcomstud.2007.06.005

Urinboyev, R. (2018). Corruption in post-Soviet Uzbekistan. In A. Farazmand (Ed.), *Global encyclopedia of public administration, public policy, and governance*. Cham, Switzerland: Springer Nature Switzerland. Retrieved on June 11, 2019, from: https://link.springer.com/content/pdf/10.1007%2F978-3-319-31816-5_3666-1.pdf

Urinboyev, R. (2019). *Everyday corruption and social norms in post-Soviet Uzbekistan*. Gothenburg, Sweden: The Program on Governance and Local Development at the University of Gothenburg. Retrieved on May 31, 2019, from: https://portal.research.lu.se/portal/files/57641563/gld_wp_19_final.pdf

Walker, C. (2011). *The Perpetual Battle: Corruption in the Former Soviet Union and the New EU Members*. Retrieved on June 12, 2019, from: https://freedomhouse.org/sites/default/files/PerpetualBattle.pdf

Warf, B. (2019). Geographically uneven landscapes of Asian corruption. In B. Warf (Ed.), *Global corruption from a geographic perspective* (pp. 143–193). Cham, Switzerland: Springer Nature Switzerland. doi:10.1007/978-3-030-03478-8_6

Wilhelm, P. G. (2002). International validation of the Corruption Perceptions Index: Implications for business ethics and entrepreneurship education. *Journal of Business Ethics, 35*(3), 177–189. doi:10.1023/A:1013882225402

Windsor, D. (2017). The role of multinationals in corruption in the Asia-Pacific region. In M. dela Rama & C. Rowley (Eds.), *The changing face of corruption in the Asia Pacific* (pp. 57–70). Amsterdam, The Netherlands: Elsevier. doi:10.1016/B978-0-08-101109-6.00004-6

Windsor, D. (2018a). Corruption in the CIS and Eurasia: Sources, consequences, and possible solutions. In O. Karnaukhova, A. Udovikina, & B. Christiansen (Eds.), *Economic and geopolitical perspectives of the Commonwealth of Independent States and Eurasia* (pp. 91–120). Hershey, PA: IGI Global. doi:10.4018/978-1-5225-3264-4.ch004

Windsor, D. (2018b). Corruption intelligence and analysis. In M. Munoz (Ed.), *Global business intelligence* (pp. 113–126). New York: Routledge.

Windsor, D. (2019). Influencing MNC strategies for managing corruption and favoritism in Pacific Asia countries: A multiple-theory configurational perspective. *Asia Pacific Business Review, 25*(4), 501–533. doi:10.1080/13602381.2019.1589769

World Bank. (2017, November 1). *Economies in Central Asia continue reform agenda.* Retrieved on June 2, 2019, from: https://www.worldbank.org/en/news/press-release/2017/11/01/economies-in-central-asia-continue-reform-agenda

World Bank. (2018). *Doing Business 2018: Reforming to create jobs.* Retrieved on June 2, 2019, from: https://www.doingbusiness.org/en/reports/global-reports/doing-business-2018

World Bank. (n.d.). *DataBank.* Retrieved on June 15, 2019, from: https://databank.worldbank.org/data/reports.aspx?Report_Name=WGI-Table&Id=ceea4d8b

World Bank Group. (n.d.). *Corruption.* Retrieved on June 15, 2019, from: https://www.enterprisesurveys.org/data/exploretopics/corruption

World Justice Project. (2019). *World Justice Project Rule of Law Index®.* Retrieved on June 1, 2019, from: https://worldjusticeproject.org/our-work/research-and-data/wjp-rule-law-index-2019

Yap, G., & Saha, S. (2013). Do political instability, terrorism, and corruption have deterring effects on tourism development even in the presence of UNESCO heritage? A cross-country panel estimate. *Tourism Analysis, 18*(5), 587–599. doi:10.3727/108354213X13782245307911

Zakharov, N. (2019). Does corruption hinder investment? Evidence from Russian regions. *European Journal of Political Economy*, *56*, 39–61. doi:10.1016/j.ejpoleco.2018.06.005

Zyglidopoulos, S., Dieleman, M., & Hirsch, P. (2019). Playing the game: Unpacking the rationale for organizational corruption in MNCs. *Journal of Management Inquiry*. doi:10.1177/1056492618817827

ADDITIONAL READING

Al-Fazari, H., & Teng, J. (2019). Adoption of One Belt and One Road initiative by Oman: Lessons from the East. *Journal for Global Business Advancement*, *12*(1), 145–166. doi:10.1504/JGBA.2019.10021555

Dabrowski, M., & Batsaikhan, U. (2017). Central Asia—Twenty-five years after the breakup of the USSR. *Russian Journal of Economics*, *3*(3), 296–320. https://bruegel.org/2017/11/central-asia-twenty-five-years-after-the-breakup-of-the-ussr/. doi:10.1016/j.ruje.2017.09.005

Denoon, D. B. H. (Ed.). (2015). *China, the United States, and the future of Central Asia*. New York: NYU Press. doi:10.18574/nyu/9781479844333.001.0001

Isaacs, R., & Frigerio, A. (Eds.). (2019). *Theorizing Central Asian politics: The state, ideology and power*. Cham, Switzerland: Palgrave Macmillan. doi:10.1007/978-3-319-97355-5

Karrar, H. H. (2019). Between border and bazaar: Central Asia's informal economy. *Journal of Contemporary Asia*, *49*(2), 272–293. doi:10.1080/00472336.2018.1532017

Pomfret, R. (2019). *The Central Asian economies in the twenty-first century: Paving a new Silk Road*. Princeton, NJ: Princeton University Press.

Rustemova, A. (2011). Political economy of Central Asia: Initial reflections on the need for a new approach. *Journal of Eurasian Studies*, *2*(1), 30–39. doi:10.1016/j.euras.2010.10.002

Sorbello, P. (2018). Oil and gas political economy in Central Asia: The international perspective. In S. Raszewski (Ed.), *The international political economy of oil and gas* (pp. 109–124). Cham, Switzerland: Palgrave Macmillan. doi:10.1007/978-3-319-62557-7_8

Tiulegenov, M. (2019). Official discourses on peace and security in post-Soviet Central Asia. In A. Kulnazarova & V. Popovski (Eds.), *The Palgrave handbook of global approaches to peace* (pp. 411–434). Cham, Switzerland: Palgrave Macmillan. doi:10.1007/978-3-319-78905-7_20

Wang, Y., Hong, S., Wang, Y., Gong, X., He, C., Lu, Z., & Zhan, F. B. (2019). What is the difference in global research on Central Asia before and after the collapse of the USSR: A bibliometric analysis. *Scientometrics, 119*(2), 909–930. doi:10.100711192-019-03069-0

KEY TERMS AND DEFINITIONS

Anti-Corruption Reform: Private, governmental, and international efforts to reduce corruption in particular countries.

Authoritarianism: An illegitimate political system concentrating authority and power to a dictator or small elite of oligarchs not constitutionally constrained by the ruled.

Central Asia: The five countries of Kazakhstan, Kyrgyzstan, Tajikistan, Turkmenistan, and Uzbekistan, previously soviet socialist republics (SSRs) within the Union of Soviet Socialist Republics (USSR), which became independent in 1991 upon USSR disintegration.

Constitutional Polity: A legitimate political system based on the rule of law defined in a constitution limiting authority and power of rulers, whether functioning as a representative republic or a direct democracy.

Corruption: Adapting the definition by Transparency International, illegitimate abuse of a position of trust or power, especially public office, for private gain obtained typically through bribery by or extortion of others.

Culture of Corruption: Attitudes, beliefs, and practices so pervasive as to make much of the population tolerant of corruption in public and private life and indifferent to anti-corruption reform through lack of confidence in the possibility of positive change.

Grand Corruption: Adapting the definition by Transparency International, corruption through bribery or extortion occurring at higher levels of government.

Petty Corruption: Adapting the definition by Transparency International, corruption through bribery or extortion occurring in daily life, including private transactions and at lower levels of government.

Political or System Corruption: Adapting the definition by Transparency International, systematic corruption and abuse of power by the top officials of government typically in combination with and furtherance of authoritarianism.

Chapter 4
The Impact of USD–TRY Forex Rate Volatility on Imports to Turkey from Central Asia

Yakup Ari

iD https://orcid.org/0000-0002-5666-5365
Alanya Alaaddin Keykubat University, Turkey

ABSTRACT

The purpose of this study is to put out the impact of volatility of the USD-TRY forex rate on imports to Turkey from Central Asia. The volatility of the USD/TRY exchange rate is analysed with a conditional variance model which is Generalised Autoregressive Conditional Heteroscedastic (GARCH) model and its extensions. The other section of the methodology is an application of Autoregressive Distributed Lag (ARDL) bounds test which is an efficient approach to determine the cointegration, long-term and short-term relations between macroeconomic variables. The exponential GARCH volatility of the exchange rate and the monthly trade data between the years 2005 and 2018 are used in the ARDL bounds test.

INTRODUCTION

The concept of Central Asian countries was formed after the declaration of independence of the five independent states of Kazakhstan, Uzbekistan, Kyrgyzstan, Uzbekistan, and Turkmenistan from the Union of Soviet Socialist Republics (USSR) in the 1990s. The sovereignty of the Central Asian countries in 1991 opened a new gateway to international and security relations. However, these relations included the special qualities that were the legacy of the USSR. The sudden disintegration

DOI: 10.4018/978-1-7998-2239-4.ch004

Copyright © 2020, IGI Global. Copying or distributing in print or electronic forms without written permission of IGI Global is prohibited.

of the Soviet Union posed a serious threat to new institutional arrangements on regional security. Following the breakup of the USSR, Turkey showed great effort to improve the political and economic cooperation with Central Asian states. After the socialist period, these countries became a great market for western countries.

Turkey's relations and cooperation with these countries, which have common language, historical and cultural ties, have developed rapidly based on common interest in many areas. Turkey's relations with Uzbekistan, Kazakhstan, and Kyrgyzstan are at the level of a strategic partnership and iyd relations with all three countries were established within the framework of the High Level Strategic Cooperation Council mechanism. It was decided to establish a Cooperation Council between Tajikistan and Turkey. Turkey's relations with Turkmenistan are developing rapidly in many areas, especially in the fields of commercial, economic, investment and contracting (www.mfa.gov.tr, 2019).

The Central Asian region is a growing market with an increasing purchasing power and a population close to 100 million. Kazakhstan, Turkmenistan and Uzbekistan are among the fastest-growing economies in the world. Central Asian countries constitute a rich geography in terms of natural resources. For example, Kazakhstan is expected to become one of the world's largest oil-producing countries and the country has a very rich geography in terms of mineral resources. Kazakhstan, which is estimated to have 15% of uranium reserves in the world, is the largest uranium producer country in the world since 2009. It is known that the coal reserves in Kazakhstan are the ninth-largest in the world. It is estimated that Turkmenistan has the world's fourth-largest natural gas reserve. Uzbekistan and Turkmenistan are among the most important cotton-producing countries in the world. Uzbekistan has the fourth-largest gold reserves in the world.

The hydroelectric potential and mineral deposits of Kyrgyzstan and Tajikistan stand out. Kumtor gold deposits in Kyrgyzstan contain the eighth largest gold reserves in the world. Tajikistan is expected to become an important player in the world aluminium market with its existing aluminium reserves (Budak, 2013). Turkey's trade volume with countries in the region in 2018 was realized 6 billion dollars, a total investment of Turkish companies in the region approached $ 15 billion. The total value of the projects undertaken by Turkish contracting firms in the region exceeded 86 billion dollars. More than 4,000 Turkish companies operate in the region (www.mfa.gov.tr, 2019).

The purpose of this study is to examine the impact of the exchange rate volatility on imports from Central Asia to Turkey. This is an important topic since the usage of national currencies for trade is often discussed today. Turkey especially wishes to eliminate the effect of foreign exchange rates on international trade because the fluctuations in the forex markets affect the economy of developing countries. The historical development of international trade between Turkey and Central Asia countries is discussed regarding trade data. Moreover, a macroeconomic descriptive analysis is applied to figure out the structure of the economies of the mentioned countries. The study is an empirical study that should include a methodology part which is briefly discussed.

The methodology of the study has two separate parts the first of which concerns the volatility and the second is the impact of volatility on trade. The volatility of the US Dollar to Turkish Lira (USD/TRY) exchange rate is analysed with a conditional variance model that is Generalised Autoregressive Conditional Heteroscedastic (GARCH) model and its extensions. The GARCH model and its extensions help us to determine volatility data. The other section of methodology is an application of Autoregressive Distributed Lag (ARDL) model which is an efficient model to determine the cointegration, long-term and short-term relations between macroeconomic variables. The monthly trade data period between the years 2005 and 2018 is used with the volatility in ARDL approach. In the last section, the discussion will be done according to the findings and outputs of empirical analysis; furthermore, the suggestions will be given for policymakers.

BRIEF LITERATURE REVIEW

Central Asia is the only regional subsystem in the world geography that does not have access to the high seas. Power asymmetry between the countries of the region and Russia continues. Similarly, the imbalance of power against the countries of the region becomes evident in developing relations with China. The unique geographic structure of Central Asia, along with its rich underground resources, and the existing power balances have created a process in which economic and technological elements are more prominent in competition. This process, in which Russia has also sought economic integration, enabled global competition in Central Asia to settle on the economic-political axis.

Central Asia, which is composed of countries that do not have access to the high seas as mentioned above, considers that global actors will focus on underground resources and commercial potential, especially oil and natural gas in the region. Therefore, it is observed that competition in Central Asia is more intensified in the economic field, especially the energy-weighted economic potential of the region which became apparent following the global financial crisis of 2008. Indeed, in the 1990s like other external actors outside Russia, Turkey has begun to implement a limited policy with more economic and cultural fields for Central Asia. It is observed that Turkey left the romantic view of the 1990s and developed a realistic approach to Central Asia in the 2000s. Economic pragmatism has been brought to the forefront in relations between Turkey and the countries in the region.

The Impact of USD-TRY Forex Rate Volatility on Imports to Turkey from Central Asia

The Central Asian Republics, which were in a transition period to the market economy during the 1990s, were confronted with many structural problems and could not achieve a sufficient level of growth. Since the beginning of the 2000s, the transition to a free market economy – and the transformation of the economy to the integration with the world economy – have resulted in great economic improvements. The Turkish Republic started to show economic improvements with the use of raw material riches, which could not be used efficiently before independence, to contribute to the industrialization of the countries after independence (Alagöz et al., 2004). However, this situation did not last long and the Central Asian Republics were affected by the 2008 international crisis like all other countries of the world. The countries that survived the post-crisis period, despite their high growth figures in 2012, 2013, and 2014, were adversely affected by the economic crisis and foreign exchange increases in Russia (Ersungur et al., 2007).

Turkey and Russia signed an agreement in 2019 that paved the way for trade between the two nations to make their own national currency. The agreement aims to use national currencies in trade between the two countries, to create an appropriate financial market, and to increase the attractiveness of national currencies for domestic institutions. Under this agreement, each country will export in its own currency. Trading in local currency will reduce the need to take positions against the dollar, reducing trade costs. Thus, mutual trade will become more advantageous and dependence on the dollar will be reduced. A similar agreement between Turkey and Central Asia can eliminate the effect of the volatility of the foreign exchange rate on trade in the long and short terms.

Asteriou et al. (2016) were to investigate the effects of volatility of the exchange rate on international trade between Mexico, Indonesia, Nigeria, and Turkey. They predicted the volatility from GARCH models and used the ARDL method to determine long-term relationship. Moreover, they applied the Granger causality test to investigate short-term effects. In the long term, with the exchange rate volatility in international trading activities outside Turkey have reached the conclusion that there is no connection. Additionally, they discovered there was no causal relationship between volatility and import for Turkey.

Beak (2013) examined the short- and long-term effects of exchange rate changes on trade flows in the context of disaggregating industry data of bilateral trade between Korea and Japan. For this purpose, the researcher used an autoregressive distributed lag (ARDL) approach. The results of the study showed that Korea's exports and imports are relatively sensitive to the bilateral exchange rate in the short-run but less responsive in the long-run.

Bakhromov (2011) estimated the effect of exchange rate volatility on international trade in Uzbekistan during the 1999-2009 period and found that the real exchange rate volatility had a substantial impact on the exports and imports of the country during the given period.

Furthermore, he used Johansen's cointegration framework to test the presence of unique cointegrating vectors linking series such as exports (imports), foreign (domestic) income, relative export (import) prices (proxied by real exchange rate) with the volatility of the real exchange rate in the long run. The results of cointegration analysis showed that increases in the volatility of the real exchange rate had a significant negative effect on equations of exports and imports in long-run dynamics.

Alper (2014) provided a literature review of the studies examining the effects of exchange rate volatility on foreign trade between 1983 and 2013 was examined. Certain studies have been compared chronologically in terms of data period, countries studied, econometric methods and findings. The study concluded the effect of exchange rate volatility on foreign trade flows remains contradictory.

GARCH MODEL

Bollerslev (1986) extended the ARCH model to the Generalized Autoregressive Conditionally Heteroscedastic (GARCH) model, which assumes that the conditional variance depends on its own p past values, and q past values of the squared error terms. The variance equation of the GARCH (p,q) model can be expressed as:

$$a_t = \sigma_t \varepsilon_t \text{ where } \varepsilon_t \sim f_v(0,1) \tag{3.1}$$

$$\sigma_t^2 = \alpha_0 + \sum_{i=1}^{p} \alpha_i a_{t-i}^2 + \sum_{i=1}^{q} \beta_i \sigma_{t-i}^2 \tag{3.2}$$

$$\sigma_t^2 = \alpha_0 + \alpha(B) a_{t-1}^2 + \beta(B) \sigma_{t-1}^2 \tag{3.3}$$

where α_0 is a constant and the innovations or residuals follow the probability density function $f_v(0,1)$ with zero mean and unit variance. In non-normal cases, v is used as additional distributional parameters for the scale and the shape of the distribution. $\alpha(B)$ is a polynomial of degree p and $\beta(B)$ is a polynomial of degree q where B is the backward shift operator.

Bollerslev (1986) has shown that the GARCH(p,q) process is covariance stationary with $E(a_t) = 0$, $\mathrm{var}(a_t) = \alpha_0 / (1 - \alpha(1) - \beta(1))$ and $\mathrm{cov}(a_t, a_s) = 0$ for t's if and only if $\alpha(1) + \beta(1) < 1$.

In this study, the Standart GARCH (Bollerslev, 1986), Integrated GARCH (Engle & Bollerslev, 1986; Nelson, 1990), Exponential GARCH (Nelson, 1991), Threshold GARCH (Zakoian, 1994), GJR-GARCH of Glosten, Jagannathan and Runkle (1993) and Absolute Value GARCH (Taylor, 1986) models are applied for modeling the volatility of foreign exchange rates. Moreover, the innovation process is allowed to follow normal distribution, skewed normal distribution, Student-t distribution, skewed Student-t distribution, Generalised Error Distribution (GED), skewed GED, normal inverse Gaussian (NIG) distribution and Johnson's SU distribution which are assumed conditional distributions for mentioned models. For details, one can read the article by Chu et al. (2017).

EGARCH Model

Nelson (1991) proposed the exponential GARCH (EGARCH) model to handle some weaknesses of the GARCH model. The positive and negative error terms have a symmetric effect on the volatility is an assumption of an ordinary GARCH model. In fact, the negative shocks on asset price have a greater influence on volatility than positive shocks if negative and positive shocks have the same magnitude. In particular, the weighted innovations are considered in the EGARCH model to allow for asymmetric effects between positive and negative asset returns. The weighted innovations can be written as follows:

$$g(\varepsilon_t) = \theta \varepsilon_t + \gamma \left[|\varepsilon_t| - E(|\varepsilon_t|) \right] \tag{3.4}$$

where $\theta, \gamma \in \mathbb{R}$. ε_t and $|\varepsilon_t| - E(|\varepsilon_t|)$ are iid sequences with zero mean and both follows continuous distributions. Thus, $E[g(\varepsilon_t)] = 0$. $g(\varepsilon_t)$ is an asymmetric function since

$$g(\varepsilon_t) = \begin{cases} (\theta + \gamma)\varepsilon_t - \gamma E(|\varepsilon_t|), & \text{if } \varepsilon_t \geq 0 \\ (\theta - \gamma)\varepsilon_t - \gamma E(|\varepsilon_t|), & \text{if } \varepsilon_t < 0 \end{cases} \tag{3.5}$$

The general form of the EGARCH(p,q) model is

$$a_t = \sigma_t \varepsilon_t, \ln(\sigma_t^2) = \alpha_0 + \left[\frac{1 + \beta_1 B + \ldots + \beta_{q-1} B^{q-1}}{1 - \alpha_1 B + \ldots + \alpha_{p-1} B^{p-1}} \right] g(\varepsilon_{t-1}) \tag{3.6}$$

where $1 + \beta_1 B + \ldots + \beta_{q-1} B^{q-1}$ and $1 - \alpha_1 B + \ldots + \alpha_{p-1} B^{p-1}$ are polynomials with zeros outside the unit circle and have no common factors (Tsay, 2012). The natural logarithm of the conditional variance enables the coefficients of the model can have negative values and $g(\varepsilon_t)$ function satisfies that the model can respond asymmetrically to positive and negative lagged values of a_t.

The normal distributed EGARCH(1,1) model is

$$a_t = \sigma_t \varepsilon_t, (1 - \alpha_1 B) \ln(\sigma_t^2) = (1 - \alpha_1) \alpha_0 + g(\varepsilon_{t-1}) \tag{3.7}$$

where the ε_t are iid standart normal. In the case of normal distiributed EGARCH(1,1) model, $E(|\varepsilon_t|) = \sqrt{2/\pi}$ and by rewritting the $g(\varepsilon_{t-1})$ the model becomes

$$(1 - \alpha_1 B) \ln(\sigma_t^2) = \begin{cases} \alpha_* + (\theta + \gamma)\varepsilon_{t-1}, & \text{if } \varepsilon_{t-1} \geq 0 \\ \alpha_* + (\gamma - \theta)(-\varepsilon_{t-1}), & \text{if } \varepsilon_{t-1} < 0 \end{cases} \tag{3.8}$$

where $\alpha_* = (1 - \alpha_1 B)\alpha_0 - (\sqrt{2/\pi})\gamma$ and the coefficients $(\theta + \gamma)$ and $(\gamma - \theta)$ show the symmetry in response to positive and negative a_{t-1} (Tsay, 2012). If the conditional distribution for the innovations is standardized Sudent-t distribution the expected mean of ε_t is

$$E(|\varepsilon_t|) = \frac{2\sqrt{v-2}\,\Gamma((v+1)/2)}{(v-1)\Gamma(v/2)\sqrt{\pi}} \tag{3.9}$$

So,

$$\alpha_* = (1 - \alpha_1 B)\alpha_0 - \left(\frac{2\sqrt{v-2}\,\Gamma((v+1)/2)}{(v-1)\Gamma(v/2)\sqrt{\pi}} \right)\gamma \tag{3.10}$$

The Impact of USD-TRY Forex Rate Volatility on Imports to Turkey from Central Asia

Autoregressive Distributed-Lag Models

The cointegration tests are applied to examine the long-term relationship between variables. Classical cointegration tests require variables to be uniformly stationary at the same order. This is a limitation for cointegration tests. However, Pesaran et al. (1996) proposed the ARDL approach, which allows testing of the relationship between different orders of stationary variables. Later, this approach is developed by Pesaran and Pesaran (1997), Pesaran and Smith (1998), Pesaran and Shin (1999) and Pesaran et al. (2001) The ARDL approach is based on the least squares method, and unlike conventional cointegration analysis, a unit root test is not required in the ARDL analysis in advance. The reason for this is that the variables do not need to be classified as $I(1)$ and $I(0)$. The main advantage of the ARDL model is that it is possible to perform cointegration test and obtain meaningful results even if the variables are $I(1)$ or $I(0)$ (Pesaran and Pesaran, 1997). However, ARDL does not work with non-stationary variables integrated of order two I(2). Another important advantage is that it can be applied to small samples. The ARDL method provides robust and consistent results for small sample sizes (Pesaran & Shin 1998; Pesaran et al., 2001' Adom et al., 2012) which is good for our setting as we have sample sizes ranging from 80-190.

A further advantage of ARDL can be considered by comparing (e.g., Vector) Autoregressive (VAR) with ARDL. If the VAR is applied to series that are required to be stationary. If they are not stationary, VAR can be utilized after taking the difference of the series. In most cases, long-run relations between series may disappear when the series are stationary at first difference (Brooks, 2014). In contrast, in an ARDL framework it is not necessary to make an adjustment to the data; hence, long-run relationships still remain possible to calculate.

There are cointegration tests in literature introduced by Engel and Granger (1987), Johansen (1988, 1991), Johansen and Juselius (1990) to determine the short-run and long-run relationships or cointegration between macroeconomic variables. These tests cannot be applied in cases of different levels of stationarity of variables. The bounds test developed by Paseran et al. (2001) allows the cointegration analysis in case of different levels of stationarity of variables. According to stationary levels of variables, the ARDL bounds test for cointegration analysis can be applied. In the ARDL models, both AR and DL part are in one regression and is written as

$$ARDL(p,q): y_t = \beta_0 + \sum_{i=0}^{p} \alpha_i y_{t-i} + \sum_{i=0}^{q} \beta_i x_{t-i} + u_t \qquad (4.1)$$

where u_t is error term with zero mean. x_t is a k-dimensional vector of explanatory variables. Typically, a constant is included by β_0. In the ARDL approach, the dependent and independent variables can be introduced in the model with lags. Thus, AR as part of the ARDL approach refers to lags of the dependent variable and DL part of the ARDL refers to the lags of explanatory variables. Inferentially, this property of ARDL model states that the effect of a change of the independent variables may or may not be instantaneous. The OLs estimation is applied to determine the parameters of ARDL model. But, OLS estimation yields biased estimates since the lagged values of the dependent variable are given presence in the model. If the error term is autocorrelated, OLS becomes inconsistent. Therefore, Instrumental Variables estimation is often used.

FINDINGS

Results of Volatility Model

The effective foreign exchange rate of the US Dollar (USD) and the Turkish Lira (TRY) monthly data in the period of years 2005-2018 were used to determine the volatility. The FOREX had a unit root according to ADF $(test - stat = 2.26, p = 1.0)$ and KPSS $(test - stat = 1.59, p = 1)$ tests. By log-returns on USD/TRY data, it became stationary $(ADF\ test - stat = -9.73, KPSS\ test - stat = 0.37\ p < .01)$. The data used in the analysis are shown in Figure 1.

The ARCH test shows that for lag 8 $(F - stat = 507.92, p < .01)$ show that there was an ARCH effect on the data. Therefore, GARCH type models can be applied to the data. GARCH, IGARCH, SGARCH, EGARCH, TGARCH, AVGARCH and GJR-GARCH were fit to data and normal distribution, skewed normal distribution, Student-t distribution, skewed Student-t distribution, Generalised Error Distribution (GED), skewed GED, normal inverse Gaussian (NIG) distribution, and Johnson's SU distribution were assumed as the conditional distributions for the innovations. The fitted models were compared according to information criteria which are given at the following table. In conclusion, the Student-t EGARCH (1,1) model was found as the best convenient model for the volatility of USD/TRY FOREX data and the parameter estimations are given in Table 2. The diagnostics test results are given in Appendix A.

The Impact of USD-TRY Forex Rate Volatility on Imports to Turkey from Central Asia

Results of ARDL Bounds Test

In this study, the short- and long-term effects of fluctuations of USD / TRY exchange rate on Turkey's imports from the Central Asian Countries (CAC) is tried to elicit. For this purpose, Turkey's total imports from these countries was accepted as a dependent variable, and volatility obtained from EGARCH model was used in the analysis as independent variables. The ARDL approach was used to elucidate the long-term relationship between imports and exchange rate volatility. In this manner, it will be determined whether or not there is cointegration between variables.

The ARDL method is based on the standard least squares regression method in which the lagged values of both the dependent variable and the explanatory variable (s) are used as the explanatory variable. In the ARDL-Bounds test approach, firstly to determine whether there is cointegration between the variables in a model, the model is transformed into an unconstrained error correction model based on the ARDL approach and is estimated with the least squares (OLS) estimator. Based on this model, the boundary test based on F statistics is performed. Based on the standard

Table 1. Model comparison

Model	Akaike	Bayes	Shibata	Hannan-Quinn	Likelihood
		Information Criteria			
sged garch	-4.459436	-4.342133	-4.462251	-4.411793	353.836
std tgarch	-4.518344	-4.420593	-4.520315	-4.478642	357.4309
ged avgarch	-4.513916	-4.377064	-4.517717	-4.458332	359.0855
std gjrgarch	-4.51862	-4.381768	-4.522422	-4.463037	359.4524
std egarch	**-4.565199**	**-4.467448**	**-4.56717**	**-4.525497**	**361.0856**
sged igarch	-4.456271	-4.378069	-4.457542	-4.424509	351.5891
nig sgarch	-4.433666	-4.335915	-4.435637	-4.393964	350.826

Table 2. Student-t EGARCH(1,1)

	Estimate	Std. Error	t value	Pr(>|t|)
	Optimal Parameters for Student-t EGARCH(1,1)			
alpha0	-4.954573	1.07923	-4.59086	0.000004
alpha1	-0.727058	0.14775	-4.9209	0.000001
beta1	0.335505	0.14516	2.31135	0.020813
gamma1	0.071535	0.20225	0.35369	0.723572
shape	10.592908	8.79518	1.2044	0.228435

The Impact of USD-TRY Forex Rate Volatility on Imports to Turkey from Central Asia

regression model, ARDL-Bounds test equation was established to determine the cointegration relationship between the variables in the model as follows:

$$\Delta ln\left(im\right)_t = \alpha_0 + \sum_{i=1}^{p}\alpha_{1i}\Delta ln\left(im\right)_{t-i} + \sum_{i=0}^{q}\alpha_{2i}\Delta ln\left(vol\right)_{t-i} + \beta_1 ln\left(im\right)_{t-1} + \beta_2 ln\left(vol\right)_{t-1} + e_t$$

(4.1)

where total import is denoted by "*im*" and the volatility of foreign Exchange rate is denoted by "*vol*". The alpha coefficients in equation 4.1 represent short-term and beta coefficients show long-term dynamics. In order to ensure the stability conditions of the estimation, firstly the optimal lag lengths (p, q) of the variables in the equation 4.1 are determined with the help of information criteria and then the bounds test is carried out from the model estimated with the appropriate lag. In the bounds test, the null hypothesis, which states that there is no long-term relationship between the variables, is tested with the F-test. The null hypothesis is tested by applying a zero constraint to the coefficients of lagged variables in equation 4.1.

Accordingly, in this study, the zero hypothesis for F-test $\left(H_0 : \beta_1 = \beta_2 = 0\right)$, the alternative hypothesis ($H_0 : \beta_i \neq 0$ *for at least one* $i; i = 1, 2$). The F-statistic is obtained by the bounds test, Pesaran et al. (2001) according to the structure of the model (restricted, constant and trend inclusion) and the number of output variables (k) in the model are compared with asymptotic critical values calculated for various confidence levels. The standard F-test used to test the null hypothesis has a non-standard distribution in some cases.

After determining there is a long-term relationship between the level values of the variables by the bounds test, the long-term relationship between the variables is examined via the ARDL method. In this study, the ARDL model to be estimated to examine the long-term relationship between variables is as follows:

$$ln\left(im\right)_t = \alpha_0 + \sum_{i=1}^{p}\alpha_{1i} ln\left(im\right)_{t-i} + \sum_{i=0}^{q}\alpha_{2i} ln\left(vol\right)_{t-i} + e_t$$

(4.2)

The short-term relationship between the variables is examined with the error correction model based on the ARDL method. This model is as follows:

$$\Delta ln\left(im\right)_t = \alpha_0 + \sum_{i=1}^{p}\alpha_{1i}\Delta ln\left(im\right)_{t-i} + \sum_{i=0}^{q}\alpha_{2i}\Delta ln\left(vol\right)_{t-i} + \delta ECT_{t-1} + e_t$$

(4.3)

where ECT is error correction term that shows how soon it is possible to correct a short-term equilibruim between dependent and explanatory variables in the model. For the error correction mechanism to work, the coefficient of this variable is expected to be negative and statistically significant.

The graph of the data sets used in this analysis is given in Figure 1. In this context, equation 4.2 will be estimated with the ARDL (2,0) model according to the appropriate lag lengths determined for the variables in order to determine the long-term relationships between the variables. ARDL long-term model estimation results and assumption tests are given in Table 3. Optimum lag lengths are determined according to the Schwarz Information Criteria.

When the diagnostic test results of ARDL (2,0) model are examined, autocorrelation according to Breusch-Godfrey LM [with 8 lag] test, and according to Breusch-Pagan-Godfrey and ARCH tests, there is no heteroskedasticity problem. It is understood the error term is not normally distributed which is a common problem in the time series analysis. There is also no model building (functional form) error according to Ramsey Reset test with 1 term added. CUSUM and CUSUM-SQ tests were performed to examine the stability of the parameters in the model and the results are shown in Figure 2 and Figure 3. According to the aforementioned graphs, CUSUM and CUSUM-SQ statistics are within the critical limits of 5% confidence level. All the mentioned diognastics test results are shown in Table 4.

Figure 1. The Plot of data sets
(Import, Log-Import, USD/TRY Forex, Volatility of USD/TRY Forex)

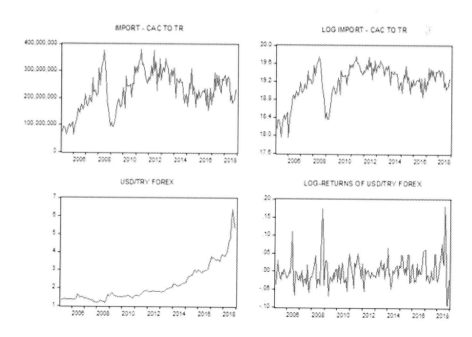

Table 3. The estimation of ARDL(2,0) for log-import

Dependent Variable: LOGIM				
Variable	Coefficient	Std. Error	t-Statistic	Prob.*
LOGIM(-1)	0.535703	0.073619	7.276679	0.0000
LOGIM(-2)	0.353262	0.071507	4.940211	0.0000
VOLATILITY	-1.720658	0.800313	-2.149981	0.0330
C	2.198904	0.679827	3.234506	0.0015
R-squared	0.804923	Mean dependent var		19.18475
Adjusted R-squared	0.801288	S.D. dependent var		0.370750
S.E. of regression	0.165270	Akaike info criterion		-0.738530
Sum squared resid	4.397576	Schwarz criterion		-0.663234
Log likelihood	64.92873	Hannan-Quinn criter.		-0.707965
F-statistic	221.4380	Durbin-Watson stat		1.988536
Prob(F-statistic)	0.000000			

According to the results of the bounds test analysis that are given in Table 5, the F-statistic (4.499855), Pesaran et al. (2001) is higher than the upper limit of 5% confidence level (4.16). According to the results of the bounds test, cointegration was determined between the series at 5% significance level, regardless of the stationary level of the series. In this case, it is concluded that there is a long-term relationship between imports and exchange rate volatility.

The results of the short-term error correction model based on the ARDL (2,0) model that reveals the short-term relationship between the variables are presented in Table 6. Short-term diagnostic tests show the stability conditions of the model are met. When the table is examined, it is understood that the coefficients in the model are statistically significant. On the other hand, the error correction term (ECT_{t-1}) coefficient was a negative sign and statistically significant as expected. Accordingly, 11.1% of deviations from long-term equilibrium due to short-term shocks will be corrected in the next period and the effect of shocks will be eliminated within 9 months and the long-term equilibrium will be approached.

Figure 2. CUSUM test for the stability of the parameters

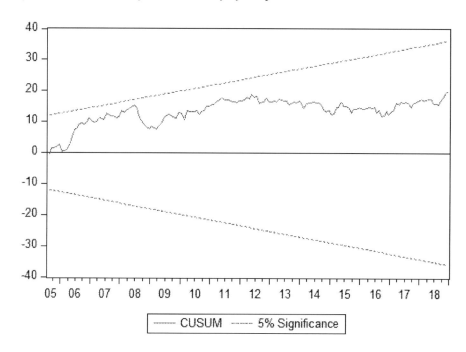

Figure 3. CUSUM-SQ test for the stability of the parameters

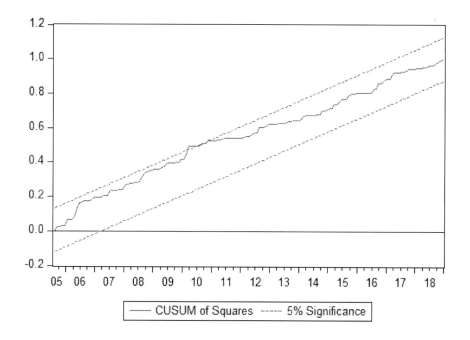

Table 4. The residual diognastics for ARDL(2,0) model

Breusch-Godfrey Serial Correlation LM Test:			
F-statistic	0.690397	Prob. F(8,153)	0.6996
Obs*R-squared	5.748839	Prob. Chi-Square(8)	0.6753
Heteroskedasticity Test: Breusch-Pagan-Godfrey			
F-statistic	1.688478	Prob. F(3,161)	0.1716
Obs*R-squared	5.032936	Prob. Chi-Square(3)	0.1694
Scaled explained SS	7.431129	Prob. Chi-Square(3)	0.0594
Ramsey RESET Test			
	Value	df	Probability
t-statistic	1.689754	160	0.0930
F-statistic	2.855268	(1, 160)	0.0930
Jarque-Bera Normality Test:			
Jarque-Bera -statistic	16.65483	Prob.	0.000242
Heteroskedasticity Test: ARCH			
F-statistic	1.157073	Prob. F(8,148)	0.3291
Obs*R-squared	9.241484	Prob. Chi-Square(8)	0.3223

CONCLUSION

In this study, short- and long-term relationships between imports of Turkey from Central Asian countries and exchange rate volatility between the period Jan 2005 and Dec 2018 and the monthly data were analyzed using the ARDL-Bounds test approach. Bounds test showed there is a significant long-term relationship between variables. According to the estimation results made by the ARDL method, it is seen that exchange rate volatility has a relatively high and statistically significant effect on import in the long-term.

According to the results of the error correction model, a total of 11.1% of the deviations from the long-term equilibrium due to short-term shocks are corrected in the next period and thus the long-term equilibrium is approached within nine months. It was observed that exchange rate volatility significantly affected imports in the short term. In this study, the most important one of the reasons the exchange rate volatility of the dependent variables is the demand of Turkey to use of national

The Impact of USD-TRY Forex Rate Volatility on Imports to Turkey from Central Asia

Table 5. ARDL long run form and bounds test results

Levels Equation				
Variable	Coefficient	Std. Error	t-Statistic	Prob.
VOLATILITY	-15.49646	8.217360	-1.885820	0.0611
C	19.80359	0.327107	60.54162	0.0000
EC = LOGIM - (-15.4965*VOLATILITY + 19.8036)				
F-Bounds Test		**Null Hypothesis: No levels relationship**		
Test Statistic	Value	Signif.	I(0)	I(1)
			Asymptotic: n=1000	
F-statistic	4.499855	10%	3.02	3.51
k	1	5%	3.62	4.16
		1%	4.94	5.58
Actual Sample Size	165		Finite Sample: n=80	
		10%	3.113	3.61
		5%	3.74	4.303
		1%	5.157	5.917

Table 6. Error correction regression for ARDL(2,0)

ECM Regression				
Variable	**Coefficient**	**Std. Error**	**t-Statistic**	**Prob.**
D(LOGIM(-1))	-0.353262	0.069680	-5.069778	0.0000
CointEq(-1)*	-0.111036	0.030035	-3.696926	0.0003
R-squared	0.210222	Mean dependent var		0.005535
Adjusted R-squared	0.205377	S.D. dependent var		0.184261
S.E. of regression	0.164253	Akaike info criterion		-0.762772
Sum squared resid	4.397576	Schwarz criterion		-0.725125
Log likelihood	64.92873	Hannan-Quinn criter.		-0.747490
Durbin-Watson stat	1.988536			

currencies in trade between neighbouring countries and Central Asia. According to the results of the study, it is seen that the exchange rate changes affect trade negatively.

As Central Asian countries are considered developing nations, they need direct foreign investment and markets to sell their products. Therefore, the trade volume they need for their economic growth is affected by the fluctuations in the foreign exchange market. Turkey and Russia signed an agreement that paves the way for trade between them to make their own national currencies. A similar agreement between Turkey and Central Asia can eliminate the effect of the volatility of the foreign exchange rate on trade in long and short terms. However, this has a minor importance to overcome the current problem.

Unfortunately, this is a virtual solution. However, Turkey's basic problems in foreign trade is not the currency which is used in trade. The problem is that all developing countries including those in Central Asia must increase the reserve of foreign exchange to reduce the current account deficit. Of course, in the long-term this alternative can be discussed in a balanced trade structure. However, the problem cannot be overcome, but in this way to increase the volume of work can be done to strengthen political unity.

Otherwise, neither it may not the way to reduce the foreign trade deficit; nor an option to eliminate the need for foreign exchange in USD and EUROs. In future studies, it will be more appropriate to carry out analyzes that include variables such as economic growth and foreign direct investment.

REFERENCES

Adom, P. K., Bekoe, W., & Akoena, S. K. K. (2012). Modelling aggregate domestic electricity demand in Ghana: An autoregressive distributed lag bounds cointegration approach. *Energy Policy, 42,* 530–537. doi:10.1016/j.enpol.2011.12.019

Alagöz, M., Yapar, S., & Uçtu, R. (2004). Türk Cumhuriyetleri İle İlişkilerimize Ekonomik Açıdan Bir Yaklaşım. *Selçuk Üniversitesi Sosyal Bilimler Enstitüsü Dergisi,* (12), 59-74.

Alper, F. (2014). Impact Of Exchange Rate Volatility On Trade: A Literature Survey. *Çukurova Üniversitesi Sosyal Bilimler Enstitüsü Dergisi, 23*(2), 29-46. Retrieved on December 22, 2017, from: https://dergipark.org.tr/tr/pub/cusosbil/issue/31959/352032

Asterious, D., Masatci, K., & Pilbeam, K. (2016). Exchange rate volatility and international trade: International evidence from the MINT countries. *Economic Modelling, 58,* 133–140. doi:10.1016/j.econmod.2016.05.006

Baek, J. (2013). Does the exchange rate matter to bilateral trade between Korea and Japan? Evidence from commodity trade data. *Economic Modelling, 30*(C), 856–862. doi:10.1016/j.econmod.2012.11.020

Baille, R. T., & Bollerslev, T. (1989). The Message in Daily Exchange Rates: A Conditional-Variance Tale. *Journal of Business & Economic Statistics*, 7, 297–305.

Bakhromov, N. (2011). The Exchange Rate Volatility and the Trade Balance: Case of Uzbekistan. *Journal of Applied Economics and Business Research*, 1(3), 149–161.

Bollerslev, T. (1986). Generalized Autoregressive Conditional Heteroskedasticity. *Journal of Econometrics*, 31(3), 307–327. doi:10.1016/0304-4076(86)90063-1

Budak, T. (2013, Fall). Orta Asya'da Küresel Jeoekonomik Rekabet ve Türkiye. *Bilge Strateji*, 5(9), 125–142.

Chu J., Chan S., Nadarajah S. and Osterrieder J. (2017). GARCH Modelling of Cryptocurrencies. *Journal of Risk and Financial Management.* doi:10.3390/jrfm10040017

Ding, Z., Engle, R. F., & Granger, C. W. J. (1993). A long memory property of stock market return and a new model. *Journal of Empirical Finance*, 1(1), 83–106. doi:10.1016/0927-5398(93)90006-D

Engle, R. F. (1982). Autoregressive conditional heteroscedasticity with estimates of the variance of United Kingdom inflation. *Econometrica*, 50(4), 987–1007. doi:10.2307/1912773

Ersungur, M., Kiziltan, A., & Karabulut, K. (2007). Türkiye İle Diğer Türk Cumhuriyetlerinin Ekonomik İlişkilerininAnalizi. Atatürk Üniversitesi Türkiyat Araştırmaları Enstitüsü Dergisi, 14(35).

Johansen, S. (1991). Estimation and hypothesis testing of cointegration vectors in Gaussian vector autoregressive models. *Econometrica*, 59(6), 1551–1580. doi:10.2307/2938278

Johensen, S. (1988). Statistical Analysis of Cointegration Vectors. *Journal of Economic Dynamics & Control*, 12(2-3), 231–254. doi:10.1016/0165-1889(88)90041-3

Nelson, D. B. (1990). Stationarity and persistence in the GARCH(1,1) models. *Econometric Theory*, 6(3), 318–334. doi:10.1017/S0266466600005296

Nelson, D. B. (1991). Conditional heteroskedasticity in asset returns: A new approach. *Econometrica*, 59(2), 347–370. doi:10.2307/2938260

Pesaran, M. H., & Shin, Y. (1998). An autoregressive distributed-lag modelling approach to cointegration analysis. *Econometric Society Monographs*, 31, 371–413. doi:10.1017/CCOL0521633230.011

Pesaran, M. H., & Shin, Y. (1999). *An Autoregressive Distributed Lag Modelling Approach to Cointegration Analysis.* Retrieved on November 11, 2018, from: http://www.econ.cam.ac.uk/faculty/pesaran/ardl.pdf

Pesaran, M. H., Shin, Y., & Smith, R. J. (2001). Bounds testing approaches to the analysis of level relationships'. *Journal of Applied Econometrics, 16*(3), 289–326. doi:10.1002/jae.616

Pesaran, M. H., & Smith, R. (1998). Structural Analysis of Cointegrating VARs. *Journal of Economic Surveys, 12*(5), 471–505. doi:10.1111/1467-6419.00065

Taylor, S. (1986). *Modelling Financial Time Series.* New York: Wiley.

Tsay, R. S. (2012). *An Introduction to Analysis of Financial Data with R.* New York: Wiley.

Zakoian, J. M. (1994). Threshold heteroscedasticity models. *Journal of Economic Dynamics & Control, 18*(5), 931–955. doi:10.1016/0165-1889(94)90039-6

The Impact of USD-TRY Forex Rate Volatility on Imports to Turkey from Central Asia

APPENDIX

Table 7. Student-t EGARCH(1,1) diognastics

```
Conditional Variance Dynamics
-----------------------------------
GARCH Model : eGARCH(1,1)
Distribution : std
Robust Standard Errors:
 Estimate Std. Error t value Pr(>|t|)
omega -4.954573 1.78940 -2.7689 0.005625
alpha1 -0.727058 0.16572 -4.3874 0.000011
beta1 0.335505 0.24472 1.3710 0.170386
gamma1 0.071535 0.14466 0.4945 0.620957
shape 10.592908 6.85351 1.5456 0.122197
Nyblom stability test
-----------------------------------
Joint Statistic: 1.0953
Individual Statistics:
omega 0.04974 alpha1 0.62495 beta1 0.05487 gamma1 0.06576 shape 0.05462
Asymptotic Critical Values (10% 5% 1%)
Joint Statistic: 1.28 1.47 1.88
Individual Statistic: 0.35 0.47 0.75
Weighted Ljung-Box Test on Standardized Residuals
-----------------------------------
 statistic p-value
Lag[1] 2.924 0.08725
Lag[2] 4.714 0.04850
Lag[5] 6.334 0.07500
H0: No serial correlation
Weighted Ljung-Box Test on Standardized Squared Residuals
-----------------------------------
 statistic p-value
Lag[1] 0.3174 0.5732
Lag[5] 2.4979 0.5063
Lag[9] 4.2094 0.5537
Weighted ARCH LM Tests
-----------------------------------
 Statistic Shape Scale P-Value
ARCH Lag[3] 0.06971 0.500 2.000 0.7918
ARCH Lag[5] 3.19693 1.440 1.667 0.2625
ARCH Lag[7] 3.90184 2.315 1.543 0.3609
Sign Bias Test
-----------------------------------
 t-value prob sig
Sign Bias 0.5636 0.5739
Negative Sign Bias 0.8746 0.3832
Positive Sign Bias 0.8944 0.3726
Joint Effect 1.8994 0.5935
Adjusted Pearson Goodness-of-Fit Test:
-----------------------------------
 group statistic p-value(g-1)
1 20 18.62 0.4817
2 30 25.54 0.6500
3 40 47.59 0.1627
4 50 52.33 0.3459
```

Chapter 5
Nation and Regional Branding of Central Asia:
Kazakhstan, Kyrgyzstan, and Uzbekistan

Gordana Pesakovic
Southern New Hampshire University, USA & OSCE Academy, Kyrgyzstan

ABSTRACT

Central Asia is defined by its history and geography, by its people and cultures, and by geopolitics and geo-economics. Therefore, analyzing a country in the region, past, present, and future should incorporate all these elements. The purpose of this chapter is to present the development of nation branding in three countries: Kazakhstan, Kyrgyzstan, and Uzbekistan. The chapter starts with the theory of nation branding. The particularity of the Central Asia as a region and three selected countries follow. Global ranking based on different indices is presented. In the fourth section, the nation branding of each country is addressed. The fifth section highlights lessons learned from the Borat case on nation branding in Kazakhstan but relevant for other countries in the region as well. The chapter ends with the section on branding the region as a whole.

INTRODUCTION

The purpose of this chapter is to present the development of nation branding in three countries: Kazakhstan, Kyrgyzstan and Uzbekistan. The paper starts with the theory of nation branding. The particularity of the Central Asia as a region and three selected countries follow. Global ranking based on different indexes is presented. In the fourth section of the paper, the nation branding of each country is addressed. The

DOI: 10.4018/978-1-7998-2239-4.ch005

Copyright © 2020, IGI Global. Copying or distributing in print or electronic forms without written permission of IGI Global is prohibited.

Nation and Regional Branding of Central Asia

fifth section of the paper highlights lessons learned from the Borat case on nation branding in Kazakhstan but relevant for other countries in the region as well. The paper ends with the section on branding the region.

Nation branding entered the big stage in the second half of the 1990s. Initially the focus of the researchers was developed economies. Recently the developing and emerging countries are also being studied. However, there has not been many studies conducted on the countries in the Central Asia. Therefore, this study will help to bridge this gap.

Why study nation branding? What are the components of nation branding? How can we measure the effectiveness of nation branding? How can nation branding help Central Asian countries and their quest for the more favorable global recognition? The goal of nation branding is to create the positive image of a country that is recognizable and respected globally. (Hurn, 2016) In return, this should increase country's competitiveness and stimulate economic, political and cultural exchanges with the world. Therefore, the country should conduct critical analysis of its internal resources, identify positive and negative challenges in order to create relevant brand image for different market segments. Rojas-Mendez (2013) argues that nation branding can result in a "positive gain for the countries as they obtain a distinctive image in a competitive global market." Today the question is not whether to design, develop and create nation branding. Instead, it is how to do it in a way that will provide the highest return to the country and all stakeholders in one nation. Successful nation branding can bring economic benefits, increase revenues from tourism, foreign direct investment and export. In addition, it may also improve international relations among countries (Fan, 2006).

NATION BRANDING

Nation branding is an emerging area of studies that requires an interdisciplinary approach. Kaneva (2011) offers her definition on nation branding "as a compendium of discourses and practices aimed at reconstituting nationhood through marketing and branding paradigms." (p. 118) Anholt, the most prolific writer in the area of nation branding, always emphasizes the difference between what he is doing, consulting governments on what to do to get where they want to be, instead of doing their public relations campaigns. Therefore, he defines nation branding as "a *component of national policy*, never as a 'campaign' that is separate from planning, governance or economic development" (Anholt, 2008, p. 23)

Kaneva (2011) has conducted a comprehensive analysis on published research (186 published sources) on this topic and has divide them in three categories:

technical-economic, political, and cultural-critical. Figure 1 summarizes the major focus of research in nation branding studies not the practice of nation branding itself.

Her research indicates the largest number of studies is focused on technical-economic approach. These studies are focused on economic growth, efficiency, and capital accumulation and include marketing, tourism, and management studies. Political studies are in the field of international relations, public relations, and international communication and are researching the impact of national images on nation-states' participation in a global system of international relations. Studies with cultural approaches are conducted in media and cultural studies, and their focus is on implication of nation branding for national and cultural identity (Kaneva 2011, p. 120). Nation branding can have an external and internal audience, and sometimes with different messages. "Branding not only explains nations to the world but also reinterprets national identity in market terms and provides new narratives for domestic consumption" (Jansen 2008, p.122).

Fetscherin (2010) states that nation branding "is complex and includes multiple levels, components, and disciplines. It entails the collective involvement of the many stakeholders it must appeal to. It concerns a country's whole image, covering political, economic, social, environmental, historical, and cultural aspects." (p.468) For Fan (2010) nation branding is "the total sum of all perceptions of a nation in the minds of international stakeholders, which may contain some of the following

Figure 1. A Conceptual Map of Nation Branding Research
Source: Kaneva 2011, p. 130

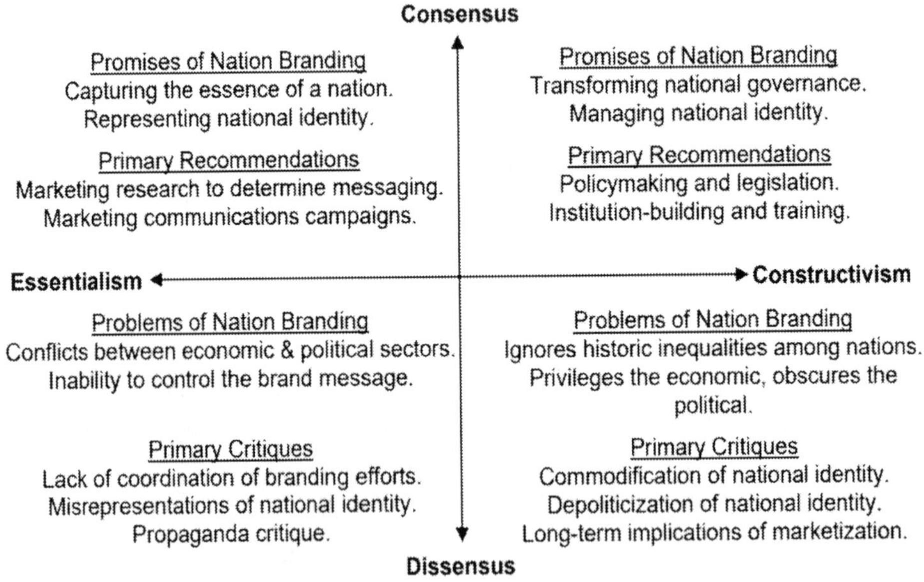

Consensus

Promises of Nation Branding
Capturing the essence of a nation.
Representing national identity.

Promises of Nation Branding
Transforming national governance.
Managing national identity.

Primary Recommendations
Marketing research to determine messaging.
Marketing communications campaigns.

Primary Recommendations
Policymaking and legislation.
Institution-building and training.

Essentialism ← → **Constructivism**

Problems of Nation Branding
Conflicts between economic & political sectors.
Inability to control the brand message.

Problems of Nation Branding
Ignores historic inequalities among nations.
Privileges the economic, obscures the political.

Primary Critiques
Lack of coordination of branding efforts.
Misrepresentations of national identity.
Propaganda critique.

Primary Critiques
Commodification of national identity.
Depoliticization of national identity.
Long-term implications of marketization.

Dissensus

elements: people, place, culture / language, history, food, fashion, famous faces (celebrities), global brands and so on." (p.98) Dinnie (2008) explains country brand as "the unique, multi-dimensional blend of elements that provide the nation with culturally grounded differentiation and relevance for all of its target audiences." (p.15)

Stock (2009) identifies nation branding elements: national identity, reference points, constructed image, current projected image, and desired future image. Every country is faced with the gap between self-image and how it is perceived by others. Therefore, it is important for these two elements to be identified as well as the existed gap. Once this process is done, the reconstructing of the new image of the country should start. Gudjonsson (2005) explains that nation branding presents application of "the tools of branding to alter, confirm or change the behavior, attitudes, identity or image of a nation in a positive way." (p.285)

Anholt points to these two characteristics of nation branding. First, nations are becoming more aware of the value of their brand as an asset. Understanding valuation helps them better comprehend the investments they make in their image and its implication for the future. The second major characteristic of nation branding is focus on the fundamental common purpose of all stakeholders (government, business and nonprofit sector) and their coordinated message (Anholt, 2007).

NATION BRANDING AND CENTRAL ASIA

Kazakhstan, Kyrgyzstan, and Uzbekistan share geography, history, and geopolitics. For centuries Central Asia was a place where big players (e.g., Darius I, Alexander the Great, Genghis Khan, Tamerlane, the British, and the Russian empire) fought for the dominance of people, land, natural resources, and strategic control. They were part of the Soviet Union until 1991. Since the disintegration of the Soviet Union, they became sovereign states for the first time. "They felt a need for self-identification and the establishment of their image in the world arena" (Lebedenko in Dinnie, 2007, p.107).

This presented a serious challenge for them, since they lacked nationhood experience and in the case of Kazakhstan, Kazakh people were not a majority (only 40%) of the total population. However, their number jumped to 65% at the beginning of 2000 (Saunders, 2016 p.122). Kyrgyzstan and Uzbekistan had a more homogenous population (around 65%). Central Asia is often "referred as a "hotbed" of destabilization, instability, violence, Islamic extremism" (Kendzior, 2013). However, it has been and still is on the radar of major powers. The newest players in the region are USA, China, and Iran. In the 21st century the leading major powers are focused on military bases (the USA had a military base in Kyrgyzsta and Russia still has one), China's Belt and Road Initiative focuses on trade, investment, and infrastructure (Chen and Fazilov, 2018). War against drug trafficking alongside with oil and gas pipelines are other areas that attract leading global powers to the region.

There is also a so-called "stan stigma". Although "stan" in Persian means "place of" or "country of," it usually comes with a negative perception. In addition to Central Asian countries, two other countries with less than best global perception, Pakistan and Afghanistan, also have this suffix. There remain frictions between some countries in the region, with mostly autocratic political regimes (an exception is Kyrgyzstan with few presidential and parliamentary elections since 1991). All these factors make the task of nation branding very challenging. The countries have different experiences with nation branding. In the case of Kazakhstan, the process was not autochthon. Instead it was triggered as a reaction to the movie Borat: Cultural Learnings of America for Make Benefit Glorious Nation of Kazakhstan.

GLOBAL RANKING OF NATION BRANDING: KAZAKHSTAN, KYRGYZSTAN AND UZBEKISTAN

There are few consulting firms that use different methodology to rank countries and their global image. Simon Anholt and Global Market Insite, a polling firm, measure the relative strengths of national brands of 35 mostly developed economies every three months. The index tracks consumer perceptions of tourism, exports, governance, people, culture and heritage, and investment.

In 2014, Anholt launched The Good Country Index. This index measures what each country contributes to the common good of humanity and to the planet (https://www.goodcountry.org/good-country/data-treatment). They use secondary data from the UN and other international organizations to present whether a country is "a net creditor to mankind, a burden on the planet, or something in between." A few other institutions have developed their indexes: Bloom Consulting Country Branding (Ranking Trade and Tourism), FutureBrand Country Brand Index, East West Global Index 200, Portland Communications -Soft Power 30 Ranking, and Digital Country Index.

Kazakhstan, Kyrgyzstan, and Uzbekistan are included in the following indexes: Nation Branding Index, the Good Country Index, Bloom Consulting Country Branding, and East West Index 200. The Bloom Consulting Country Branding measures the following four variables: economic performance (Foreign Direct Investment), Digital Demand (Business environment, Socio Economic factors, Strategic Sector), CBS rating (Country Brand Strategy) and Online Performance (Facebook, Twitter, LinkedIn websites). East West Index 200 is based on how a country is described in major media. This Index has been recorded for these three countries in 2011. The tables below show ranking of Kazakhstan, Kyrgyzstan and

Nation and Regional Branding of Central Asia

Uzbekistan. Unfortunately, the countries are not ranked every year, and as stated only 4 institutions rank these countries.

In addition, Bloom Consulting Country Brand Ranking provides the ranking of countries based on the region. Their ranking for Asia in the area of tourism, puts Kazakhstan at 29th, and Kyrgyzstan at 38th out of 48 countries. Uzbekistan has not been ranked (https://www.bloom-consulting.com/en/pdf/rankings/Bloom_Consulting_Country_Brand_Ranking_Tourism.pdf). The ranking for Asia in the area of trade puts Kazakhstan at 13th, Uzbekistan at 33rd, and Kyrgyzstan at the very last, 48th place (https://www.bloom-consulting.com/en/pdf/rankings/Bloom_Consulting_Country_Brand_Ranking_Trade.pdf).

NATION BRANDING BY COUNTRY

Three countries differ in size, population, natural resources, major industries, and somewhat in political structure. Kazakhstan is the 9th largest country in the world, Uzbekistan is the largest country in the region based on population (40% of total population of Central Asia), and Kyrgyzstan is regarded as the most democratic country ("Island of democracy") in the region. However, all of them share the major goal of nation branding: to attract new investment, tourist, and donors. The messages they communicate are focused on domestic and international audiences,

Table 1. Nation Branding Ranking: Kyrgyzstan

Kyrgyzstan	Rank 2011	Rank 2012	Rank 2013	Rank 2014	Rank 2015	Rank 2016	Rank 2017
Anholt – Gfk Roper Nation Brands Index	-	-	-	-	-	-	-
Anholt – The Good Country Index	-	-	-	74	-	115	-
Bloom Consulting Country Branding Ranking Trade	-	-	-	158	-	-	173
Bloom Consulting Country Branding Ranking Tourism	-	-	-	147	-	-	145
FutureBrand Country Brand Index	-	-	-	-	-	-	-
East West Global Index 200	121	-	-	-	-	-	-
Portland Communications - Soft Power 30 Ranking	-	-	-	-	-	-	-
Digital Country Index	-	-	-	-	-	-	176

Source: http://countrybrandingwiki.org/index.php/Kyrgyzstan

Table 2. Nation Branding Ranking: Kazakhstan

Kazakhstan	Rank 2011	Rank 2012	Rank 2013	Rank 2014	Rank 2015	Rank 2016	Rank 2017
Anholt – Gfk Roper Nation Brands Index	-	-	-	-	-	-	-
Anholt – The Good Country Index	-	-	-	80	-	120	-
Bloom Consulting Country Branding Ranking Trade	-	-	-	37	-	-	36
Bloom Consulting Country Branding Ranking Tourism	-	-	-	85	-	-	98
FutureBrand Country Brand Index	-	-	-	-	-	-	-
East West Global Index 200	27	-	-	-	-	-	-
Portland Communications - Soft Power 30 Ranking	-	-	-	-	-	-	-
Digital Country Index	-	-	-	-	-	-	96

Source: http://countrybrandingwiki.org/index.php/Kazakhstan

Table 3. Nation Branding Ranking: Uzbekistan

Uzbekistan	Rank 2011	Rank 2012	Rank 2013	Rank 2014	Rank 2015	Rank 2016	Rank 2017
Anholt – Gfk Roper Nation Brands Index	-	-	-	-	-	-	-
Anholt – The Good Country Index	-	-	-	-	-	-	-
Bloom Consulting Country Branding Ranking Trade	-	-	-	96	-	-	109
Bloom Consulting Country Branding Ranking Tourism	-	-	-	-	-	-	-
FutureBrand Country Brand Index	-	-	-	-	-	-	-
East West Global Index 200	91	-	-	-	-	-	-
Portland Communications - Soft Power 30 Ranking	-	-	-	-	5	-	-
Digital Country Index	-	-	-	-	-	-	153

Source: http://countrybrandingwiki.org/index.php/Uzbekistan

whereas in the case of Uzbekistan that message differs based on the audience. In the case of Kyrgyzstan their focus is mostly on promoting tourism. Kazakhstan's two big nation branding projects were focus on the country's promotion for the OSCE Chairmanship (2010) and EXPO 2017.

Kazakhstan

Kazakhstan promotes its country as a center of Eurasia with the slogan "The Heart of Eurasia". It has even moved the capital city from Almaty to Astana to demonstrate this central role in Eurasia. Emphasis is also on multiculturalism and linking positive sides of two worlds, the East and the West

Kazakhstan uses mostly mass media, commemorative books, conferences, and public events (through its embassies around the world). Under the Ministry of Foreign Affairs, the Department of International Information was created. Kazakhstan also used its international agency to promote the country.

Kyrgyzstan

Kyrgyzstan's first president was on the quest toward developing a new national identity and started with the message "Kyrgyzstan it our common home". The purpose of this project was to unite different ethnic groups and attract skilled Russians to stay in the country after the disintegration of USSR. This campaign had some positive results. However, the other two, Manas – 1000 (promoting national hero and epic) alienated non-Kyrgyz ethnic groups. The other projects, 2200 Years of Kyrgyz Statehood, Clean hands were less successful. The first brand images to be promoted was under the slogans "Switzerland of Central Asia" and "the Island of Democracy."". The focus was on foreign direct investors and tourism. However, when the government started to suppress the opposition in the late 1990s the interest for FDI has declined. This again demonstrates that when there is a gap between the country's perception and the world's perception of a country the results are missing.

Since Kyrgyzstan did not have a centralized message to the world, different actors (businessmen and opposition leaders) were promoting the country based on their interests (Marat, 2009). Triggered by the Swedish consulting firm's initiative that Kyrgyzstan can be the "land of Santa Claus" (2007), the new image of the country started to develop. It is interesting how the Muslim dominated country can become a center for a Christian symbol! Based on the personal experience (2012-2019) I have not heard from the local people about this slogan. However, the first one "Switzerland of Central Asia" seems to be accepted and was mentioned with a sense of pride. Kyrgyzstan is currently focusing on ecological tourism and attracting tourist who are looking for untouched nature. However, what is still lacking is a good infrastructure and developed service sector.

Uzbekistan

Uzbekistan has been promoting its brand mostly via diplomatic means, business, and diplomatic channels. Emphasis is on ancient tradition and modern culture. The country is promoted as "a cultural gem," and "Crossroad of Civilizations."". The major tourist attractions during and after the Soviet time have not changed: Samarkand, Bukhara and Khiva. Since the country had only one President (1989-2016), Islam Karimov, creating messages for the international and local population was monopolized by the ruling elite. This approach has somewhat changed with the new President Mirziyoyev. He has marked 2017 as the "Year of Dialogue with People and Human Interests." He has started a new nation branding project. The modernization of the capital city Tashkent has raised many different reactions.

The goal of the Tashkent City Project is to "redesign the capital and rebrand Uzbekistan as a country interested in political reform, economic investment, and friendly relations with the rest of the world" (Matyabukova, 2018). However, the project is not taking into consideration local citizens' interests and concerns, therefore it is igniting criticism at home. This case emphasizes another characteristic of country's approach in nation branding: for domestic consumption another for global consumption. Another example for dual messages is focus on ancient tradition and culture when promotion is focused to international actors, while using Amir Timur heritage for the domestic promotion.

THE BORAT EFFECT

The movie, *Borat: Cultural Learnings of America for Make Benefit Glorious Nation of Kazakhstan*, has demonstrated the power of the modern era, no longer characterized with analog but digital transmission, which Saunders calls "digital nationality" (2016). Initially the movie generated an outpouring of defensive reactions from the government of Kazakhstan that interpreted movie as a mockery of Kazakh people, culture, and country. In order to communicate the preferable narrative about their country, ads were placed in the leading US media: the New York Times, The International Herald Tribune, US News and World Report, The Washington Post, and Foreign Affairs. There were also TV ads that run on CNN and ABC's local affiliate in Washington D.C.

However, contrary to the expectations of Kazakhstani officials, the movie had more positive than negative effects on perceptions of people in the USA and UK, for example. The biggest winner in Kazakhstan was the tourist industry. In December, the website hotels.com reported that during one week, there was a 300 percent jump in internet searches for hotel accommodations in Kazakhstan's capital Astana (Mangan, 2006). The Kazakhstanis Embassies in London and Washington registered a significant increase in tourist requests and tourists visa applications. (Collinson, 2006; Mangan, 2006). Tourist agencies in Kazakhstan reacted to this new demand by designing special Borat-themed tours.

Stock (2009) has analyzed this phenomenon and suggested that there were six key perspectives of Kazakhstan image: Kazakhstan's national identity, the construed image, point of reference: USA, Kazakhstan's actual image, projected image, desired future image (Figure 2). The crucial action is focused on mapping the gap between those perspectives with an ultimate purpose of closing the gap.

The purpose of nation branding, in general, is to identify the gap between the country's perception about its own image and the perceptions of others about a country. The Borat effect has demonstrated the gap in these perceptions. Kazakhstan was reactive in this case but did not fully take advantage of this opportunity. It did

Figure 2. Six perspectives of Borat effect
Source: Stock (2009). p. 190

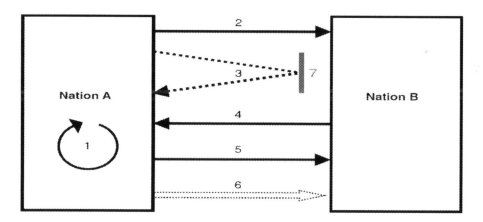

1 Nation A self-perception: i.e. *National identity*

2 Nation A's perception of Nation B: *Reference point*

3 What Nation A believes Nation B perceives it as: *Construed image*

4 How Nation A is actually perceived by Nation B: *Reputation / Actual image*

5 How Nation A is promoting itself to Nation B: *Current projected image*

6 How Nation A wants to be perceived by Nation B: *Desired future image*

7 The Borat Effect

not improve some of its own shortcomings, like the poorly developed embassy's website. The movie introduced the country to the world. Anholt argues that the movie made people open to listening to information coming out of Kazakhstan. The country "could have spent 20 million dollars a year for the previous 10 years trying to promote Kazakhstan and it wouldn't have had any effect at all - after Borat, they could have spent US$5 million a year and had 20 times more effect" (Stock F. interview with Anholt, 2008 as seen in Stock, 2009).

SOLUTIONS AND RECOMMENDATIONS

The first goal of the countries in Central Asia, since gaining their statehood was self-identification and the establishment of their image in the world arena" (Lebedenko in Dinnie, 2007, p.107). This was a challenging process with different outcomes. Regardless of nation branding approach, all countries in the region are still faced with a region's deficit. The case of Africa demonstrates the impact region's (continent) deficit plays for all countries in the region. Cover pages of the Economics from 2000 and 2011 showed the power of perception.

Zbigniew Brzezinski portrays Central Asia as "Eurasian Balkans." The region is often "perceived as a "hotbed" of destabilization, instability, violence, Islamic extremism." (Kendzior, 2013) Since names of all countries in the region end with

Figure 3. Front-page covers for The Economist in 2000 and 2011
Source: The Economist

suffix "stan" as in the case with Pakistan and Afghanistan, this in addition puts a negative perception on them. Therefore, we suggest that for the individual country to benefit from nation branding strategy it is important that all countries in the region to start parallelly to work on the region's brand. With changing perception of the region all countries will benefit. Few of the potential unifying themes for the region could be: Nomad games, Naruz celebration, national cuisine, snow leopard, high mountains and ecological tourism.

Two countries are in the process or have already changed their official name. Kyrgyzstan changed its name to Kyrgyz Republic in 1993. However, the old name is still used globally. During his presidency, Nazarbayev suggested the name change: "The ending of our country's name is -stan, like the other countries in Central Asia. At the same time, many foreigners are drawn to Mongolia, a country of just two million people whose country does not have the -stan ending." In January 2019, the name change topic has been raised again (Kumenov, 2019) .

Central Asia is a challenging but a promising region as well. Nation branding strategies for individual countries as well as for the region, while developed as a long-term plan not a short-term campaign could give positive results and close the perception gap between a country and the world.

FUTURE RESEARCH DIRECTIONS

The existed research on nation branding of Kazakhstan, Kyrgyzstan and Uzbekistan is limited. Thus, future research is needed. The countries in the region individually and as a group should encourage more studies in this area. The concept of nation branding should be promoted in educational system across the region. This will give additional impetus to students, professors, business and political leaders to work in a more sophisticated and coordinated way on nation branding. Since this is a multidimensional and multidisciplinary topic coordinated research between economist, marketing experts, political researches, cultural and sociological researcher is required. The emphasis of the research should be on quantifiable results of the nation branding campaigns where the costs of the campaign will be linked to the outcomes.

Case study research of nation branding is the area that can give new light to this topic. This way the best practices for nation branding could be developed. Comparative studies in this area are also welcomed. Soft versus hard diplomacy also deserve a place in future research of this topic.

The potential topics for research include branding the region which requires more coordination between all Central Asian countries. Global agencies that measure nation branding index sporadically include Central Asian counties. However, these are the agencies that are highly respected and influential in the world and can persuade potential investors or tourist where to invest their money or where to spend their vacation. Therefore, Central Asian countries should encourage these agencies to include all countries from Central Asia in their research. This will give the region higher visibility.

CONCLUSION

Nation branding in Central Asia is emerging. Some countries have engaged in nation branding by reacting to the outside events (Borat effect) while others were more proactive (Kyrgyzstan in the 1990s). In Kazakhstan and Uzbekistan, the nation branding activates were more centralized, while this was not the case in Kyrgyzstan. Few of the global agencies measure nation branding. However, not all of them include countries from Central Asia. The leading global powers, USA, China, Russia, have strategic interest in this region (from military base to Belt and Road Initiative). Therefore, the study of this region is necessary. In this chapter the comprehensive analysis of the topic was presented. Nation branding in the region went through different stages and with different results. The goal of nation branding was to attract more foreign investment, tourists and donors. Uzbekistan had two approaches for nation branding: one for domestic consumption and another for global consumption. Sometimes this method triggered negative reactions from the local population.

The Borat Effect presents a valuable case study of the reactive approach in nation branding. The special lesson from this case is linked to six different perspectives and mapping of a gap. The crucial action is focused on mapping the gap between those perspectives with an ultimate purpose of closing the gap. The chapter suggests a need for region's branding. Central Asia suffers from region's deficit and derived negative consequences on countries. Therefore, working only on nation branding without region's branding would not be effective. Nation branding strategies for individual country as well as for the region, while developed as a long-term plan not a short-term campaign could give positive results and close the perception gap between a country and the world.

REFERENCES

Ahn, M. J., & Wu, H. (2015). The art of nation branding: National branding value and the role of government and the arts and culture sector. *Public Organization Review*, *15*(1), 157–173. doi:10.100711115-013-0255-6

Anholt, S. (2006). Why brand? Some practical considerations for nation branding. *Place Branding and Public Diplomacy*, *2*(2), 97–107. doi:10.1057/palgrave. pb.5990048

Anholt, S. (2008). From *nation branding* to *competitive identity* – The role of brand management as a component of national policy. In K. Dinnie (Ed.), *Nation branding: concepts, issues, practice* (pp. 22–23). Oxford, UK: Butterworth-Heinemann.

Anholt. (2007, November 6). *Countries Must Earn Better Images through Smart Policy*. An Interview, Council on Foreign Relations.

Anonymous. (2010). The New Great Game, Central Asia Special. *Spiegel online*. Retrieved on June 2, 2012, from: https://www.spiegel.de/international/world/spiegel-central-asia-special-the-new-great-game-a-722173.html

Chen, X., & Fazilov, F. (2018). Re-centering Central Asia: China's "New Great game" in the old Eurasian Heartland. *Palgrave Communications*, *4*(1), 71. doi:10.105741599-018-0125-5

Collins, O., & Gbadamosi, A. (2011). Re-branding Africa. *Marketing Intelligence & Planning*, *29*(3), 284–304. doi:10.1108/02634501111129257

Collinson, S. (2006). Joke on Borat as Kazakhstan 'makes benefit' tourism. *Mail & Guardian Online*. Retrieved on September 9, 2017, from: https://www.mg.co.za/article/2006-11-16-joke-on-borat-as-kazakhstan-makes-benefit-tourism

Dinnie, K. (2007). *Nation Branding: Concepts, Issues, Practice*. Oxford, UK: Butterworth Heinemann.

Dinnie, K. (2010). *Nation Branding: Concepts, Issues, Practice*. Routledge. Retrieved on October 7, 2013, from: https://search.proquest.com/abicomplete/legacydocview/EBC/535091?accountid=167104

Dinnie, K., Melewar, T. C., Seidenfuss, K.-U., & Musa, G. (2010). Nation branding and integrated marketing communication: An ASEAN perspective. *International Marketing Review*, *27*(4), 388–403. doi:10.1108/02651331011058572

Domeisen, N. (2003). Is there a case for national branding? *International Trade Forum*, *14*(1). Retrieved from https://prx-herzing.lirn.net/login?url=https://search.proquest.com/docview/231424853?accountid=167104

Fan, Y. (2010). Branding the nation: Towards a better understanding. *Place Branding and Public Diplomacy*, *6*(2), 97–103. doi:10.1057/pb.2010.16

Fetscherin, M. (2010). The determinants and measurement of a country brand: The country brand strength index. *International Marketing Review*, *27*(4), 466–479. doi:10.1108/02651331011058617

Fullerton, J., Kendrick, A., & Wallis, C. (2008). Brand Borat? Americans' reaction to a Kazakhstani place branding campaign. *Place Branding and Public Diplomacy*, *4*(2), 159–168. doi:10.1057/pb.2008.6

Gudjonsson, H. (2005). Nation branding. *Place Branding*, *1*(3), 283–298. doi:10.1057/palgrave.pb.5990029

Harrison-Walker, L. J. (2011). Strategic positioning of nation as brands. *Journal of International Business Research*, *10*(2), 135–147.

Herstein, R. (2012). Thin line between country, city, and region branding. *Journal of Vacation Marketing*, *18*(2), 147–155. doi:10.1177/1356766711435976

Hurn, B. J. (2016). The role of cultural diplomacy in nation branding. *Industrial and Commercial Training*, *48*(2), 80–85. doi:10.1108/ICT-06-2015-0043

Jansen, S. C. (2008). Designer nations: Neo-liberal nation branding — Brand Estonia. *Social Identities*, *14*(1), 121–142. doi:10.1080/13504630701848721

Kaneva, N. (2011). Nation branding: Toward an agenda of critical research. *International Journal of Communication*, *5*, 117–141.

Kendzior, S. (2013). The Curse of Stability in Central Asia. *Foreign Policy*. Retrieved on March 16, 2017, from: https://foreignpolicy.com/2013/02/19/the-curse-of-stability-in-central-asia/

Kotler, P., & Gertner, D. (2002). Country as brand, product, and beyond: A place marketing and brand management perspective. *Journal of Brand Management*, *9*(4/5), 249–261. doi:10.1057/palgrave.bm.2540076

Kumenov, A. (2019). Kazakhstan MP suggests changing country's name. *Eurasianet*. Retrieved on October 7, 2019, from: https://eurasianet.org/kazakhstan-mp-suggests-changing-countrys-name

Mangan, D. (2006) Kazakhstan tourism's Borat boom. *New York Post*. Retrieved on August 20, 2008, from: https://www.nypost.com/seven/12042006/news/nationalnews/kazakh_tourisms_borat_boom_nationalnews_dan_mangan.htm

Marat, E. (2009). Nation Branding in Central Asia: A New Campaign to Present Ideas about the State and the Nation. *Europe-Asia Studies*, *61*(7), 1123–1136. doi:10.1080/09668130903068657

Matyabukova, D. (2018). Who Is "Tashkent City" For? Nation-Branding and Public Dialogue in Uzbekistan. *Voices on Central Asia*. Retrieved on July 9, 2019, from: https://voicesoncentralasia.org/who-is-tashkent-city-for-nation-branding-and-public-dialogue-in-uzbekistan/

Rojas-Méndez, J. (2013). The nation brand molecule. *Journal of Product and Brand Management, 22*(7), 462–472. doi:10.1108/JPBM-09-2013-0385

Rojas-Méndez, J. I., Papadopoulos, N., & Murphy, S. A. (2013). Measuring and positioning nation brands: A comparative brand personality approach. *Corporate Reputation Review, 16*(1), 48–65. doi:10.1057/crr.2012.25

Saunders, R. A. (2007). In defense of Kazakshilik: Kazakhstan's war on Sacha Baron Cohen. *Identity, 14*(3), 225–255. doi:10.1080/10702890601162682

Saunders, R. A. (2008). Buying into brand Borat: Kazakhstan's cautious embrace of its unwanted 'son'. *Slavic Review, 67*(1), 63–80. doi:10.2307/27652767

Saunders, R. A. (2016). *Popular Geopolitics and Nation Branding in the Post-Soviet Realm*. New York: Routledge. doi:10.4324/9781315737386

Stock, F. (2009). The Borat effect. *Place Branding and Public Diplomacy, 5*(3), 180–191. doi:10.1057/pb.2009.12

Stock, F. (2009). Identity, image and brand: A conceptual framework. *Place Branding and Public Diplomacy, 5*(2), 118–125. doi:10.1057/pb.2009.2

Szondi, G. (2007). The role and challenges of country branding in transition countries: The Central and Eastern European experience. *Place Branding and Public Diplomacy, 3*(1), 8–20. doi:10.1057/palgrave.pb.6000044

Szondi, G. (2007). The role and challenges of country branding in transition countries: The Central and Eastern European experience. *Place Branding and Public Diplomacy, 3*(1), 8–20. doi:10.1057/palgrave.pb.6000044

van Ham, P. (2001). The rise of the brand state. *Foreign Affairs, 80*(5), 2–6. doi:10.2307/20050245

Volcic, Z., & Andrejevic, M. (2011). Nation branding in the era of commercial nationalism. *International Journal of Communication, 5*, 598–618.

Wu, L. (2017). Relationship building in nation branding: The central role of nation brand commitment. *Place Branding and Public Diplomacy, 13*(1), 65–80. doi:10.1057/pb.2015.16

Chapter 6

Brand Consciousness and Brand Loyalty:
A Study on Foreign Brand Beauty and Skin Care Products

Asmat Nizam Abdul-Talib
iD https://orcid.org/0000-0001-6820-2918
Universiti Utara Malaysia, Malaysia

Nadia Japeri
Universiti Utara Malaysia, Malaysia

ABSTRACT

It is often argued that consumers become loyal to a particular brand based on their perception of the brand itself. This study investigates the relationship between brand consciousness and three key variables: perceived quality, emotional value, and brand involvement. It also examines the influence of these three variables on students' brand loyalty to foreign-brand beauty and skin care products. A total of 318 female students from a public university in Malaysia participated in the survey. Using multiple regression analysis, the study found that brand consciousness is positively related to perceived quality and emotional value, but not brand involvement. Perceived quality and emotional value positively influence loyalty toward foreign beauty and skin care products, while brand involvement negatively influences brand loyalty.

DOI: 10.4018/978-1-7998-2239-4.ch006

Copyright © 2020, IGI Global. Copying or distributing in print or electronic forms without written permission of IGI Global is prohibited.

INTRODUCTION

Although the marketing literature has largely focused on the study of foreign brands, very limited research has been conducted on brand loyalty in Asian markets. Against the background of major changes in the marketplace in global brands, scholars strive to understand the reasons why consumers are loyal to a brand choice and the key factors that influence their loyalty to their brand choice. People want a better standard of living, and improvements in technology, science, economics, and education stimulate the desire for current styles and new products. In the era of globalization, consumers exposed to foreign products seek to consume foreign products from foreign countries and are more aware of branded products as a way to represent their identity and image. Malaysians are no exception, especially in the area of beauty and skincare products.

As the Malaysian economy becomes stronger, the income level of the general population gets higher as well. The rising income has led to a change in a new lifestyle. According to Hassan, Rahman, and Sade (2015), Saat, Shaari, and Ahmad Fauzi (2017), and Idowu, Ja'afar, Shari, and Dahlan (2018), Malaysians are becoming more westernized, sophisticated and cosmopolitan. One product that has shown a considerable increase in demand over the last decade is the beauty and skincare product category. Skincare products are designed to moisturize, cleanse, tone, and maintain the skin (Yee, Chin, & Suan, 2012; Jan et al., 2019), and Malaysians are now more than ever concerned with beauty regimens, such as skin and hair care, out of a desire to look beautiful, young and trendy.

In Malaysia, skin care was one of the most dynamic product categories in 2014 (Euromonitor.com, 2014). Make-up brands and skincare products made in Malaysia are now coming to the fore. Meanwhile, the younger crowd, heavily influenced by Korean music and drama series, go for branded Korean make-up and skincare products used by their favorite celebrities. Continuous innovation by industry players, especially foreign brands, has also attracted consumer attention to skincare products.

Due to marketing and advertising, beauty and skincare products are in high demand, including home-grown cosmetic products. The strong performance of home-grown cosmetic products can be attributed to many factors. Rapid urbanization has resulted in many people having an office job. As a result, many see that a professional and well-groomed appearance is required. Social media, such as Instagram, Facebook, and Twitter, which are primarily founded by fashion entrepreneurs, professional make-up artists, and celebrities, as well as social media influencers, also contribute toward the growth of home-grown cosmetic products (Badarudin, 2018).

There is a high demand for cosmetic products due to age-related skin problems in Malaysia (countrymeters.info, 2015). As people age, their skin changes. Women consumers in their 20s to 40s use beauty and skincare products to maintain a youthful appearance. The products are used primarily to reduce wrinkles and dull skin. In general, women are the biggest consumers of beauty and skincare products to maintain their self-image, and such products are seen to be able to enhance their self-confidence. Malaysian consumers spend an estimated USD500 million on cosmetic products (Eze, Tan, & Yeo, 2012). According to Eze, Tan, and Yeo (2012), Malaysia is a net importer of cosmetic and toiletry products and equipment, importing US$156 million in 2006, US$167 million in 2007, and US$225 million in 2008. Malaysia's total trade volume for personal care and cosmetics products was about US$2.24 billion (RM8.9 billion) in 2015. Over 50 percent of the demand was met by US$1.3 billion in imports, mainly from China, Thailand, France, the European Union, the United States, South Korea, and Japan.

In Malaysia, both local and international manufacturers have entered the market, attracted by the rising demand for beauty and skincare products. However, international players, such as L'Oreal, continue to dominate the local market. L'Oreal, based in France, is the world's largest cosmetics company and the leading provider of skincare products in the Malaysian market with a 12% retail market share in 2013 (Euromonitor.com, 2014; Zamani, Abdul-Talib and Ashari, 2016). Procter & Gamble continued to lead beauty and personal care in Malaysia in 2018. Premium beauty and personal care players continue their rapid expansion in Malaysia, with the opening of first outlets by brands, such as Tom Ford Beauty and Maison Christian Dior Fragrance Boutique, and the rapid expansion of outlets by Estée Lauder and Sulwhasoo (Euromonitor.com, 2019).

Che Wel, Alam, and Mohd Nor (2011), Aluri, Price, and McIntyre (2019), and Song, Wang, and Han (2019) argued that it is hard to earn consumer loyalty because of the many factors that encourage customers to change brands. Marketers must understand consumer loyalty and its effect on consumer buying behavior, as well as the factors that affect consumer loyalty to a brand. For marketers, brand loyalty is a way of measuring a consumer's buying patterns in order to encourage them to repurchase a product – in this case, a foreign brand of beauty and skincare product. To measure consumer's brand loyalty to a foreign-branded beauty and skincare product, marketers need an accurate picture of their target consumer's behavior toward that product. Marketers face a challenging environment because consumers nowadays are more demanding, and their needs are hard to satisfy. Marketers need to be concerned with consumer's perception of their brand since such perception affects consumer's repurchase intention toward a product.

This study examines how brand consciousness affects three components of brand perception: perceived quality, emotional value, and brand involvement. Malaysian consumers are increasingly familiar with and willing to consider buying foreign branded products over local ones (Kamaruddin, 2002; Azmi Hassali et al., 2015; Karmakar & Ahmed, 2019). Hence, brand consciousness plays an important role

Brand Consciousness and Brand Loyalty

in encouraging consumers to make a purchase. Also, this study seeks to understand whether perceived quality, emotional value, and brand involvement have any effect on their brand loyalty.

This chapter is organized as follows: a review of the related literature is followed by an elaborate description of the research framework. Next, we discuss the methods used to collect the data, followed by data analysis and results. Finally, we highlight the research implications and limitations and suggest directions for future research.

CONCEPTUAL FRAMEWORK AND HYPOTHESIS DEVELOPMENT

Brand Consciousness and Perceived Quality

Quality is an important factor in consumer choice of which brand to buy (Che Wel, Alam, & Mohd Nor, 2011; Chadwick & Piartrini, 2019; Chung & Lee, 2019). Doyle (2001) stated that consumers form their perception of a brand based on the quality of the products. Consumers with a favorable perception will continue to purchase a branded product over a period of time. However, Yim et al. (2014) claimed that consumers with low brand consciousness tend to ignore brands in their decision-making process. It is difficult to evaluate a product's quality quickly, and it takes time for brand consciousness to act; as a shortcut, consumers tend to believe that higher price equates higher quality (Keller, 2013). Consumers are willing to pay a premium for well-known brands since they believe that well-known brands are better made and more durable.

Past research has investigated the relationship between brand consciousness and perceived quality. Lee et al. (2008), in their study on factors affecting Mexican college students' purchase intentions toward a US apparel brand, found that brand consciousness is positively related to perceived quality. Brand consciousness would bring about a positive image on the product quality of foreign products. Since brands of foreign origin products have the above advantages, consumers may associate their brand image as perceived positively with quality. Thus, it can be argued that college students who are brand conscious will look upon highly the quality of foreign products. Therefore, we propose the following:

Hypothesis 1: Brand consciousness is positively related to perceived quality of a foreign beauty and skincare products.

Brand Consciousness and Emotional Value

Brands also provide an emotional value to consumers, making them happy and giving them enjoyment and pleasure from using the product. The emotional value especially applies to foreign brand products. Familiarity with a brand engenders in consumers a positive feeling toward it (Mouangue, 2019; Yee & Sidek, 2008). Consumers in developing countries prefer foreign brand products over local ones because the former offers more emotional benefits (Shen et al., 2002).

Lee et al. (2009), in their study on factors affecting Mexican college students' purchase intention toward a US apparel brand, found that brand consciousness is positively related to the emotional value associated with the US brand. Asian consumers tend to perceive that products originating from the developed countries are more attractive, have higher quality, and more prestigious (Lee & Nguyen, 2017; Rodrigo, Khan, & Ekinci, 2019). They also often emulate western consumption practices and purchase brands that symbolize western lifestyles associated with affluence. They also view foreign goods as superior to domestic goods because they believe that ownership of foreign products, especially high-end brand names, demonstrate their status in society (Haryonto, Febrianto & Cahyono, 2019; Nguyen & Kuan, 2011). Therefore, we provide the following:

Hypothesis 2: Brand consciousness is positively related to the emotional value obtained from a foreign beauty and skincare products.

Brand Consciousness and Brand Involvement

Brands serve a social function by providing informational, interactional, and symbolic benefits to their customers (Holt, 2006; Hanson, Jiang, & Dahl, 2019). Customers need information about a product to understand its perceived personal relevance to them. Consumers learn about a brand and then combine this new knowledge with existing knowledge, creating new structures in their memory; in other words, they interpret the meaning of a brand. This investment of effort is referred to as involvement. Past studies have found that consumers who are much concerned about their status and highly susceptible to interpersonal influence are prone to favor luxury brands, which direct their desire for status consumption (e.g., O'Cass & McEwen, 2004; Wiedmann, Hennigs, & Siebels, 2009; Shao, Grace, & Ross, 2019). Increasing levels of consumers' brand consciousness are expected to influence their brand involvement directly. Thus, often, brand-conscious consumers tend to get involved with the brand that leads to a purchase decision. Therefore, we hypothesize that:

Brand Consciousness and Brand Loyalty

Hypothesis 3: Brand consciousness is positively related to brand involvement with a foreign beauty and skincare products.

Perceived Quality and Brand Loyalty

Consumers, especially in South East Asia, have high expectations of foreign brands because the products tend to be perceived as superior in both features and performance to local brands and assume that a foreign brand's quality is consistently maintained at a high standard. Kumar, Kim, and Pelton (2009) stated that "consumers may purchase the brand with higher quality" (pp. 511). According to Yee and Sidek (2008), consumers tend to repurchase a brand or switch to another brand based on the quality of the product. Consumers may develop brand loyalty – that is, some degree of commitment toward a brand – as a function of repetitive purchases (Aluri, Price, & McIntyre, 2019; Che Wel, Alam, & Mohd Nor, 2011; Song, Wang, & Han, 2019).

Che Wel, Alam, and Mohd Nor (2011) found that perceived product quality is the major factor affecting brand loyalty in Malaysia. Yee and Sidek (2008) found that product quality is one of seven key factors that influence brand loyalty, and their findings are consistent with those of Sharma et al. (2013) and Lau et al. (2006). These studies found that product quality is an important factor in brand loyalty because higher product quality may enhance consumers emotionally, thus providing a more gratifying experience with the brand. The positive relationship between quality and brand loyalty is expected to apply to Malaysian consumers, regardless of whether they are loyal to a foreign or local brand product. Thus, we hypothesize the following:

Hypothesis 4: Consumer perception of brand quality will have a positive influence on brand loyalty.

Emotional Value and Brand Loyalty

A customer's emotional value on a particular brand is linked to three major factors, including customer's self-connection with the brand, the feeling of warmth towards the brand, and having an intense liking for the brand (Chang et al., 2019; Thomson et al., 2005). Some researchers observed that consumers give more weight to emotional value when purchasing a product or brand than to the perceived quality of the product. It seems reasonable to expect that consumers will become loyal to brands that can satisfy their emotional needs, and emotional value will thus have a particularly positive impact on brand loyalty toward foreign products, from which customers expect high emotional benefits.

Brand loyalty reflects the commitment of a consumer toward a brand; it represents a long-term relationship (Abdul-Talib & Mohd-Adnan, 2017; Nelson & McLeod,

2005). Emotional attachment to a brand increases the emotional value consumers place on the brand (Saini & Singh, 2019; So, Parsons, & Yap, 2013). It strengthens consumers' connection to the brand and their desire to maintain their relationship with the brand. In short, it makes consumers loyal to the brand.

Lee, Back, and Kim (2009) found that emotions play an important role in explaining satisfaction and brand loyalty. This positive relationship between emotional value and brand loyalty is also expected to apply to Malaysian consumers, whether they become loyal to a foreign brand or a local brand. Therefore, we hypothesize the following:

Hypothesis 5: Consumer perception of a brand's emotional value will have a positive influence on brand loyalty.

Brand Involvement and Brand Loyalty

Product involvement refers to consumer or user engagement with a product in the form of thoughts, feelings, and behavioral responses (Gordon, McKeage, & Fox 1998; Abdul-Talib, Abd-Latif, & Abd-Razak, 2016; Junaid, Hou, Hussain, & Kirmani, 2019). The central idea of the relationship between brand involvement and brand loyalty centers on the premise that consumers who are more involved with a particular brand are more committed, and hence, more loyal to that brand. High involvement has also been suggested as a precondition to loyalty (Beatty & Kahle, 1988). Furthermore, Menidjel, Benhabib, and Bilgihan (2017) argued that the cognitive definition of brand loyalty represents a commitment, and therefore, involvement with the brand. Thus, consumers' involvement in a product will have a positive effect on their loyalty to a brand.

Consumers with high product involvement experience have an increased interest in a product, which, in turn, may motivate them to purchase it. According to Quester and Lim (2003) and Mathew and Thomas (2019), interest in a product category arises from a consumer's perception that the product or brand meets his or her values and/or goals. The expected values can motivate consumers to purchase the product or brand and make them loyal to the brand.

Quester and Lim (2003) and Parihar, Dawra, and Sahay (2019) found that product involvement is positively associated with brand loyalty. Similarly, So, Parsons, and Yap (2013) found that the higher a customer's emotional attachment, the greater their brand loyalty. Thus, we hypothesize the following:

Hypothesis 6: High consumer involvement in foreign beauty and skincare products will have a positive influence on brand loyalty.

Figure 1 illustrates the conceptual framework that outlines the research quests of this study.

METHODOLOGY

Measures

Six questions on brand consciousness adapted from Nelson and McLeod (2005) were employed. Six questions on perceived quality and five on emotional value were adapted from Sweeney and Soutar (2001). Twenty questions on brand involvement were adapted from Zaichkowsky (1985). Four questions on brand loyalty were adapted from Carrol and Ahuvia (2006). The total number of questions in both Section A and Section B was 52. Brand involvement was measured using closed-ended bipolar questions (two extreme answers at the opposite ends of the scale), while the Likert seven-point scale was used to evaluate brand consciousness, perceived quality, emotional value, and brand loyalty. We made several adjustments to the items to make them more relevant and suitable to the Malaysian context.

Figure 1. Research framework

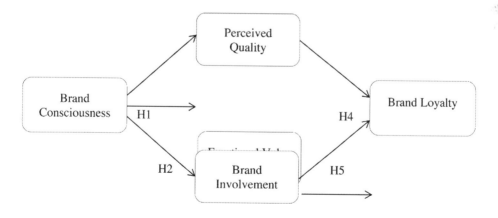

H3   H6

Data Collection and Sample

Our sample consisted of female students at Universiti Utara Malaysia, Kedah, Malaysia. Students were used as the sample for several reasons. Firstly, according to Azuizkulov (2013), students use beauty and skincare products in their daily lives to promote beauty and personality. Secondly, students are a young demographic; therefore, they represent potential future consumers (Abdul-Latif & Abdul-Talib, 2017; Bakar & Abdul-Talib, 2013; Zakaria, Wan-Ismail & Abdul-Talib, 2015). In total, 350 questionnaires were distributed using convenience sampling, and 326 were returned. Eight questionnaires filled out by non-Malaysian respondents were discarded since the target population was Malaysian, resulting in a sample size of 318. The questionnaire consisted of two sections. Section A collected demographic information, while Section B collected information pertaining to all of the variables. The questionnaires asked participants to rate more than 60 brands of beauty and skincare products, covering both global and local players in the Malaysian market.

Results

Most of the respondents were Malay (68.6%) and Muslim (70.4%). In terms of education, most were full-time students (95.6%). Some participants had a master's degree (37.4%), and a few had a Ph.D. (6.3%). Most students had financial loans (77.4%). In terms of purchasing habits, 89.4% of the participants reported using or purchasing beauty and skincare products, and 73.9% reported using a global brand. Regarding how often beauty and skincare products were purchased, 34.4% reported purchasing such products once every three months, and 34% reported purchasing them once a month. In total, 177 used a global brand, while 103 used a local brand. Six other participants used global and local brands randomly. Safi was at the top of the list (25%), followed by Fair & Lovely (20%), Garnier (18%), Nano White (16%), and SKII (15%), with other brands clustered at the bottom (e.g., L'Oreal, Nivea, Clinique, and Bio-Essence). A summary of the findings from this study is presented in Table 1.

Model Estimation

Before testing the hypotheses, we ran exploratory factor analysis (EFA), and a correlation matrix was generated to test the relationship between all the variables in the study. Table 2 shows a significant positive relationship between brand consciousness and perceived quality ($r = 0.584$, $p=0.000$). There is also a significant positive relationship between brand consciousness and emotional value ($r = 0.643$,

Brand Consciousness and Brand Loyalty

Table 1. Demographic profile of respondents

	Demographic group	Response	Frequency	Percentage (%)
1.	Race	Malay	218	68.6
		Chinese	61	19.2
		Indian	33	10.4
		Other	5	1.6
2.	Religion	Islam	224	70.4
		Christian	35	11.0
		Buddhist	33	10.4
		Hindu	26	8.2
3.	Level of study	Masters	119	37.4
		PhD	20	6.3
		Other Degree	179	56.3
4.	Current student status	Full Time	304	95.6
		Part Time	13	4.1
5.	Student loan	Yes	246	77.4
		No	55	17.3
6.	Use of beauty and skin care products	Yes	284	89.3
		No	16	5.0
7.	Use of foreign beauty and skin care products	Yes	235	73.9
		No	79	24.8
8.	How often respondent purchases beauty and skin care products	More than once a month	68	21.4
		Once a month	108	34.0
		Once in three month	109	34.3
		Others	23	7.2

p=0.001). There is a positive relationship between brand consciousness and brand loyalty (r = 0.063, p=0.000), but it is not significant since r < 0.10 (p=0.000).

There is also a moderately positive relationship between perceived quality and brand loyalty (r = 0.476, p=0.001). Emotional value and brand loyalty show a significant positive relationship (r = 0.513, p=0.000), as do emotional value and brand loyalty (r > 0.5 for both, p=0.000). Finally, there is a positive relationship between brand involvement and brand loyalty (r = 0.031), but it is not significant since r < 0.10 (p=0.000).

Cross-loading factors were removed following the EFA. All remaining measures had loading greater than 0.4. Following Hair's (2015) recommendation, the values met the threshold value, suggesting that they were appropriate for further analysis. Table 3 lists all the finalized items used in testing the model. Cronbach's alpha values for all five items after factor analysis (excluding the eliminated factors) were listed. According to Hair (2015), values above 0.7 are considered acceptable, while

Table 2. Pearson correlations for all variables

	Brand consciousness	Perceived quality	Emotional value	Brand involvement	Brand loyalty
Brand consciousness	1				
Perceived quality	.584**	1			
Emotional value	.643**	.654**	1		
Brand involvement	.063	.052	.180**	1	
Brand loyalty	.371**	.476**	.513**	.031	1
** Correlation is significant at the 0.01 level (2-tailed). * Correlation is significant at the 0.05 level (2-tailed).					

values above 0.8 are preferable. Table 3 shows that all of Cronbach's alpha values were comfortably above 0.7. Hence, all measures used in the subsequent analysis were highly reliable.

Multiple regression analysis was performed to test the hypotheses. Table 4 presents the results. For a summary of the hypothesis results, see Table 5.

In the case of H1, brand consciousness has a significant impact on perceived quality (t=12.784, p<0.05). Hence, the first hypothesis is supported. In the case of H2, brand consciousness has a positive impact on emotional value, supporting H2 (t=14.912, p<0.05). However, in the case of H3, no significant relationship between brand consciousness and brand involvement (t=1.124, p>0.05) is found. Hence, H3 is not supported. In the cases of H4 and H5, the t values are 3.642 (p=0.000) and 5.388 (p=0.000, respectively, indicating both hypothesized relationships are supported. In the case of H6, no significant relationship between brand consciousness and brand loyalty is observed (=-0.806, p>0.05). Hence, H6 is not supported.

DISCUSSION AND CONCLUSION

This research has important implications for current and future local and international retailers and marketers in the Malaysian beauty and skincare industry. Because perceived quality and emotional value are important factors in consumers' choice of brands, marketers (especially foreign companies) should focus on the quality and emotional aspects of their brand to attract Malaysian consumers, especially those who are new to the brand. Consumers who are brand conscious are likely to have high expectations of quality and emotional value (Abdul-Talib and Abdul-Latif, 2015; Jamal and Goode (2001) stated that brand-conscious consumers are likely to

Brand Consciousness and Brand Loyalty

Table 3. Final measurement items

Variable	Item	Loading in EFA	Cronbach's alpha
Brand consciousness	1. I pay attention to the brand names of the beauty and skin care product that I buy.	0.759	0.908
	2. Brand names tell me something about the quality of the beauty and skin care product.	0.852	
	3. Brand names tell me something about how 'cool' an item of beauty and skin care product is.	0.830	
	4. Sometimes I am willing to pay more money for beauty and skin care product because of its brand name.	0.630	
	5. Brand name beauty and skin care product that cost a lot of money are good quality.	0.708	
	6. I pay attention to the brand names of most of the products I buy.	0.679	
Perceived quality	1. Foreign brand of beauty and skin care product has consistent quality.	0.540	0.862
	2. Foreign brand of beauty and skin care product is well made.	0.503	
	3. Foreign brand of beauty and skin care product has an acceptable standard of quality.	0.656	
	4. Foreign brand of beauty and skin care product has poor workmanship.	0.582	
	5. Foreign brand of beauty and skin care product would not last a long time.	0.612	
	6. Foreign brand of beauty and skin care product would perform consistently.	0.572	
Emotional value	1. Foreign brand of beauty and skin care product is one that I would enjoy.	0.613	0.933
	2. Foreign brand of beauty and skin care product would make me want to use it.	0.615	
	3. Foreign brand of beauty and skin care product is one that I would feel relaxed about using.	0.782	
	4. Foreign brand of beauty and skin care product would make me feel good.	0.748	
	5. Foreign brand of beauty and skin care product would give me pleasure.	0.729	
Brand involvement	The foreign brand is _____ to me.		
	1. Important … Unimportant	0.676	0.812
	2. Of no concern … Of concern	0.522	
	3. Relevant … Irrelevant*	-	
	4. Means a lot … Means nothing	0.732	
	5. Useless … Useful	0.585	
	6. Valuable … Worthless	0.744	
	7. Trivial … Nontrivial	-0.616	
	8. Beneficial … Not beneficial	0.788	
	9. Matters … Doesn't matter	0.816	
	10. Uninterested … Interested	0.653	
	11. Significant … Not significant	0.714	
	12. Vital … Not vital	0.714	

continued on following page

Brand Consciousness and Brand Loyalty

Table 3. Continued

Variable	Item	Loading in EFA	Cronbach's alpha
	13. Boring … Interesting	0.716	
	14. Unexciting … Exciting	0.794	
	15. Appealing … Unappealing	0.664	
	16. Mundane … Not mundane	-0.521	
	17. Essential … Inessential	0.722	
	18. Undesirable … Desirable	0.739	
	19. Wanted … Unwanted	0.671	
	20. Not needed … Needed	0.701	
Brand loyalty	1. Foreign brand of beauty and skin care is only product that I will buy.	0.691	0.903
	2. When I go shopping, I don't even notice local brands.	0.800	
	3. If the store is out of foreign brand of beauty and skin care product, I'll postpone buying or go to another store.	0.736	
	4. I'll 'do without' rather than buy local brands.	0.846	
* Item deleted			

Table 4. Standardized coefficients and t-statistics for the structural model

Hypothesis	Structural path	B	Standard error	t-values	Sig
H1	Brand consciousness and perceived quality	0.584	0.038	12.784	0.000
H2	Brand consciousness and emotional value	0.643	0.043	14.912	0.000
H3	Brand consciousness and brand involvement	0.063	0.031	1.124	0.262
H4	Perceived quality and brand loyalty	0.240	0.085	3.642	0.000
H5	Emotional value and brand loyalty	0.359	0.071	5.388	0.000
H6	Brand involvement and brand loyalty	-0.040	0.097	-0.806	0.421

consider a brand name when evaluating a particular product. When local or foreign brands offer emotional satisfaction and consistently high quality, consumers are more likely to be loyal to the brand.

Both local and international marketers should pay attention to young consumers, such as students at higher learning institutions. Despite lacking much purchasing power, this market segment is the potential future consumers. Student consumers offer tremendous market potentials for companies to develop brand loyalty. Marketers

Brand Consciousness and Brand Loyalty

Table 5. Summary of hypotheses-testing results

Hypotheses		Findings
H1	Brand consciousness is positively related to perceived quality of foreign beauty and skin care product	Supported
H2	Brand consciousness is positively related to emotional value of foreign beauty and skin care product.	Supported
H3	Brand consciousness is positively related to brand involvement of foreign beauty and skin care product.	Not supported
H4	Consumers' brand perception of quality will have a positive influence on their brand loyalty.	Supported
H5	Consumers' brand perception of emotional value will have a positive influence on their brand loyalty.	Supported
H6	Consumers who are high involvement toward foreign beauty and skin care product will have positive influence on their brand loyalty.	Not supported

should take advantage of this to attract this market segment by implementing appropriate marketing strategies to make them involved with the products and, in particular, the brands. As a result, the young consumers would become more aware of the products they use, evaluate them, make their purchasing decision, and finally get involved with the product.

This study has several limitations. Firstly, the sample for this study was limited to students at one university. As a result, the findings may not be generalizable to all consumers in Malaysia. Future research should include a larger group of participants and should expand its focus to a larger geographic area. Also, future research should be conducted with samples from non-student populations to increase the credibility and generalizability of the findings. Secondly, this study was limited to female consumers. Future studies could examine the factors affecting male customers' brand loyalty toward foreign beauty and skincare products and make a gendered comparison.

Future researchers should include men in their sample since men are increasingly conscious of their body, concerned with beauty, and sensitive to cosmetics (Souiden & Diagne, 2009; Zakaria and Abdul-Talib, 2011). Thirdly, convenience sampling was chosen since it was the fastest way to obtain information from the participants. However, this method could limit the generalizability of the findings. Hence, future studies should consider using other methods, such as random sampling. Finally, previous studies have not measured the relationship between brand consciousness and brand involvement with which to compare the present study's findings. Future researchers need to explore brand consciousness and brand involvement to get a clearer picture of the relationship.

This study has underlined the factors affecting female university students' brand loyalty toward foreign brands of beauty and skincare products by exploring brand loyalty in terms of brand consciousness, perceived quality, emotional value, and brand involvement. The findings showed that brand consciousness has a significant positive relationship with perceived quality and emotional value. However, no significant relationship was found between brand consciousness and brand involvement. In terms of brand loyalty, perceived quality and emotional value were found to influence brand loyalty, but brand involvement has no impact on brand loyalty.

This study offers managers and foreign marketers a deeper understanding of brand loyalty in Malaysia, which may help them better satisfy their potential consumers' needs and wants. For example, since perceived quality and emotional value were found to influence brand loyalty, foreign beauty and skincare product marketers should focus on maintaining and standardizing the quality of their products to make consumers loyal to their brands. The same is true of emotional value: foreign beauty and skincare product marketers should focus on the emotional aspect of their brand to appeal to consumers (in this case, female university students), especially those who are brand conscious, to make them loyal toward the brand.

REFERENCES

Abdul-Latif, S. A., & Abdul-Talib, A. N. (2017). Consumer racism: A scale modification. *Asia Pacific Journal of Marketing and Logistics*, *29*(3), 616–633. doi:10.1108/APJML-02-2016-0026

Abdul-Talib, A. N., Abd-Latif, S. A., & Abd-Razak, I. S. (2016). A study on the boycott motivations of Malaysian non-Muslims. *Journal of Islamic Marketing*, *7*(3), 264–287. doi:10.1108/JIMA-11-2014-0071

Abdul-Talib, A. N., & Abdul-Latif, S. A. (2015). Antecedents to willingness to Boycotts among Malaysian muslims. In *Emerging Research on Islamic Marketing and Tourism in the Global Economy* (pp. 70–106). Hershey, PA: IGI Global. doi:10.4018/978-1-4666-6272-8.ch004

Abdul-Talib, A. N., & Mohd Adnan, M. M. (2017). Determinants of consumer's willingness to boycott surrogate products. *Journal of Islamic Marketing*, *8*(3), 345–360. doi:10.1108/JIMA-08-2015-0065

Aluri, A., Price, B. S., & McIntyre, N. H. (2019). Using machine learning to co-create value through dynamic customer engagement in a brand loyalty program. *Journal of Hospitality & Tourism Research (Washington, D.C.)*, *43*(1), 78–100. doi:10.1177/1096348017753521

Azmi Hassali, M., Al-Tamimi, S. K., Dawood, O. T., Verma, A. K., & Saleem, F. (2015). Malaysian cosmetic market: Current and future prospects. *Pharmaceutical Regulatory Affairs, 4*(4), 4. doi:10.4172/2167-7689.1000155

Azuizkulov, D. (2013). Country of origin and brand loyalty on cosmetic products among Universiti Utara Malaysia students. *Atlantic Review of Economics, 2*, 3443. Retrieved on May 3, 2016, from: https://www.econstor.eu/handle/10419/146555

Badarudin, N. (2018, January 17). *Rise of local cosmetic brands*. Retrieved on June 19, 2018, from: https://www.nst.com.my/lifestyle/flair/2018/01/325908/rise-local-cosmetic-brands

Bakar, A., Rahim, A., & Abdul-Talib, A. N. (2013). A case study of an internationalization process of a private higher education institution in Malaysia. *Gadjah Mada International Journal of Business, 15*(3), 211–230. doi:10.22146/gamaijb.5444

Beatty, S. E., & Kahle, L. R. (1988). Alternative hierarchies of the attitude-behavior relationship: The impact of brand commitment and habit. *Journal of the Academy of Marketing Science, 16*(2), 1–10. doi:10.1007/BF02723310

Carrol, A. A., & Ahuvia, A. C. (2006). Some antecedents and outcomes of brand love. *Marketing Letters, 17*(2), 79–89. doi:10.100711002-006-4219-2

Chadwick, C., & Piartrini, P. S. (2019). Product quality, convenience and brand loyalty: A case study of Silverqueen's adolescent consumers. *Proceedings of the 12th International Conference on Business and Management Research (ICBMR 2018)*. Retrieved on March 30, 2019, from: https://www.atlantis-press.com/proceedings/icbmr-18/55914310

Chang, Y., Li, Y., Yan, J., & Kumar, V. (2019). Getting more likes: The impact of narrative person and brand image on customer–brand interactions. *Journal of the Academy of Marketing Science, 195*(47), 1–19. doi:10.100711747-019-00632-2

Che Wel, C. A., Alam, S. H., & Mohd Nor, S. (2011). Factors affecting brand loyalty: An empirical study in Malaysia. *Australian Journal of Basic and Applied Sciences, 5*(12), 777–783.

Chung, H., & Lee, E. (2019). Impact of category-specific demand environment on store brand quality positioning: Empirical evidence. Paper presented at the International Conference on Advances in National Brand and Private Label Marketing 2019. *Springer Proceedings in Business and Economics*. Springer. Retrieved on June 1, 2019, from: https://link.springer.com/chapter/10.1007/978-3-030-18911-2_2

Countrymeters.info. (2015). *Malaysia population*. Retrieved from https://countrymeters.info/en/Malaysia

Department of Statistics Malaysia. (2018, July 31). *Current Population Estimates, Malaysia, 2017-2018*. Retrieved on January 7, 2019, from: https://www.dosm.gov.my/v1/index.php?r=column/cthemeByCat&cat=155&bul_id=c1pqTnFjb29HSnNYNUpiTmNWZHArdz09&menu_id=L0pheU43NWJwRWVSZklWdzQ4TlhUUT09

Doyle, P. (2001). Shareholder-value-based brand strategies. *Brand Management*, 9(1), 20–30. doi:10.1057/palgrave.bm.2540049

Euromonitor International. (2015). *Skin care in Malaysia*. Retrieved on June 13, 2019, from: https://www.euromonitor.com/skin-care-in-malaysia/report

Euromonitor International. (2019, Jun). *Beauty and personal care in Malaysia*. Retrieved on June 13, 2019, from: https://www.euromonitor.com/beauty-and-personal-care-in-malaysia/report

Eze, U. C., Tan, C. B., & Yeo, L. Y. (2012). Purchasing cosmetic products: A preliminary perspective of Gen-Y. *Contemporary Management Research*, 8(1), 51–60. doi:10.7903/cmr.10149

Gordon, M. E., McKeage, K., & Fox, M. A. (1998). Relationship marketing effectiveness: The role of involvement. *Psychology and Marketing*, 15(5), 443–459. doi:10.1002/(SICI)1520-6793(199808)15:5<443::AID-MAR3>3.0.CO;2-7

Hair, J. F. (2015). *Essentials of business research methods*. New York: ME Sharpe.

Hanson, S., Jiang, L., & Dahl, D. (2019). Enhancing consumer engagement in an online brand community via user reputation signals: A multi-method analysis. *Journal of the Academy of Marketing Science*, 47(2), 349–367. doi:10.100711747-018-0617-2

Haryanto, B., Febrianto, A., & Cahyono, E. (2019). Lifestyle and consumer preferences in choosing local or foreign brands: A study of consumer behavior in Surakarta Indonesia. *Jurnal Manajemen dan Kewirausahaan, 21*(1), 74-88.

Hassan, H., Rahman, M. S., & Sade, A. B. (2015). Shopping day and time preferences of malaysian hypermarket consumers. *Australian Journal of Business and Economic Studies, 1*(1), 61–68.

Holt, D. B. (2006). Toward a sociology of branding. *Journal of Consumer Culture*, 6(3), 299–302. doi:10.1177/1469540506068680

Idowu, I. A., Ja'afar, M. F. Z., Shari, Z., & Dahlan, N. D. (2018). Indoor Environmental Quality performance of mixed-mode ventilated shopping malls in. *International Journal Of Built Environment And Sustainability, 5*(3), 187–200. doi:10.11113/ijbes.v5.n3.289

Jamal, A., & Goode, M. M. (2001). Consumers and brands: A study of the impact of self-image congruence on brand preference and satisfaction. *Marketing Intelligence & Planning, 19*(7), 482–492. doi:10.1108/02634500110408286

Jan, M. T., Haque, A., Abdullah, K., Anis, Z., & Alam, F. E. (2019). Elements of advertisement and their impact on buying behaviour: A study of skincare products. *Management Science Letters, 9*, 1519–1528. doi:10.5267/j.msl.2019.5.033

Junaid, M., Hou, F., Hussain, K., & Kirmani, A. A. (2019). Brand love: The emotional bridge between experience and engagement, generation-M perspective. *Journal of Product and Brand Management, 28*(2), 200–215. doi:10.1108/JPBM-04-2018-1852

Kamaruddin, A. (2002). Ethnocentrism orientation and choice decisions of Malaysian consumers: The effects of socio-cultural and demographic factors. *Asia Pacific Management Review, 7*(4), 555–574.

Kumar, A., Kim, Y. K., & Pelton, L. (2009). Indian consumers' purchase behavior toward US versus local brands. *International Journal of Retail & Distribution Management, 376*(6), 510–526. doi:10.1108/09590550910956241

Lau, M. M., Chang, M. S., Moon, K., & Liu, W. S. (2006). The brand loyalty of sportswear in Hong Kong. *Journal of Textile and Apparel. Technology and Management, 5*, 1–13.

Lee, J., & Nguyen, M. J. (2017). Product attributes and preference for foreign brands among Vietnamese consumers. *Journal of Retailing and Consumer Services, 35*, 76–83. doi:10.1016/j.jretconser.2016.12.001

Lee, M. Y., Kim, Y. K., Pelton, L., Knight, D., & Forney, J. (2008). Factors affecting Mexican college students' purchase intention toward a US apparel brand. *Journal of Fashion Marketing and Management, 12*(3), 294–307. doi:10.1108/13612020810889263

Lee, Y., Back, K., & Kim, J. (2009). Family restaurant brand personality and its impact on customer's emotion, satisfaction and brand loyalty. *Journal of Hospitality & Tourism Research (Washington, D.C.), 33*(3), 305–328. doi:10.1177/1096348009338511

Mathew, V., & Thomas, S. (2019). Direct and indirect effect of brand experience on true brand loyalty: Role of involvement. *Asia Pacific Journal of Marketing and Logistics, 30*(3), 725–748. doi:10.1108/APJML-08-2017-0189

Menidjel, C., Benhabib, A., & Bilgihan, A. (2017). Examining the moderating role of personality traits in the relationship between brand trust and brand loyalty. *Journal of Product and Brand Management, 26*(6), 631–649. doi:10.1108/JPBM-05-2016-1163

Mouangue, R. L. (2019). Getting over discomfort in luxury brand stores: How pop-up stores affect perceptions of luxury, embarrassment, and store evaluations. *Journal of Retailing and Consumer Services, 49*, 77–85. doi:10.1016/j.jretconser.2019.03.005

Nelson, M., & McLeod, L. (2005). Adolescent brand consciousness and product placements: Awareness, liking and perceived effects on self and others. *International Journal of Consumer Studies, 29*(6), 515–528. doi:10.1111/j.1470-6431.2005.00429.x

Nguyen, M. N., & Kuan, T. S. (2011). Antecedents and consequences of status consumption among urban Vietnamese consumers. *Organizations and Markets in Emerging Economies, 2*(1), 75–98. doi:10.15388/omee.2011.2.1.14291

O'Cass, A., & McEwen, H. (2004). Exploring consumer status and conspicuous consumption. *Journal of Consumer Behaviour, 4*(1), 25–39. doi:10.1002/cb.155

Parihar, P., Dawra, J., & Sahay, V. (2019). The role of customer engagement in the involvement-loyalty link. *Marketing Intelligence & Planning, 37*(1), 66–79. doi:10.1108/MIP-11-2017-0318

Quester, P., & Lim, A. L. (2003). Product involvement/brand loyalty: Is there a link? *Journal of Product and Brand Management, 12*(1), 22–38. doi:10.1108/10610420310463117

Rodrigo, P., Khan, H., & Ekinci, Y. (2019). The determinants of foreign product preference amongst elite consumers in an emerging market. *Journal of Retailing and Consumer Services, 46*, 139–148. doi:10.1016/j.jretconser.2018.04.012

Saat, M. K., Shaari, S. A., & Ahmad Fauzi, T. (2017). Materialism and consumerism through urban social. Paper presented at the Advances in Economics. *Business and Management Research (AEBMR), 41, 4th Bandung Creative Movement International Conference on Creative Industries 2017 (BCM 2017),* 303-307. Retrieved on June 12, 2019, from: https://libraryeproceeding.telkomuniversity.ac.id/index.php/bcm/article/view/5918/5900

Saini, S., & Singh, J. (2019). Cultivating emotional branding through customer experience management: From the holistic experience perspective. In *Brand culture and identity: Concepts, methodologies, tools, and applications* (pp. 1346–1361). Hershey, PA: IGI Global. doi:10.4018/978-1-5225-7116-2.ch072

Shao, W., Grace, D., & Ross, M. (2019). Consumer motivation and luxury consumption: Testing moderating effects. *Journal of Retailing and Consumer Services*, *46*, 33–44. doi:10.1016/j.jretconser.2018.10.003

Sharma, A., & Bhola, S., Malyan, S., & Patni, N. (2013). Impact of brand loyalty on buying behavior of women consumers for beauty care products - Delhi region. *Global Journal of Management and Business Studies*, *3*, 817–824.

Sharpe Kumar, A., Kim, Y. K., & Pelton, L. (2009). Indian Consumers' Purchase Behavior Toward US Versus Local Brands. *International Journal of Retail & Distribution Management*, *37*(6), 510–526. doi:10.1108/09590550910956241

Shen, D., Lennon, S., Dickson, M. A., Montalto, C., & Zhang, L. (2002). Chinese consumers' attitudes toward US and PRC made clothing from a cultural perspective. *Family and Consumer Sciences Research Journal*, *31*(1), 19–49. doi:10.1177/107 7727X02031001002

So, J. T., Parsons, A. G., & Yap, S. F. (2013). Corporate branding, emotional attachment and brand loyalty: The case of luxury fashion branding. *Journal of Fashion Marketing and Management*, *17*(4), 403–423. doi:10.1108/JFMM-03-2013-0032

Song, H., Wang, J., & Han, H. (2019). Effect of image, satisfaction, trust, love, and respect on loyalty formation for name-brand coffee shops. *International Journal of Hospitality Management*, *79*, 50–59. doi:10.1016/j.ijhm.2018.12.011

Souiden, N., & Diagne, M. (2009). Canadian and French men's consumption of cosmetics: A comparison of their attitudes and motivations. *Journal of Consumer Marketing*, *26*(2), 97–109. doi:10.1108/07363760910940465

Sweeney, J. C., & Soutar, G. N. (2001). Consumer perceived value: The development of a multiple item scale. *Journal of Retailing*, *77*(2), 203–220. doi:10.1016/S0022-4359(01)00041-0

Thomson, M., MacInnis, D. J., & Park, C. W. (2005). The ties that bind measuring the strength of consumers' emotional attachments to brands. *Journal of Consumer Psychology*, *15*(1), 77–91. doi:10.120715327663jcp1501_10

Wiedmann, K., Hennigs, N., & Siebels, A. (2009). Value-based segmentation of luxury consumption behavior. *Psychology and Marketing*, *26*(7), 625–651. doi:10.1002/mar.20292

Yee, F. S., Chin, S., & Suan, T. (2012). Analysis of the purchasing behavior on skin care products among what? *International Journal of Economics and Management*, *6*(2), 22–36.

Yee, W. F., & Sidek, Y. (2008). Influence of brand loyalty on consumer sportswear. *International Journal of Economics and Management*, *2*(2), 221–236.

Yim, M. Y., Sauer, P. L., Williams, J., Lee, S., & Macrury, I. (2014). Drivers of attitudes toward luxury brands: A cross-national investigation into the roles of interpersonal influence and brand consciousness. *International Marketing Review*, *31*(4), 363–389. doi:10.1108/IMR-04-2011-0121

Zaichkowsky, J. L. (1985). Measuring the involvement inventory: Reduction, revision and application to advertising. *Journal of Advertising*, *23*(4), 59–69. doi:10.1080/00913367.1943.10673459

Zakaria, N., & Talib, A. N. A. (2011). What did you say? A cross-cultural analysis of the distributive communicative behaviors of global virtual teams. In *2011 International Conference on Computational Aspects of Social Networks (CASoN)* (pp. 7-12). IEEE. 10.1109/CASON.2011.6085910

Zakaria, N., Wan-Ismail, W. N. A., & Abdul-Talib, A. N. (2015). Superfluous or Moderation?: The Effect of Religious Value on Conspicuous Consumption Behavior for Luxury Products. In *Emerging Research on Islamic Marketing and Tourism in the Global Economy* (pp. 1–18). Hershey, PA: IGI Global. doi:10.4018/978-1-4666-6272-8.ch001

Zamani, S. N. M., Abdul-Talib, A. N., & Ashari, H. (2016). Strategic orientations and new product success: The mediating impact of innovation speed. International Information Institute (Tokyo) Information, 19(7B), 2785.

Chapter 7
The Context of the Tourism Market in Kazakhstan:
State, Firms, Old and New Practices

Onur Dirlik
Eskişehir Osmangazi University, Turkey

Janset Özen-Aytemur
Akdeniz University, Turkey

Murat Atalay
Akdeniz University, Turkey

ABSTRACT

This chapter is designed to reveal the development of the tourism sector in Kazakhstan as an example of the process of integrating Central Asia countries into the capitalist world economy at various levels in the post-Soviet period. The study aims to understand the effects of some contextual elements that affect the development process of the tourism sector in Kazakhstan. For this purpose, interviews were conducted with the managers of foreign tour operators operating in Kazakhstan. It is expected some context-based elements may be observed by the managers and to obtain some clues about the distinctive path of developing capitalist economy of the country. Following a brief literature review about the role of the state and tourism sector in Kazakhstan, the rest of the chapter includes the authors' findings on the characteristics of the institutional context of the tourism market in Kazakhstan.

DOI: 10.4018/978-1-7998-2239-4.ch007

Copyright © 2020, IGI Global. Copying or distributing in print or electronic forms without written permission of IGI Global is prohibited.

INTRODUCTION

In social sciences, interest in market economies, more specifically in capitalism, goes back to the 1800s. The current position of interested parties in market economies is the result of a series of developments from the late 1800s to the present. Since the great *Methodenstreit* in Germany in the late nineteenth century (Louzek, 2011) the studies of capitalism have been divided into two groups. The first group assumes that capitalism is shaped by the eternal market forces and that the regulations and social arrangements shape the market with their invisible jobs. This group seeks to identify universal structures and argues that these structures have normative effects. The second group adopts the political economy perspective and assumes that capitalism is formed by divergent historical forms. In order to understand the characteristics of a market, this group pursues the historical patterns of institutions, the history of political economy and the historical patterns of contexts. In order to understand market relations, they refer to the critical transition periods and relations between the past and existing institutions.

In this perspective, economic processes are embedded in institutions that form, transform, and substantiate the economic process and its inherent contradictions (Kristensen & Lilja, 2011). Although capitalism has diffused in recent years with increasing acceleration along with globalization, studies show that the diffusion in question triggers the emergence of different market forms contrary to expectations (Hall & Soskice, 2001). Therefore, it is possible to say that the opinions regarding the existence of uniform markets, which were emphasized in previous discussions in the literature, have weakened. This study has been designed with the framework of the institutionalism tradition of the second group, in terms of the distinction mentioned briefly in the above lines, in investigating the markets. Different conceptual frameworks, models and approaches have been developed in the studies on the relationship of organizations with their institutional environment. According to the authors, in order to understand economic organizations with a macro-level analysis, it is necessary to analyze them on the basis of their relations with the 'market'. It is because understanding the capitalist dynamics in a context is one of the best ways to understand how organizations are influenced by the market and to understand how organizations shape their environment by accepting its power as an institutional actor. This approach provides an opportunity to understand market relations in an institutional environment based framework.

The literature on the different institutional contexts of various economies in different countries raises two approaches -Varieties of Capitalism (Hall & Soskice, 2001) and National Business Systems (Whitley, 1999). The Varieties of Capitalism approach classifies the advanced economies into two as liberal and coordinated markets. Allocation mechanisms of resources, profits and risk are the basic criteria

The Context of the Tourism Market in Kazakhstan

for that classification. As the last phase of the literature of "varieties of capitalism", the studies focus on 'the initiatives of actors to reshape their firms and institutions'; 'the internationalization of economic activity and the variety of ways in which this is achieved'; and 'how different forms of state establish conditions for institutional change and experimentation' (Kristensen & Morgan, 2012: 37).

On the other hand, the National Business Systems approach focuses on "distinctive ways of structuring economic activities with different kinds of actors following contrasting priorities and logics" (Whitley, 1998a: 449) and deeply interested in the institutions which are intrinsic to the state, financial markets, social capital, and human capital. Although both approaches are functional in explaining the nature of various mechanisms that formalize the economic actors and activities in different countries, they are not completely suited for describing the institutional structures of newly-developed, emerging or developing economies (Fainshmidt et al., 2018). The Varieties of Capitalism framework has been criticized for not to being interested in the institutional context of the developing world, which the relationship between the state and economic actors and all the social norms are embedded in (Wilkinson, Wood & Deeg, 2014).

Likewise, the National Business System framework has not been evaluated as sufficient to represent many economic systems that have recently adopted capitalism and experience incremental changes in the institutional context (Wilkinson, Wood & Deeg, 2014; Tsui-Auch & Lee, 2003). Some of the institutional mechanisms identified by the Varieties of Capitalism or the National Business System approach are either absent or peripheral in many understudied economies. Instead, the main actor that determine and formalize the institutional structure formalizing the economic activity is the state or the big capital-owned families (Boyer, 2005; Morck & Steiner, 2005). To determine the distinctive features that are related to 'imitated' institutional contexts in Asia, Latin America or the Middle East, a recently discussed framework is developed named the Varieties of Institutional Systems. This framework integrates the Varieties of Capitalism and the National Business Systems frameworks, and also includes the role of the state and powerful family-owned firms. In order to catch a more deeply understanding of that economies, five institutional dimensions as "the role of the state", "the role of financial markets", "the role of human capital", "the role of social capital" and "the role of corporate governance institutions" are included in this framework (Fainshmidt et al., 2018).

Although the increase in the level of economic development of East Asian countries in recent years and the fact that countries such as China and South Korea have attracted the attention of the whole world have led to the diversification of studies in this field, research for understanding different contexts are still not sufficient. However, these studies are especially necessary to understand regional differences and context-specific governance structures that play an important role in development. As mentioned above, given the policies, models, and transitions between countries in their development adventures, the path to development is not the only one. Each market develops its own rules and creates its institutional diversity through the influence of its sociological and historical reality, in the process of articulation to international economic mobility.

One of the interesting subjects in the field of capitalism research is the Central Asian countries which have made very fast attempts and institutional arrangements to open up international markets in the post-Soviet period. Based on this, Kazakhstan is one of the Central Asian countries that has been analyzed with the dimensions of the Varieties of Institutional Systems which is the latest comprehensive framework of capitalism studies (Fainshmidt et al., 2018). According to the institutional variables of 68 economies (see Table 3 in Fainshmidt et al., 2018, p.314), in Kazakhstan, which is a developmental state exerts intense control over the economy with an expectation of long term national interests exists. The findings reveal that the *direct dominance of the state* is not observed but the *indirect intervention of the state* is confirmed. In other words, the Kazakhstan government, particularly the executive branch, engages in the formalization of business sectors via developing industrial policies (Fainshmidt et al., 2018; Charman, 2007).

This chapter is designed with the inspiration from these advances in the extant literature and has traced the development of the tourism sector in Kazakhstan as an example of the process of integrating Central Asia countries into the capitalist world economy at various levels in the post-Soviet period. The study aims to understand the effects of some contextual elements that directly or indirectly affect the development process of the tourism sector in Kazakhstan.

For this purpose, interviews were conducted with the managers of foreign tour operators operating in Kazakhstan. It is expected to find out some context-based elements which may be observed by the managers and to get some clues about the distinctive path of developing capitalist economy of the country. The first part of the chapter includes a brief literature review about the role of the state and tourism sector in Kazakhstan, which is on the way to becoming a strong liberal market. And the rest of the chapter includes the authors' findings on the characteristics of the institutional context of the tourism market in Kazakhstan which is based on interviews with the managers of the foreign tour operators[1].

Kazakhstan's Economy in Transition to a "Liberal Market" and the Role of State

The Republic of Kazakhstan left the Soviet Union in December 1991 and declared its independence, and the first constitution was adopted in 1995 (Bhuiyan & Amagoh, 2011: 230). Kazakhstan is the world's largest landlocked country (Aslan

The Context of the Tourism Market in Kazakhstan

& Bozyiğit, 2014) and is regarded as the main economic power of Central Asia (OECD, 2011: 17). It has a land area equal to that of Western Europe but one of the lowest population densities globally (in 2018, the population of the country is 18,2 million). Strategically, she links the large and fast-growing markets of China and South Asia and those of Russia and Western Europe by road, rail, and a port on the Caspian Sea. Kazakhstan has succeeded in the transition from lower-middle-income to upper-middle income status in less than two decades. Since 2002, GDP per capita has risen six fold (annually 6,8% increase between 2001 and 2016) and poverty incidence has fallen sharply (The World Bank, 2018: 11; 2019a: 1). Kazakhstan, having the highest sustained rates of growth of all the former centrally planned economies (Charman, 2007) by 2005, is still the fastest growing economy among all Central Asian countries (OECD, 2017: 13).

Kazakhstan followed Russia's economic reform policies for the transition to a liberal market economy after independence in December 1991. The two important steps to adopt a market economy were 'price liberalisation' and 'privatisation of state enterprises' (Minbaeva et al., 2007: 353). As the Soviet bloc crumbled, like other Central Asian republics, Kazakhstan faced some problems of transition like 'external economic effects', 'establishing the institutions of a market-based economy' and 'political transition' (Saner et al., 2008). Among these countries, the most active and focused reformer was the Republic of Kazakhstan with its distinctive methods. "Decentralization in all political and administrative decisions", "bringing civil service closer to western standards", "e-governance" and "increasing the role of civil society" are important public sector reforms of Kazakhstan (Bhuiyan and Amagoh, 2011: 234).

According to the OECD report (2014: 11), the significant reforms declared in Kazakhstan's agenda were 'the rules driven fiscal framework', 'the strengthening of its public administration processes', 'providing a business climate for effective market relations', and 'the allocation of resources for improved social services and infrastructure to stabilize growth'. The government has initiated a remarkable program to develop the investment climate. Kazakhstan authorities have planned and implemented 43 reforms since 2008 which aim to build an institutional structure that would position Kazakhstan as a powerful market economy. This attempt is ongoing as part of the Business Roadmap 2020 and then with the Kazakhstan 2050 Strategy, which aims to position the country among the 30 most developed nations by 2050 (The World Bank, 2019b). The role of the state is explicit and irreplaceable in the reform process and it is the central coordinator of the economy (Charman, 2007).

Kazakhstan's economy is fragile to external effects and this is the main difficulty in attaining sustainable development. External demand from Kazakhstan's main trading partners, China and the Russian Federation, and also the global oil demand and prices, will continuously impact Kazakhstan's economic performance (The

131

The Context of the Tourism Market in Kazakhstan

World Bank, 2019a: 1). The huge amount of acquisition from hydrocarbons and metals have ensured the growth in recent decades. The extractive industry accounts for nearly 30% of Gross Domestic Product (GDP), two-thirds of exports, three-quarters of the stock of Foreign Direct Investment (FDI) and half of government revenues. Like other economies with less industrial diversification, Kazakhstan is vulnerable to commodity-price fluctuations and some other issues associated with resource-based development. For sustainable productivity over the long term, Kazakhstan needs to put into practice a wide range of structural reforms (OECD, 2018: 14-18). Especially the instant decreases in oil prices have shown that the Kazakhstan economy is unsustainable and that structural reforms are inevitable.

After a serious drop in oil prices, oil production stabilized and growth came mainly from non-tradable services. The largest job-creating sectors included publicly provided services like education, health, and other social services, along with construction, trade, and transport and storage on the private sector side (The World Bank, 2018: 12-14). Several reasons for lower elasticity of long-term employment in Kazakhstan summarized as follows: a) in the oil industry, productivity rates are directly related to oil-extraction activities which are carried out by large capital investments. Employment is limited at that oil-extracting regions; b) an immature private sector cannot provide enough employment opportunities. Despite the meaningful steps for privatization, many critical industries are subject to state control and intervention.

Besides, the private sector still experience various limitations and is not growing enough to satisfy the work applicants; c) 22 percent of employed people work in public institutions. As an important employer, public institutions provide employees with more wages and benefits than the private sector offers. High levels of government employment, which means using the labour force for less productive public services, could limit private investment and limit economic growth, leading to the lack of staff in the private sector in the coming years; d) in spite of the fact that there is a salient demand for personnel with higher education and vocational knowledge, there is a supply of a workforce with general secondary school education and below. Kazakhstan still has not been able to provide qualified employees to the labour market (IMF, 2014: 7).

The purpose of the present reforms for establishing or restructuring institutions is to restrict the role of the state in the economy and pave the way for the development of an effective, innovative and productive non-oil industry (The World Bank, 2019a: 1). All the industrial and service sectors of Kazakhstan are driven by the state-owned enterprises and the economy in the country relies heavily on extractive industries. The companies owned by Kazakhstan's national holding company Samruk-Kazyna are the dominant actors not only in the extractive sector but also almost in every industry like transport, logistics, information and telecommunications (The World Bank, 2019b:

The Context of the Tourism Market in Kazakhstan

2). The economy in Kazakhstan is dependent on the export of a limited range of natural resources that make it as fragile as the other "less-diversified economies".

Resource dependency causes some macroeconomic disadvantages including vulnerability to external effects and important institutional weaknesses. Kazakhstan's policymakers have to consider these challenges while discussing on the structural reforms, as establishing new institutions may be striving because of resource-dependency. The economic heritage of communism is still evident all across Kazakhstan. The structures and processes of the Soviet system are apparent in public administration. A highly formalised bureaucratic structure still dominates public administration and a hierarchical reporting system is in force. Public decisions and actions are applied in an inflexible hierarchical manner, based on a rigid traditional command-and-control approach.

The country achieved a spectacular progress in establishing institutions for an effective liberal market economy, but many of the challenges of transition remain prevailing. These include "composing of efficient markets and setting up rules for the security of property rights"; "the restriction of the state's intervener role in the market; struggling for the issues of centralised administration system, politicisation of decision-making, limited delegation of authority to regional administrators, lack of transparency, and corruption"; "changing the case that state-owned enterprises are the dominant actors of the economy; reducing their preferential position to access the resources, markets, licenses, and finance; changing the conditions that inhibit growing and diversifying of private firms"; "the completion of reforms to transform the Soviet-era structures and practices" and "ensuring equal access to higher education and labour market opportunities" (OECD, 2018: 14-38).

In a survey conducted in 2013, 19% of the companies stated that corruption is the most important obstacle for doing business in Kazakhstan. It is the biggest administrative challenge for firms. Corruption induces an untrustworthy business environment by undermining the fairness perceptions of businessmen, reducing the operational efficiency of firms and raising the costs (The World Bank, 2013: 9). The practices of the informal sector (15%), inadequately educated workforce (13,1%), tax rates (11,3%) and access to finance (10,6%), respectively follow the corruption problem (The World Bank, 2013: 4). Kazakhstan adopted a new anti-corruption strategy for 2015-2025, which aims to reduce corruption in critical fields, including in the public service.

In procurement in public services Kazakhstan implemented reforms to provide and sustain transparency. The government's actions aimed at preventing corruption in the private sectors are also precious. But corruption remains a major problem despite recent reforms. According to the 2016 Transparency International Kazakhstan Report, 29% of respondents indicated that they have to pay bribes (Transparency International Kazakhstan, 2016). Among enterprises, a total of 26.7% stated that

The Context of the Tourism Market in Kazakhstan

they expect to pay at least one bribe, against an average for OECD countries of 1.9%. Briefly, despite preventive precautions, corruption is seen as being deeply institutionalized in Kazakhstan and prevalent at high levels of public authority (OECD, 2018).

The Tourism Industry in Kazakhstan

After the disintegration of the Soviet Union, Kazakhstan became an available destination for international travellers like other Central Asian countries, and tourism development in the country began. However, as in all sectors, deterioration was observed also in the tourism sector in the early years of independence. In the years when social security policies were dominant, large-scale health hotels were built, but as a result of ignoring the market mechanism, they faced lots of problems such as amortization problems and most of them were bankrupted due to decreased demand. Between 1991 and 1999, the share of tourism in national GDP had steadily dropped. This ratio was 0.3% in 1991 and dropped to 0.09 in 1999.

In 2010, the Strategic Development Plan of the Republic of Kazakhstan aimed at the development of the economy through diversification was accepted, and the tourism industry was selected as one of the main industries to be developed. With this plan, a competitive tourism industry was aimed to be structured (Abubakirova et al., 2016: 5-6). A program of tourism has been developed by the government, envisaged to be implemented by 2023.

For the tourism sector, which accounts for 1% of GDP in 2017, the target for 2023 was set by the government to be 8% of GDP. In addition, the country was ranked 81st in the World Economic Forum in terms of tourism competitiveness in 2017 and is expected to rise to 50th in 2023. The priorities of the tourism program of the Republic of Kazakhstan developed for the year 2023 are; development of tourism infrastructure, implementation of liberalization policy in visa and immigration procedures, development and improvement of the transportation infrastructure to touristic facilities and destinations, increasing efficiency of the travel marketing field, creating new jobs for the community, more efficient use and development of the state support in tourism, improvement of service standards, personnel qualification, culture and tourism information environment (Ministry of Culture and Sports of the Republic of Kazakhstan, 2018).

Kazakhstan, one of the largest countries in the world, facilitates trade between Europe and Asia due to its geographical location where the important trade routes connect east and west, and the rich geographical and cultural assets it has brought to the present day provide Kazakhstan with rich tourism potential. Economic and social reasons suggesting that tourism is a priority area for national development in Kazakhstan can be listed as follows (Shevyakova et al., 2018: 604-605):

134

The Context of the Tourism Market in Kazakhstan

- Tourism has the potential to create about 250,000 new jobs, including the rural areas of the country so that families and small and medium-sized enterprises will benefit from it.
- Providing a very positive contribution to the development of different remote regions and rural areas in Kazakhstan. Particularly providing the development of these remote areas in terms of transportation, infrastructure, and engineering.
- Tourism in particular, has the potential to trigger the development of these sectors such as agriculture, infrastructure and food and beverage.
- Tourism has the potential to socially accelerate the development of cross cultural relations

Tourism in Kazakhstan, as in other Commonwealth of Independent States (CIS) countries, is progressing mainly in outbound tourism (Mukhambetov et al., 2014: 42). Furthermore, the tourism sector is seen as one of the most promising sectors in terms of the economy and is perceived as the sector that will save the country from its dependence on natural resources (Mamanova & Sadyrova, 2013). Kazakhstan offers many opportunities in terms of tourism diversity such as history, ecotourism, observation of rare species of flora and fauna, adventure travel, and other varieties. In addition to over 100 therapeutic facilities in the country, there are around 9000 archaeological and historic sites.

Tourism in Kazakhstan has a progressive structure and this is evident from the increasing number of visitors every year. For Kazakhstan, which is among the 50 most competitive countries in the world, developing tourism industry has become a priority. According to the State Tourism Development Program, the tourism sector is one of the seven priority non-primary sectors. The reason for this is to increase the country's economic diversification and improve its competitiveness. For example, NASA, which is also a popular tourist destination in the United States; the First Space Harbour on the Planet Project in Baikonur in Kazakhstan is a destination that has the same touristic potential.

The First Space Harbour on the Planet Project will also include trips covering the history of the space industry. In addition, many new hotel facilities are being built around the country, developments related to beach and cruise tourism are taking place along the Caspian Sea coast, Great silk road route is being revived, national parks, historical cities, and places such as Shybulak ski tourism areas are being given more importance. In addition to these, sports facilities for the development of tourism in the country are also given emphasis and important agreements are signed with various states (Sultanov, 2010: 278-279). Table 1 shows a SWOT analysis table including the strengths and weaknesses of Kazakhstan's tourism sector, as well as the opportunities and threats for this sector.

135

Tourism revenues in Kazakhstan, which were US$155 million in 1995, accelerated with market economy transformation efforts and rose to US$1.99 billion in 2017. The number of visitors from abroad, a total of 202,000 in 1996, reached 7.7 million in 2017 (Ceicdata, 2018a). In addition, the number of people going abroad for touristic purposes is increasing day by day. The number of residents going abroad increased from 3.6 million in 2006 to 10.2 million in 2017 (Ceicdata, 2018b). Turkey stands at the top of Kazakh tourists' foreign destination choice, and it is followed by Thailand, Dubai, Egypt, Arab Emirates, Russia, Uzbekistan and Kyrgyzstan respectively (T.C. Kültür ve Turizm Bakanlığı, 2018: 1).

Table 1. SWOT analysis of the tourism sector in Kazakhstan

Strengths	Weaknesses
1. The advantage of the location of the country and variety of the natural landscape 2. Significant natural, historical, cultural and recreational potential 3. Experience in international sports, music and other organizations (Asian Games, musical competitions) 4. The interest of the state and the public in the development of tourism 5. Low electricity and construction costs. 6. Government support for the tourism sector (Tourism Development Programs) 7. The relatively high level of competition in the market, the formation of a professional community of travel agents (CTA - Kazakhstan Tourism Association) 8. Stable increasing tourism demand and tourism revenues	1. Underdeveloped tourism infrastructure that meets international standards. 2. Depreciation of hotel stock, low rate of modern buildings 3. Corruption and inefficiency of the authorities 4. Weak marketing promotion of tourism products in the domestic and international markets. 5. Lack of visibility and attractiveness of the image of Kazakhstan in the world 6. Lack of industry statistics, providing information and management support for the development of tourism 7. The insufficient number of trained and qualified personnel in the tourism industry 8. Underdeveloped transport scheme delivery of tourists in the distal and rural regions, and high prices for air travel, absence of national low-cost carriers 9. Lack of motivation factors for the development of inbound and outbound tourism
Opportunities	**Threats**
1. Availability of fiscal space, allowing for targeted financial support for the tourism industry 2. Implementation of major economic projects (FIID, the Roadmap, Western China-Western Europe) that improve the tourism infrastructure 3. Stable purchasing power in the country on tourist products, the trend of growth in domestic tourism 4. The increased interest of the citizens to the historical and cultural heritage and its own attractions 5. Selling tour packages through online platforms, and expansion of e-commerce 6. Rising demand for the niche and adventure tourism	1. The limited consumer market due to large areas and small population 2. Low attractiveness of the industry to local and foreign investors 3. Lack of development of small business 4. The growing competition among the Central Asian countries in tourism 5. The low efficiency of the state apparatus in the implementation of the tourism development 6. The corruption in access to land 7. Tax laws are unfavourable to tourism activities 8. Exchange rate instability and high inflation 9. The high cost of long-distance trips.

Source: Adapted from Mamanova and Sadyrova: 2013; Mamanova et al., 2013; Shevyakova et al., 2018.

136

The Context of the Tourism Market in Kazakhstan

In terms of inbound tourism in Kazakhstan, the interest of foreign tourists coming to the country remains low. Kazakhstan ranks 78th place among the countries that attract tourists, especially when it comes to criteria such as pricing and service quality, it can be said that tourism services in Kazakhstan are still not competitive (Shevyakova et al., 2018: 614). In short, it can be said that the current situation of tourism industry in Kazakhstan is still underdeveloped, but it has great potential for the future (See Baisakalova & Garkavenko, 2015).

Findings on Institutional Context in Kazakhstan's Tourism Market

The countries which have not yet completed the process of transition to free-market economy show specific samples of market mechanism with old business practices accompanying the formation and spread of necessary institutional processes and embedded institutions. Kazakhstan is one such country. We can say that active companies in the tourism sector, whose development is given much importance by Kazakhstan in the latest years, have different organizational practices due to this special contextual pattern. These practices differing from classical rational business practices defined for free market mechanism throughout the literature are the fruit of tourism organisations' survival efforts to adapt to the institutional context in Kazakhstan. Below there are some findings that can be used for defining the institutional context of Kazakhstan's tourism market based on the expressions of foreign tour operator interviewees.

Old Dominating Institutional Practices That do not Correspond to Free Market Economy

Moving more motivated and faster compared to other old Soviet bloc countries to integrate the global market, having the best economic potential in Central Asia, recent high growth performance and geographical proximity to East Asia country group, one of the most important economic mobility centers, have made Kazakhstan a strong economic actor with a high and clear potential in Central Asia. However, no matter how much it tries, Kazakhstan exhibits some contextual features drifting apart from global free market mechanisms in terms of its economic organizational structure and practices. It is possible to see that existing instutional context has some features that do not fully match with market conditions. Throughout this study, we have found that active organizations in Kazakhstan's tourism market have had to adapt to some institutionalised mechanisms during historical processes of the country apart from the rules of free-market even though the country has become one of the most important economic actors of Central Asia thanks to its ambitious growth.

According to the interviewee managers of international tour operators, one of the challenging local practices they face from time to time and have to adapt is the institutionalized corruption mechanism. The managers have stated that they developed some organizational practices taking this rooted corruption mechanism into account. Especially, it can be understood that when they first arrived in Kazakhstan, these tourism organizations had no idea about "what to do with this unknown, unrecognized local practice" and they had to try some methods. This expression of an interviewee offers a proof: "Kazakhstan seemed like the most promising, modern and developed country to us.

Our first method to enter into there was being an agency. However, since so much corruption was at stake during the business, someone from the company instead of a Kazakh agent was thought to be better to launch". It can be argued that this long-lasting existence of corruption mechanism in market relations and in relations of companies with public institutions makes it necessary for tourism sector investors to have an experience and knowledge about "how this situation is reflected on an operational level and how it is implemented". These words of an interviewee give the impression that the corruption is known and legitimate to a certain extent for public bodies: "Corruption… statesmen also say this… What we sell is obvious and we have never been faced with a serious alarm about corruption up to now but this is constantly spoken. It is always argued that it exists."

Another interviewee's words for the public permissions to their activities also attract attention: "… we tried so hard to complete everything. We asked. They do not reject it, they sweep it underneath the rug. It took for months, we discussed with relevant departments and they promised to help. We sought support from the companies with a word in the market. We tried to make use of bureaucrat but nothing happened. There is a huge corruption pyramid in Central Asia. No matter what you do, it is almost impossible to make progress without corruption in the high volume business." In spite of these experiences, managers utter that they are satisfied with the existence of Anti-Corruption Committee and the state takes important measures to prevent the corruption. Anti-Corruption Committee is a state institution working with the state prosecutor, Tax Committee, Ministry of Finance and national security services (Kobonbaev & Eicher, 2016). According to interviewees, the work of this Committee can be seen as an important example of the struggle of the Kazakhstan state to reach a more institutionalized market structure for all sectors.

Another contextual feature specified as influential is the "reflection of power relations on business relations". An interviewee says that "We have got used to the case that some people who consider themselves important call you at 3.00 am and say 'Just make the plane wait, my passenger is coming'", which is the proof of the abovesaid. Another interviewee who emphasizes that personal relations are more determining than business contracts talks regarding the case as such: "Someone from

The Context of the Tourism Market in Kazakhstan

here wants to see the person with whom he will do business face to face without any doubt, in case of conflict, the opposing party is normally expected to open the agreement and look but this is not how things work here.

No matter what is written in the agreement, parties see each other face to face. I want to regard this as something positive, nevertheless this is still open to abuse. Even though there has been some improvement in recent years, this kind of trade is still unprofessional." The managers who express that power relations on a local level affect the business relations emphasize that rather than resisting, they try to build strong networks and adapt to this context-specific structure of the market. As one of the interviewees emphasize, "Knowing as many people as possible is so important in Central Asia. And your strength is the second most important factor. The more people you know, the faster your work is done." This sentence is an example of networking reflex of tourism organizations.

It can be inferred that interviewees are aware that "building strong political relations creates the opportunity for having a word in the market and influence on market dynamics." While discussing the tourism market in Kazakhstan, managers often emphasize that "close relations to bureaucracy determine the direction of the competition in the market." Moreover, personal relations with bureaucracy "can be seen as the world's way of trade to a certain extent", as stressed by the managers, but they also do not skip saying that "in Kazakhstan, these relations overshadow the sanction power of legal bodies, which is very important for a free market."

An interviewee expressed that "We got really tired of dealing with this… It is not just about carrying passengers… We have a brand. So, we decided to steer a middle course and not to quarrel with the state", which could signal this may be backbreaking from time to time. Sayings of interviewees like "personal relations are of secondary importance in countries where legal systems determine the commercial relations but here they are of primary importance" and "in Kazakhstan, you cannot exist without building a relation to bureaucracy…you cannot prove it on paper but it is known by everyone" indicate this feature of the market.

Effect Of The State On Free Market Dynamics

The State as the Pioneer of the Transformation: Effort for Institutionalization of Free Market Dynamics

That the main actor in the transition to a market economy in Kazakhstan is the state itself, which struggles for creating an ideal market mechanism, is reflected in what the interviewees have said. The managers express that Kazakhstan is a country that wants to integrate with the global liberal arena, for which legal arrangements are made to change old institutions. When asked about the state's intervention style, they also utter that "the state has no effort in controlling but tries to regulate the most problematic fields." Interviewees' such expressions as "…we did not feel the existence of the state directly… they are lustful for the sector… they asked our opinion, they said they wanted our support, they were open to anything and the state was with us" indicate that the state is open to collaborating with companies to meet international market standards in tourism. However, expressions like "… they say but it is not practised, maybe the bureaucracy really affects it" and "the state has support for tourism… Union of Hoteliers helps… Ministries support by giving advertisement… They do it but the original idea, the drive always comes from the sector" show that the state must collaborate more with stronger actors in the period of transition to a liberal economy.

Financial institutions which have a great importance in terms of free-market operations reassure the foreign investors in Kazakhstan, which is considered as the advantage of Kazakhstan compared to other Central Asian countries. Interviewee expressions like "…we do not have much trouble in banking here. Doing business in Kazakhstan is much more comfortable compared to the other Central Asian countries since Kazakhstan is a more liberal country, which makes it the strongest link of banking… Kazakhstan is the financial centre of Central Asia, it opens its doors to foreigners, its laws are similar to European laws, which is more suitable for capitalism" show that reassuring infrastructure of finance services give comfort to tourism organizations. This translates to that the banking sector has advanced to an important extent during this neoliberal transformation process.

The manager interviewees state that Non-Government Organizations (NGOs), professional societies and commercial organizations as the significant actors in free-market mechanisms apart from the state and capitalists began to be founded. A manager expresses that "… we have a union of agencies and another union of operators. The state tries to catch the common language with market agents compared to previous years, it invites them and tries to talk to them", which signals the state's tendency to recognize market actors. Now, the state is expected to flex institutionalized autocratical and central decision mechanisms in keeping with liberal economy goal of the state for the good of the private sector. Likewise, the expectation of a strong tourism market corresponds to societal needs and Kazakhs' demands for various destinations increase. The interviewees argue that they can meet this demand, which will contribute to a more mature tourism sector in Kazakhstan, as long as the state makes room for it.

Interviewee expressions such as "The passenger has a trouble while choosing the brand. Those who call the tour operator and make a conscious choice are not more than 10%. When we came here, the relationship between agency and tour operator became clear. Now, it was seen that everything has a system in the tourism sector… The market develops so slowly in Kazakhstan. Old Soviet institutions have a certain

The Context of the Tourism Market in Kazakhstan

influence on it, however the latest years have witnessed much improvement, legal arrangements are on the way… we can say that the tourism sector is also maturing… holiday culture of the passengers are improving but tour operators are making great efforts to it" prove that the state's effort for creating free market dynamics is taken kindly and supportively by the investors.

This picture should be evaluated considering the hardness of changing traditional bureaucratic practices. While the state's effort for regulating the market is appreciated by tourism organizations, some sustained state practices complicate doing business within the sector.

The State as a Barrier to Transformation: Old Practices Still in the Market

States are main actors that create, regulate and control the market mechanism of the relevant country. Especially, states in markets with a central organization history and governed by autocratic structures show their strength in a clearer way compared to those in free markets. Transforming the structures of these states with rooted bureaucracies requires a difficult and painful process. It is stated that Kazakhstan has not broken away with its old bureaucratic traditions although it tries to set the free market mechanism. "When you submit the papers, the setting up of the company may last for a month although you are informed about three days… Completing the setup process in a week requires finding a friend working there" says a manager, which indicates to a slow and arbitrary bureaucracy. Company managers utter that when they encounter any kind of problem or conflict, they use their own methods instead of existing legal solutions. An interviewee says: "… The European citizen goes to court immediately but here they try to figure it out with you individually. People rarely go to court… It is not practical, it lasts too long… It may take several months" It may be thought that a quick and efficient legal system that lays the basis of free-market mechanism, regulates and controls market relations has not developed fully, yet.

It is also seen that the state has put strict rules at the expense of preventing the formation of an ideal free market in order not to lose its traditional power. As to the managers, to make things difficult on charter flights by foreign airlines in Kazakhstan is an example of this repressive attitude. "…to found an airline company is very difficult. Actually, inhibiting does not solve anything. It destroys competition… the competition would be good for the passenger… You can change the cost of flight and accommodation in the competition. If you cannot decrease flight costs, the passenger has to fly expensively, which does not fit the market logic … even though tourism goes fast, the state does not seem intending to flex its hegemony on the market." It can be argued that just like other countries chasing after a liberal

The Context of the Tourism Market in Kazakhstan

transformation, all institutions and the attitude of the Kazakhstan state must change in a way to adapt to an ideal free market mechanism.

Missing Practices of a Free-Market

Some institutitons and practices expected to be institutionalized in an ideal market mechanism have not been matured in Kazakhstan despite the state's pioneer role in the development of the tourism sector and private sector tourism organizations' struggle. This is also the case for the reflection of the tourism market on the social level. For example; a manager defines a Kazakh citizen's perception and demand about tourism's treatment with these words: "Like Germany the 90s... some style based on personal relations instead of brand loyalty in which relatives gather and travel somewhere. A market whose portfolio is made up of close relations not advertisement. The more people you know, the more customers you have... however, the passenger must have a touristic culture, make conscious choices and plan her/his own holiday on time."

Another manager evaluates the situation as such: "...It took us so much time to tell that they can find their answers on the web. They sometimes call us and ask each and every aspect of any destination or hotel. There is hardly any work about the product or tour packages here... Actually, there is some potential, the market has a thirst for information and new destinations...tour operators have the mission of teaching tourism to everyone in the field." Another important topic for the neoliberal turn in the tourism sector is to fill in the deficiencies in the infrastructure. The sentences of managers like "it would be best to make some changes in airports. The duration of passport control or waiting periods must change. Hotels must be built, roads must change. The country has a touristic aspect to sell but the roads going to these places are not good enough. There are even no place for a passenger to stop and refresh... The market must be professional in every term" summarises a whole situation. These comments of managers show that Kazakhstan has a long way to go in terms of creating a constant demand in the tourism market and meeting this demand professionally with free market principles.

In addition to state and a strong private sector, NGOs and professional organizations with a right to speak and sanction power are of the utmost importance in the operation of a free market. Interviewees state that private enterprises and NGOs in the tourism sector are not in adequate numbers to develop the market. According to them, "a mechanism in which NGOs and other civil entities develop the market in collaboration with the state or work together for drafting the laws is not available in Kazakhstan's tourism market."

Interviewees announce that Kazakhstan's hosting of many international brands and many foreign companies especially active in the petrol and gas sector make

142

The Context of the Tourism Market in Kazakhstan

powerful commercial contracts possible and improve the laws. It is also emphasized that once Kazakhstan had declared independence, it began modeling genuine liberal countries in terms of regulations to accelerate in adapting to global capitalism. However, the managers put the problem of quick modeling of the countries that are cradles of industrialization and neoliberal economy this way: "...the problem is that they make laws not based on needs but dreams and force the whole market to comply with them... They do not make laws based on their own needs... For example, they made a law for exactly the same thing as in Britain, but there is a difference: England is the first place where tourism, finance and banking started in the world. If you model some British implementations dating back to 100-150 years ago for an emerging market in Kazakhstan, you will have difficulty in practice. In spite of the struggle for development and mobility expressed by managers as such "there is always a law transfer, culture transfer and work transfer", it is also indicated that legal regulations have been modeled so fast that they cannot match with the realities of the market.

Development Potential of the Tourism Market in Kazakhstan

Managers of foreign tour operators define Kazakhstan as an attractive market they do not want to give up on despite all the challenges they have mentioned. One of the managers who emphasized that Kazakhstan would be a more profitable investment area in the near future thanks to contributions from all the actors in the tourism market said that: "... 60% of the tourists coming from Russia go to economic hotels while 40% of them go to Delux and five-star ones. In Kazakhstan, 54% of them go to Delux and five-star ones... These rates encourage each tour operator to invest. Such a big volume...".

Interviewees exhibit some organizational practices to contribute to the development of the tourism market and with their own words they "teach those in the market to do business in the tourism sector". For example, those interviewees who define the labor force in Kazakhstan as "partially qualified" make the labour force specialized with their own means. A manager puts it that way: "labor market...there are universities to find qualified employees. Education is given importance, a remnant from the Soviets. But, when it comes to business, I think we must recruit and train our own staff. There are some tourism faculties and departments providing basic knowledge but we are the ones to deal with this adaptation thing." Another manager signals that they are motivated to train the labor force in accordance with market needs and states that "...putting flight for destinations is not enough, we need to tell the qualities of these countries those working in the field... We have a market that is really open to develop." Based on this, it is possible to argue that some basic and routine practices encountered in professionalized organizations are so new to the

Kazakhstan market and tourism organizations spread their work experiences and knowledge by exhibiting these practices in Kazakhstan's market. The high tourism potential of Kazakhstan is defined as an important motivator for the struggle of tourism actors.

CONCLUSION

Throughout the literature of Varieties of Capitalism and National Business Systems, which try to examine the differences in the processes of being capitalist in different contexts, the role of the state is generally defined as something static. Dealing with the relationship between the state and the market, these approaches assume that governmental bodies behave rationally and ignore that the ideological nature of the state makes its own actions seem different (Schmidt, 2009). One of the important reasons for this assumption is that empirical studies in the literature were carried out with the data of developed countries, where the market with its institutionalized structure is an influential actor in the presence of the state and has the capacity to control, organize, and re-produce.

Even though some researchers (Whitley, 1991, 1998; Witt & Redding, 2014) have scrutinized East Asian countries, a region developed later than other parts of the world, they discussed the states' methods and capacities to shape the market from an Anglo-Saxon framework. There is a tendency in literature to understand capitalizing processes in different contexts based on many more countries from a deeper point. Designed with such a perspective, this chapter examines the market dynamics of Kazakhstan, a very important country in Central Asia, specifically within the framework of the tourism sector. The tourism sector in Kazakhstan is a field on which the struggle for creating institutions and practices are necessary for a free market economy during a time when the neoliberal turn is reflected. In this chapter, certain findings regarding the influence of traditional or new practices on the shaping of the Kazakhstan's tourism sector context and the behaviors of companies have been reached. And certain clues about what kind of different practices Kazakhstan has specifically followed while trying to create its tourism sector on the axis of a free-market economy's logic have been obtained.

The findings of this study can be evaluated on two levels. The operational level, which allows us to view the issue from the perspective of foreign tour operators who play a role in the development of Kazakhstan's tourism market in accordance within the norms of a global free-market, gives us the opportunity to understand the activities of the state and firms in the market. On this level, stronger networks that determine the extent of corruption mechanisms and business relations can be defined as the elements complicating the operation of the free-market. Conscious

The Context of the Tourism Market in Kazakhstan

consumers necessary for the market's operation, adequate infrastructure (airport, roads, tour packages, etc.), a powerful private sector and civil organizations show themselves as the elements whose absence are really felt in Kazakhstan's tourism sector.

On the second level that signals the capitalizing process, the findings indicate that Kazakhstan's state has a two-dimensional determining effect in this liberal transformation process. In addition to its function as a trigger actor during the transformation process, the state is a structure containing institutions that sustain old bureaucratic practices. In Kazakhstan, the state is witnessed to struggle for transforming both the market and itself. It would run short if we regard contextually embedded actors of the Kazakhstan market, a candidate to be an empowering liberal market, as only some institutional structures that support or resist the transformation. The findings of this study give clues to consider the behaviors of the state and the company, their old and new practices, market relations, etc. as structures that are inherent in the context and transform together within Kazakhstan, where traditional institutions and practices sustain. The effect of specific institutions in the context becomes involved in developing countries' struggle in integrating with international markets. Regarding these institutions separately and analyzing them as some external variables would be a mistake.

Thus, it is not right to handle the state as a single actor in spite of its power of affecting the market. The comprehension of the transformation requires the understanding of patterns formed by various institutional regulations to come together (Amable, 2000). If the existence of an institution affects, supports and legitimizes another institution, these two institutions can be regarded as complementary (Hall and Soskice, 2001). To understand the effect of an institution or institutional arrangement, its connection with other institutional complementaries must be discovered (Höpner, 2005). In this chapter, old institutional patterns that conflict with the free-market mechanism in Kazakhstan have been detected. When such practices as the existence of corruption and strong political relations within Kazakhstan come together with the bureaucratic tradition of the state, they create this institutional complementary blocking the liberalization of the market. The findings on the two levels in this chapter may offer a guiding framework for studies designed to scrutinize the outlines of Kazakhstan's capitalization and existing business systems.

According to Morgan and Whitley (2012), samples from different countries in the global system must be known and systems of especially developing economies must be examined to have more knowledge about national business systems. Business system studies where perspectives from different disciplines, (especially politics, sociology and economic geography) are offered, different socioeconomic contexts and the conditions of capitalist systems are analysed and the effects of institutional environments are discussed on multi-levels are necessary to understand the differences.

145

Studies that will analyze the other sectors in Kazakhstan in addition to the tourism industry and understand the behaviors of the state, which is the main actor of the transformation as a historical carrier, will contribute to the literature of Varieties of Capitalism and National Business Systems.

REFERENCES

Abubakirova, A., Syzdykova, A., Kelesbayev, D., Dandayeva, B., & Ermankulova, R. (2016). Place of tourism in the economy of Kazakhstan Republic. *Procedia Economics and Finance, 39*, 3–6. doi:10.1016/S2212-5671(16)30232-5

Amable, B. (2000). Institutional complementarity and diversity of social systems of innovation and production. *Review of International Political Economy, 7*(4), 645–687. doi:10.1080/096922900750034572

Aslan, D. H., & Bozyigit, D. (2014). Turkey-Kazakhstan relations: An overview of mutual relations since the collapse of the Soviet Union. *Kwartalnik Naukowy Uczelni Vistula, 4*(42), 133–145.

Baisakalova, A., & Garkavenko, V. (2015). Competitiveness of tourism industry in Kazakhstan. In K. Kantarci, M. Uysal, & V. Magnini (Eds.), *Tourism in Central Asia: Cultural Potential and Challenges* (pp. 15–40). Boca Raton, FL: CRC Press.

Bhuiyan, S. H., & Amagoh, F. (2011). Public sector reform in Kazakhstan: Issues and perspectives. *International Journal of Public Sector Management, 24*(3), 227–249. doi:10.1108/09513551111121356

Boyer, R. (2005). How and why capitalisms differ. *Economy and Society, 34*(4), 509–557. doi:10.1080/03085140500277070

Ceicdata. (2018a). *Related Indicators for Kazakhstan Tourism Revenue*. Retrieved on October 22, 2018, from: https://www.ceicdata.com/en/indicator/kazakhstan/tourism-revenue

Ceicdata. (2018b). *Kazakshtan Resident Departures*. Retrieved on October 22, 2018, from: https://www.ceicdata.com/en/kazakhstan/resident-departures/resident-departures

Charman, K. (2007). Kazakhstan: A state-led liberalized market economy? In D. S. Lane & M. R. Myant (Eds.), *Varieties of Capitalism in Post-Communist Countries* (pp. 165–182). London: Palgrave Macmillan. doi:10.1057/9780230627574_9

Fainshmidt, S., Judge, W. Q., Aguilera, R. V., & Smith, A. (2018). Varieties of institutional systems: A contextual taxonomy of understudied countries. *Journal of World Business*, *53*(3), 307–322. doi:10.1016/j.jwb.2016.05.003

Hall, P. A., & Soskice, D. (2001). *An introduction to varieties of capitalism.* Academic Press.

Hall, P. A., & Soskice, D. (Eds.). (2001). *Varieties of capitalism: The institutional foundations of comparative advantage.* Oxford, UK: Oxford University Press. doi:10.1093/0199247757.001.0001

Höpner, M. (2005). What connects industrial relations and corporate governance? Explaining institutional complementarity. *Socio-economic Review*, *3*(2), 331–358. doi:10.1093/SER/mwi014

IMF. (2014). *Republic of Kazakhstan, Selected Issues.* International Monetary Fund. Retrieved on September 2, 2017, from: https://www.imf.org/external/pubs/ft/scr/2014/cr14243.pdf

Kobenbaev, M., & Eicher, S. (2009). Exploring Corruption in the Petroleum Sector. In S. Eicher (Ed.), Corruption in International Business (pp.81–90). Cornwell, UK: Gower Publishing.

Kristensen, P. H., & Lilja, K. (Eds.). (2011). *Nordic capitalisms and globalization: New forms of economic organization and welfare institutions.* Oxford, UK: Oxford University Press. doi:10.1093/acprof:oso/9780199594535.001.0001

Kristensen, P. H., & Morgan, G. (2012). Theoretical contexts and conceptual frames for the study of twenty-first century capitalisms. In G. Morgan & R. Whitley (Eds.), *Capitalisms and Capitalism in the Twenty-first Century* (pp. 11–43). Oxford, UK: Oxford University Press. doi:10.1093/acprof:oso/9780199694761.003.0002

Louzek, M. (2011). The battle of methods in economics: The classical Methodenstreit-Menger vs. Schmoller. *American Journal of Economics and Sociology*, *70*(2), 439–463. doi:10.1111/j.1536-7150.2011.00780.x

Mamanova, K. M., & Sadyrova, M. S. (2013). Reality and Perspectives of Tourism Development in Kazakhstan: Sociological Analysis. *World Academy of Science, Engineering and Technology*, *75*, 244–251.

Mamanova, K. M., Sadyrova, M. S., & Tufekcioglu, H. (2013). Social aspects of tourism formation and development in Kazakhstan and in Turkey: Comparative analysis. *Middle East Journal of Scientific Research*, *15*(11), 1496–1504.

Minbaeva, D. B., Hutchings, K., & Thomson, S. B. (2007). Hybrid human resource management in post-Soviet Kazakhstan. *European Journal of International Management, 1*(4), 350–371. doi:10.1504/EJIM.2007.015656

Ministry of Culture and Sports of the Republic of Kazakhstan. (2018). *Tourism in the Rebuplic of Kazakhstan, Report Presentation.* Retrieved on October 1, 2018, from: https://www.carecprogram.org/uploads/2b.-Presentation-KAZ.pdf

Morck, R., & Steier, L. (2005). The global history of corporate governance: An introduction. In R. Morck (Ed.), *A history of corporate governance around the world: Family business groups to professional managers* (pp. 1–64). Chicago: University of Chicago Press. doi:10.7208/chicago/9780226536835.001.0001

Morgan, G., & Whitley, R. (2012). *Capitalisms and Capitalism in the Twenty-first Century.* Oxford, UK: Oxford University Press. doi:10.1093/acprof:oso/9780199694761.001.0001

Mukhambetov, T. I., Janguttinav, G. O., Esaidar, U. S., Myrzakulova, G. R., & Imanbekova, B. T. (2014). The life cycle of sustainable eco-tourism: A Kazakhstan case study. *WIT Transactions on Ecology and the Environment, 187*, 39–49. doi:10.2495/ST140041

OECD. (2011). *Competitiveness and Private Sector Development: Kazakhstan 2010 – Sector Competitiveness, Strategy.* OECD Publishing. doi:10.1787/9789264089792-en

OECD. (2014). *Kazakhstan: Review of the Central Administration, OECD Public Governance Reviews.* OECD Publishing. doi:10.1787/9789264224605-en

OECD. (2017). OECD Investment Policy Reviews: Kazakhstan 2017. OECD Publishing. doi:10.1787/9789264269606-en

OECD. (2018). *Reforming Kazakhstan: Progress, Challenges and Opportunities.* Retrieved on October 22, 2018, from: https://www.oecd.org/eurasia/countries/OECD-Eurasia-Reforming-Kazakhstan-EN.pdf

Saner, R., Toseva, G., Atamanov, A., Mogilevsky, R., & Sahov, A. (2008). Government governance (GG) and inter-ministerial policy coordination (IMPC) in Eastern and Central Europe and Central Asia. *Public Organization Review, 8*(3), 215–231. doi:10.100711115-008-0051-x

Schmidt, V. A. (2009). Putting the political back into political economy by bringing the state back in yet again. *World Politics, 61*(3), 516–546. doi:10.1017/S0043887109000173

Shevyakova, A., Tyugina, I., Arystan, M., & Munsh, E. (2018). Transformation of economy towards tourism: Case of Kazakhstan. *Journal of Security & Sustainability Issues, 7*(3), 601–616. doi:10.9770/jssi.2018.7.3(19)

Sultanov, B. K. (2010). *Kazakhstan Today*. Almaty: The Kaz. Inst. for Strategic Studies under the President of the Republic of Kazakhstan.

T.C. Kültür ve Turizm Bakanlığı. (2018). *Bilgi Notu Formu Kazakistan / Astana Kültür ve Tanıtma Müşavirliği 2018 Yılı I. Dönem Raporu*. Retrieved on September 19, 2018, from: http://www.tanitma.gov.tr/TR-209741/kazakistan-pazar-raporu.html

The World Bank. (2013). *Kazakhstan Country Profile Enterprise Surveys 2013*. Retrieved on July 4, 2015, from: https://www.enterprisesurveys.org/~/media/GIAWB/EnterpriseSurveys/Documents/Profiles/English/kazakhstan-2013.pdf

The World Bank. (2018). *A New Growth Model For Building A Secure Middle Class: Kazakhstan Systematic Country Diagnostic*. Report No. 125611-KZ. Retrieved on November 3, 2018, from: http://documents.worldbank.org/curated/en/664531525455037169/pdf/KAZ-SCD-April-2018-FINAL-eng-with-IDU-05012018.pdf

The World Bank. (2019a). *The World Bank in Kazakhstan Country Snaphot Report*. Retrieved on June 2, 2019, from: http://pubdocs.worldbank.org/en/753441554997978839/Kazakhstan-Snapshot-Apr2019.pdf

The World Bank. (2019b). *Doing Business In Kazakhstan 2019*. Retrieved on June 2, 2019, from: https://www.doingbusiness.org/en/reports/subnational-reports/kazakhstan

Tsui-Auch, L. S., & Lee, Y. J. (2003). The state matters: Management models of Singaporean Chinese and Korean business groups. *Organization Studies, 24*(4), 507–534. doi:10.1177/0170840603024004001

Whitley, R. (1998). East Asian and Anglo-American business systems. In G. Thompson (Ed.), *Economic Dynamism in the Asia-Pacific* (pp. 213–249). New York: Routledge.

Whitley, R. (1998a). Internationalization and varieties of capitalism: The limited effects of cross-national coordination of economic activities on the nature of business systems. *Review of International Political Economy, 5*(3), 445–481. doi:10.1080/096922998347480

Whitley, R. D. (1991). The social construction of business systems in East Asia. *Organization Studies, 12*(1), 1–28. doi:10.1177/017084069101200102

Whitley, R. D. (1999). *Divergent Capitalism: The Social Stucturing and Change of Business Systems*. Oxford, UK: Oxford University Press.

Wilkinson, A., Wood, G., & Deeg, R. (Eds.). (2014). *The Oxford Handbook of Employment Relations: Comparative Employment Systems*. Oxford, UK: Oxford University Press. doi:10.1093/oxfordhb/9780199695096.001.0001

Witt, M. A., & Redding, G. (Eds.). (2014). *The Oxford Handbook of Asian Business Systems*. OUP Oxford. doi:10.1093/oxfordhb/9780199654925.001.0001

ENDNOTE

[1] Since there are a certain number of foreign tour operators operating in Kazakhstan, no information has been provided about the interviewees, at their request, in order to keep the names of the companies confidential.

Chapter 8

A Temporal and Situational Approach in Tourism Education as a Mechanism for Economic Growth and Development

Evangelina Cruz Barba

 https://orcid.org/0000-0002-3185-889X
University of Guadalajara, Mexico

ABSTRACT

The argument of this chapter is that tourism education can generate a positive impact on the economic growth of a country by fostering a link between education and work, including economic development. A review of the literature based on the use of bibliometric techniques is performed, but quantification of the work is not conducted; however, Web of Science and Scopus, among other databases, are consulted in relation to economic growth, economic development, human capital and tourism education. All this around the theoretical economic and sociological framework that sustains this work.

INTRODUCTION

The division of labor and specialization as sources of the wealth of nations was proposed in 1776 (Smith, 1987). Currently, the challenge of economic development in the world suggests, among other things, a transformation of the productive structure

DOI: 10.4018/978-1-7998-2239-4.ch008

Copyright © 2020, IGI Global. Copying or distributing in print or electronic forms without written permission of IGI Global is prohibited.

in countries to incorporate the redefinition of human capital and its strong burden on new knowledge into economic activities. This may be the fundamental instrument for the thrust of sectors such as services (where tourism is located), and not only in the extractive industry. The diversification of productive activities in the countries is expressed in their economic performance from job creation, welfare, and social inclusion. The challenge is to manage knowledge from human capital to incorporate it into the economic and social fabric (Ferrer, 2010).

Knowledge management refers to the professions, which according to their origin and knowledge skills, are classified as liberal and modern, the first that arise from the Middle Ages as philosophy, law and medicine, as a manifestation of theoretical thinking, and the modern ones that originate in praxis as a result of the evolution of jobs. Both professions depend on a social structure, whose performance depends on a balance of diverse social forces within a field of knowledge (Parsons, 1939). Thus, the tourism job is institutionalized when professional validation is required in the world in response to national and international market requirements. Starting in 1893, university studies in tourism began with a technical training aimed at hospitality, specifically at the school in Lausanne, Switzerland, with the support of local hotel associations (Formica, 1996), since then, education in the world gradually expanded to all latitudes.

From the emergence of education in tourism in the world, this goes hand in hand with the processes of globalization of tourism activity. However it is not the same in all countries, for instance, in Central Asia, international demand for tourism is emerging internationally according to the World Tourism Organization, Kazakhstan, which is the most dynamic country in Central Asia, barely registered about three million international tourists, followed by Uzbekistan with almost 1 million tourists (UNWTO, 2018, p.15). Unlike other regions of the world, the empirical evidence shows tourism as one of the fastest-growing industries in the world, the tourism sector has been seen as an increasingly important driver of growth and prosperity for many countries, the authors Dias, Costa, Pita and Costa (2017); Le, McDonald, and Klieve (2018); Velempini and Martin (2019); Fahimi, Saint, Seraj and Akadiri (2018); Folarin, Oladipupo, Ajogbeje and Adeniyi (2017); Di Liberto (2013) and Saleh, Assaf, Ihalanayake and Lung (2015) argue that tourism activity has become a crucial source of income for many countries. From this idea, questions arise about the link between economic growth, economic development and tourism education that has been little studied to date.

Specifically, in Central Asia, Spoor (2005) argues that economic growth in that region, after the Russian financial crisis of 1998, is mainly due to the expansion of extractive industries (oil, gas, metals), and the export of crops such as cotton. Almost all Foreign Direct Investment (FDI) is directed to these subsectors, especially to Kazakhstan, for their provision of resources in extractive industry capabilities and

A Temporal and Situational Approach in Tourism Education as a Mechanism

mineral wealth. Therefore, the Gross Domestic Product (GDP) figures between 1997 and 2004 indicate a recovery in the economic growth of Central Asia, among other things, due to the international prices of these goods. However, agriculture and services are relegated. Thus, the analysis of the role of education in tourism, as an externality of human capital in the services sector, suggests a possible improvement of economic growth indicators thanks to the possibility of diversifying economic activities when considering the tourism sector and not only extractive industry.

In the understanding that economic growth is not synonymous with economic development, without going into the discussion about whether economic growth refers to the quantitative growth of wealth like the GDP, while development is a broader concept that also implies a qualitative improvement in the welfare of the population, there is no disagreement that the processes of growth and economic development must necessarily involve human capital as a factor that allows the generation of a surplus, it is known that both are related by the consideration of human capital. In this sense, we focus our attention on specialized tourism education to serve an economic sector that generates jobs; promotes investment both locally in access routes and abroad in hotel chains that favor foreign direct investment and, therefore, promotes international tourism demand in a country.

The importance of focus on tourism sector lies in the fact that countries evolve at different levels of growth according to their main productive activities, and tourism is one of the most contributing to GDP. Identifying the factors that determine economic growth is essential to understand how certain productive activities increase the living standards of the population of a country, and consequently the approach to economic development. This, according to the explanation of the Structuralist Theory of the development of Prebisch (1950), who, based on Keynes' ideas, analyzes historical and contextual differences of the countries to approximate the explanation of the differences in economic development.

The argument in this chapter is that tourism education can generate a positive impact on the economic growth of a country by fostering a link between education and work, as in Romer (1986), where it "offers an alternative view of long-term perspectives for growth"(p.1003). From here, tourism education can translate into a proportional increase in visitors and the entry of foreign currency income. In addition to the entry of foreign income, knowledge of the management of tourism, that a country has, is what can generate a measure of economic growth in modern societies. According to Becker (1993), human capital is an influential conceptual vision in the context of globalization, because this approach establishes education as an investment which generates profits in the future and favors economic growth in several ways, including economic development in some particular cases.

Historically in tourism, human capital begins as an externality of "learning by doing" in an elitist activity. Later, when the interest in the economic benefits

153

generated by this activity is aroused, the "formal education" arises. The conditions that determine the ability of countries to respond to the challenges and opportunities of tourism in globalization are based on the management of knowledge of human capital, therefore, one option is to improve multidisciplinary tourism education to move to a transdisciplinary curriculum that provides tools for economic, sociological, psychological and geographical analysis that encourages the growth of tourism with added value for tourists thanks to the generation of diversified tourism products and, by Therefore, contribute favorably to the economy of a country.

In this chapter, with the intention of reviewing the topic of tourism education as a mechanism for economic growth and development, a review of the literature is carried out from an economic and sociological perspective. We use bibliometric techniques as an important element of the information science that allows the quantitative study of the bibliographic material. Even when we do not make any quantification of the works on literature, we do a general description of empirical evidence with econometric modeling on economic growth and tourism, and the literature on tourism education from the sociological point of view, with the intention of giving a look at the curriculum in tourism education.

The bibliometric process is based on the search for keywords such as tourism education, tourism, economic growth or economic development with Boolean operators, in order to carry out filters to focus our attention on the literature that only relates tourism, education and economic growth -econometric models- and development, which specifically correspond to the interest of this chapter.

The literature review is organized according to the structure presented in this chapter: Economic Development and Economic Growth; later, Empirical evidence: Tourism, Education and Economic Growth; the tourist education and sociological point of view with the look in the tourist curriculum; to end with an epistemological approach on the curriculum and solutions and recommendations.

Economic Development

Economic development models try to explain the economic reality and the problems that countries face by showing differences in their levels of development. Economic development presents some challenges that were exposed decades ago by Prebish (1950), who focuses its attention on the structural inequality of countries with less technological development in Latin America. These countries provide primary agricultural goods with no added value, a situation that promotes disadvantages in terms of international trade in relation to Europe and North America mainly.

In economic development, the issue of structural and contextual differences of the countries becomes relevant in Central Asia because, with the dissolution of the Soviet bloc, it has developed a set of transformations in the political, economic,

154

A Temporal and Situational Approach in Tourism Education as a Mechanism

social and cultural structures of the countries for generating new order. Hence, in Central Asia, there were low poverty rates in the 1970s that increased as of 1998 due to the increase in inequality. However, their poverty rates are low compared to other Latin American countries (Barro and Sala-i-Martin, p.9-10).

Although Prebish (1950) focuses his attention on the structural dynamics of Latin America differentiated from European countries, Ferrer (2010) argues that the development challenges remain. A particular case is Central Asia where Spoor (2005) argues that the countries of Central Asia have developed economies with a high level of inequality. This inequality arises first, due to the focus placed exclusively on the extractive industries sector, which causes differentials in human capital, and second, due to political and ethnic tensions given their geographical position and common borders with Iran (Turkmenistan), Afghanistan (Uzbekistan and Tajikistan) and China (Kazakhstan and Kyrgyzstan).

In general terms, Prebisch's argument is that, given these structural differences, economic development begins within countries with the capacity for knowledge and production of goods that are generated and multiplied over time. Prebisch remarks about the importance that economic growth and economic development take human capital as an externality (either with technological advancement or as a form of knowledge management). Because economic development implies certain characteristics in the population of a country, such as health, life expectancy, literacy and the growth of per capita income (Ray, 1998). However, economic growth, even though it does not capture all aspects of development, is one of the most important factors for improving health and education in the population. It has been argued that development is a complex process.

Economic Growth

Historically, economists have been concerned with the explanation of economic growth. The phrase "economic growth" embraces a diverse body of theoretical and empirical work that emerged with the neoclassical view of economic growth explained by the factors of production in Solow (1956), who develop the first theoretical modeling, but mathematically it becomes complex and moves away from reality to explain long-term growth (Barro & Sala-i-Martin, 2009).

After Solow, Kaldor (1963, as cited in Barro & Sala-i-Martin, 2009, p.10) identified stylized facts to typify the process of economic growth, such as: per capita production grows over time and its growth rate is not decreasing; physical capital per worker grows over time; the ratio of physical capital between production is approximately constant; the growth rate of production per worker is very different in different countries. Additionally, Kuznets (1981, p. 59 as cited in Barro & Sala-i-Martin, 2009, p.10) adds that the rapid pace of structural transformation, to explain economic growth, for example, the shift from agriculture to industry and services requires changes in the structure of the labor market, and therefore specialized human capital. The case of tourism is a clear example of countries like Mexico that has increased the demand for higher education in specific sectors such as tourism in recent years.

However, economic growth can be analyzed from two theoretical perspectives, on the one hand, exogenous growth models arise from the premises of neoclassical economics models (Solow, 1956) who emphasizes physical capital as a source of growth. On the other hand, endogenous growth models, as in Romer (1986), considers human capital as endogenous factors for economic growth. Romer "departs from both the Ramsey-Cass Koopmans model and the Arrow model by assuming that knowledge is a capital asset with an increasing marginal product" (1986, p. 1006). Romer considers that "investment in knowledge suggests a natural externality" (p. 1003). Thus, human capital generates externalities that reinforce the productivity of physical capital and cause sustainable economic growth in the long term.

The important thing about Romer's work is the return to the classic positions of increasing returns based on Adam Smith when he refers to the increasing specialization and division of labor by identifying technological change as endogenous. Romer (1986) refers to the abandonment of the assumption of diminishing returns of Solow's theory. In that sense, the endogenous growth approach refers to long-term growth, where externalities can be identified from the accumulation of human capital as a way to strengthen the productivity of physical capital. In addition, Sala-i-Martin (2010) identifies three more decisive elements for growth: First, the accumulation of factors: physical and human capital. Second, a variety of market-friendly institutions, and third, openness to trade and capital, technology, ideas, foreign direct investment, and information.

EMPIRICAL EVIDENCE: TOURISM, EDUCATION AND ECONOMIC GROWTH

The main objective of this section is to review the efforts to investigate the effect of tourism on the economic growth of countries based on different econometric models from the 1970s to date (Table 1), where a large part of the models consider variables related to enrollment in education and /or variables related to international tourism.

Empirical evidence of this economic approach based on econometric modeling in tourism to analyze the returns of higher education on the economic growth of Pakistan since 1972-2008, is shown by Aziz, Khan, and Aziz (2008) who start from a Cobb-Douglas production function, the authors consider the dependent variable GDP, and as explanatory variables: the enrollment in higher education, spending

A Temporal and Situational Approach in Tourism Education as a Mechanism

on higher education, the employment rate, the labor force, the participation rate in the labor force and per capita income. Within its results, there is evidence that enrollment in higher education and expenditure in higher education has a positive impact on GDP.

Adopting the Solow (1956) residual method and the Cobb-Douglas production function, Zuo and Bao (2008) estimate the Productivity Growth rates of the Total Tourism Factor (TTFP) and identify the sources of economic growth of tourism for the period of 1992 to 2005 in China and its 30 provinces. They conclude that China's tourism industry belongs to an economy based on factors with cheap labor that contributed 63.69% to total economic growth. In addition, the average growth rate of TTFP is slightly positive at 2.91% during the sample period thanks to the effect of tourism education, the encouraging policy and better provision of information, but growth thanks to tourism can be hampered by the investment in infrastructure.

Brida, Carrera, Risso, and Schubert (2008) analyze the impact of tourism on economic growth. Postulating that the growth of tourism exports is one of the key determinants of economic growth for Mexico. Given that for Mexico, tourism is one of the most important economic sectors, representing 9.4% of the GDP. Follow the cointegration analysis model developed by Johansen and the Granger causality tests for the period 1980-2006, they conclude that there is a positive shock in tourism activities that positively impact real GDP in the long term.

Di Liberto (2013) shows empirical evidence about tourism as one of the fastest-growing industries in the world and a favorable strategy for economic growth. With the idea of leaving this evidence, the author analyzes the role of human capital, based on a panel model of 72 countries (1980-2005), which showed results that confirm that the indicator of the tourism sector is always positive and significant in growth, regressions also show that the increase in education contributes to growth and that the role of the tourism sector is significantly greater in countries with higher aggregate levels of human capital.

Li, Mahmood, Abdullah, and Chuan (2013) identify how, tourism is one of the largest and fastest-growing industries in the world, which makes it a potential strategic factor for Malaysia's economic growth, as it is the second-largest contributor to foreign exchange earnings after manufacturing. Therefore, for the period 1974-2010 determined the long and short term causal relationship with a cointegration model and the Granger test between economic growth and tourism income with macroeconomic variables such as government spending on tourism, physical capital, education, health and exports as control variables. The long-term model shows that economic growth, income from tourism and health complement each other (bidirectional causality), while public spending on tourism, physical capital, education and exports to economic growth are in unidirectional causes. In addition, the increase in physical capital, education, health, exports, and government spending on tourism precede tourism income; all this, in turn, indirectly leads to economic growth.

The paper for Saleh et al. (2015) examines the contribution of the tourism industry to GDP from three selected destinations in the Middle East region: Bahrain, Jordan, and Saudi Arabia. From a functional quadratic form in a dynamic model of cointegration of advanced panels, the evidence is shown that with the variables of receptive tourism, investment in education, direct foreign investment, and formation of fixed capital for the period 1981-2008. The results show a long-term relationship between tourism growth and GDP. They also show that tourism is a sector with more dynamism in the economy than other related sectors.

Additionally, Obadic and Pehar (2016) correlate macroeconomic variables for examines the influence of the tourism industry on GDP, employment and capital investments in selected Mediterranean countries (Croatia, France, Greece, Italy, and Spain). In addition, it identifies the contribution that tourism has to economic activity, capital investment and the labor market. The analysis synthesizes data on tourism employment and employment according to educational level. The results show that the quality of human capital is increasing; however, there are gender differences with men in a higher percentage who occupy positions of senior management and decision making. Finally, a strong contribution to GDP and the problem of seasonality that impacts on employment are also identified and identify that the level of educational attainment in tourism is improving.

In the discourse of Economic Development in Africa, Folarin et al. (2017) identify that tourism has been seen as a source of job creation, an increase in GDP that increases the standard of living, income in foreign currency and government income through taxes, due, on the one hand, the high influx of tourists to the continent, as well as the relative size of tourism income to GDP. The authors examine the effect of tourism development on the development of human capital in Africa, by using data in a panel of 25 African countries in the period from 1998 to 2014. The results provide evidence that the development of tourism had a positive and significant effect on the development of human capital in Africa.

Moreover, the authors Aberg and Müller (2018) based on the micro-level data of the total Swedish labor force during the years 2000-2010, they explore the educational aspect of the tourism sector compared to the total and two other sectors of low training, the results show that the educational aspects of tourism is more related to geography than to economic sectors and, contrary to general assumptions, the labor force within the tourism sector has a higher level of formal education than the other sectors selected in regions with generally low educational levels.

In another recent study for Fahimi et al. (2018) investigate the contribution of the tourism sector to the economic growth of the micro-states during 1995-2015, from a panel model incorporating investment in human capital as an additional

A Temporal and Situational Approach in Tourism Education as a Mechanism

variable. The causal relationship and interaction between tourism, investment in human capital and economic growth is analyzed using the Granger causality test approach. The empirical results show evidence in support of the growth induced by tourism, the development of human capital induced by tourism and the growth induced by the development of human capital.

The evidence from econometric models try to provide coverage of the different regions of the world (Table 1), however it is recognized that studies of the United States, United Kingdom, and Canada are not included, not because tourism is not important in these countries, but these countries have developed high levels in tourism due to the structure of different productive sectors. From here, we can deduce that the countries that have more concern on the impact of tourism in economic growth are rather emerging economies, so it is argued that ideas from the structuralist theory of development even in force to the realities of these countries.

As mentioned repeatedly in this work, there are two types of prediction: neoclassical, which is a type of exogenous growth of Solow (1956), and the endogenous growth model of Romer (1986) from the externalities of capital. In general terms, the empirical evidence shown in Table 1 considers GDP as a dependent variable to explain economic growth according to economic theory. However, the theoretical approach to economic growth with independent variables is not empirically supported a neoclassical model or an endogenous model (Sala-i-Martin, 2010). The vast majority do not have consensus with a theoretical backing on the human capital. It is well known, the approach that explains the growth of the countries depends on the context of the country itself depending on the assumptions of how their savings rates are; the population growth rate and the process of capital accumulation of the economy, which allow determining more clearly the causes of economic growth.

In what if there is consensus is, regardless of the level of development in countries, the empirical evidence with econometric models indicates tourism activity and human capital as a favorable outcome for economic growth. Even in Africa, it is part of the economic development discourse. However, not much detail is given of the theoretical approach in which they consider human capital in econometric modeling. So, it is considered important to look at the sociological approach and what countries refer to education in tourism in the following section. According to Sala-i-Martín (2010), the constant link between theory and practice and the flexibility that generates creativity in education. For this reason, the policy to generate economic growth must be formulated from within the countries, because the people, history, institutions, climate, and geography are different and the countries are not comparable to agglutinate in a Panel Model.

Empirical evidence based on econometric modeling gives an idea of the degree of difficulty in clearly presenting the impact of tourism-specific education and the economic growth or development of countries. Arguments supported by Sala-i-

159

A Temporal and Situational Approach in Tourism Education as a Mechanism

Table 1. Econometrics models: Tourism-economic growth

Author	Model	Analysis	Period	Country
Zuo and Bao (2008)	Production function Cobb-Douglas	Productivity Growth rates of the Total Tourism Factor.	1992 - 2005	China
Aziz et al. (2008)	Production function Cobb-Douglas	Returns of higher education on the economic growth.	1972 -2008	Pakistan
Brida et al. (2008)	Cointegration Model	The tourism impact on economic growth.	1980-2006	Mexico
Di Liberto (2013)	Panel Model	The role of human capital, tourism as one of the fastest-growing industries.	1980-2005	72 countries
Li, et al. (2013)	Cointegration Model	Measuring the relationship between government tourism expenditure and economic growth.	1974-2010	Malaysia
Saleh, et al. (2015)	Dynamic Model of Cointegration of Advanced Panels	Contribution of the tourism industry to GDP.	1981-2008	East region: Bahrain, Jordan, and Saudi Arabia.
Obadic and Pehar (2016)	Correlate Macroeconomic Variables	Influence of the tourism industry on GDP.	2000-2015	Mediterranean countries: Croatia, France, Greece, Italy, and Spain
Folarin, et al. (2017)	Panel Model	Effect of tourism development on the development of human capital.	1998 - 2014	25 countries in Africa
Aberg and Müller (2018)	Panel Model	The educational aspect of the tourism sector compared with two other sectors.	2000-2010	Sweden
Fahimi, et al. (2018)	Panel Model	Contribution of the tourism sector to the economic growth.	1995-2015	Barbados, Cyprus, Dominican R. Fiji, Cuba, Iceland, Malta, Mauritius, Haiti, Trinidad.

Source: Author based on literature review

Martin (2010), like Bills (2016) who argues that the empirical relationships between schooling and economic growth are problematic and education in economic growth is not so clear because "the relationship between education and growth may not be directly observable." In fact, "education" and "economic growth" are large, complex and dynamic. To date, the theoretical and empirical literature on education and development has received much attention when conceptualizing an educational entry that leads to an unequivocal economic exit (p.242).

A Temporal and Situational Approach in Tourism Education as a Mechanism

However, this is a reductionist vision because of the existence of a socially established identification process what Collins (1979) calls "credentialism". In this sense, differences are observed in the econometric models in that economists are concerned about productivity and wages and do not necessarily see this as different things. "Sociologists are concerned about occupations, jobs, and limitations of open labor markets" (Granovetter, 1988 as cited in Bills, 2003, p.443). Therefore, it is important to pay attention to the interior of the countries in terms of what happens with education, in the case of this work: Tourism education.

Tourism Education

It is well known that the educational policy changed drastically in many countries with the arriving of the neoliberal model, so that, some results of structural adjustment consisted of conceiving the university as a company. This ideological influence of neoliberalism in higher education in tourism is appreciated from a perspective of political discourse analysis (Ayikoru & Tribe, 2009). For instance, Clancy (2001) argues that the neoliberal process favored the dynamism of tourism due to the minimal protectionist barriers in Mexico. Echtner (1995, p. 130) when analyzing the academic formation in the higher level of tourism in the world, identifies that the type of education offered in a country is a function of its political system.

The number of tourist education courses has increased significantly in recent decades to meet the demands of the skilled workforce. In light of current global challenges, Barkathunnisha, Lee, and Price (2017) identify the need to reorient and to rethink tourism education. With the intention of moving towards an educational platform that includes ethics, values, and spirituality, the latter is a way to advance in higher education of tourism that goes beyond the transmission of knowledge and compromises the transforming spirit of students. However, tourism education will need to consider different skills to face the challenges of this highly competitive and demanding industry in a global world. Following the idea of improving tourism education Dias et al., (2017) describe an innovative teaching program called "Learning to be", focused on fostering attitudes and business skills in tourism education.

The diversity of tourism education programs in countries makes formal education in tourism particularly difficult for developing countries. The work of Theunis and Rasheed (1983) summarizes the guidelines for the choice of programs by examining two tourism education approaches, one focusing on the demand and the other on the offer. In this sense, it is intuited that the differences in tourism education are given in terms of the country's resources and the capacity of a country of hotel infrastructure, as well as communications and transport. The reason why the development of tourism in developing countries is associated with public policy and the interest that a country has in the economic spillover generated by tourism activity.

Analyzing the case of Vietnam, where tourism has little participation in the economy, Le et al. (2018) explore in depth the aspects of this industry. Mainly, explore higher education in hospitality in Vietnam as a support to the continuous development of tourism through human resources, based on qualitative research with 26 in-depth interviews with industry professionals, hospitality academics and university hospitality students. Their findings provide information on the relevance of higher education for hospitality in Vietnam, to prepare for the expansion of the tourism sector. Another case in Botswana, this country cannot fully exploit this potential due to the lack of human resource capacity within the tourism industry. An important factor in the lack of capacity is due to an inadequate educational curriculum in the area of hospitality and tourism (Velempini & Martin, 2019).

The work of Goh, Muskat, and Tan (2017) explore the attitudes of students of hospitality in "generation Y" and perceptions about ecological and sustainable tourism practices of four and five-star hotels in Australia. From qualitative research with 12 semi-structured interviews to students of hotel management in Australia, they identified a positive attitude towards the care of the environment, therefore, relevant topics to include in their academic curriculum to provide an ecological and sustainable hotel environment; "students also perceive that this subject would allow them to practice change management skills and become effective agents of change" (p.247).

Andrades and Dimanche (2017) identify that thanks to new border policies and infrastructure development, international tourism to Russia has experienced double-digit growth in recent years. However, the authors acknowledge the challenges Russia faces for sustainable and competitive tourism development. Therefore, they emphasize the problem of the image of the destination, the development of the infrastructure, the training and education of the labor force, the management of the quality and the sustainable management, the previous thing to take into account by the Russian universities to prepare to tourism professionals. Under the idea that tourism education has to change:

The perception that education is to suit only the employment requirements of the industry may not be the most effective or desired purpose of a college education, nor provide qualified individuals as contributors not only as tourism professionals, but also as thoughtful participants in a global society (Inui, Wheeler, & Lankford 2010, p 31).

For instance, globalization often forgets certain communities in countries with developing economies, the work of Makoena (2018) analyzes the research design used in a service-learning project of Tourism Management in South Africa, to contribute to the body of knowledge of learning research service. To explore, among other things, the social benefits for the participating communities, action research was carried out. The post-project reflections of all participants were collected immediately after the completion of each project. The results of the research pointed to positive and personal business developments for the participating communities and greater business awareness among the students. 80% of the students obtained critical business skills from the project, and 100% of the community participants responded affirmatively to their businesses, benefiting positively from the project.

In the same sense, as a special case, recently Central Asia joins this logic of tourism and economic growth, in this regard, Brijesh (2019) identify that tourism in Kazakhstan has been raised to a governmental priority with the creation of the Ministry of Tourism and Sports to facilitate the industry (p.119). In fact, by focusing on ecotourism, argues that "the development of the postgraduate study plan in tourism is a necessity" (p.123). It is intuited that if the government considers the inclusion of communities in tourism projects, better economic results would be obtained in regions and countries.

In the same order of ideas, Zholdasbekov, Berkinbaev, and Tasbolat (2008, p.5) argue that Kazakhstan is stressed that the maintenance of the tourist branch staff so far remains unsatisfactory. Therefore, state educational standards on a specialty of this type do not fully meet the requirements of society and region in the preparation of experts in accordance with the realization of the Tourism Development Concept.

As a discussion of the literature, the lack of inclusion of communities in tourism projects endangers the natural resources of the tourist site and destabilizes social relations in communities that live in nearby areas, because in countries with developing economies and with a low level of education in communities have gone from being peasants to integrate into the market economy is located in the lowest link in the tourism industry. With the development of mass tourism, the inhabitants of communities are forced to change their activity to produce and sell souvenirs with low-profit margins.

The future growth of international tourism is challenged by concerns of countries in terms of economic policy, border policies, the image of the destination, the development of the infrastructure, and environmental impact. However, the role of tourism education is crucial to solving the challenges of a global world, because globalization has increased competition in tourism markets, and destinations are exposed to tough competition from tourism products.

Differences are identified in terms of the level of development of the countries and the level of education, it is intuited that the developed countries have greater clarity in what they should teach and how to equip skills in the tourism curriculum. Indeed, it is important to mention that in most of the developing countries, touristic activity presents the peculiarity of seasonality, this affects in terms of employment. Given these challenges and the desire of countries with developing economies in the world the development of human resources is fundamental to the success of tourism that is reflected in the trade balances of the recipient countries, that is, it generates economic growth and economic development. As countries become more concerned with higher education in tourism, many of them can improve the impact on their country's economy, reaching levels of competitiveness required in a globalized world.

The Sociological Point of View: The Curriculum Like Resource

First, we take the conceptualization of curriculum of Dussel (1997) who argues that the academic curriculum is a cultural proposal expressed in thematic contents that in itself defines social and economic elements of a country. Likewise, many sociologists have contributed to the literature on education and economic growth in a country, but the field is dominated by economists. For this reason, it is important to take into consideration the institutions, resources, markets and other processes and structures of the Meso-level (Bill, 2016, p.254).

As in the economic perspective, there is consensus in the association between education and economic growth from the sociological point of view. About that, this chapter has the sociological vision in which Bills (2003) reiterates that the sociology of education maintains that formal schooling is strongly related to socioeconomic development and discusses the theoretical part that sustains the relationship between educational achievement and credentialism with the socio-economic aspect. Particularly the Institutional Theory emphasizes the role of educational credentials, more closely the literature associated with Meyer (Bills, 2003, p.451)

The reminder that "correlation is not causality" is more than an adage learned in Sociology, and acquires a particular force when applied to such heterogeneous concepts and as education and development. A more common explanation for the contribution of education to economic growth is that it provides students with the types of cognitive skills that employer's value and on which economic expansion depends. Although the theory of human capital has seldom been presented so simply, many of its followers would certainly be satisfied explanation focused on cognitive skills (Bills, 2016, p.245).

Hence, the importance of considering the management of specific knowledge in a curriculum, which for tourism is not the solution to expand the levels of education in graduate courses in tourism, but to provide tourism education with theoretical and conceptual tools, that gives them the ability to analyze with a multicultural view. In a transdisciplinary way, among the economic, psychological, sociological,

A Temporal and Situational Approach in Tourism Education as a Mechanism

geographic, and other disciplines, for the good management of the tourist resources available to a country.

Bills (2003) argues that the theory of human capital is wrong to ignore school learning, but this topic is simply not a focus of institutional theory (p.452). Therefore, it is important to recognize that the quantification of people with a level of educational instruction is not enough, because this has social effects in terms of what is learned or not in school in the different educational levels. Indeed, it is important to look at the concept of human capital and to care about what they learn and how to learn to have a positive impact on the labor market. In this regard, we finally focus attention on a specific tourism curriculum, which is consistent with the needs of a country with shape experience in the tourism sector.

The other vision is given by the multidimensionality of human capital which Klomp and De Haan (2013) identifies from macroeconomic variables, over the period 2000-2008, sixteen human capital indicators at the national level around 120 countries, and apply FA (Factor Analysis) with the intention of avoiding the problem that some previous works only represent formal education. For instance, Benhabib and Spiegel (1994) who from the production function of Cobb-Douglas and estimation through the stock of the physical and human capital country, associated with Romer (1986) theory of endogenous growth, model the technological progress, or the growth of the productivity total factors, depending on the level of education or human capital.

In this sense, the work of Klomp and De Haan (2013) considers different levels of education as well as skills as a non-formal level of instruction; in addition, they include five indicators of science and technological development, the relationship between different dimensions of the political regime in place and human capital using a two-step structural equation model, they found "The level of income has a significant positive relationship with both types of human capital" distinguish between 'basic human capital' and 'advanced human capital´ (p.56).

The work of Hsu, Xiao, and Chen (2017) synthesize and evaluates research on hospitality and tourism education for the period 2005-2014. From a qualitative methodology, the authors analyze 644 articles. From a process of coding and analysis of each article, present the evidence of five distinctive meta-themes in the tourism education literature, they based on 30 sub-themes in the tourism curriculum. Among the results of its analysis, the first topic is that of teaching and learning, in terms of tools, new technologies and experiential learning among some sub-themes of it. As a second topic the skills and competences of the students, followed by the design of the curriculum and the revision of the countries. This review provides a complete source of information for professionals in education and industry committed to human capital, educational practices for the development of professionals in tourism and above all notes that there are curricular differences between countries.

The Tourism Curriculum: An Epistemological Approach

As explained above, it is worth mentioning some epistemological characteristics that involve the touristic sector. The tourism profession's nature obeys a very particular practice according to the vision of each country because it is recognized that tourism is not a profession that is born as other professions such as law, medicine, biology or economics, those professions arise from an own theoretical body that was consolidating from theoretical principles.

However, Tourism is a modern profession according to what is established by Parsons (1939), a field of knowledge has a social function that translates into a profession. We understand that since its origin in Europe, tourism training in universities focused its attention on technical training in which priority was given to operational problems of hospitality, and then the need to train hotel managers with tools related to business administration, due to the interest of both the public and private sectors, given the rapid growth of tourism activity, which led to the establishment of specialized tourism departments in some universities (Inui et al., 2010, p.26). Now there are issues of ecotourism and the environment.

With this epistemological approach in mind, Wallerstein (2002, p.249) recognizes a division of knowledge intellectually as disciplines; organizationally as corporate structures and culturally as communities of scholars that share certain elementary premises. On the other hand, Foucault (1998) defines the discipline as a set of methods, a corpus of propositions considered true, a set of rules and definitions, techniques and instruments. It is a principle of control of the production of discourse, sets limits for the game of an identity that has the form of a permanent updating of the rules.

Hence, it is possible to identify an intellectual problem of this disciplinary division, which is appreciated with the world changes after the Second World War in 1945, due to the influence of the United States. Thus by 1970, the borders between disciplines were no longer clear and institutionalization has been seen as a way to preserve and reproduce practices, seeking not to discipline the intellect but practice (Wallerstein, 2002). New labor practices, that overlap in several disciplines, gives rise to the emergence of modern professions, for example, tourism that begins with a technical vocation and extends after the Second World War until the seventies, the creation of Bachelor's degrees in tourism was reflected throughout the world.

The disciplines form "tribes" that defend their territory, perhaps the disciplines that predominate in the tourism curriculum correspond to soft-pure according to Becher's classification (1989), such disciplines as the economy, and accounting and management. These have a nature of functional knowledge, utilitarian, and largely concerned with the improvement of the practice, in search of results with procedures that often limit the creativity of the tourism student.

A Temporal and Situational Approach in Tourism Education as a Mechanism

Therefore, this chapter proposes transdisciplinarity in tourism education, which is essential to theoretically locate the impact of tourism development through the identification of social, cultural and environmental costs that are difficult to evaluate with a single disciplinary view. "The trans prefix refers simultaneously between disciplines" (Davalos 2005, p.89), where there is "the confluence of knowledge, in their reciprocal interaction and integration, or in their transformation and improvement" (Molina, 2007, p. 138), this in order to contribute to the field of scientific research in tourism.

It is desirable that transdisciplinary is reflected in an academic curriculum of tourism according to the changing needs of the global world. For this, Sanchez and Perez (2011) identify four fundamental axes of a transdisciplinary and complex curricular practice: epistemological-philosophical, this is to rethink the pedagogical theories; the eco-politics that requires the participation of actors from different disciplines that connect the new social realities; The axiological axis that guarantees the presence of values in cultural and environmental differences and, finally, the praxeological methodology that assumes the exercise of a complex, hermeneutic, transdisciplinary and reflective thought of the diversity and cultural reality of the context.

As shown in Figure 1, tourism has different perspectives on the very nature of the human being; as an example, this scheme is manifested in the form of a network of some keywords that have an impact on economic development and tourism. In terms of temporality, we observe that economic development discourse, Asia and developing countries was present 2000, so after 2010 issues such as education, culture and tourism development take relevance.

The transdisciplinarity in the tourist curriculum makes sense among other things, for instance, according to Van der Zee, Gerrets, and Vanneste (2017) identify that tourist destinations are complex systems of interrelated entities without a hierarchical chain of command. The author refers to the authentic tourism experience with a perspective of management based on networks as a promising way to make the tourism industry more innovative and competitive.

Therefore, a qualitative study with in-depth interviews with 12 network administrators in Flanders (Belgium) provides an example of the way networks currently operate. The main conclusion is that although the interviewees (managers) stated that they had adopted a 'network approach', most of them still devoted most of their time to the traditional tasks related to the provision of top-down information, the lobbying and the representation of the network towards external actors. In conclusion, we can appreciate the importance of increasing the professionalization of the sector, including specific training and education.

Figure 1.

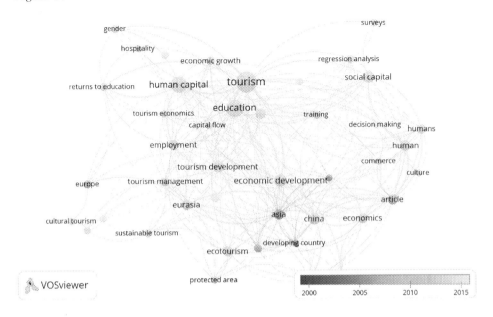

SOLUTIONS AND RECOMMENDATIONS

In short, education in economic growth is not so clear in many educational indexes, such as university enrollment, do not seem clearly correlation with the growth in econometric models, due to the credentialing effect, however, more attention can be paid to the tourism curriculum.

It should be noted that the understanding of tourism has been fetishized as an economic activity that generates resources for a country (Franklin & Crang, 2001). In particular, the economic aspect has been given greater emphasis, due to its implications of foreign currency revenues, minimizing the analysis of the social, cultural and environmental problem that mass tourism implies, for instance, the improper use of natural resources. For this reason, it is important to take into account the importance of human capital in tourism, which values economic, cultural and environmental aspects, since these express a connection with all productive activity.

Additionally, a large number of studies of tourism frequently privilege exotic and strange geographic sites. These studies reflect the anthropological legacy to analyze the contrasts between locals and visitors. According to Franklin and Crang, (2001) many academic works carry out a large number of case studies that remain at a descriptive level and appreciate tourism as an activity with taxonomy or classification represented superficially in sociology and psychology. These authors argue that there is a divorce between market research and scientific research on tourism. To this, we add in this chapter the econometric studies that analyze the impact of tourism on macroeconomic variables in a global way, but they are not enough to understand the real benefit of tourism that leads to the economic development of the countries.

In order to better understanding of tourism education, we can only reiterate that scientific knowledge is of a complex order, through the history of humanity and, above all, based on the postulates of the philosophy of science. It is shown that science arises from questions of the very nature of the human being in the dialectic between what he sees and what he feels (the myth of the cave). What objectifies and what is not characteristic of objectification. Therefore, it is not about discovering new theories of tourism, because from our understanding, it is necessary to investigate from the philosophy of science of Popper (1999) in the search of situations, events or tourist phenomena that cannot be explained with the existing theoretical referents, and consider a paradigmatic change in the explanation of tourism according to Kunh (1962).

However, in terms of tourism education, it is important to emphasize that the limitation of this profession, in terms of its own theoretical framework, first obeys that tourism was born as an activity and not a theoretical body like the liberal professions, and second, that it is the result of the convergence of multiple disciplines. Given the dramatic increase in tourism demand in the world, each country has its own perception of education according to its own requirements emphasizing the importance of economic growth. In this sense, the academic community does not incorporate the education phenomenon for its understanding and the explanation has been, for example, from econometric modeling identifying variables that impact on the demand of tourism exports, being studied by economic science. Therefore, efforts to investigate this phenomenon of tourism do not allow identifying the tourism education process in the economic impact.

The curriculum is not about just including "sociological and philosophical perspectives" as argued by Inui et al. (2010, p. 33), or values and spirituality, but to reinforce according to Morin (1994) complex thinking involves rendering accounts about the articulation of theoretical bodies from various disciplines considered as part of a whole that identifies what interferes and what interacts. Adopting a new way of thinking, of organizing knowledge and acting on the reality of things, recognizing the complexity of the environment in which individuals develop and the changing tourist activity.

We can summarize that the social, political, economic, cultural and geographical context is inherent to the understanding of tourism education and its impact on the economic development of countries. Because historically tourism activity has evolved, so must the need to make adjustments in tourism education. We cannot leave aside the genealogy of tourism activity or the origin of the profession. Both are necessary to understand how the tourism professional has been constituted within the educational institutions in the world, and how this knowledge in tourism has been sheltered by other sciences in a multidisciplinary way, however, tourism education needs to adapt to the complexity of tourism. A global world requires a professional with a global mind in a current requirement of the profession to open up to transdisciplinarity and action more open to a global society, with the recognition that each country has its own historical and contextual reality with its own natural and cultural resources.

FUTURE RESEARCH DIRECTIONS

In future work, econometric modeling can be carried out including categorical variables that identify the levels of development of the countries to mark structural differences, that Prebish theoretically proposed in his explanation of the different levels of development of the countries, because given the complex and limiting education in tourism in many developing countries. There is a large amount of capital repatriation by multinationals and tour operators, which generates few economic benefits and a low multiplier effect of local tourism investment in emerging countries. Additionally, an in-depth analysis of the tourism curriculum can be deepened by identifying particularities in countries with different levels of economic development.

REFERENCES

Aberg, K. G., & Müller, D. K. (2018). The development of geographical differences in education levels within the Swedish tourism industry. *Tourism Geographies*, *20*(1), 67–84. doi:10.1080/14616688.2017.1400093

Andrades, L., & Dimanche, F. (2017). Destination competitiveness and tourism development in Russia: Issues and challenges. *Tourism Management*, *62*, 360–376. doi:10.1016/j.tourman.2017.05.008

Ayikoru, M., Tribe, J., & Airey, D. (2009). Reading tourism education: Neoliberalism unveiled. *Annals of Tourism Research*, *36*(2), 191–221. doi:10.1016/j. annals.2008.11.001

Aziz, B., Khan, T., & Aziz, S. (2008) Impact of Higher Education on Economic Growth of Pakistan. *University Library of Munich, 6*(2), 15-19. Retrieved on September 9, 2017, from: https://mpra.ub.uni-muenchen.de/22912/

A Temporal and Situational Approach in Tourism Education as a Mechanism

Barkathunnisha, A. B., Lee, D., & Price, A. (2017). Transcending towards a spirituality-based platform in tourism higher education: A contemplation of the pedagogical implications. *Journal of Hospitality, Leisure, Sport and Tourism Education*, *21*, 174–184. doi:10.1016/j.jhlste.2016.11.003

Barro, J. R., & Sala-i-Martin, X. (2009). *Crecimiento Económico*. Barcelona: Reverté.

Becher, T. (1989). *Tribus y territorios académicos. La indagación intelectual y las culturas de las disciplinas*. Barcelona: Gedisa.

Becker, G. (1993). *Human Capital: A theoretical and empirical analysis with special references to education*. Chicago: The University of Chicago Press. doi:10.7208/chicago/9780226041223.001.0001

Benhabib, J., & Spiegel, M. M. (1994). The role of human capital in economic development evidence from aggregate cross-country data. *Journal of Monetary Economics*, *34*(2), 143–173. doi:10.1016/0304-3932(94)90047-7

Bills, D. B. (2003). Credentials, signals, and screens: Explaining the relationship between schooling and job assignment. *Review of Educational Research*, *73*(4), 441–449. doi:10.3102/00346543073004441

Bills, D. B. (2016). Education and Development. In G. Hooks (Ed.), *The sociology of development handbook* (pp. 241–262). Oakland, CA: University of California Press.

Brida, J. G., Carrera, J. S. E., Risso, A. W., & Schubert, F. (2008). Tourism Impact in the Long-Run Mexican Economic Growth. *Anatolia: An International Journal of Tourism and Hospitality Research*, 265-278.

Brijesh, T. (2019). Ecotourism Education and Development in Kazakhstan. *Journal of Hospitality & Tourism Education*, *31*(2), 119–124. doi:10.1080/10963758.201 8.1485499

Clancy, M. (2001). *Exporting Paradise Tourism and Development. Evidence from México*. London: Pergamon.

Collins, R. (1979). *La sociedad credencialista. Sociología histórica de la educación y la estratificación*. Madrid: Akal.

Contreras, D. L. M. (2007). Ejes transversales en el currículo universitario: Experiencia en la carrera de derecho. *Ciências & Cognição*, *10*, 132–146. Retrieved from http://pepsic.bvsalud.org/scielo.php?script=sci_arttext&pid=S1806-58212007000100013

Davalos Gamboa, M. (2005). Implicaciones epistemológicas del curriculum transdisciplinario. *Gaceta Médica Boliviana*, 28(2), 81–92. Retrieved from http://www.scielo.org.bo/scielo.php?script=sci_arttext&pid=S1012-29662005000200015&lng=es&tlng=es

Di Liberto, A. (2013). High skills, high growth: Is tourism an exception? *The Journal of International Trade & Economic Development*, 22(5), 749–785. doi:10.1080/09638199.2011.603054

Dias, A. D., Costa, R. A., Pita, M., & Costa, C. (2017). Tourism Education: What about entrepreneurial skills? *Journal of Hospitality and Tourism Management*, 30, 65–72. doi:10.1016/j.jhtm.2017.01.002

Echtner, C. M. (1995). Entrepreneurial Training in Developing Countries. *Annals of Tourism Research*, 22(1), 119–134. doi:10.1016/0160-7383(94)00065-Z

Fahimi, A., Saint, A. S., Seraj, M., & Akadiri, A. C. (2018). Testing the role of tourism and human capital development in economic growth. A panel causality study of micro states. *Tourism Management Perspectives*, 28, 62–70. doi:10.1016/j.tmp.2018.08.004

Ferrer, A. (2010). Raul Prebisch y el dilemma del desarrollo en el mundo global. *Revista de CEPAL*, (101), 7-15.

Folarin, O., Oladipupo, E., Ajogbeje, K., & Adeniyi, O. (2017). Does tourism development contribute to human capital development in Africa? *Turizam: međunarodni znanstveno-stručni časopis*, 65(3), 314-329.

Formica, S. (1996). European hospitality and tourism education: Differences with the American model and future trends. *Journal of Hospitality Management*, 15(4), 317–323. doi:10.1016/S0278-4319(96)00039-4

Foucault, M. (1998). El orden del discurso. Traducción de Alberto González Trovan. Argentina: Fábula Tusquets Editores.

Franklin, A., & Crang, M. (2001). *The trouble with tourism and travel theory?* Sage Publications. Retrieved on April 11, 2017, from: https://www.nyu.edu/classes/bkg/tourist/a019893.pdf

Goh, E., Muskat, B., & Tan, A. H. T. (2017). The nexus between sustainable practices in hotels and future Gen Y hospitality students' career path decisions. *Journal of Teaching in Travel & Tourism*, 17(4), 237–253. doi:10.1080/15313220.2017.1362971

A Temporal and Situational Approach in Tourism Education as a Mechanism

Hsu, C. H., Xiao, H., & Chen, N. (2017). Hospitality and tourism education research from 2005 to 2014: "Is the past a prologue to the future? *International Journal of Contemporary Hospitality Management, 29*(1), 141–160. doi:10.1108/IJCHM-09-2015-0450

Inui, Y., Wheeler, D., & Lankford, S. (2010). Rethinking Tourism Education: What Should Schools Teach? *Journal of Hospitality, Leisure, Sport and Tourism Education, 5*(2), 25–32. doi:10.3794/johlste.52.122

Klomp, J., & de Haan, J. (2013). Political regime and human capital: A cross-country analysis. *Social Indicators Research, 111*(1), 45–73. doi:10.100711205-011-9983-6 PMID:23378681

Kuhn Thomas, S. (1962). *La estructura de las revoluciones científicas.* D. F., México: Fondo de Cultura Económica.

Le, A. H., McDonald, C. V., & Klieve, H. (2018). Hospitality higher education in Vietnam: Voices from stakeholders. *Tourism Management Perspectives, 27*, 68–82. doi:10.1016/j.tmp.2018.05.002

Li, C. C., Mahmood, R., Abdullah, H., & Chuan, O. S. (2013). Economic growth, tourism, and selected macroeconomic variables: A triangular causal relationship in Malaysia. *Margin - the Journal of Applied Economic Research, 7*(2), 185–206. doi:10.1177/0973801013483503

Molina Contreras, D. L. (2007). Ejes transversales en el currículo universitario: Experiencia en la carrera de derecho. *Ciências & Cognição, 10*, 132–146.

Morin, E. (1994). *Introducción al pensamiento complejo.* Barcelona: Gedisa.

Obadic, A., & Pehar, L. (2016). Employment, Capital and Seasonality in Selected Mediterranean Countries. *Zagreb International Review of Economics and Business, 19*(1), 43–58. doi:10.1515/zireb-2016-0012

Parsons, T. (1939). The professions and social structure. *Social Forces, 17*(4), 457–467. doi:10.2307/2570695

Popper, K. R. (1999). *La lógica de la investigación científica.* Madrid: Tecnos.

Prebisch, R. (1950). Crecimiento, desequilibrio y disparidades: interpretación del proceso de desarrollo económico. *Estudio Económico de América Latina y el Caribe, Naciones Unidas Comisión Económica para América Latina y el Caribe (CEPAL), 1110.*

Ray, D. (1998). *Development Economics.* London: Princeton University Press.

Romer, P. M. (1986). Increasing Returns and Log-Run Growth. *Journal of Political Economy, 94*(5), 1002–1037. doi:10.1086/261420

Sala-i-Martin, X. (2001, Aug.). La apertura y la flexibilidad son ingredientes importantes del crecimiento económico. *Boletín del FMI*, 20.

Saleh, A. S., Assaf, A. G., Ihalanayake, R., & Lung, S. (2015). A panel cointegration analysis of the impact of tourism on economic growth: Evidence from the Middle East region. *International Journal of Tourism Research, 17*(3), 209–220. doi:10.1002/jtr.1976

Sánchez, J., & Pérez, C. (2011) Hacia un currículo transdisciplinario: una mirada desde el pensamiento complejo. *Revista de Teoría y Didáctica de las Ciencias Sociales,* (17), 143-164. Retrieved on October 7, 2015, from: https://www.redalyc.org/pdf/652/65221619010.pdf

Smith, A. (1987). *Investigación sobre la naturaleza y causas de la riqueza de las naciones.* México: Fondo de Cultura Económica.

Solow, R. M. (1956). A Contribution to the Theory of Economic Growth. *The Quarterly Journal of Economics, 70*(1), 65–94. doi:10.2307/1884513

Theunis, H. L., & Rasheed, A. (1983). Alternative approaches to tertiary tourism education with special reference to developing countries. *Tourism Management, 4*(1), 42–51. doi:10.1016/0261-5177(83)90049-3

Van der Zee, E., Gerrets, A. M., & Vanneste, D. (2017). Complexity in the governance of tourism networks: Balancing between external pressure and internal expectations. *Journal of Destination Marketing & Management, 6*(4), 296–308. doi:10.1016/j.jdmm.2017.07.003

Velempini, K., & Martin, B. (2019). Place-based education as a framework for tourism education in secondary schools: A case study from the Okavango Delta in Southern Africa. *Journal of Hospitality, Leisure, Sport and Tourism Education, 25,* 100–197. doi:10.1016/j.jhlste.2019.100197

Wallerstein, I. (2002). *El legado de la sociología, la promesa de la ciencia social en Conocer el mundo. El fin de lo aprendido.* México: Una ciencia social para el Siglo XXI-UNAM.

World Tourism Organization (UNWTO). (2018). *Panorama OMT del turismo internacional.* Retrieved on March 4, 2019, from: https://www.e-unwto.org/doi/pdf/10.18111/9789284419890

Zholdasbekov, A., Berkinbaev, K. M., & Tasbolat, B. (2008). Modern Tendencies of Professional Training of Specialists in the Sphere of Tourism in Kazakhstan. *Anatolia: An International Journal of Tourism and Hospitality Research*, 3-11.

Zuo, B., & Bao, J. G. (2008). Tourism total factor productivity and its regional variation in China from 1992 to 2005. *Acta Geographica Sinica*, *63*(4), 417–427.

Compilation of References

Abdimomunova, L., Boutenko, V., Chin, V., Nuriyev, R., Perapechka, S., Raji, M., . . . Türpitz, A. (2018, December 23). *Investing in Central Asia: One region, many opportunities.* Retrieved on June 8, 2019, from: https://www.bcg.com/en-ru/perspectives/205272

Abdul-Latif, S. A., & Abdul-Talib, A. N. (2017). Consumer racism: A scale modification. *Asia Pacific Journal of Marketing and Logistics, 29*(3), 616–633. doi:10.1108/APJML-02-2016-0026

Abdul-Talib, A. N., Abd-Latif, S. A., & Abd-Razak, I. S. (2016). A study on the boycott motivations of Malaysian non-Muslims. *Journal of Islamic Marketing, 7*(3), 264–287. doi:10.1108/JIMA-11-2014-0071

Abdul-Talib, A. N., & Abdul-Latif, S. A. (2015). Antecedents to willingness to Boycotts among Malaysian muslims. In *Emerging Research on Islamic Marketing and Tourism in the Global Economy* (pp. 70–106). Hershey, PA: IGI Global. doi:10.4018/978-1-4666-6272-8.ch004

Abdul-Talib, A. N., & Mohd Adnan, M. M. (2017). Determinants of consumer's willingness to boycott surrogate products. *Journal of Islamic Marketing, 8*(3), 345–360. doi:10.1108/JIMA-08-2015-0065

Aberg, K. G., & Müller, D. K. (2018). The development of geographical differences in education levels within the Swedish tourism industry. *Tourism Geographies, 20*(1), 67–84. doi:10.1080/1 4616688.2017.1400093

Abubakirova, A., Syzdykova, A., Kelesbayev, D., Dandayeva, B., & Ermankulova, R. (2016). Place of tourism in the economy of Kazakhstan Republic. *Procedia Economics and Finance, 39*, 3–6. doi:10.1016/S2212-5671(16)30232-5

Adom, P. K., Bekoe, W., & Akoena, S. K. K. (2012). Modelling aggregate domestic electricity demand in Ghana: An autoregressive distributed lag bounds cointegration approach. *Energy Policy, 42*, 530–537. doi:10.1016/j.enpol.2011.12.019

Aghion, P., Bloom, N., Blundell, R., Griffith, R., & Howitt, P. (2005). Competion and innovation: An inverted U relationship. *The Quarterly Journal of Economics, 120*(2), 701–728.

Compilation of References

Ahn, M. J., & Wu, H. (2015). The art of nation branding: National branding value and the role of government and the arts and culture sector. *Public Organization Review, 15*(1), 157–173. doi:10.100711115-013-0255-6

Ahrens, J., & Hoen, H. W. (2019). The emergence of state capitalism in Central Asia: The absence of Normative Power Europe. In M. Neuman (Ed.), *Democracy promotion and the Normative Power Europe framework: The European Union in South Eastern Europe, Eastern Europe, and Central Asia* (pp. 81–97). Cham, Switzerland: Springer. doi:10.1007/978-3-319-92690-2_5

Alagöz, M., Yapar, S., & Uçtu, R. (2004). Türk Cumhuriyetleri İle İlişkilerimize Ekonomik Açıdan Bir Yaklaşım. *Selçuk Üniversitesi Sosyal Bilimler Enstitüsü Dergisi,* (12), 59-74.

Alper, F. (2014). Impact Of Exchange Rate Volatility On Trade: A Literature Survey. *Çukurova Üniversitesi Sosyal Bilimler Enstitüsü Dergisi, 23*(2), 29-46. Retrieved on December 22, 2017, from: https://dergipark.org.tr/tr/pub/cusosbil/issue/31959/352032

Aluri, A., Price, B. S., & McIntyre, N. H. (2019). Using machine learning to co-create value through dynamic customer engagement in a brand loyalty program. *Journal of Hospitality & Tourism Research (Washington, D.C.), 43*(1), 78–100. doi:10.1177/1096348017753521

Amable, B. (2000). Institutional complementarity and diversity of social systems of innovation and production. *Review of International Political Economy, 7*(4), 645–687. doi:10.1080/096922900750034572

Andersson, S., & Heywood, P. M. (2009). The politics of perception: Use and abuse of Transparency International's approach to measuring corruption. *Political Studies, 57*(4), 746–767. doi:10.1111/j.1467-9248.2008.00758.x

Andrades, L., & Dimanche, F. (2017). Destination competitiveness and tourism development in Russia: Issues and challenges. *Tourism Management, 62,* 360–376. doi:10.1016/j.tourman.2017.05.008

André, F. J., Cardenete, M. A., & Romero, C. (2009). A goal programming approach for a joint design of macroeconomic and environmental policies: A methodological proposal and an application to the Spanish economy. *Environmental Management, 43*(5), 888–898. doi:10.100700267-009-9276-x PMID:19224273

Anholt. (2007, November 6). *Countries Must Earn Better Images through Smart Policy.* An Interview, Council on Foreign Relations.

Anholt, S. (2006). Why brand? Some practical considerations for nation branding. *Place Branding and Public Diplomacy, 2*(2), 97–107. doi:10.1057/palgrave.pb.5990048

Anholt, S. (2008). From *nation branding* to *competitive identity* – The role of brand management as a component of national policy. In K. Dinnie (Ed.), *Nation branding: concepts, issues, practice* (pp. 22–23). Oxford, UK: Butterworth-Heinemann.

Anonymous. (2010). The New Great Game, Central Asia Special. *Spiegel online.* Retrieved on June 2, 2012, from: https://www.spiegel.de/international/world/spiegel-central-asia-special-the-new-great-game-a-722173.html

Anti-Corruption Digest. (2019, February 5). *Corruption in Eastern Europe & Central Asia is on the rise.* Retrieved on May 31, 2019, from: https://anticorruptiondigest.com/2019/02/05/corruption-in-eastern-europe-central-asia-is-on-the-rise/#axzz5pVaWYDXg

Apergis, N., & Payne, J. E. (2010). Natural gas consumption and economic growth : A panel investigation of 67 countries. *Applied Energy, 87*(8), 2759–2763. doi:10.1016/j.apenergy.2010.01.002

Ashyrov, G., & Masso, J. (2019, February 5). *Does corruption affect local and foreign owned companies differently? Evidence from the BEEPS survey.* The University of Tartu FEBA Working Papers. doi:10.2139srn.3329236

Aslan, D. H., & Bozyigit, D. (2014). Turkey-Kazakhstan relations: An overview of mutual relations since the collapse of the Soviet Union. *Kwartalnik Naukowy Uczelni Vistula, 4*(42), 133–145.

Asterious, D., Masatci, K., & Pilbeam, K. (2016). Exchange rate volatility and international trade: International evidence from the MINT countries. *Economic Modelling, 58,* 133–140. doi:10.1016/j.econmod.2016.05.006

Audretsch, D. B., Keilbach, M. C., & Lehmann, E. E. (2006). *Entrepreneurship and economic growth.* New York: Oxford University Press. doi:10.1093/acprof:oso/9780195183511.001.0001

Ayikoru, M., Tribe, J., & Airey, D. (2009). Reading tourism education: Neoliberalism unveiled. *Annals of Tourism Research, 36*(2), 191–221. doi:10.1016/j.annals.2008.11.001

Aziz, B., Khan, T., & Aziz, S. (2008) Impact of Higher Education on Economic Growth of Pakistan. *University Library of Munich, 6*(2), 15-19. Retrieved on September 9, 2017, from: https://mpra.ub.uni-muenchen.de/22912/

Azmi Hassali, M., Al-Tamimi, S. K., Dawood, O. T., Verma, A. K., & Saleem, F. (2015). Malaysian cosmetic market: Current and future prospects. *Pharmaceutical Regulatory Affairs, 4*(4), 4. doi:10.4172/2167-7689.1000155

Azuizkulov, D. (2013). Country of origin and brand loyalty on cosmetic products among Universiti Utara Malaysia students. *Atlantic Review of Economics, 2,* 3443. Retrieved on May 3, 2016, from: https://www.econstor.eu/handle/10419/146555

Badarudin, N. (2018, January 17). *Rise of local cosmetic brands.* Retrieved on June 19, 2018, from: https://www.nst.com.my/lifestyle/flair/2018/01/325908/rise-local-cosmetic-brands

Badawi, A., & AlQudah, A. (2019). The impact of anti-corruption policies on the profitability and growth of firms listed in the stock market: Application on Singapore with a panel data analysis. *Journal of Developing Areas, 53*(1), 179–204. doi:10.1353/jda.2019.0011

Compilation of References

Baek, J. (2013). Does the exchange rate matter to bilateral trade between Korea and Japan? Evidence from commodity trade data. *Economic Modelling, 30*(C), 856–862. doi:10.1016/j.econmod.2012.11.020

Baille, R. T., & Bollerslev, T. (1989). The Message in Daily Exchange Rates: A Conditional-Variance Tale. *Journal of Business & Economic Statistics, 7,* 297–305.

Baisakalova, A., & Garkavenko, V. (2015). Competitiveness of tourism industry in Kazakhstan. In K. Kantarci, M. Uysal, & V. Magnini (Eds.), *Tourism in Central Asia: Cultural Potential and Challenges* (pp. 15–40). Boca Raton, FL: CRC Press.

Bakar, A., Rahim, A., & Abdul-Talib, A. N. (2013). A case study of an internationalization process of a private higher education institution in Malaysia. *Gadjah Mada International Journal of Business, 15*(3), 211–230. doi:10.22146/gamaijb.5444

Bakhromov, N. (2011). The Exchange Rate Volatility and the Trade Balance: Case of Uzbekistan. *Journal of Applied Economics and Business Research, 1*(3), 149–161.

Balan, D. J., & Knack, S. (2012). The correlation between human capital and morality and its effect on economic performance: Theory and evidence. *Journal of Comparative Economics, 40*(3), 457–475. doi:10.1016/j.jce.2011.12.005

Barkathunnisha, A. B., Lee, D., & Price, A. (2017). Transcending towards a spirituality-based platform in tourism higher education: A contemplation of the pedagogical implications. *Journal of Hospitality, Leisure, Sport and Tourism Education, 21,* 174–184. doi:10.1016/j.jhlste.2016.11.003

Barro, J. R., & Sala-i-Martin, X. (2009). *Crecimiento Económico.* Barcelona: Reverté.

Beatty, S. E., & Kahle, L. R. (1988). Alternative hierarchies of the attitude-behavior relationship: The impact of brand commitment and habit. *Journal of the Academy of Marketing Science, 16*(2), 1–10. doi:10.1007/BF02723310

Becher, T. (1989). *Tribus y territorios académicos. La indagación intelectual y las culturas de las disciplinas.* Barcelona: Gedisa.

Becker, G. (1993). *Human Capital: A theoretical and empirical analysis with special references to education.* Chicago: The University of Chicago Press. doi:10.7208/chicago/9780226041223.001.0001

Benhabib, J., & Spiegel, M. M. (1994). The role of human capital in economic development evidence from aggregate cross-country data. *Journal of Monetary Economics, 34*(2), 143–173. doi:10.1016/0304-3932(94)90047-7

Bhuiyan, S. H., & Amagoh, F. (2011). Public sector reform in Kazakhstan: Issues and perspectives. *International Journal of Public Sector Management, 24*(3), 227–249. doi:10.1108/09513551111121356

Bildirici, M. E., & Bakirtas, T. (2014). The relationship among oil, natural gas and coal consumption and economic growth in BRICTS (Brazil, Russian, India, China, Turkey and South Africa) countries. *Energy, 65*, 134–144. doi:10.1016/j.energy.2013.12.006

Bildirici, M. E., & Kayıkçı, F. (2013). Effects of oil production on economic growth in Eurasian Countries: Panel ARDL Approach. *Energy, 49*, 156–161. doi:10.1016/j.energy.2012.10.047

Bills, D. B. (2003). Credentials, signals, and screens: Explaining the relationship between schooling and job assignment. *Review of Educational Research, 73*(4), 441–449. doi:10.3102/00346543073004441

Bills, D. B. (2016). Education and Development. In G. Hooks (Ed.), *The sociology of development handbook* (pp. 241–262). Oakland, CA: University of California Press.

Bollerslev, T. (1986). Generalized Autoregressive Conditional Heteroskedasticity. *Journal of Econometrics, 31*(3), 307–327. doi:10.1016/0304-4076(86)90063-1

Boyer, R. (2005). How and why capitalisms differ. *Economy and Society, 34*(4), 509–557. doi:10.1080/03085140500277070

BP. (2019). *Statistical Review of World Energy*. Author.

Breusch, T. S., & Pagan, A. R. (1980). The lagrange multipler test and its applications to model specification in econometrics. *The Review of Economic Studies, 47*(1), 239–253. doi:10.2307/2297111

Brida, J. G., Carrera, J. S. E., Risso, A. W., & Schubert, F. (2008). Tourism Impact in the Long-Run Mexican Economic Growth. *Anatolia: An International Journal of Tourism and Hospitality Research*, 265-278.

Brijesh, T. (2019). Ecotourism Education and Development in Kazakhstan. *Journal of Hospitality & Tourism Education, 31*(2), 119–124. doi:10.1080/10963758.2018.1485499

Budak, T. (2013, Fall). Orta Asya'da Küresel Jeoekonomik Rekabet ve Türkiye. *Bilge Strateji, 5*(9), 125–142.

Carayannis, E. G., Barth, T. D., & Campbell, D. F. J. (2012). The Quintuple Helix innovation model: Global warming as a challenge and driver for innovation. *Journal of Innovation and Entrepreneurship, 1*, 1–12. doi:10.1186/2192-5372-1-1

Carayannis, E. G., & Campbell, D. F. (2006). *Knowledge creation, diffusion, and use in innovation networks and knowledge clusters. A comparative systems approach across the United States, Europe, and Asia*. London: Praeger.

Carree, M. A., & Thurik, A. R. (2003). The impact of entrepreneurship on economic growth. In J. Acs & D. B. Audretsch (Eds.), *Handbook of entrepreneurship research* (pp. 437–471). Boston: Kluwer Academic.

Compilation of References

Carree, M. A., Van Stel, A., Thurik, R., & Wennekers, S. (2007). The relationship between economic development and business ownership revisited. *Entrepreneurship and Regional Development, 19*(3), 281–291. doi:10.1080/08985620701296318

Carrol, A. A., & Ahuvia, A. C. (2006). Some antecedents and outcomes of brand love. *Marketing Letters, 17*(2), 79–89. doi:10.100711002-006-4219-2

Cassin, H. (2019, March 7). *DOJ indicts [Gulnara] Karimova for taking $866 million in bribes.* Retrieved on May 31, 2019, from: http://www.fcpablog.com/blog/2019/3/7/doj-indicts-karimova-for-taking-866-million-in-bribes.html

Ceicdata. (2018a). *Related Indicators for Kazakhstan Tourism Revenue.* Retrieved on October 22, 2018, from: https://www.ceicdata.com/en/indicator/kazakhstan/tourism-revenue

Ceicdata. (2018b). *Kazakshtan Resident Departures.* Retrieved on October 22, 2018, from: https://www.ceicdata.com/en/kazakhstan/resident-departures/resident-departures

Central Intelligence Agency. (n.d.). *The world factbook.* Retrieved on June 13, 2019, from: https://www.cia.gov/library/publications/the-world-factbook/

Chadwick, C., & Piartrini, P. S. (2019). Product quality, convenience and brand loyalty: A case study of Silverqueen's adolescent consumers. *Proceedings of the 12th International Conference on Business and Management Research (ICBMR 2018).* Retrieved on March 30, 2019, from: https://www.atlantis-press.com/proceedings/icbmr-18/55914310

Chang, T., Gupta, R., Inglesi-Lotz, R., Masabala, L. S., Simo-Kengne, B. D., & Weideman, J. P. (2016). The causal relationship between natural gas consumption and economic growth : Evidence from the G7 countries. *Applied Economics Letters, 23*(1), 38–46. doi:10.1080/13504 851.2015.1047085

Chang, Y., Li, Y., Yan, J., & Kumar, V. (2019). Getting more likes: The impact of narrative person and brand image on customer–brand interactions. *Journal of the Academy of Marketing Science, 195*(47), 1–19. doi:10.100711747-019-00632-2

Charman, K. (2007). Kazakhstan: A state-led liberalized market economy? In D. S. Lane & M. R. Myant (Eds.), *Varieties of Capitalism in Post-Communist Countries* (pp. 165–182). London: Palgrave Macmillan. doi:10.1057/9780230627574_9

Charnes, A., & Cooper, W. W. (1952). Chance constraints and normal deviates. *Journal of the American Statistical Association, 57*(297), 134–148. doi:10.1080/01621459.1962.10482155

Charnes, A., & Cooper, W. W. (1959). Chance-constrained programming. *Management Science, 6*(1), 73–80. doi:10.1287/mnsc.6.1.73

Charnes, A., & Cooper, W. W. (1961). *Management models and industrial applications of linear programming.* New York: Wiley.

Charnes, A., Cooper, W. W., & Ferguson, R. (1955). Optimal estimation of executive compensation by linear programming. *Management Science, 1*(2), 138–151. doi:10.1287/mnsc.1.2.138

Charron, N. (2016). Do corruption measures have a perception problem? Assessing the relationship between experiences and perceptions of corruption among citizens and experts. *European Political Science Review, 8*(1), 147–171. doi:10.1017/S1755773914000447

Chayes, S. (2016). *The structure of corruption in Kyrgyzstan.* Retrieved on May 31, 2019, from: https://carnegieendowment.org/files/9_Kyrgyzstan_Full_Web1.pdf

Che Wel, C. A., Alam, S. H., & Mohd Nor, S. (2011). Factors affecting brand loyalty: An empirical study in Malaysia. *Australian Journal of Basic and Applied Sciences, 5*(12), 777–783.

Chen, X., & Fazilov, F. (2018). Re-centering Central Asia: China's "New Great game" in the old Eurasian Heartland. *Palgrave Communications, 4*(1), 71. doi:10.105741599-018-0125-5

Chu J., Chan S., Nadarajah S. and Osterrieder J. (2017). GARCH Modelling of Cryptocurrencies. *Journal of Risk and Financial Management.* doi:10.3390/jrfm10040017

Chung, H., & Lee, E. (2019). Impact of category-specific demand environment on store brand quality positioning: Empirical evidence. Paper presented at the International Conference on Advances in National Brand and Private Label Marketing 2019. *Springer Proceedings in Business and Economics.* Springer. Retrieved on June 1, 2019, from: https://link.springer.com/chapter/10.1007/978-3-030-18911-2_2

Clancy, M. (2001). *Exporting Paradise Tourism and Development. Evidence from México.* London: Pergamon.

Colapinto, C. (2007). A way to foster innovation: A venture capital district from Silicon Valley and route 128 to Waterloo Region. *International Review of Economics, 54*(3), 319–343. doi:10.100712232-007-0018-1

Colapinto, C., & Porlezza, C. (2012). Innovation in creative industries: From the quadruple-helix model to the systems theory. *Journal of the Knowledge Economy, 3*(4), 343–353. doi:10.100713132-011-0051-x

Collins, O., & Gbadamosi, A. (2011). Re-branding Africa. *Marketing Intelligence & Planning, 29*(3), 284–304. doi:10.1108/02634501111129257

Collinson, S. (2006). Joke on Borat as Kazakhstan 'makes benefit' tourism. *Mail & Guardian Online.* Retrieved on September 9, 2017, from: https://www.mg.co.za/article/2006-11-16-joke-on-borat-as-kazakhstan-makes-benefit-tourism

Collins, R. (1979). *La sociedad credencialista. Sociología histórica de la educación y la estratificación.* Madrid: Akal.

Consultancy.asia. (2019, March 19). *BCG outlines $170 billion FDI potential for Central Asia over next decade.* Retrieved on June 7, 2019, from: https://www.consultancy.asia/news/2078/bcg-outlines-170-billion-fdi-potential-for-central-asia-over-next-decade

Compilation of References

Contreras, D. L. M. (2007). Ejes transversales en el currículo universitario: Experiencia en la carrera de derecho. *Ciências & Cognição*, *10*, 132–146. Retrieved from http://pepsic.bvsalud.org/scielo.php?script=sci_arttext&pid=S1806-58212007000100013

Countrymeters.info. (2015). *Malaysia population*. Retrieved from https://countrymeters.info/en/Malaysia

d'Agostino, G., & Pieroni, L. (2019). Modelling corruption perceptions: Evidence from Eastern Europe and Central Asian countries. *Social Indicators Research*, *142*(1), 311–341. doi:10.100711205-018-1886-3

Das, A., McFarlane, A. A., & Chowdhury, M. (2013). The dynamics of natural gas consumption and GDP in Bangladesh. *Renewable & Sustainable Energy Reviews*, *22*, 269–274. doi:10.1016/j.rser.2013.01.053

Das, J., & Dirienzo, C. E. (2010). Tourism competitiveness and corruption: A cross-country analysis. *Tourism Economics*, *16*(3), 477–492. doi:10.5367/000000010792278392

Davalos Gamboa, M. (2005). Implicaciones epistemológicas del curriculum transdisciplinario. *Gaceta Médica Boliviana*, *28*(2), 81–92. Retrieved from http://www.scielo.org.bo/scielo.php?script=sci_arttext&pid=S1012-29662005000200015&lng=es&tlng=es

Department of Statistics Malaysia. (2018, July 31). *Current Population Estimates, Malaysia, 2017-2018*. Retrieved on January 7, 2019, from: https://www.dosm.gov.my/v1/index.php?r=column/cthemeByCat&cat=155&bul_id=c1pqTnFjb29HSnNYNUpiTmNWZHArdz09&menu_id=L0pheU43NWJwRWVSZklWdzQ4TlhUUT09

Di Liberto, A. (2013). High skills, high growth: Is tourism an exception? *The Journal of International Trade & Economic Development*, *22*(5), 749–785. doi:10.1080/09638199.2011.603054

Dias, A. D., Costa, R. A., Pita, M., & Costa, C. (2017). Tourism Education: What about entrepreneurial skills? *Journal of Hospitality and Tourism Management*, *30*, 65–72. doi:10.1016/j.jhtm.2017.01.002

Ding, Z., Engle, R. F., & Granger, C. W. J. (1993). A long memory property of stock market return and a new model. *Journal of Empirical Finance*, *1*(1), 83–106. doi:10.1016/0927-5398(93)90006-D

Dinnie, K. (2010). *Nation Branding: Concepts, Issues, Practice*. Routledge. Retrieved on October 7, 2013, from: https://search.proquest.com/abicomplete/legacydocview/EBC/535091?accountid=167104

Dinnie, K. (2007). *Nation Branding: Concepts, Issues, Practice*. Oxford, UK: Butterworth Heinemann.

Dinnie, K., Melewar, T. C., Seidenfuss, K.-U., & Musa, G. (2010). Nation branding and integrated marketing communication: An ASEAN perspective. *International Marketing Review*, *27*(4), 388–403. doi:10.1108/02651331011058572

183

Dixit, A. K. (2016). Corruption: Supply-side and demand-side solutions. In S. M. Dev & P. G. Babu (Eds.), *Development in India: Micro and macro perspectives* (pp. 57–68). New Delhi: Springer India. doi:10.1007/978-81-322-2541-6_4

Domeisen, N. (2003). Is there a case for national branding? *International Trade Forum, 14*(1). Retrieved from https://prx-herzing.lirn.net/login?url=https://search.proquest.com/docview/231 424853?accountid=167104

Doyle, P. (2001). Shareholder-value-based brand strategies. *Brand Management, 9*(1), 20–30. doi:10.1057/palgrave.bm.2540049

Duerrenberger, N., & Warning, S. (2018). Corruption and education in developing countries: The role of public vs. private funding of higher education. *International Journal of Educational Development, 62*, 217–225. doi:10.1016/j.ijedudev.2018.05.002

Echtner, C. M. (1995). Entrepreneurial Training in Developing Countries. *Annals of Tourism Research, 22*(1), 119–134. doi:10.1016/0160-7383(94)00065-Z

El Bahnasawy, N. G., & Revier, C. F. (2012). The determinants of corruption: Cross-country-panel-data analysis. *The Developing Economies, 50*(4), 311–333. doi:10.1111/j.1746-1049.2012.00177.x

Engle, R. F. (1982). Autoregressive conditional heteroscedasticity with estimates of the variance of United Kingdom inflation. *Econometrica, 50*(4), 987–1007. doi:10.2307/1912773

Ersungur, M., Kiziltan, A., & Karabulut, K. (2007). Türkiye İle Diğer Türk Cumhuriyetlerinin Ekonomik İlişkilerininAnalizi. Atatürk Üniversitesi Türkiyat Araştırmaları Enstitüsü Dergisi, 14(35).

Etkzowitz, H., Webster, A., Gebhardt, C., & Cantisano Terra, B. R. (2000). The future of the university and the university of the future: Evolution of ivory tower to entrepreneurial paradigm. *Research Policy, 29*(2), 313–331. doi:10.1016/S0048-7333(99)00069-4

Etzkowitz, H., & Leydesdorff, L. (2000). The Dynamics of Innovation: From National Systems and 'Mode 2' to a Triple Helix of University-Industry-Government Relations. *Research Policy, 29*(2), 109–123. doi:10.1016/S0048-7333(99)00055-4

Etzkowitz, H., & Zhou, C. (2006). Triple Helix twins: Innovation and sustainability. *Science & Public Policy, 33*(1), 77–83.

Euromonitor International. (2015). *Skin care in Malaysia*. Retrieved on June 13, 2019, from: https://www.euromonitor.com/skin-care-in-malaysia/report

Euromonitor International. (2019, Jun). *Beauty and personal care in Malaysia*. Retrieved on June 13, 2019, from: https://www.euromonitor.com/beauty-and-personal-care-in-malaysia/report

Eze, U. C., Tan, C. B., & Yeo, L. Y. (2012). Purchasing cosmetic products: A preliminary perspective of Gen-Y. *Contemporary Management Research, 8*(1), 51–60. doi:10.7903/cmr.10149

Compilation of References

Fahimi, A., Saint, A. S., Seraj, M., & Akadiri, A. C. (2018). Testing the role of tourism and human capital development in economic growth. A panel causality study of micro states. *Tourism Management Perspectives*, *28*, 62–70. doi:10.1016/j.tmp.2018.08.004

Fainshmidt, S., Judge, W. Q., Aguilera, R. V., & Smith, A. (2018). Varieties of institutional systems: A contextual taxonomy of understudied countries. *Journal of World Business*, *53*(3), 307–322. doi:10.1016/j.jwb.2016.05.003

Fan, Y. (2010). Branding the nation: Towards a better understanding. *Place Branding and Public Diplomacy*, *6*(2), 97–103. doi:10.1057/pb.2010.16

Ferrer, A. (2010). Raul Prebisch y el dilemma del desarrollo en el mundo global. *Revista de CEPAL*, (101), 7-15.

Fetscherin, M. (2010). The determinants and measurement of a country brand: The country brand strength index. *International Marketing Review*, *27*(4), 466–479. doi:10.1108/02651331011058617

Folarin, O., Oladipupo, E., Ajogbeje, K., & Adeniyi, O. (2017). Does tourism development contribute to human capital development in Africa? *Turizam: medunarodni znanstveno-stručni časopis*, *65*(3), 314-329.

Formica, S. (1996). European hospitality and tourism education: Differences with the American model and future trends. *Journal of Hospitality Management*, *15*(4), 317–323. doi:10.1016/S0278-4319(96)00039-4

Foucault, M. (1998). El orden del discurso. Traducción de Alberto González Trovan. Argentina: Fábula Tusquets Editores.

Franklin, A., & Crang, M. (2001). *The trouble with tourism and travel theory?* Sage Publications. Retrieved on April 11, 2017, from: https://www.nyu.edu/classes/bkg/tourist/a019893.pdf

Freedom House. (2018). *Turkmenistan*. Retrieved on May 31, 2019, from: https://freedomhouse.org/report/nations-transit/2018/turkmenistan

Freedom House. (2019). *Freedom in the World 2019*. Retrieved on June 4, 2019, from: https://freedomhouse.org/report/freedom-world/freedom-world-2019

Fullerton, J., Kendrick, A., & Wallis, C. (2008). Brand Borat? Americans' reaction to a Kazakhstani place branding campaign. *Place Branding and Public Diplomacy*, *4*(2), 159–168. doi:10.1057/pb.2008.6

Furstenberg, S. (2018). State responses to reputational concerns: The case of the Extractive Industries Transparency Initiative in Kazakhstan. *Central Asian Survey*, *37*(2), 286–304. doi:10.1080/02634937.2018.1428789

Furuoka, F. (2016). Natural gas consumption and economic development in China and Japan : An empirical examination of the Asian context. *Renewable & Sustainable Energy Reviews*, *56*, 100–115. doi:10.1016/j.rser.2015.11.038

Gephart, M. (2015). Contested meanings in the anti-corruption discourse: International and local narratives in the case of Paraguay. *Critical Policy Studies*, *9*(2), 119–138. doi:10.1080/19 460171.2014.951668

Goh, E., Muskat, B., & Tan, A. H. T. (2017). The nexus between sustainable practices in hotels and future Gen Y hospitality students' career path decisions. *Journal of Teaching in Travel & Tourism*, *17*(4), 237–253. doi:10.1080/15313220.2017.1362971

Gordon, M. E., McKeage, K., & Fox, M. A. (1998). Relationship marketing effectiveness: The role of involvement. *Psychology and Marketing*, *15*(5), 443–459. doi:10.1002/(SICI)1520-6793(199808)15:5<443::AID-MAR3>3.0.CO;2-7

Government of Kazakhstan. (2016). *About Joint Business support and development Program "Business Roadmap - 2020"*. Retrieved on June 2, 2017, from: http://egov.kz/cms/en/articles/road_business_map

Gründler, K., & Potrafke, N. (2019). Corruption and economic growth: New empirical evidence. *European Journal of Political Economy*. doi:10.1016/j.ejpoleco.2019.08.001

Gudjonsson, H. (2005). Nation branding. *Place Branding*, *1*(3), 283–298. doi:10.1057/palgrave. pb.5990029

Hair, J. F. (2015). *Essentials of business research methods*. New York: ME Sharpe.

Hale, H. E. (2010). Eurasian polities as hybrid regimes: The case of Putin's Russia. *Journal of Eurasian Studies*, *1*(1), 33–41. doi:10.1016/j.euras.2009.11.001

Hall, P. A., & Soskice, D. (2001). *An introduction to varieties of capitalism*. Academic Press.

Hall, P. A., & Soskice, D. (Eds.). (2001). *Varieties of capitalism: The institutional foundations of comparative advantage*. Oxford, UK: Oxford University Press. doi:10.1093/0199247757.001.0001

Hanson, S., Jiang, L., & Dahl, D. (2019). Enhancing consumer engagement in an online brand community via user reputation signals: A multi-method analysis. *Journal of the Academy of Marketing Science*, *47*(2), 349–367. doi:10.100711747-018-0617-2

Harrison-Walker, L. J. (2011). Strategic positioning of nation as brands. *Journal of International Business Research*, *10*(2), 135–147.

Haryanto, B., Febrianto, A., & Cahyono, E. (2019). Lifestyle and consumer preferences in choosing local or foreign brands: A study of consumer behavior in Surakarta Indonesia. *Jurnal Manajemen dan Kewirausahaan*, *21*(1), 74-88.

Hassan, H., Rahman, M. S., & Sade, A. B. (2015). Shopping day and time preferences of malaysian hypermarket consumers. *Australian Journal of Business and Economic Studies*, *1*(1), 61–68.

Heidari, H., Katircioglu, S. T., & Saeidpour, L. (2013). Natural gas consumption and economic growth : Are we ready to natural gas price liberalization in Iran? *Energy Policy*, *63*, 638–645. doi:10.1016/j.enpol.2013.09.001

Compilation of References

Henriques, C. O., & Antunes, C. H. (2012). Interactions of economic growth, energy consumption and the environment in the context of the crisis - A study with uncertain data. *Energy, 48*(1), 415–422. doi:10.1016/j.energy.2012.04.009

Herstein, R. (2012). Thin line between country, city, and region branding. *Journal of Vacation Marketing, 18*(2), 147–155. doi:10.1177/1356766711435976

Holmes, L. (2018). A fish rots from the head: corruption scandals in post-Communist Russia. In O. E. Hawthorne & S. Magu (Eds.), *Corruption scandals and their global impacts* (pp. 57–76). London: Routledge. doi:10.4324/9781315142722-4

Holt, D. B. (2006). Toward a sociology of branding. *Journal of Consumer Culture, 6*(3), 299–302. doi:10.1177/1469540506068680

Höpner, M. (2005). What connects industrial relations and corporate governance? Explaining institutional complementarity. *Socio-economic Review, 3*(2), 331–358. doi:10.1093/SER/mwi014

Hornberger, J. (2018). A ritual of corruption: How young middle-class South Africans get their driver's licenses. *Current Anthropology, 59*(S18), S138–S148. doi:10.1086/696099

Hsu, C. H., Xiao, H., & Chen, N. (2017). Hospitality and tourism education research from 2005 to 2014: "Is the past a prologue to the future? *International Journal of Contemporary Hospitality Management, 29*(1), 141–160. doi:10.1108/IJCHM-09-2015-0450

Huang, C.-J. (2016). Is corruption bad for economic growth? Evidence from Asia-Pacific countries. *The North American Journal of Economics and Finance, 35*, 247–256. doi:10.1016/j.najef.2015.10.013

Hurn, B. J. (2016). The role of cultural diplomacy in nation branding. *Industrial and Commercial Training, 48*(2), 80–85. doi:10.1108/ICT-06-2015-0043

Hyde-Price, A. (2005). 'Normative' power Europe: A realist critique. *Journal of European Public Policy, 13*(2), 217–234. doi:10.1080/13501760500451634

Idowu, I. A., Ja'afar, M. F. Z., Shari, Z., & Dahlan, N. D. (2018). Indoor Environmental Quality performance of mixed-mode ventilated shopping malls in. *International Journal Of Built Environment And Sustainability, 5*(3), 187–200. doi:10.11113/ijbes.v5.n3.289

IEA, 2016

IMF. (2014). *Republic of Kazakhstan, Selected Issues.* International Monetary Fund. Retrieved on September 2, 2017, from: https://www.imf.org/external/pubs/ft/scr/2014/cr14243.pdf

Integrity Business Anti-Corruption Portal, G. A. N. (2016a, May). *Turkmenistan Corruption Report.* Retrieved on May 31, 2019, from: https://www.business-anti-corruption.com/country-profiles/turkmenistan/

Integrity Business Anti-Corruption Portal, G. A. N. (2016b, July). *Kazakhstan Corruption Report*. Retrieved on May 31, 2019, from: https://www.business-anti-corruption.com/country-profiles/kazakhstan/

Integrity Business Anti-Corruption Portal, G. A. N. (2016c, July). *Kyrgyzstan Corruption Report*. Retrieved on May 31, 2019, from: https://www.business-anti-corruption.com/country-profiles/kyrgyzstan/

Integrity Business Anti-Corruption Portal, G. A. N. (2016d, August). *Tajikistan Corruption Report*. Retrieved on May 31, 2019, from: https://www.business-anti-corruption.com/country-profiles/tajikistan/

Integrity Business Anti-Corruption Portal, G. A. N. (2017, June). *Uzbekistan Corruption Report*. Retrieved on May 31, 2019, from: https://www.business-anti-corruption.com/country-profiles/uzbekistan/

International Monetary Fund (IMF). (2014). The Caucasus and Central Asia: Transitioning to Emerging Markets. Washington, DC: IMF.

International Monetary Fund (IMF). (2018). Opening Up in the Caucasus and Central Asia: Policy Frameworks to Support Regional and Global Integration. IMF Departmental Paper, 18/07. Washington, DC: IMF.

International Monetary Fund (IMF). (2019). *Regional Economic Outlook Update Caucasus and Central Asia*. Washington, DC: IMF.

Inui, Y., Wheeler, D., & Lankford, S. (2010). Rethinking Tourism Education: What Should Schools Teach? *Journal of Hospitality, Leisure, Sport and Tourism Education*, *5*(2), 25–32. doi:10.3794/johlste.52.122

Işik, C. (2010). Natural gas consumption and economic growth in Turkey : A bound test approach. *Energy Syst*, *1*(4), 441–456. doi:10.100712667-010-0018-1

Jamal, A., & Goode, M. M. (2001). Consumers and brands: A study of the impact of self-image congruence on brand preference and satisfaction. *Marketing Intelligence & Planning*, *19*(7), 482–492. doi:10.1108/02634500110408286

Jan, M. T., Haque, A., Abdullah, K., Anis, Z., & Alam, F. E. (2019). Elements of advertisement and their impact on buying behaviour: A study of skincare products. *Management Science Letters*, *9*, 1519–1528. doi:10.5267/j.msl.2019.5.033

Jansen, S. C. (2008). Designer nations: Neo-liberal nation branding — Brand Estonia. *Social Identities*, *14*(1), 121–142. doi:10.1080/13504630701848721

Jayaraman, R., Colapinto, C., La Torre, D., & Malik, T. (2017a). A Weighted Goal Programming model for planning sustainable development applied to Gulf Cooperation Council Countries. *Applied Energy*, *185*(Part 2, 1), 1931-1939.

Compilation of References

Jayaraman, R., Colapinto, C., La Torre, D., & Malik, T. (2015). Multi-criteria model for sustainable development using goal programming applied to the United Arab Emirates. *Energy Policy, 87,* 447–454. doi:10.1016/j.enpol.2015.09.027

Jayaraman, R., Colapinto, C., Liuzzi, D., & La Torre, D. (2017c). Planning sustainable development through a scenario-based stochastic goal programming model. *Operations Research, 17*(3), 789–805. doi:10.100712351-016-0239-8

Jayaraman, R., Liuzzi, D., Colapinto, C., & Malik, T. (2017b). A fuzzy goal programming model to analyse energy, environmental and sustainability goals of the United Arab Emirates. *Annals of Operations Research, 251*(1–2), 255–270. doi:10.100710479-015-1825-5

Johansen, S. (1991). Estimation and hypothesis testing of cointegration vectors in Gaussian vector autoregressive models. *Econometrica, 59*(6), 1551–1580. doi:10.2307/2938278

Johensen, S. (1988). Statistical Analysis of Cointegration Vectors. *Journal of Economic Dynamics & Control, 12*(2-3), 231–254. doi:10.1016/0165-1889(88)90041-3

Junaid, M., Hou, F., Hussain, K., & Kirmani, A. A. (2019). Brand love: The emotional bridge between experience and engagement, generation-M perspective. *Journal of Product and Brand Management, 28*(2), 200–215. doi:10.1108/JPBM-04-2018-1852

Junisbai, B., & Junisbai, A. (2019). Regime type versus patronal politics: A comparison of "ardent democrats" in Kazakhstan and Kyrgyzstan. *Post-Soviet Affairs, 35*(3), 240–257. doi:10.1080/1060586X.2019.1568144

Kalyuzhnova, Y., & Belitski, M. (2019). The impact of corruption and local content policy in on firm performance: Evidence from Kazakhstan. *Resources Policy, 61,* 67–76. doi:10.1016/j.resourpol.2019.01.016

Kamaruddin, A. (2002). Ethnocentrism orientation and choice decisions of Malaysian consumers: The effects of socio-cultural and demographic factors. *Asia Pacific Management Review, 7*(4), 555–574.

Kaneva, N. (2011). Nation branding: Toward an agenda of critical research. *International Journal of Communication, 5,* 117–141.

Kar, M., Nazlıoğlu, Ş., & Ağır, H. (2011). Financial development and economic growth nexus in the MENA countries : Bootstrap panel granger causality analysis. *Economic Modelling, 28*(1-2), 685–693. doi:10.1016/j.econmod.2010.05.015

Kassab, H. S., & Rosen, J. D. (2019). Central Asia and Middle East. In *Corruption, institutions, and fragile states* (pp. 65–84). Cham, Switzerland: Palgrave Macmillan. doi:10.1007/978-3-030-04312-4_4

Kaufmann, D., & Vicente, P. C. (2011). Legal corruption. *Economics and Politics, 23*(2), 195–219. doi:10.1111/j.1468-0343.2010.00377.x

Kendzior, S. (2013). The Curse of Stability in Central Asia. *Foreign Policy*. Retrieved on March 16, 2017, from: https://foreignpolicy.com/2013/02/19/the-curse-of-stability-in-central-asia/

Kendzior, S. (2013, February 19). *The curse of stability in Central Asia: The autocrats of Central Asia like to tout the virtues of stability. But they're really making excuses for decay.* Retrieved on June 3, 2019, from: https://foreignpolicy.com/2013/02/19/the-curse-of-stability-in-central-asia/

Kirişci, K., & Le Corre, P. (2018, January 2). *The new geopolitics of Central Asia: China vies for influence in Russia's backyard: What will it mean for Kazakhstan?* Retrieved on May 14, 2019, from: https://www.brookings.edu/blog/order-from-chaos/2018/01/02/the-new-geopolitics-of-central-asia-china-vies-for-influence-in-russias-backyard/

Klomp, J., & de Haan, J. (2013). Political regime and human capital: A cross-country analysis. *Social Indicators Research*, *111*(1), 45–73. doi:10.100711205-011-9983-6 PMID:23378681

Knack, S. (2007). Measuring corruption: A critique of indicators in Eastern Europe and Central Asia. *Journal of Public Policy*, *27*(3), 255–291. doi:10.1017/S0143814X07000748

Kobenbaev, M., & Eicher, S. (2009). Exploring Corruption in the Petroleum Sector. In S. Eicher (Ed.), Corruption in International Business (pp.81–90). Cornwell, UK: Gower Publishing.

Koç, S., & Saidmurodov, S. (2018). Orta Asya Ülkelerinde elektrik enerjisi, doğrudan yabancı yatırımı ve ekonomik büyüme ilişkisi. *Ege Akademik Bakış, 18*(2), 321–328.

Koellinger, P. D., & Roy Thurik, A. (2012). Entrepreneurship and the business cycle. *The Review of Economics and Statistics, 94*(4), 1143–1156. doi:10.1162/REST_a_00224

Ko, K., & Samajdar, A. (2010). Evaluation of international corruption indexes: Should we believe them or not? *The Social Science Journal, 47*(3), 508–540. doi:10.1016/j.soscij.2010.03.001

Kónya, L. (2006). Exports and growth: Granger causality analysis on OECD countries with a panel data approach. *Economic Modelling, 23*(6), 978–992. doi:10.1016/j.econmod.2006.04.008

Kotchegura, A. (2018). Preventing corruption risk in legislation: Evidence from Russia, Moldova, and Kazakhstan. *International Journal of Public Administration, 41*(5-6), 377–387. doi:10.108 0/01900692.2018.1426011

Kotler, P., & Gertner, D. (2002). Country as brand, product, and beyond: A place marketing and brand management perspective. *Journal of Brand Management, 9*(4/5), 249–261. doi:10.1057/palgrave.bm.2540076

Kristensen, P. H., & Lilja, K. (Eds.). (2011). *Nordic capitalisms and globalization: New forms of economic organization and welfare institutions.* Oxford, UK: Oxford University Press. doi:10.1093/acprof:oso/9780199594535.001.0001

Kristensen, P. H., & Morgan, G. (2012). Theoretical contexts and conceptual frames for the study of twenty-first century capitalisms. In G. Morgan & R. Whitley (Eds.), *Capitalisms and Capitalism in the Twenty-first Century* (pp. 11–43). Oxford, UK: Oxford University Press. doi:10.1093/ac prof:oso/9780199694761.003.0002

Compilation of References

Kudaibergenova, D. T., & Shin, B. (2018). Authors and authoritarianism in Central Asia: Failed agency and nationalising authoritarianism in Uzbekistan and Kazakhstan. *Asian Studies Review*, *42*(2), 304–322. doi:10.1080/10357823.2018.1447549

Kuhn Thomas, S. (1962). *La estructura de las revoluciones científicas*. D. F., México: Fondo de Cultura Económica.

Kumar, A., Kim, Y. K., & Pelton, L. (2009). Indian consumers' purchase behavior toward US versus local brands. *International Journal of Retail & Distribution Management*, *376*(6), 510–526. doi:10.1108/09590550910956241

Kumenov, A. (2019). Kazakhstan MP suggests changing country's name. *Eurasianet.* Retrieved on October 7, 2019, from: https://eurasianet.org/kazakhstan-mp-suggests-changing-countrys-name

Kum, H., Ocal, O., & Aslan, A. (2012). The relationship among natural gas energy consumption, capital and economic growth : Bootstrap-corrected causality tests from G-7 countries. *Renewable & Sustainable Energy Reviews*, *16*(5), 2361–2365. doi:10.1016/j.rser.2012.01.041

Lau, M. M., Chang, M. S., Moon, K., & Liu, W. S. (2006). The brand loyalty of sportswear in Hong Kong. *Journal of Textile and Apparel. Technology and Management*, 5, 1–13.

Le, A. H., McDonald, C. V., & Klieve, H. (2018). Hospitality higher education in Vietnam: Voices from stakeholders. *Tourism Management Perspectives*, *27*, 68–82. doi:10.1016/j.tmp.2018.05.002

Lee, J., & Nguyen, M. J. (2017). Product attributes and preference for foreign brands among Vietnamese consumers. *Journal of Retailing and Consumer Services*, *35*, 76–83. doi:10.1016/j.jretconser.2016.12.001

Lee, M. Y., Kim, Y. K., Pelton, L., Knight, D., & Forney, J. (2008). Factors affecting Mexican college students' purchase intention toward a US apparel brand. *Journal of Fashion Marketing and Management*, *12*(3), 294–307. doi:10.1108/13612020810889263

Lee, Y., Back, K., & Kim, J. (2009). Family restaurant brand personality and its impact on customer's emotion, satisfaction and brand loyalty. *Journal of Hospitality & Tourism Research (Washington, D.C.)*, *33*(3), 305–328. doi:10.1177/1096348009338511

Li, C. C., Mahmood, R., Abdullah, H., & Chuan, O. S. (2013). Economic growth, tourism, and selected macroeconomic variables: A triangular causal relationship in Malaysia. *Margin - the Journal of Applied Economic Research*, *7*(2), 185–206. doi:10.1177/0973801013483503

Lim, H., & Yoo, S. (2012). Natural gas consumption and economic growth in Korea : A causality analysis. *Energy Sources. Part B, Economics, Planning, and Policy*, *7*(2), 169–176. doi:10.1080/15567240902882864

Louzek, M. (2011). The battle of methods in economics: The classical Methodenstreit-Menger vs. Schmoller. *American Journal of Economics and Sociology*, *70*(2), 439–463. doi:10.1111/j.1536-7150.2011.00780.x

Mamanova, K. M., & Sadyrova, M. S. (2013). Reality and Perspectives of Tourism Development in Kazakhstan: Sociological Analysis. *World Academy of Science, Engineering and Technology, 75*, 244–251.

Mamanova, K. M., Sadyrova, M. S., & Tufekcioglu, H. (2013). Social aspects of tourism formation and development in Kazakhstan and in Turkey: Comparative analysis. *Middle East Journal of Scientific Research, 15*(11), 1496–1504.

Mangan, D. (2006) Kazakhstan tourism's Borat boom. *New York Post.* Retrieved on August 20, 2008, from: https://www.nypost.com/seven/12042006/news/nationalnews/kazakh_tourisms_borat_boom_nationalnews_dan_mangan.htm

Marantidou, V., & Cossa, R. A. (2014, October 1). *China and Russia's Great Game in Central Asia: "The real problem is that wherever Russia turns it encounters China and vice-versa."* Retrieved on May 14, 2019, from: https://nationalinterest.org/blog/the-buzz/china-russias-great-game-central-asia-11385

Marat, E. (2009). Nation Branding in Central Asia: A New Campaign to Present Ideas about the State and the Nation. *Europe-Asia Studies, 61*(7), 1123–1136. doi:10.1080/09668130903068657

Mathew, V., & Thomas, S. (2019). Direct and indirect effect of brand experience on true brand loyalty: Role of involvement. *Asia Pacific Journal of Marketing and Logistics, 30*(3), 725–748. doi:10.1108/APJML-08-2017-0189

Matyabukova, D. (2018). Who Is "Tashkent City" For? Nation-Branding and Public Dialogue in Uzbekistan. *Voices on Central Asia.* Retrieved on July 9, 2019, from: https://voicesoncentralasia.org/who-is-tashkent-city-for-nation-branding-and-public-dialogue-in-uzbekistan/

McMann, K. M. (2014). *Corruption as a last resort: Adapting to the market in Central Asia.* Ithaca, NY: Cornell University Press.

Meadows, D. H., Meadows, D. L., Randers, J., & Behrens, W. W. III. (1972). *The Limits to Growth. A Report for the Club of Rome's Project on the Predicament of Mankind.* New York: Universe Books.

Menidjel, C., Benhabib, A., & Bilgihan, A. (2017). Examining the moderating role of personality traits in the relationship between brand trust and brand loyalty. *Journal of Product and Brand Management, 26*(6), 631–649. doi:10.1108/JPBM-05-2016-1163

Menyah, K., Nazlioglu, S., & Wolde-Rufael, Y. (2014). Financial development, trade openness and economic growth in African countries : New insights from a panel causality approach. *Economic Modelling, 37*, 386–394. doi:10.1016/j.econmod.2013.11.044

Minbaeva, D. B., Hutchings, K., & Thomson, S. B. (2007). Hybrid human resource management in post-Soviet Kazakhstan. *European Journal of International Management, 1*(4), 350–371. doi:10.1504/EJIM.2007.015656

Compilation of References

Ministry of Culture and Sports of the Republic of Kazakhstan. (2018). *Tourism in the Rebuplic of Kazakhstan, Report Presentation*. Retrieved on October 1, 2018, from: https://www.carecprogram.org/uploads/2b.-Presentation-KAZ.pdf

Morck, R., & Steier, L. (2005). The global history of corporate governance: An introduction. In R. Morck (Ed.), *A history of corporate governance around the world: Family business groups to professional managers* (pp. 1–64). Chicago: University of Chicago Press. doi:10.7208/chicago/9780226536835.001.0001

Morgan, G., & Whitley, R. (2012). *Capitalisms and Capitalism in the Twenty-first Century.* Oxford, UK: Oxford University Press. doi:10.1093/acprof:oso/9780199694761.001.0001

Morin, E. (1994). *Introducción al pensamiento complejo.* Barcelona: Gedisa.

Mouangue, R. L. (2019). Getting over discomfort in luxury brand stores: How pop-up stores affect perceptions of luxury, embarrassment, and store evaluations. *Journal of Retailing and Consumer Services, 49*, 77–85. doi:10.1016/j.jretconser.2019.03.005

Mukhambetov, T. I., Janguttinav, G. O., Esaidar, U. S., Myrzakulova, G. R., & Imanbekova, B. T. (2014). The life cycle of sustainable eco-tourism: A Kazakhstan case study. *WIT Transactions on Ecology and the Environment, 187*, 39–49. doi:10.2495/ST140041

Nazarbayev, N. (2012). *Strategy Kazakhstan-2050: New political course of the established state.* Retrieved on November 11, 2014, from: https://strategy2050.kz/en/multilanguage/

Nazlioglu, S., Lebe, F., & Kayhan, S. (2011). Nuclear energy consumption and economic growth in OECD countries: Cross-sectionally dependent heterogeneous panel causality analysis. *Energy Policy, 39*(10), 6615–6621. doi:10.1016/j.enpol.2011.08.007

Nelson, D. B. (1990). Stationarity and persistence in the GARCH(1,1) models. *Econometric Theory, 6*(3), 318–334. doi:10.1017/S0266466600005296

Nelson, D. B. (1991). Conditional heteroskedasticity in asset returns: A new approach. *Econometrica, 59*(2), 347–370. doi:10.2307/2938260

Nelson, M., & McLeod, L. (2005). Adolescent brand consciousness and product placements: Awareness, liking and perceived effects on self and others. *International Journal of Consumer Studies, 29*(6), 515–528. doi:10.1111/j.1470-6431.2005.00429.x

Nguyen, M. N., & Kuan, T. S. (2011). Antecedents and consequences of status consumption among urban Vietnamese consumers. *Organizations and Markets in Emerging Economies, 2*(1), 75–98. doi:10.15388/omee.2011.2.1.14291

Nichol, J. (2014, March 21). *Central Asia: Regional developments and implications for U.S. interests.* Congressional Research Service. Retrieved on May 31, 2019, from: https://fas.org/sgp/crs/row/RL33458.pdf

Nordhaus, W. (1991). To Slow or Not to Slow: The Economics of the Greenhouse Effect. *Economic Journal (London), 101*(407), 920–937. doi:10.2307/2233864

Nordhaus, W. (2008). *A Question of Balance: Weighing the Options on Global Warming Policies.* New Haven, CT: Yale University Press.

Nur-tegin, K., & Jakee, K. (2019). Does corruption grease or sand the wheels of development? New results based on disaggregated data. *Quarterly Review of Economics and Finance.* doi:10.1016/j.qref.2019.02.001

Nur-tegin, K., & Czap, H. J. (2012). Corruption: Democracy, autocracy, and political stability. *Economic Analysis and Policy, 42*(1), 51–66. doi:10.1016/S0313-5926(12)50004-4

O'Cass, A., & McEwen, H. (2004). Exploring consumer status and conspicuous consumption. *Journal of Consumer Behaviour, 4*(1), 25–39. doi:10.1002/cb.155

Obadic, A., & Pehar, L. (2016). Employment, Capital and Seasonality in Selected Mediterranean Countries. *Zagreb International Review of Economics and Business, 19*(1), 43–58. doi:10.1515/zireb-2016-0012

OECD. (2011). *Competitiveness and Private Sector Development: Kazakhstan 2010 – Sector Competitiveness, Strategy.* OECD Publishing. doi:10.1787/9789264089792-en

OECD. (2014). *Kazakhstan: Review of the Central Administration, OECD Public Governance Reviews.* OECD Publishing. doi:10.1787/9789264224605-en

OECD. (2017). *Building inclusive labour markets in Kazakhstan: a focus on youth, older workers, and people with disabilities.* Paris: OECD Publishing.

OECD. (2017). OECD Investment Policy Reviews: Kazakhstan 2017. OECD Publishing. doi:10.1787/9789264269606-en

OECD. (2018). *Reforming Kazakhstan: Progress, Challenges and Opportunities.* Retrieved on October 22, 2018, from: https://www.oecd.org/eurasia/countries/OECD-Eurasia-Reforming-Kazakhstan-EN.pdf

OECD. (2018). *SME and Entrepreneurship Policy in Kazakhstan 2018, OECD Studies on SMEs and Entrepreneurship.* Paris: OECD Publishing.

Oliveira, C., & Antunes, C. H. (2010). A macro-level multi-objective model with uncertain data for sustainability studies. *Proceedings of the 23rd International Conference on Efficiency, Cost, Optimization, Simulation, and Environmental Impact of Energy Systems. Ecos, 2010,* 329–336.

Omirgazy, D. (2016, November 30). *More Kazakh citizens see progress in fight against corruption, according to Global Corruption Barometer.* Retrieved on June 12, 2019, from: https://astanatimes.com/2016/11/more-kazakh-citizens-see-progress-in-fight-against-corruption-according-to-global-corruption-barometer/

Organisation for Economic Co-operation and Development. (2008). *The Istanbul Anti-Corruption Action Plan: Progress and Challenges.* Retrieved on June 12, 2019, from: http://www.oecd.org/daf/anti-bribery/42740427.pdf

Compilation of References

Organisation for Economic Co-operation and Development. (2016). *Anti-corruption Reforms in Eastern Europe and Central Asia: Progress and Challenges, 2013-2015*. Retrieved on June 12, 2019, from: http://www.oecd.org/corruption/acn/Anti-Corruption-Reforms-Eastern-Europe-Central-Asia-2013-2015-ENG.pdf

Organisation for Economic Co-operation and Development. (2018). *Anti-corruption reforms in Kyrgyzstan 4th round of monitoring of the Istanbul Anti-Corruption Action Plan*. Retrieved on May 31, 2019, from: https://www.oecd.org/corruption/acn/OECD-ACN-Kyrgyzstan-4th-Round-Monitoring-Report-2018-ENG.pdf

Organisation for Economic Co-operation and Development. (n.d.). *Anti-Corruption Network › Istanbul Action Plan*. Retrieved on June 12, 2019, from: http://www.oecd.org/corruption/acn/istanbulactionplan/

Osipian, A. L. (2012). Education corruption, reform, and growth: Case of Post-Soviet Russia. *Journal of Eurasian Studies*, *3*(1), 20–29. doi:10.1016/j.euras.2011.10.003

Ozturk, I. (2010). A literature survey on energy-growth nexus. *Energy Policy*, *38*(1), 340–349. doi:10.1016/j.enpol.2009.09.024

Pannier, B. (2016, June 4). The perfect storm of corruption in Central Asia. *RadioFreeEuropeRadioLiberty*. Retrieved on May 31, 2019, from: https://www.rferl.org/a/corruption-central-asia/27779246.html

Papyrakis, E., & Gerlagh, R. (2004). The resource curse hypothesis and its transmission channels. *Journal of Comparative Economics*, *32*(1), 181–193. doi:10.1016/j.jce.2003.11.002

Parihar, P., Dawra, J., & Sahay, V. (2019). The role of customer engagement in the involvement-loyalty link. *Marketing Intelligence & Planning*, *37*(1), 66–79. doi:10.1108/MIP-11-2017-0318

Parsons, T. (1939). The professions and social structure. *Social Forces*, *17*(4), 457–467. doi:10.2307/2570695

Payne, J. E. (2011). US disaggregate fossil fuel consumption and Real GDP : An Empirical Note. *Energy Sources. Part B, Economics, Planning, and Policy*, *6*(1), 63–68. doi:10.1080/15567240902839278

Persson, A., Rothstein, B., & Teorell, J. (2013). Why anticorruption reforms fail—Systemic corruption as a collective action problem. *Governance: An International Journal of Policy, Administration and Institutions*, *26*(3), 449–471. doi:10.1111/j.1468-0491.2012.01604.x

Pertiwi, K. (2018). Contextualizing corruption: A cross-disciplinary approach to studying corruption in organizations. *Administrative Sciences*, *8*(2), 12. doi:10.3390/admsci8020012

Pesaran, M. H. (2004). *General diagnostic tests for cross section dependence in panels*. CESifo Working Paper Series, No. 1229; IZA Discussion Paper No. 1240. Available at SSRN: https://ssrn.com/abstract=572504

Pesaran, M. H., & Shin, Y. (1999). *An Autoregressive Distributed Lag Modelling Approach to Cointegration Analysis.* Retrieved on November 11, 2018, from: http://www.econ.cam.ac.uk/faculty/pesaran/ardl.pdf

Pesaran, M. H., & Shin, Y. (1998). An autoregressive distributed-lag modelling approach to cointegration analysis. *Econometric Society Monographs, 31*, 371–413. doi:10.1017/CCOL0521633230.011

Pesaran, M. H., Shin, Y., & Smith, R. J. (2001). Bounds testing approaches to the analysis of level relationships'. *Journal of Applied Econometrics, 16*(3), 289–326. doi:10.1002/jae.616

Pesaran, M. H., & Smith, R. (1998). Structural Analysis of Cointegrating VARs. *Journal of Economic Surveys, 12*(5), 471–505. doi:10.1111/1467-6419.00065

Pesaran, M. H., Ullah, A., & Yamagata, T. (2008). A bias-adjusted LM test of error cross-section independence. *The Econometrics Journal, 11*(1), 105–127. doi:10.1111/j.1368-423X.2007.00227.x

Pesaran, M. H., & Yamagata, T. (2008). Testing slope homogeneity in large panels. *Journal of Econometrics, 142*(1), 50–93. doi:10.1016/j.jeconom.2007.05.010

Pollack, E., & Allern, S. (2018). Disclosure of Scandinavian telecom companies' corruption in Uzbekistan: The role of investigative journalists. *European Journal of Communication, 33*(1), 73–88. doi:10.1177/0267323117750697

Popper, K. R. (1999). *La lógica de la investigación científica.* Madrid: Tecnos.

Poprawe, M. (2015). A panel data analysis of the effect of corruption on tourism. *Applied Economics, 47*(23), 2399–2412. doi:10.1080/00036846.2015.1005874

Prasad, M., da Silva, M. B. M., & Nickow, A. (2019). Approaches to corruption: A synthesis of the scholarship. *Studies in Comparative International Development, 54*(1), 96–132. doi:10.100712116-018-9275-0

Prebisch, R. (1950). Crecimiento, desequilibrio y disparidades: interpretación del proceso de desarrollo económico. *Estudio Económico de América Latina y el Caribe, Naciones Unidas Comisión Económica para América Latina y el Caribe (CEPAL),* 1110.

Putz, C. (2018, October 29). *Another Atambayev ally faces corruption charges in Kyrgyzstan: Ikramjan Ilmiyanov, a former adviser to previous Kyrgyz President Almazbek Atambayev, faces corruption charges.* Retrieved on May 31, 2019, from: https://thediplomat.com/tag/corruption-in-central-asia/

Quester, P., & Lim, A. L. (2003). Product involvement/brand loyalty: Is there a link? *Journal of Product and Brand Management, 12*(1), 22–38. doi:10.1108/10610420310463117

Raimondi, P. P. (2019, May 13). *Central Asia oil and gas industry – The external powers' energy interests in Kazakhstan, Turkmenistan and Uzbekistan.* Fondazione Eni Enrico Mattei Working Papers 1265. Retrieved on May 31, 2019, from: https://services.bepress.com/feem/paper1265/

Compilation of References

Ray, D. (1998). *Development Economics*. London: Princeton University Press.

Reiche, D. (2010). Renewable energy policies in the Gulf countries – a case study of the carbon-neutral "Masdar City" in Abu Dhabi. *Energy Policy, 38*(1), 378–382. doi:10.1016/j.enpol.2009.09.028

REN-21. (2016). *Renewables – Global Status Report: 2016*. Retrieved on June 4, 2017, from: http://www.ren21.net/wp-content/uploads/2016/05/GSR_2016_Full_Report_lowres.pdf

Rodrigo, P., Khan, H., & Ekinci, Y. (2019). The determinants of foreign product preference amongst elite consumers in an emerging market. *Journal of Retailing and Consumer Services, 46*, 139–148. doi:10.1016/j.jretconser.2018.04.012

Rodríguez-Merino, P. A. (2019). Old "counter-revolution", new "terrorism": Historicizing the framing of violence in Xinjiang by the Chinese state. *Central Asian Survey, 38*(1), 27–45. doi:10.1080/02634937.2018.1496066

Rojas-Méndez, J. (2013). The nation brand molecule. *Journal of Product and Brand Management, 22*(7), 462–472. doi:10.1108/JPBM-09-2013-0385

Rojas-Méndez, J. I., Papadopoulos, N., & Murphy, S. A. (2013). Measuring and positioning nation brands: A comparative brand personality approach. *Corporate Reputation Review, 16*(1), 48–65. doi:10.1057/crr.2012.25

Romero, C. (1991). *Handbook of Critical Issues in Goal Programming*. Oxford, UK: Pergamon Press.

Romer, P. M. (1986). Increasing Returns and Log-Run Growth. *Journal of Political Economy, 94*(5), 1002–1037. doi:10.1086/261420

Rubasundram, G. A., & Rasiah, R. (2019). Corruption and good governance: An analysis of ASEAN's E-Governance experience. *Journal of Southeast Asian Economies, 36*(1), 57–70. https://www.muse.jhu.edu/article/722710. doi:10.1355/ae36-1f

Rumer, E., Sokolsy, R., & Stronski, P. (2016, January 25). *U.S. policy toward Central Asia 3.0*. Retrieved on June 3, 2019, from: https://carnegieendowment.org/2016/01/25/u.s.-policy-toward-central-asia-3.0-pub-62556

Rusch, J. J. (2019, February 7). *Sorry, but corruption can be measured*. Retrieved on June 1, 2019, from: http://www.fcpablog.com/blog/2019/2/7/sorry-but-corruption-can-be-measured.html

Saad, M., Zawdie, G., & Malairaja, C. (2008). The triple helix strategy for universities in developing countries: The experiences in Malaysia and Algeria. *Science & Public Policy, 35*(6), 431–443. doi:10.3152/030234208X323316

Saat, M. K., Shaari, S. A., & Ahmad Fauzi, T. (2017). Materialism and consumerism through urban social. Paper presented at the Advances in Economics. *Business and Management Research (AEBMR), 41, 4th Bandung Creative Movement International Conference on Creative Industries 2017 (BCM 2017),* 303-307. Retrieved on June 12, 2019, from: https://libraryeproceeding. telkomuniversity.ac.id/index.php/bcm/article/view/5918/5900

Saha, S., & Yap, G. (2015). Corruption and tourism: An empirical investigation in a non-linear framework. *International Journal of Tourism Research, 17*(3), 272–281. doi:10.1002/jtr.1985

Saini, S., & Singh, J. (2019). Cultivating emotional branding through customer experience management: From the holistic experience perspective. In *Brand culture and identity: Concepts, methodologies, tools, and applications* (pp. 1346–1361). Hershey, PA: IGI Global. doi:10.4018/978-1-5225-7116-2.ch072

Sala-i-Martin, X. (2001, Aug.). La apertura y la flexibilidad son ingredientes importantes del crecimiento económico. *Boletín del FMI,* 20.

Saleh, A. S., Assaf, A. G., Ihalanayake, R., & Lung, S. (2015). A panel cointegration analysis of the impact of tourism on economic growth: Evidence from the Middle East region. *International Journal of Tourism Research, 17*(3), 209–220. doi:10.1002/jtr.1976

San Cristóbal, J. R. (2012). A goal programming model for environmental policy analysis: Application to Spain. *Energy Policy, 43,* 303–307. doi:10.1016/j.enpol.2012.01.007

Sánchez, J., & Pérez, C. (2011) Hacia un currículo transdisciplinario: una mirada desde el pensamiento complejo. *Revista de Teoría y Didáctica de las Ciencias Sociales,* (17), 143-164. Retrieved on October 7, 2015, from: https://www.redalyc.org/pdf/652/65221619010.pdf

Sandholtz, W., & Taagepera, R. (2005). Corruption, culture, and communism. *International Review of Sociology, 15*(1), 109–131. doi:10.1080/03906700500038678

Saner, R., Toseva, G., Atamanov, A., Mogilevsky, R., & Sahov, A. (2008). Government governance (GG) and inter-ministerial policy coordination (IMPC) in Eastern and Central Europe and Central Asia. *Public Organization Review, 8*(3), 215–231. doi:10.100711115-008-0051-x

Saunders, R. A. (2007). In defense of Kazakshilik: Kazakhstan's war on Sacha Baron Cohen. *Identity, 14*(3), 225–255. doi:10.1080/10702890601162682

Saunders, R. A. (2008). Buying into brand Borat: Kazakhstan's cautious embrace of its unwanted 'son'. *Slavic Review, 67*(1), 63–80. doi:10.2307/27652767

Saunders, R. A. (2016). *Popular Geopolitics and Nation Branding in the Post-Soviet Realm.* New York: Routledge. doi:10.4324/9781315737386

Schenkkan, N. (2016, January 22). *A perfect storm in Central Asia: For years, the five ex-Soviet republics have enjoyed surprising stability. But Russia's economic crisis is shaking their foundations.* Retrieved on May 31, 2019, from: https://foreignpolicy.com/2016/01/22/a-perfect-storm-in-central-asia/

Compilation of References

Schmidt, V. A. (2009). Putting the political back into political economy by bringing the state back in yet again. *World Politics, 61*(3), 516–546. doi:10.1017/S0043887109000173

Schumpeter, J. A. (1943). *Capitalism, socialism and democracy.* New York: Routledge.

Sciutto, J. (2019). *The shadow war: Inside Russia's and China's secret operations to defeat America.* New York: Harper.

Scott, I., & Gong, T. (2015). Evidence-based policy-making for corruption prevention in Hong Kong: A bottom-up approach. *Asia Pacific Journal of Public Administration, 37*(2), 87–101. doi:10.1080/23276665.2015.1041222

Shane, S. (2009). Why encouraging more people to become entrepreneurs is bad public policy. *Small Business Economics, 33*(2), 141–149. doi:10.100711187-009-9215-5

Shao, W., Grace, D., & Ross, M. (2019). Consumer motivation and luxury consumption: Testing moderating effects. *Journal of Retailing and Consumer Services, 46*, 33–44. doi:10.1016/j.jretconser.2018.10.003

Sharma, A., & Bhola, S., Malyan, S., & Patni, N. (2013). Impact of brand loyalty on buying behavior of women consumers for beauty care products - Delhi region. *Global Journal of Management and Business Studies, 3*, 817–824.

Shen, D., Lennon, S., Dickson, M. A., Montalto, C., & Zhang, L. (2002). Chinese consumers' attitudes toward US and PRC made clothing from a cultural perspective. *Family and Consumer Sciences Research Journal, 31*(1), 19–49. doi:10.1177/1077727X02031001002

Shevyakova, A., Tyugina, I., Arystan, M., & Munsh, E. (2018). Transformation of economy towards tourism: Case of Kazakhstan. *Journal of Security & Sustainability Issues, 7*(3), 601–616. doi:10.9770/jssi.2018.7.3(19)

Smith, A. (1987). *Investigación sobre la naturaleza y causas de la riqueza de las naciones.* México: Fondo de Cultura Económica.

So, J. T., Parsons, A. G., & Yap, S. F. (2013). Corporate branding, emotional attachment and brand loyalty: The case of luxury fashion branding. *Journal of Fashion Marketing and Management, 17*(4), 403–423. doi:10.1108/JFMM-03-2013-0032

Solarin, A. S., & Ozturk, I. (2016). The relationship between natural gas consumption and economic growth in OPEC members. *Renewable & Sustainable Energy Reviews, 58*, 1348–1356. doi:10.1016/j.rser.2015.12.278

Solow, R. M. (1956). A Contribution to the Theory of Economic Growth. *The Quarterly Journal of Economics, 70*(1), 65–94. doi:10.2307/1884513

Song, H., Wang, J., & Han, H. (2019). Effect of image, satisfaction, trust, love, and respect on loyalty formation for name-brand coffee shops. *International Journal of Hospitality Management, 79*, 50–59. doi:10.1016/j.ijhm.2018.12.011

Souiden, N., & Diagne, M. (2009). Canadian and French men's consumption of cosmetics: A comparison of their attitudes and motivations. *Journal of Consumer Marketing, 26*(2), 97–109. doi:10.1108/07363760910940465

Stock, F. (2009). Identity, image and brand: A conceptual framework. *Place Branding and Public Diplomacy, 5*(2), 118–125. doi:10.1057/pb.2009.2

Stock, F. (2009). The Borat effect. *Place Branding and Public Diplomacy, 5*(3), 180–191. doi:10.1057/pb.2009.12

Sultanov, B. K. (2010). *Kazakhstan Today.* Almaty: The Kaz. Inst. for Strategic Studies under the President of the Republic of Kazakhstan.

Swamy, P. A. V. B. (1970). Efficient inference in a random coefficient regression model. *Econometrica, 38*(2), 311–323. doi:10.2307/1913012

Swartz, B., Wadsworth, F., & Wheat, J. (2011). Perceptions of corruption in Central Asian countries. *International Business & Economics Research Journal, 7*(3), 71–78. doi:10.19030/iber.v7i3.3235

Sweeney, J. C., & Soutar, G. N. (2001). Consumer perceived value: The development of a multiple item scale. *Journal of Retailing, 77*(2), 203–220. doi:10.1016/S0022-4359(01)00041-0

Syzdykova, A. (2018). Orta Asya Ülkelerinde enerji tüketimi ve ekonomik büyüme ilişkisi: Panel veri analizi. *AKÜ İktisadi ve İdari Bilimler Fakültesi Dergisi, 20*(1), 87–99. doi:10.5578/jeas.67162

Szondi, G. (2007). The role and challenges of country branding in transition countries: The Central and Eastern European experience. *Place Branding and Public Diplomacy, 3*(1), 8–20. doi:10.1057/palgrave.pb.6000044

T.C. Kültür ve Turizm Bakanlığı. (2018). *Bilgi Notu Formu Kazakistan / Astana Kültür ve Tanıtma Müşavirliği 2018 Yılı I. Dönem Raporu.* Retrieved on September 19, 2018, from: http://www.tanitma.gov.tr/TR-209741/kazakistan-pazar-raporu.html

Tan, Y., Shuai, C., Jiao, L., & Shen, L. (2017). An adaptive neuro-fuzzy inference system (ANFIS) approach for measuring country sustainability performance. *Environmental Impact Assessment Review, 65*, 29–40. doi:10.1016/j.eiar.2017.04.004

Taylor, S. (1986). *Modelling Financial Time Series.* New York: Wiley.

The World Bank. (2013). *Kazakhstan Country Profile Enterprise Surveys 2013.* Retrieved on July 4, 2015, from: https://www.enterprisesurveys.org/~/media/GIAWB/EnterpriseSurveys/Documents/Profiles/English/kazakhstan-2013.pdf

The World Bank. (2018). *A New Growth Model For Building A Secure Middle Class: Kazakhstan Systematic Country Diagnostic.* Report No. 125611-KZ. Retrieved on November 3, 2018, from: http://documents.worldbank.org/curated/en/664531525455037169/pdf/KAZ-SCD-April-2018-FINAL-eng-with-IDU-05012018.pdf

Compilation of References

The World Bank. (2019a). *The World Bank in Kazakhstan Country Snaphot Report*. Retrieved on June 2, 2019, from: http://pubdocs.worldbank.org/en/753441554997978839/Kazakhstan-Snapshot-Apr2019.pdf

The World Bank. (2019b). *Doing Business In Kazakhstan 2019*. Retrieved on June 2, 2019, from: https://www.doingbusiness.org/en/reports/subnational-reports/kazakhstan

Theunis, H. L., & Rasheed, A. (1983). Alternative approaches to tertiary tourism education with special reference to developing countries. *Tourism Management, 4*(1), 42–51. doi:10.1016/0261-5177(83)90049-3

Thomson, M., MacInnis, D. J., & Park, C. W. (2005). The ties that bind measuring the strength of consumers' emotional attachments to brands. *Journal of Consumer Psychology, 15*(1), 77–91. doi:10.120715327663jcp1501_10

Trabelsi, M. A., & Trabelsi, H. (2014). *At what level of corruption does economic growth decrease?* Retrieved from https://mpra.ub.uni-muenchen.de/81279/

Transparency International. (2011, November 2). *Bribe Payers Index 2011*. Retrieved on June 12, 2019, from: https://www.transparency.org/whatwedo/publication/bpi_2011

Transparency International. (2015). *Corruption Perceptions Index 2015*. Retrieved on June 12, 2019, from: https://www.transparency.org/cpi2015

Transparency International. (2016, November 16). *People and corruption: Europe and Central Asia 2016*. Retrieved on June 11, 2019, from: https://www.transparency.org/whatwedo/publication/people_and_corruption_europe_and_central_asia_2016

Transparency International. (2017a, March 7). *People and corruption: Asia Pacific – Global Corruption Barometer*. Retrieved on June 11, 2019, from: https://www.transparency.org/whatwedo/publication/people_and_corruption_asia_pacific_global_corruption_barometer

Transparency International. (2017b, November 14). *People and corruption: Citizen's voices from around the world*. Retrieved on June 11, 2019, from: https://www.transparency.org/whatwedo/publication/people_and_corruption_citizens_voices_from_around_the_world

Transparency International. (2019a, January). *Corruption Perceptions Index*. Retrieved on June 5, 2019, from: https://www.transparency.org/research/cpi/overview

Transparency International. (2019b, January 29). *Eastern Europe & Central Asia: Weak checks and balances threat anti-corruption efforts: Corruption flourishing across the region while the quality of democracy continues to falter or stagnate*. Retrieved on May 31, 2019, from: https://www.transparency.org/news/feature/weak_checks_and_balances_threaten_anti_corruption_efforts_across_eastern_eu

Tsay, R. S. (2012). *An Introduction to Analysis of Financial Data with R*. New York: Wiley.

Tsui-Auch, L. S., & Lee, Y. J. (2003). The state matters: Management models of Singaporean Chinese and Korean business groups. *Organization Studies, 24*(4), 507–534. doi:10.1177/0170840603024004001

Tudoroiu, T. (2007). Rose, Orange, and Tulip: The failed post-Soviet revolutions. *Communist and Post-Communist Studies, 40*(3), 315–342. doi:10.1016/j.postcomstud.2007.06.005

Urinboyev, R. (2018). Corruption in post-Soviet Uzbekistan. In A. Farazmand (Ed.), *Global encyclopedia of public administration, public policy, and governance.* Cham, Switzerland: Springer Nature Switzerland. Retrieved on June 11, 2019, from: https://link.springer.com/content/pdf/10.1007%2F978-3-319-31816-5_3666-1.pdf

Urinboyev, R. (2019). *Everyday corruption and social norms in post-Soviet Uzbekistan.* Gothenburg, Sweden: The Program on Governance and Local Development at the University of Gothenburg. Retrieved on May 31, 2019, from: https://portal.research.lu.se/portal/files/57641563/gld_wp_19_final.pdf

Uzgören, E., & Aslan, V. (2019). Seçili MENA Ülkelerinde doğalgaz tüketimi ile iktisadi büyüme arasındaki ilişki. *Dumlupınar Üniversitesi Sosyal Bilimler Dergisi, 59,* 13–20.

Van der Zee, E., Gerrets, A. M., & Vanneste, D. (2017). Complexity in the governance of tourism networks: Balancing between external pressure and internal expectations. *Journal of Destination Marketing & Management, 6*(4), 296–308. doi:10.1016/j.jdmm.2017.07.003

van Ham, P. (2001). The rise of the brand state. *Foreign Affairs, 80*(5), 2–6. doi:10.2307/20050245

Velempini, K., & Martin, B. (2019). Place-based education as a framework for tourism education in secondary schools: A case study from the Okavango Delta in Southern Africa. *Journal of Hospitality, Leisure, Sport and Tourism Education, 25,* 100–197. doi:10.1016/j.jhlste.2019.100197

Vié, A., Liuzzi, D., Colapinto, C., & La Torre, D. (2019). The long-run sustainability of the European Union countries: Assessing the Europe 2020 strategy through a fuzzy goal programming model. *Management Decision, 57*(2), 523–542. doi:10.1108/MD-05-2018-0518

Volcic, Z., & Andrejevic, M. (2011). Nation branding in the era of commercial nationalism. *International Journal of Communication, 5,* 598–618.

Walker, C. (2011). *The Perpetual Battle: Corruption in the Former Soviet Union and the New EU Members.* Retrieved on June 12, 2019, from: https://freedomhouse.org/sites/default/files/PerpetualBattle.pdf

Wallerstein, I. (2002). *El legado de la sociología, la promesa de la ciencia social en Conocer el mundo. El fin de lo aprendido.* México: Una ciencia social para el Siglo XXI-UNAM.

Warf, B. (2019). Geographically uneven landscapes of Asian corruption. In B. Warf (Ed.), *Global corruption from a geographic perspective* (pp. 143–193). Cham, Switzerland: Springer Nature Switzerland. doi:10.1007/978-3-030-03478-8_6

Compilation of References

Wennekers, S., Van Wennekers, A., Thurik, R., & Reynolds, P. D. (2005). Nascent entrepreneurship and the level of economic development. *Small Business Economics, 24*(3), 293–309. doi:10.100711187-005-1994-8

Whitley, R. (1998). East Asian and Anglo-American business systems. In G. Thompson (Ed.), *Economic Dynamism in the Asia-Pacific* (pp. 213–249). New York: Routledge.

Whitley, R. (1998a). Internationalization and varieties of capitalism: The limited effects of cross-national coordination of economic activities on the nature of business systems. *Review of International Political Economy, 5*(3), 445–481. doi:10.1080/096922998347480

Whitley, R. D. (1991). The social construction of business systems in East Asia. *Organization Studies, 12*(1), 1–28. doi:10.1177/017084069101200102

Whitley, R. D. (1999). *Divergent Capitalism: The Social Stucturing and Change of Business Systems.* Oxford, UK: Oxford University Press.

Wiedmann, K., Hennigs, N., & Siebels, A. (2009). Value-based segmentation of luxury consumption behavior. *Psychology and Marketing, 26*(7), 625–651. doi:10.1002/mar.20292

Wilhelm, P. G. (2002). International validation of the Corruption Perceptions Index: Implications for business ethics and entrepreneurship education. *Journal of Business Ethics, 35*(3), 177–189. doi:10.1023/A:1013882225402

Wilkinson, A., Wood, G., & Deeg, R. (Eds.). (2014). *The Oxford Handbook of Employment Relations: Comparative Employment Systems.* Oxford, UK: Oxford University Press. doi:10.1093/oxfordhb/9780199695096.001.0001

Windsor, D. (2017). The role of multinationals in corruption in the Asia-Pacific region. In M. dela Rama & C. Rowley (Eds.), *The changing face of corruption in the Asia Pacific* (pp. 57–70). Amsterdam, The Netherlands: Elsevier. doi:10.1016/B978-0-08-101109-6.00004-6

Windsor, D. (2018a). Corruption in the CIS and Eurasia: Sources, consequences, and possible solutions. In O. Karnaukhova, A. Udovikina, & B. Christiansen (Eds.), *Economic and geopolitical perspectives of the Commonwealth of Independent States and Eurasia* (pp. 91–120). Hershey, PA: IGI Global. doi:10.4018/978-1-5225-3264-4.ch004

Windsor, D. (2018b). Corruption intelligence and analysis. In M. Munoz (Ed.), *Global business intelligence* (pp. 113–126). New York: Routledge.

Windsor, D. (2019). Influencing MNC strategies for managing corruption and favoritism in Pacific Asia countries: A multiple-theory configurational perspective. *Asia Pacific Business Review, 25*(4), 501–533. doi:10.1080/13602381.2019.1589769

Witt, M. A., & Redding, G. (Eds.). (2014). *The Oxford Handbook of Asian Business Systems.* OUP Oxford. doi:10.1093/oxfordhb/9780199654925.001.0001

World Bank Group. (n.d.). *Corruption.* Retrieved on June 15, 2019, from: https://www.enterprisesurveys.org/data/exploretopics/corruption

World Bank. (2015). *KZ Skills and Jobs Project*. Retrieved on December 2, 2017, from: https://projects.worldbank.org/P150183?lang=en

World Bank. (2017, November 1). *Economies in Central Asia continue reform agenda*. Retrieved on June 2, 2019, from: https://www.worldbank.org/en/news/press-release/2017/11/01/economies-in-central-asia-continue-reform-agenda

World Bank. (2018). *Doing Business 2018: Reforming to create jobs*. Retrieved on June 2, 2019, from: https://www.doingbusiness.org/en/reports/global-reports/doing-business-2018

World Bank. (n.d.). *DataBank*. Retrieved on June 15, 2019, from: https://databank.worldbank.org/data/reports.aspx?Report_Name=WGI-Table&Id=ceea4d8b

World Justice Project. (2019). *World Justice Project Rule of Law Index®*. Retrieved on June 1, 2019, from: https://worldjusticeproject.org/our-work/research-and-data/wjp-rule-law-index-2019

World Tourism Organization (UNWTO). (2018). *Panorama OMT del turismo internacional*. Retrieved on March 4, 2019, from: https://www.e-unwto.org/doi/pdf/10.18111/9789284419890

Wu, L. (2017). Relationship building in nation branding: The central role of nation brand commitment. *Place Branding and Public Diplomacy, 13*(1), 65–80. doi:10.1057/pb.2015.16

Yap, G., & Saha, S. (2013). Do political instability, terrorism, and corruption have deterring effects on tourism development even in the presence of UNESCO heritage? A cross-country panel estimate. *Tourism Analysis, 18*(5), 587–599. doi:10.3727/108354213X13782245307911

Yazar, Y. (2011). *Enerji İlişkileri Bağlamında Türkiye ve Orta Asya Ülkeleri*. Ahmet Yesevi Üniversitesi. Retrieved on April 15, 2019, from: http://www.ayu.edu.tr/static/kitaplar/enerji_raporu.pdf

Yee, F. S., Chin, S., & Suan, T. (2012). Analysis of the purchasing behavior on skin care products among what? *International Journal of Economics and Management, 6*(2), 22–36.

Yee, W. F., & Sidek, Y. (2008). Influence of brand loyalty on consumer sportswear. *International Journal of Economics and Management, 2*(2), 221–236.

Yim, M. Y., Sauer, P. L., Williams, J., Lee, S., & Macrury, I. (2014). Drivers of attitudes toward luxury brands: A cross-national investigation into the roles of interpersonal influence and brand consciousness. *International Marketing Review, 31*(4), 363–389. doi:10.1108/IMR-04-2011-0121

Zaichkowsky, J. L. (1985). Measuring the involvement inventory: Reduction, revision and application to advertising. *Journal of Advertising, 23*(4), 59–69. doi:10.1080/00913367.1943.10673459

Zakaria, N., & Talib, A. N. A. (2011). What did you say? A cross-cultural analysis of the distributive communicative behaviors of global virtual teams. In *2011 International Conference on Computational Aspects of Social Networks (CASoN)* (pp. 7-12). IEEE. 10.1109/CASON.2011.6085910

Compilation of References

Zakaria, N., Wan-Ismail, W. N. A., & Abdul-Talib, A. N. (2015). Superfluous or Moderation?: The Effect of Religious Value on Conspicuous Consumption Behavior for Luxury Products. In *Emerging Research on Islamic Marketing and Tourism in the Global Economy* (pp. 1–18). Hershey, PA: IGI Global. doi:10.4018/978-1-4666-6272-8.ch001

Zakharov, N. (2019). Does corruption hinder investment? Evidence from Russian regions. *European Journal of Political Economy*, *56*, 39–61. doi:10.1016/j.ejpoleco.2018.06.005

Zakoian, J. M. (1994). Threshold heteroscedasticity models. *Journal of Economic Dynamics & Control*, *18*(5), 931–955. doi:10.1016/0165-1889(94)90039-6

Zamani, S. N. M., Abdul-Talib, A. N., & Ashari, H. (2016). Strategic orientations and new product success: The mediating impact of innovation speed. International Information Institute (Tokyo) Information, 19(7B), 2785.

Zamani, M. (2007). Energy consumption and economic activities in Iran. *Energy Economics*, *29*(6), 1135–1140. doi:10.1016/j.eneco.2006.04.008

Zholdasbekov, A., Berkinbaev, K. M., & Tasbolat, B. (2008). Modern Tendencies of Professional Training of Specialists in the Sphere of Tourism in Kazakhstan. *Anatolia: An International Journal of Tourism and Hospitality Research*, 3-11.

Zuo, B., & Bao, J. G. (2008). Tourism total factor productivity and its regional variation in China from 1992 to 2005. *Acta Geographica Sinica*, *63*(4), 417–427.

Zyglidopoulos, S., Dieleman, M., & Hirsch, P. (2019). Playing the game: Unpacking the rationale for organizational corruption in MNCs. *Journal of Management Inquiry*. doi:10.1177/1056492618817827

Related References

To continue our tradition of advancing information science and technology research, we have compiled a list of recommended IGI Global readings. These references will provide additional information and guidance to further enrich your knowledge and assist you with your own research and future publications.

Abtahi, M. S., Behboudi, L., & Hasanabad, H. M. (2017). Factors Affecting Internet Advertising Adoption in Ad Agencies. *International Journal of Innovation in the Digital Economy*, 8(4), 18–29. doi:10.4018/IJIDE.2017100102

Agrawal, S. (2017). The Impact of Emerging Technologies and Social Media on Different Business(es): Marketing and Management. In O. Rishi & A. Sharma (Eds.), *Maximizing Business Performance and Efficiency Through Intelligent Systems* (pp. 37–49). Hershey, PA: IGI Global. doi:10.4018/978-1-5225-2234-8.ch002

Alnoukari, M., Razouk, R., & Hanano, A. (2016). BSC-SI: A Framework for Integrating Strategic Intelligence in Corporate Strategic Management. *International Journal of Social and Organizational Dynamics in IT*, 5(2), 1–14. doi:10.4018/IJSODIT.2016070101

Alnoukari, M., Razouk, R., & Hanano, A. (2016). BSC-SI, A Framework for Integrating Strategic Intelligence in Corporate Strategic Management. *International Journal of Strategic Information Technology and Applications*, 7(1), 32–44. doi:10.4018/IJSITA.2016010103

Altındağ, E. (2016). Current Approaches in Change Management. In A. Goksoy (Ed.), *Organizational Change Management Strategies in Modern Business* (pp. 24–51). Hershey, PA: IGI Global. doi:10.4018/978-1-4666-9533-7.ch002

Related References

Alvarez-Dionisi, L. E., Turner, R., & Mittra, M. (2016). Global Project Management Trends. *International Journal of Information Technology Project Management*, 7(3), 54–73. doi:10.4018/IJITPM.2016070104

Anantharaman, R. N., Rajeswari, K. S., Angusamy, A., & Kuppusamy, J. (2017). Role of Self-Efficacy and Collective Efficacy as Moderators of Occupational Stress Among Software Development Professionals. *International Journal of Human Capital and Information Technology Professionals*, 8(2), 45–58. doi:10.4018/IJHCITP.2017040103

Aninze, F., El-Gohary, H., & Hussain, J. (2018). The Role of Microfinance to Empower Women: The Case of Developing Countries. *International Journal of Customer Relationship Marketing and Management*, 9(1), 54–78. doi:10.4018/IJCRMM.2018010104

Arsenijević, O. M., Orčić, D., & Kastratović, E. (2017). Development of an Optimization Tool for Intangibles in SMEs: A Case Study from Serbia with a Pilot Research in the Prestige by Milka Company. In M. Vemić (Ed.), *Optimal Management Strategies in Small and Medium Enterprises* (pp. 320–347). Hershey, PA: IGI Global. doi:10.4018/978-1-5225-1949-2.ch015

Aryanto, V. D., Wismantoro, Y., & Widyatmoko, K. (2018). Implementing Eco-Innovation by Utilizing the Internet to Enhance Firm's Marketing Performance: Study of Green Batik Small and Medium Enterprises in Indonesia. *International Journal of E-Business Research*, 14(1), 21–36. doi:10.4018/IJEBR.2018010102

Atiku, S. O., & Fields, Z. (2017). Multicultural Orientations for 21st Century Global Leadership. In N. Baporikar (Ed.), *Management Education for Global Leadership* (pp. 28–51). Hershey, PA: IGI Global. doi:10.4018/978-1-5225-1013-0.ch002

Atiku, S. O., & Fields, Z. (2018). Organisational Learning Dimensions and Talent Retention Strategies for the Service Industries. In N. Baporikar (Ed.), *Global Practices in Knowledge Management for Societal and Organizational Development* (pp. 358–381). Hershey, PA: IGI Global. doi:10.4018/978-1-5225-3009-1.ch017

Ávila, L., & Teixeira, L. (2018). The Main Concepts Behind the Dematerialization of Business Processes. In M. Khosrow-Pour, D.B.A. (Ed.), Encyclopedia of Information Science and Technology, Fourth Edition (pp. 888-898). Hershey, PA: IGI Global. doi:10.4018/978-1-5225-2255-3.ch076

Bartens, Y., Chunpir, H. I., Schulte, F., & Voß, S. (2017). Business/IT Alignment in Two-Sided Markets: A COBIT 5 Analysis for Media Streaming Business Models. In S. De Haes & W. Van Grembergen (Eds.), *Strategic IT Governance and Alignment in Business Settings* (pp. 82–111). Hershey, PA: IGI Global. doi:10.4018/978-1-5225-0861-8.ch004

Bashayreh, A. M. (2018). Organizational Culture and Organizational Performance. In W. Lee & F. Sabetzadeh (Eds.), *Contemporary Knowledge and Systems Science* (pp. 50–69). Hershey, PA: IGI Global. doi:10.4018/978-1-5225-5655-8.ch003

Bedford, D. A. (2018). Sustainable Knowledge Management Strategies: Aligning Business Capabilities and Knowledge Management Goals. In N. Baporikar (Ed.), *Global Practices in Knowledge Management for Societal and Organizational Development* (pp. 46–73). Hershey, PA: IGI Global. doi:10.4018/978-1-5225-3009-1.ch003

Benmoussa, F., Nakara, W. A., & Jaouen, A. (2016). The Use of Social Media by SMEs in the Tourism Industry. In I. Lee (Ed.), *Encyclopedia of E-Commerce Development, Implementation, and Management* (pp. 2159–2170). Hershey, PA: IGI Global. doi:10.4018/978-1-4666-9787-4.ch155

Berger, R. (2016). Indigenous Management and Bottom of Pyramid Countries: The Role of National Institutions. In U. Aung & P. Ordoñez de Pablos (Eds.), *Managerial Strategies and Practice in the Asian Business Sector* (pp. 107–123). Hershey, PA: IGI Global. doi:10.4018/978-1-4666-9758-4.ch007

Bharwani, S., & Musunuri, D. (2018). Reflection as a Process From Theory to Practice. In M. Khosrow-Pour, D.B.A. (Ed.), Encyclopedia of Information Science and Technology, Fourth Edition (pp. 1529-1539). Hershey, PA: IGI Global. doi:10.4018/978-1-5225-2255-3.ch132

Bhatt, G. D., Wang, Z., & Rodger, J. A. (2017). Information Systems Capabilities and Their Effects on Competitive Advantages: A Study of Chinese Companies. *Information Resources Management Journal*, *30*(3), 41–57. doi:10.4018/IRMJ.2017070103

Bhushan, M., & Yadav, A. (2017). Concept of Cloud Computing in ESB. In R. Bhadoria, N. Chaudhari, G. Tomar, & S. Singh (Eds.), *Exploring Enterprise Service Bus in the Service-Oriented Architecture Paradigm* (pp. 116–127). Hershey, PA: IGI Global. doi:10.4018/978-1-5225-2157-0.ch008

Bhushan, S. (2017). System Dynamics Base-Model of Humanitarian Supply Chain (HSCM) in Disaster Prone Eco-Communities of India: A Discussion on Simulation and Scenario Results. *International Journal of System Dynamics Applications*, *6*(3), 20–37. doi:10.4018/IJSDA.2017070102

Related References

Biswas, A., & De, A. K. (2017). On Development of a Fuzzy Stochastic Programming Model with Its Application to Business Management. In S. Trivedi, S. Dey, A. Kumar, & T. Panda (Eds.), *Handbook of Research on Advanced Data Mining Techniques and Applications for Business Intelligence* (pp. 353–378). Hershey, PA: IGI Global. doi:10.4018/978-1-5225-2031-3.ch021

Bücker, J., & Ernste, K. (2018). Use of Brand Heroes in Strategic Reputation Management: The Case of Bacardi, Adidas, and Daimler. In A. Erdemir (Ed.), *Reputation Management Techniques in Public Relations* (pp. 126–150). Hershey, PA: IGI Global. doi:10.4018/978-1-5225-3619-2.ch007

Bureš, V. (2018). Industry 4.0 From the Systems Engineering Perspective: Alternative Holistic Framework Development. In R. Brunet-Thornton & F. Martinez (Eds.), *Analyzing the Impacts of Industry 4.0 in Modern Business Environments* (pp. 199–223). Hershey, PA: IGI Global. doi:10.4018/978-1-5225-3468-6.ch011

Buzady, Z. (2017). Resolving the Magic Cube of Effective Case Teaching: Benchmarking Case Teaching Practices in Emerging Markets – Insights from the Central European University Business School, Hungary. In D. Latusek (Ed.), *Case Studies as a Teaching Tool in Management Education* (pp. 79–103). Hershey, PA: IGI Global. doi:10.4018/978-1-5225-0770-3.ch005

Campatelli, G., Richter, A., & Stocker, A. (2016). Participative Knowledge Management to Empower Manufacturing Workers. *International Journal of Knowledge Management*, *12*(4), 37–50. doi:10.4018/IJKM.2016100103

Căpusneanu, S., & Topor, D. I. (2018). Business Ethics and Cost Management in SMEs: Theories of Business Ethics and Cost Management Ethos. In I. Oncioiu (Ed.), *Ethics and Decision-Making for Sustainable Business Practices* (pp. 109–127). Hershey, PA: IGI Global. doi:10.4018/978-1-5225-3773-1.ch007

Carneiro, A. (2016). Maturity in Health Organization Information Systems: Metrics and Privacy Perspectives. *International Journal of Privacy and Health Information Management*, *4*(2), 1–18. doi:10.4018/IJPHIM.2016070101

Chan, R. L., Mo, P. L., & Moon, K. K. (2018). Strategic and Tactical Measures in Managing Enterprise Risks: A Study of the Textile and Apparel Industry. In K. Strang, M. Korstanje, & N. Vajjhala (Eds.), *Research, Practices, and Innovations in Global Risk and Contingency Management* (pp. 1–19). Hershey, PA: IGI Global. doi:10.4018/978-1-5225-4754-9.ch001

Related References

Chandan, H. C. (2016). Motivations and Challenges of Female Entrepreneurship in Developed and Developing Economies. In N. Baporikar (Ed.), *Handbook of Research on Entrepreneurship in the Contemporary Knowledge-Based Global Economy* (pp. 260–286). Hershey, PA: IGI Global. doi:10.4018/978-1-4666-8798-1.ch012

Charlier, S. D., Burke-Smalley, L. A., & Fisher, S. L. (2018). Undergraduate Programs in the U.S: A Contextual and Content-Based Analysis. In J. Mendy (Ed.), *Teaching Human Resources and Organizational Behavior at the College Level* (pp. 26–57). Hershey, PA: IGI Global. doi:10.4018/978-1-5225-2820-3.ch002

Chaudhuri, S. (2016). Application of Web-Based Geographical Information System (GIS) in E-Business. In U. Panwar, R. Kumar, & N. Ray (Eds.), *Handbook of Research on Promotional Strategies and Consumer Influence in the Service Sector* (pp. 389–405). Hershey, PA: IGI Global. doi:10.4018/978-1-5225-0143-5.ch023

Choudhuri, P. S. (2016). An Empirical Study on the Quality of Services Offered by the Private Life Insurers in Burdwan. In U. Panwar, R. Kumar, & N. Ray (Eds.), *Handbook of Research on Promotional Strategies and Consumer Influence in the Service Sector* (pp. 31–55). Hershey, PA: IGI Global. doi:10.4018/978-1-5225-0143-5.ch002

Dahlberg, T., Kivijärvi, H., & Saarinen, T. (2017). IT Investment Consistency and Other Factors Influencing the Success of IT Performance. In S. De Haes & W. Van Grembergen (Eds.), *Strategic IT Governance and Alignment in Business Settings* (pp. 176–208). Hershey, PA: IGI Global. doi:10.4018/978-1-5225-0861-8.ch007

Damnjanović, A. M. (2017). Knowledge Management Optimization through IT and E-Business Utilization: A Qualitative Study on Serbian SMEs. In M. Vemić (Ed.), *Optimal Management Strategies in Small and Medium Enterprises* (pp. 249–267). Hershey, PA: IGI Global. doi:10.4018/978-1-5225-1949-2.ch012

Daneshpour, H. (2017). Integrating Sustainable Development into Project Portfolio Management through Application of Open Innovation. In M. Vemić (Ed.), *Optimal Management Strategies in Small and Medium Enterprises* (pp. 370–387). Hershey, PA: IGI Global. doi:10.4018/978-1-5225-1949-2.ch017

Daniel, A. D., & Reis de Castro, V. (2018). Entrepreneurship Education: How to Measure the Impact on Nascent Entrepreneurs. In A. Carrizo Moreira, J. Guilherme Leitão Dantas, & F. Manuel Valente (Eds.), *Nascent Entrepreneurship and Successful New Venture Creation* (pp. 85–110). Hershey, PA: IGI Global. doi:10.4018/978-1-5225-2936-1.ch004

Related References

David, F., van der Sijde, P., & van den Besselaar, P. (2016). Enterpreneurial Incentives, Obstacles, and Management in University-Business Co-Operation: The Case of Indonesia. In J. Saiz-Álvarez (Ed.), *Handbook of Research on Social Entrepreneurship and Solidarity Economics* (pp. 499–518). Hershey, PA: IGI Global. doi:10.4018/978-1-5225-0097-1.ch024

David, R., Swami, B. N., & Tangirala, S. (2018). Ethics Impact on Knowledge Management in Organizational Development: A Case Study. In N. Baporikar (Ed.), *Global Practices in Knowledge Management for Societal and Organizational Development* (pp. 19–45). Hershey, PA: IGI Global. doi:10.4018/978-1-5225-3009-1.ch002

Delias, P., & Lakiotaki, K. (2018). Discovering Process Horizontal Boundaries to Facilitate Process Comprehension. *International Journal of Operations Research and Information Systems*, 9(2), 1–31. doi:10.4018/IJORIS.2018040101

Denholm, J., & Lee-Davies, L. (2018). Success Factors for Games in Business and Project Management. In *Enhancing Education and Training Initiatives Through Serious Games* (pp. 34–68). Hershey, PA: IGI Global. doi:10.4018/978-1-5225-3689-5.ch002

Deshpande, M. (2017). Best Practices in Management Institutions for Global Leadership: Policy Aspects. In N. Baporikar (Ed.), *Management Education for Global Leadership* (pp. 1–27). Hershey, PA: IGI Global. doi:10.4018/978-1-5225-1013-0.ch001

Deshpande, M. (2018). Policy Perspectives for SMEs Knowledge Management. In N. Baporikar (Ed.), *Knowledge Integration Strategies for Entrepreneurship and Sustainability* (pp. 23–46). Hershey, PA: IGI Global. doi:10.4018/978-1-5225-5115-7.ch002

Dezdar, S. (2017). ERP Implementation Projects in Asian Countries: A Comparative Study on Iran and China. *International Journal of Information Technology Project Management*, 8(3), 52–68. doi:10.4018/IJITPM.2017070104

Domingos, D., Martinho, R., & Varajão, J. (2016). Controlled Flexibility in Healthcare Processes: A BPMN-Extension Approach. In M. Cruz-Cunha, I. Miranda, R. Martinho, & R. Rijo (Eds.), *Encyclopedia of E-Health and Telemedicine* (pp. 521–535). Hershey, PA: IGI Global. doi:10.4018/978-1-4666-9978-6.ch040

Domingos, D., Respício, A., & Martinho, R. (2017). Reliability of IoT-Aware BPMN Healthcare Processes. In C. Reis & M. Maximiano (Eds.), *Internet of Things and Advanced Application in Healthcare* (pp. 214–248). Hershey, PA: IGI Global. doi:10.4018/978-1-5225-1820-4.ch008

Dosumu, O., Hussain, J., & El-Gohary, H. (2017). An Exploratory Study of the Impact of Government Policies on the Development of Small and Medium Enterprises in Developing Countries: The Case of Nigeria. *International Journal of Customer Relationship Marketing and Management*, 8(4), 51–62. doi:10.4018/ IJCRMM.2017100104

Durst, S., Bruns, G., & Edvardsson, I. R. (2017). Retaining Knowledge in Smaller Building and Construction Firms. *International Journal of Knowledge and Systems Science*, 8(3), 1–12. doi:10.4018/IJKSS.2017070101

Edvardsson, I. R., & Durst, S. (2017). Outsourcing, Knowledge, and Learning: A Critical Review. *International Journal of Knowledge-Based Organizations*, 7(2), 13–26. doi:10.4018/IJKBO.2017040102

Edwards, J. S. (2018). Integrating Knowledge Management and Business Processes. In M. Khosrow-Pour, D.B.A. (Ed.), Encyclopedia of Information Science and Technology, Fourth Edition (pp. 5046-5055). Hershey, PA: IGI Global. doi:10.4018/978-1-5225-2255-3.ch437

Ejiogu, A. O. (2018). Economics of Farm Management. In *Agricultural Finance and Opportunities for Investment and Expansion* (pp. 56–72). Hershey, PA: IGI Global. doi:10.4018/978-1-5225-3059-6.ch003

Ekanem, I., & Abiade, G. E. (2018). Factors Influencing the Use of E-Commerce by Small Enterprises in Nigeria. *International Journal of ICT Research in Africa and the Middle East*, 7(1), 37–53. doi:10.4018/IJICTRAME.2018010103

Ekanem, I., & Alrossais, L. A. (2017). Succession Challenges Facing Family Businesses in Saudi Arabia. In P. Zgheib (Ed.), *Entrepreneurship and Business Innovation in the Middle East* (pp. 122–146). Hershey, PA: IGI Global. doi:10.4018/978-1-5225-2066-5.ch007

El Faquih, L., & Fredj, M. (2017). Ontology-Based Framework for Quality in Configurable Process Models. *Journal of Electronic Commerce in Organizations*, 15(2), 48–60. doi:10.4018/JECO.2017040104

El-Gohary, H., & El-Gohary, Z. (2016). An Attempt to Explore Electronic Marketing Adoption and Implementation Aspects in Developing Countries: The Case of Egypt. *International Journal of Customer Relationship Marketing and Management*, 7(4), 1–26. doi:10.4018/IJCRMM.2016100101

Related References

Entico, G. J. (2016). Knowledge Management and the Medical Health Librarians: A Perception Study. In J. Yap, M. Perez, M. Ayson, & G. Entico (Eds.), *Special Library Administration, Standardization and Technological Integration* (pp. 52–77). Hershey, PA: IGI Global. doi:10.4018/978-1-4666-9542-9.ch003

Faisal, M. N., & Talib, F. (2017). Building Ambidextrous Supply Chains in SMEs: How to Tackle the Barriers? *International Journal of Information Systems and Supply Chain Management*, *10*(4), 80–100. doi:10.4018/IJISSCM.2017100105

Fernandes, T. M., Gomes, J., & Romão, M. (2017). Investments in E-Government: A Benefit Management Case Study. *International Journal of Electronic Government Research*, *13*(3), 1–17. doi:10.4018/IJEGR.2017070101

Fouda, F. A. (2016). A Suggested Curriculum in Career Education to Develop Business Secondary Schools Students' Career Knowledge Management Domains and Professional Thinking. *International Journal of Technology Diffusion*, *7*(2), 42–62. doi:10.4018/IJTD.2016040103

Gallardo-Vázquez, D., & Pajuelo-Moreno, M. L. (2016). How Spanish Universities are Promoting Entrepreneurship through Your Own Lines of Teaching and Research? In L. Carvalho (Ed.), *Handbook of Research on Entrepreneurial Success and its Impact on Regional Development* (pp. 431–454). Hershey, PA: IGI Global. doi:10.4018/978-1-4666-9567-2.ch019

Gao, S. S., Oreal, S., & Zhang, J. (2018). Contemporary Financial Risk Management Perceptions and Practices of Small-Sized Chinese Businesses. In I. Management Association (Ed.), Global Business Expansion: Concepts, Methodologies, Tools, and Applications (pp. 917-931). Hershey, PA: IGI Global. doi:10.4018/978-1-5225-5481-3.ch041

Garg, R., & Berning, S. C. (2017). Indigenous Chinese Management Philosophies: Key Concepts and Relevance for Modern Chinese Firms. In B. Christiansen & G. Koc (Eds.), *Transcontinental Strategies for Industrial Development and Economic Growth* (pp. 43–57). Hershey, PA: IGI Global. doi:10.4018/978-1-5225-2160-0.ch003

Gencer, Y. G. (2017). Supply Chain Management in Retailing Business. In U. Akkucuk (Ed.), *Ethics and Sustainability in Global Supply Chain Management* (pp. 197–210). Hershey, PA: IGI Global. doi:10.4018/978-1-5225-2036-8.ch011

Giacosa, E. (2016). Innovation in Luxury Fashion Businesses as a Means for the Regional Development. In L. Carvalho (Ed.), *Handbook of Research on Entrepreneurial Success and its Impact on Regional Development* (pp. 206–222). Hershey, PA: IGI Global. doi:10.4018/978-1-4666-9567-2.ch010

Giacosa, E. (2018). The Increasing of the Regional Development Thanks to the Luxury Business Innovation. In L. Carvalho (Ed.), *Handbook of Research on Entrepreneurial Ecosystems and Social Dynamics in a Globalized World* (pp. 260–273). Hershey, PA: IGI Global. doi:10.4018/978-1-5225-3525-6.ch011

Gianni, M., & Gotzamani, K. (2016). Integrated Management Systems and Information Management Systems: Common Threads. In P. Papajorgji, F. Pinet, A. Guimarães, & J. Papathanasiou (Eds.), *Automated Enterprise Systems for Maximizing Business Performance* (pp. 195–214). Hershey, PA: IGI Global. doi:10.4018/978-1-4666-8841-4.ch011

Gianni, M., Gotzamani, K., & Linden, I. (2016). How a BI-wise Responsible Integrated Management System May Support Food Traceability. *International Journal of Decision Support System Technology*, 8(2), 1–17. doi:10.4018/IJDSST.2016040101

Glykas, M., & George, J. (2017). Quality and Process Management Systems in the UAE Maritime Industry. *International Journal of Productivity Management and Assessment Technologies*, 5(1), 20–39. doi:10.4018/IJPMAT.2017010102

Glykas, M., Valiris, G., Kokkinaki, A., & Koutsoukou, Z. (2018). Banking Business Process Management Implementation. *International Journal of Productivity Management and Assessment Technologies*, 6(1), 50–69. doi:10.4018/IJPMAT.2018010104

Gomes, J., & Romão, M. (2017). The Balanced Scorecard: Keeping Updated and Aligned with Today's Business Trends. *International Journal of Productivity Management and Assessment Technologies*, 5(2), 1–15. doi:10.4018/IJPMAT.2017070101

Gomes, J., & Romão, M. (2017). Aligning Information Systems and Technology with Benefit Management and Balanced Scorecard. In S. De Haes & W. Van Grembergen (Eds.), *Strategic IT Governance and Alignment in Business Settings* (pp. 112–131). Hershey, PA: IGI Global. doi:10.4018/978-1-5225-0861-8.ch005

Grefen, P., & Turetken, O. (2017). Advanced Business Process Management in Networked E-Business Scenarios. *International Journal of E-Business Research*, 13(4), 70–104. doi:10.4018/IJEBR.2017100105

Haider, A., & Saetang, S. (2017). Strategic IT Alignment in Service Sector. In S. Rozenes & Y. Cohen (Eds.), *Handbook of Research on Strategic Alliances and Value Co-Creation in the Service Industry* (pp. 231–258). Hershey, PA: IGI Global. doi:10.4018/978-1-5225-2084-9.ch012

Related References

Haider, A., & Tang, S. S. (2016). Maximising Value Through IT and Business Alignment: A Case of IT Governance Institutionalisation at a Thai Bank. *International Journal of Technology Diffusion, 7*(3), 33–58. doi:10.4018/IJTD.2016070104

Hajilari, A. B., Ghadaksaz, M., & Fasghandis, G. S. (2017). Assessing Organizational Readiness for Implementing ERP System Using Fuzzy Expert System Approach. *International Journal of Enterprise Information Systems, 13*(1), 67–85. doi:10.4018/IJEIS.2017010105

Haldorai, A., Ramu, A., & Murugan, S. (2018). Social Aware Cognitive Radio Networks: Effectiveness of Social Networks as a Strategic Tool for Organizational Business Management. In H. Bansal, G. Shrivastava, G. Nguyen, & L. Stanciu (Eds.), *Social Network Analytics for Contemporary Business Organizations* (pp. 188–202). Hershey, PA: IGI Global. doi:10.4018/978-1-5225-5097-6.ch010

Hall, O. P. Jr. (2017). Social Media Driven Management Education. *International Journal of Knowledge-Based Organizations, 7*(2), 43–59. doi:10.4018/IJKBO.2017040104

Hanifah, H., Halim, H. A., Ahmad, N. H., & Vafaei-Zadeh, A. (2017). Innovation Culture as a Mediator Between Specific Human Capital and Innovation Performance Among Bumiputera SMEs in Malaysia. In N. Ahmad, T. Ramayah, H. Halim, & S. Rahman (Eds.), *Handbook of Research on Small and Medium Enterprises in Developing Countries* (pp. 261–279). Hershey, PA: IGI Global. doi:10.4018/978-1-5225-2165-5.ch012

Hartlieb, S., & Silvius, G. (2017). Handling Uncertainty in Project Management and Business Development: Similarities and Differences. In Y. Raydugin (Ed.), *Handbook of Research on Leveraging Risk and Uncertainties for Effective Project Management* (pp. 337–362). Hershey, PA: IGI Global. doi:10.4018/978-1-5225-1790-0.ch016

Hass, K. B. (2017). Living on the Edge: Managing Project Complexity. In Y. Raydugin (Ed.), *Handbook of Research on Leveraging Risk and Uncertainties for Effective Project Management* (pp. 177–201). Hershey, PA: IGI Global. doi:10.4018/978-1-5225-1790-0.ch009

Hassan, A., & Privitera, D. S. (2016). Google AdSense as a Mobile Technology in Education. In J. Holland (Ed.), *Wearable Technology and Mobile Innovations for Next-Generation Education* (pp. 200–223). Hershey, PA: IGI Global. doi:10.4018/978-1-5225-0069-8.ch011

Hassan, A., & Rahimi, R. (2016). Consuming "Innovation" in Tourism: Augmented Reality as an Innovation Tool in Digital Tourism Marketing. In N. Pappas & I. Bregoli (Eds.), *Global Dynamics in Travel, Tourism, and Hospitality* (pp. 130–147). Hershey, PA: IGI Global. doi:10.4018/978-1-5225-0201-2.ch008

Hawking, P., & Carmine Sellitto, C. (2017). Developing an Effective Strategy for Organizational Business Intelligence. In M. Tavana (Ed.), *Enterprise Information Systems and the Digitalization of Business Functions* (pp. 222–237). Hershey, PA: IGI Global. doi:10.4018/978-1-5225-2382-6.ch010

Hawking, P., & Sellitto, C. (2017). A Fast-Moving Consumer Goods Company and Business Intelligence Strategy Development. *International Journal of Enterprise Information Systems*, *13*(2), 22–33. doi:10.4018/IJEIS.2017040102

Hawking, P., & Sellitto, C. (2017). Business Intelligence Strategy: Two Case Studies. *International Journal of Business Intelligence Research*, *8*(2), 17–30. doi:10.4018/IJBIR.2017070102

Haynes, J. D., Arockiasamy, S., Al Rashdi, M., & Al Rashdi, S. (2016). Business and E Business Strategies for Coopetition and Thematic Management as a Sustained Basis for Ethics and Social Responsibility in Emerging Markets. In M. Al-Shammari & H. Masri (Eds.), *Ethical and Social Perspectives on Global Business Interaction in Emerging Markets* (pp. 25–39). Hershey, PA: IGI Global. doi:10.4018/978-1-4666-9864-2.ch002

Hee, W. J., Jalleh, G., Lai, H., & Lin, C. (2017). E-Commerce and IT Projects: Evaluation and Management Issues in Australian and Taiwanese Hospitals. *International Journal of Public Health Management and Ethics*, *2*(1), 69–90. doi:10.4018/IJPHME.2017010104

Hernandez, A. A. (2018). Exploring the Factors to Green IT Adoption of SMEs in the Philippines. *Journal of Cases on Information Technology*, *20*(2), 49–66. doi:10.4018/JCIT.2018040104

Hernandez, A. A., & Ona, S. E. (2016). Green IT Adoption: Lessons from the Philippines Business Process Outsourcing Industry. *International Journal of Social Ecology and Sustainable Development*, *7*(1), 1–34. doi:10.4018/IJSESD.2016010101

Hollman, A., Bickford, S., & Hollman, T. (2017). Cyber InSecurity: A Post-Mortem Attempt to Assess Cyber Problems from IT and Business Management Perspectives. *Journal of Cases on Information Technology*, *19*(3), 42–70. doi:10.4018/JCIT.2017070104

Related References

Igbinakhase, I. (2017). Responsible and Sustainable Management Practices in Developing and Developed Business Environments. In Z. Fields (Ed.), *Collective Creativity for Responsible and Sustainable Business Practice* (pp. 180–207). Hershey, PA: IGI Global. doi:10.4018/978-1-5225-1823-5.ch010

Ilahi, L., Ghannouchi, S. A., & Martinho, R. (2016). A Business Process Management Approach to Home Healthcare Processes: On the Gap between Intention and Reality. In M. Cruz-Cunha, I. Miranda, R. Martinho, & R. Rijo (Eds.), *Encyclopedia of E-Health and Telemedicine* (pp. 439–457). Hershey, PA: IGI Global. doi:10.4018/978-1-4666-9978-6.ch035

Iwata, J. J., & Hoskins, R. G. (2017). Managing Indigenous Knowledge in Tanzania: A Business Perspective. In P. Jain & N. Mnjama (Eds.), *Managing Knowledge Resources and Records in Modern Organizations* (pp. 198–214). Hershey, PA: IGI Global. doi:10.4018/978-1-5225-1965-2.ch012

Jabeen, F., Ahmad, S. Z., & Alkaabi, S. (2016). The Internationalization Decision-Making of United Arab Emirates Family Businesses. In N. Zakaria, A. Abdul-Talib, & N. Osman (Eds.), *Handbook of Research on Impacts of International Business and Political Affairs on the Global Economy* (pp. 1–22). Hershey, PA: IGI Global. doi:10.4018/978-1-4666-9806-2.ch001

Jain, P. (2017). Ethical and Legal Issues in Knowledge Management Life-Cycle in Business. In P. Jain & N. Mnjama (Eds.), *Managing Knowledge Resources and Records in Modern Organizations* (pp. 82–101). Hershey, PA: IGI Global. doi:10.4018/978-1-5225-1965-2.ch006

Jamali, D., Abdallah, H., & Matar, F. (2016). Opportunities and Challenges for CSR Mainstreaming in Business Schools. *International Journal of Technology and Educational Marketing*, 6(2), 1–29. doi:10.4018/IJTEM.2016070101

James, S., & Hauli, E. (2017). Holistic Management Education at Tanzanian Rural Development Planning Institute. In N. Baporikar (Ed.), *Management Education for Global Leadership* (pp. 112–136). Hershey, PA: IGI Global. doi:10.4018/978-1-5225-1013-0.ch006

Janošková, M., Csikósová, A., & Čulková, K. (2018). Measurement of Company Performance as Part of Its Strategic Management. In R. Leon (Ed.), *Managerial Strategies for Business Sustainability During Turbulent Times* (pp. 309–335). Hershey, PA: IGI Global. doi:10.4018/978-1-5225-2716-9.ch017

Jean-Vasile, A., & Alecu, A. (2017). Theoretical and Practical Approaches in Understanding the Influences of Cost-Productivity-Profit Trinomial in Contemporary Enterprises. In A. Jean Vasile & D. Nicolò (Eds.), *Sustainable Entrepreneurship and Investments in the Green Economy* (pp. 28–62). Hershey, PA: IGI Global. doi:10.4018/978-1-5225-2075-7.ch002

Jha, D. G. (2016). Preparing for Information Technology Driven Changes. In S. Tiwari & L. Nafees (Eds.), *Innovative Management Education Pedagogies for Preparing Next-Generation Leaders* (pp. 258–274). Hershey, PA: IGI Global. doi:10.4018/978-1-4666-9691-4.ch015

Joia, L. A., & Correia, J. C. (2018). CIO Competencies From the IT Professional Perspective: Insights From Brazil. *Journal of Global Information Management*, 26(2), 74–103. doi:10.4018/JGIM.2018040104

Juma, A., & Mzera, N. (2017). Knowledge Management and Records Management and Competitive Advantage in Business. In P. Jain & N. Mnjama (Eds.), *Managing Knowledge Resources and Records in Modern Organizations* (pp. 15–28). Hershey, PA: IGI Global. doi:10.4018/978-1-5225-1965-2.ch002

K., I., & A, V. (2018). Monitoring and Auditing in the Cloud. In K. Munir (Ed.), *Cloud Computing Technologies for Green Enterprises* (pp. 318-350). Hershey, PA: IGI Global. doi:10.4018/978-1-5225-3038-1.ch013

Kabra, G., Ghosh, V., & Ramesh, A. (2018). Enterprise Integrated Business Process Management and Business Intelligence Framework for Business Process Sustainability. In A. Paul, D. Bhattacharyya, & S. Anand (Eds.), *Green Initiatives for Business Sustainability and Value Creation* (pp. 228–238). Hershey, PA: IGI Global. doi:10.4018/978-1-5225-2662-9.ch010

Kaoud, M. (2017). Investigation of Customer Knowledge Management: A Case Study Research. *International Journal of Service Science, Management, Engineering, and Technology*, 8(2), 12–22. doi:10.4018/IJSSMET.2017040102

Kara, M. E., & Fırat, S. Ü. (2016). Sustainability, Risk, and Business Intelligence in Supply Chains. In M. Erdoğdu, T. Arun, & I. Ahmad (Eds.), *Handbook of Research on Green Economic Development Initiatives and Strategies* (pp. 501–538). Hershey, PA: IGI Global. doi:10.4018/978-1-5225-0440-5.ch022

Katuu, S. (2018). A Comparative Assessment of Enterprise Content Management Maturity Models. In N. Gwangwava & M. Mutingi (Eds.), *E-Manufacturing and E-Service Strategies in Contemporary Organizations* (pp. 93–118). Hershey, PA: IGI Global. doi:10.4018/978-1-5225-3628-4.ch005

Related References

Khan, M. A. (2016). MNEs Management Strategies in Developing Countries: Establishing the Context. In M. Khan (Ed.), *Multinational Enterprise Management Strategies in Developing Countries* (pp. 1–33). Hershey, PA: IGI Global. doi:10.4018/978-1-5225-0276-0.ch001

Khan, M. A. (2016). Operational Approaches in Organizational Structure: A Case for MNEs in Developing Countries. In M. Khan (Ed.), *Multinational Enterprise Management Strategies in Developing Countries* (pp. 129–151). Hershey, PA: IGI Global. doi:10.4018/978-1-5225-0276-0.ch007

Kinnunen, S., Ylä-Kujala, A., Marttonen-Arola, S., Kärri, T., & Baglee, D. (2018). Internet of Things in Asset Management: Insights from Industrial Professionals and Academia. *International Journal of Service Science, Management, Engineering, and Technology, 9*(2), 104–119. doi:10.4018/IJSSMET.2018040105

Klein, A. Z., Sabino de Freitas, A., Machado, L., Freitas, J. C. Jr, Graziola, P. G. Jr, & Schlemmer, E. (2017). Virtual Worlds Applications for Management Education. In L. Tomei (Ed.), *Exploring the New Era of Technology-Infused Education* (pp. 279–299). Hershey, PA: IGI Global. doi:10.4018/978-1-5225-1709-2.ch017

Kożuch, B., & Jabłoński, A. (2017). Adopting the Concept of Business Models in Public Management. In M. Lewandowski & B. Kożuch (Eds.), *Public Sector Entrepreneurship and the Integration of Innovative Business Models* (pp. 10–46). Hershey, PA: IGI Global. doi:10.4018/978-1-5225-2215-7.ch002

Kumar, J., Adhikary, A., & Jha, A. (2017). Small Active Investors' Perceptions and Preferences Towards Tax Saving Mutual Fund Schemes in Eastern India: An Empirical Note. *International Journal of Asian Business and Information Management, 8*(2), 35–45. doi:10.4018/IJABIM.2017040103

Lassoued, Y., Bouzguenda, L., & Mahmoud, T. (2016). Context-Aware Business Process Versions Management. *International Journal of e-Collaboration, 12*(3), 7–33. doi:10.4018/IJeC.2016070102

Lavassani, K. M., & Movahedi, B. (2017). Applications Driven Information Systems: Beyond Networks toward Business Ecosystems. *International Journal of Innovation in the Digital Economy, 8*(1), 61–75. doi:10.4018/IJIDE.2017010104

Lazzareschi, V. H., & Brito, M. S. (2017). Strategic Information Management: Proposal of Business Project Model. In G. Jamil, A. Soares, & C. Pessoa (Eds.), *Handbook of Research on Information Management for Effective Logistics and Supply Chains* (pp. 59–88). Hershey, PA: IGI Global. doi:10.4018/978-1-5225-0973-8.ch004

Lederer, M., Kurz, M., & Lazarov, P. (2017). Usage and Suitability of Methods for Strategic Business Process Initiatives: A Multi Case Study Research. *International Journal of Productivity Management and Assessment Technologies*, 5(1), 40–51. doi:10.4018/IJPMAT.2017010103

Lee, I. (2017). A Social Enterprise Business Model and a Case Study of Pacific Community Ventures (PCV). In V. Potocan, M. Üngan, & Z. Nedelko (Eds.), *Handbook of Research on Managerial Solutions in Non-Profit Organizations* (pp. 182–204). Hershey, PA: IGI Global. doi:10.4018/978-1-5225-0731-4.ch009

Lee, L. J., & Leu, J. (2016). Exploring the Effectiveness of IT Application and Value Method in the Innovation Performance of Enterprise. *International Journal of Enterprise Information Systems*, 12(2), 47–65. doi:10.4018/IJEIS.2016040104

Lee, Y. (2016). Alignment Effect of Entrepreneurial Orientation and Marketing Orientation on Firm Performance. *International Journal of Customer Relationship Marketing and Management*, 7(4), 58–69. doi:10.4018/IJCRMM.2016100104

Leon, L. A., Seal, K. C., Przasnyski, Z. H., & Wiedenman, I. (2017). Skills and Competencies Required for Jobs in Business Analytics: A Content Analysis of Job Advertisements Using Text Mining. *International Journal of Business Intelligence Research*, 8(1), 1–25. doi:10.4018/IJBIR.2017010101

Leu, J., Lee, L. J., & Krischke, A. (2016). Value Engineering-Based Method for Implementing the ISO14001 System in the Green Supply Chains. *International Journal of Strategic Decision Sciences*, 7(4), 1–20. doi:10.4018/IJSDS.2016100101

Levy, C. L., & Elias, N. I. (2017). SOHO Users' Perceptions of Reliability and Continuity of Cloud-Based Services. In M. Moore (Ed.), *Cybersecurity Breaches and Issues Surrounding Online Threat Protection* (pp. 248–287). Hershey, PA: IGI Global. doi:10.4018/978-1-5225-1941-6.ch011

Levy, M. (2018). Change Management Serving Knowledge Management and Organizational Development: Reflections and Review. In N. Baporikar (Ed.), *Global Practices in Knowledge Management for Societal and Organizational Development* (pp. 256–270). Hershey, PA: IGI Global. doi:10.4018/978-1-5225-3009-1.ch012

Lewandowski, M. (2017). Public Organizations and Business Model Innovation: The Role of Public Service Design. In M. Lewandowski & B. Kożuch (Eds.), *Public Sector Entrepreneurship and the Integration of Innovative Business Models* (pp. 47–72). Hershey, PA: IGI Global. doi:10.4018/978-1-5225-2215-7.ch003

Related References

Lhannaoui, H., Kabbaj, M. I., & Bakkoury, Z. (2017). A Survey of Risk-Aware Business Process Modelling. *International Journal of Risk and Contingency Management, 6*(3), 14–26. doi:10.4018/IJRCM.2017070102

Li, J., Sun, W., Jiang, W., Yang, H., & Zhang, L. (2017). How the Nature of Exogenous Shocks and Crises Impact Company Performance?: The Effects of Industry Characteristics. *International Journal of Risk and Contingency Management, 6*(4), 40–55. doi:10.4018/IJRCM.2017100103

Lu, C., & Liu, S. (2016). Cultural Tourism O2O Business Model Innovation-A Case Study of CTrip. *Journal of Electronic Commerce in Organizations, 14*(2), 16–31. doi:10.4018/JECO.2016040102

Machen, B., Hosseini, M. R., Wood, A., & Bakhshi, J. (2016). An Investigation into using SAP-PS as a Multidimensional Project Control System (MPCS). *International Journal of Enterprise Information Systems, 12*(2), 66–81. doi:10.4018/IJEIS.2016040105

Malega, P. (2017). Small and Medium Enterprises in the Slovak Republic: Status and Competitiveness of SMEs in the Global Markets and Possibilities of Optimization. In M. Vemić (Ed.), *Optimal Management Strategies in Small and Medium Enterprises* (pp. 102–124). Hershey, PA: IGI Global. doi:10.4018/978-1-5225-1949-2.ch006

Malewska, K. M. (2017). Intuition in Decision-Making on the Example of a Non-Profit Organization. In V. Potocan, M. Üngan, & Z. Nedelko (Eds.), *Handbook of Research on Managerial Solutions in Non-Profit Organizations* (pp. 378–399). Hershey, PA: IGI Global. doi:10.4018/978-1-5225-0731-4.ch018

Maroofi, F. (2017). Entrepreneurial Orientation and Organizational Learning Ability Analysis for Innovation and Firm Performance. In N. Baporikar (Ed.), *Innovation and Shifting Perspectives in Management Education* (pp. 144–165). Hershey, PA: IGI Global. doi:10.4018/978-1-5225-1019-2.ch007

Martins, P. V., & Zacarias, M. (2017). A Web-based Tool for Business Process Improvement. *International Journal of Web Portals, 9*(2), 68–84. doi:10.4018/IJWP.2017070104

Matthies, B., & Coners, A. (2017). Exploring the Conceptual Nature of e-Business Projects. *Journal of Electronic Commerce in Organizations, 15*(3), 33–63. doi:10.4018/JECO.2017070103

McKee, J. (2018). Architecture as a Tool to Solve Business Planning Problems. In M. Khosrow-Pour, D.B.A. (Ed.), Encyclopedia of Information Science and Technology, Fourth Edition (pp. 573-586). Hershey, PA: IGI Global. doi:10.4018/978-1-5225-2255-3.ch050

McMurray, A. J., Cross, J., & Caponecchia, C. (2018). The Risk Management Profession in Australia: Business Continuity Plan Practices. In N. Bajgoric (Ed.), *Always-On Enterprise Information Systems for Modern Organizations* (pp. 112–129). Hershey, PA: IGI Global. doi:10.4018/978-1-5225-3704-5.ch006

Meddah, I. H., & Belkadi, K. (2018). Mining Patterns Using Business Process Management. In R. Hamou (Ed.), *Handbook of Research on Biomimicry in Information Retrieval and Knowledge Management* (pp. 78–89). Hershey, PA: IGI Global. doi:10.4018/978-1-5225-3004-6.ch005

Mendes, L. (2017). TQM and Knowledge Management: An Integrated Approach Towards Tacit Knowledge Management. In D. Jaziri-Bouagina & G. Jamil (Eds.), *Handbook of Research on Tacit Knowledge Management for Organizational Success* (pp. 236–263). Hershey, PA: IGI Global. doi:10.4018/978-1-5225-2394-9.ch009

Mnjama, N. M. (2017). Preservation of Recorded Information in Public and Private Sector Organizations. In P. Jain & N. Mnjama (Eds.), *Managing Knowledge Resources and Records in Modern Organizations* (pp. 149–167). Hershey, PA: IGI Global. doi:10.4018/978-1-5225-1965-2.ch009

Mokoqama, M., & Fields, Z. (2017). Principles of Responsible Management Education (PRME): Call for Responsible Management Education. In Z. Fields (Ed.), *Collective Creativity for Responsible and Sustainable Business Practice* (pp. 229–241). Hershey, PA: IGI Global. doi:10.4018/978-1-5225-1823-5.ch012

Muniapan, B. (2017). Philosophy and Management: The Relevance of Vedanta in Management. In P. Ordóñez de Pablos (Ed.), *Managerial Strategies and Solutions for Business Success in Asia* (pp. 124–139). Hershey, PA: IGI Global. doi:10.4018/978-1-5225-1886-0.ch007

Muniapan, B., Gregory, M. L., & Ling, L. A. (2016). Marketing Education in Sarawak: Looking at It from the Employers' Viewpoint. In B. Smith & A. Porath (Eds.), *Global Perspectives on Contemporary Marketing Education* (pp. 112–130). Hershey, PA: IGI Global. doi:10.4018/978-1-4666-9784-3.ch008

Murad, S. E., & Dowaji, S. (2017). Using Value-Based Approach for Managing Cloud-Based Services. In A. Turuk, B. Sahoo, & S. Addya (Eds.), *Resource Management and Efficiency in Cloud Computing Environments* (pp. 33–60). Hershey, PA: IGI Global. doi:10.4018/978-1-5225-1721-4.ch002

Related References

Mutahar, A. M., Daud, N. M., Thurasamy, R., Isaac, O., & Abdulsalam, R. (2018). The Mediating of Perceived Usefulness and Perceived Ease of Use: The Case of Mobile Banking in Yemen. *International Journal of Technology Diffusion*, 9(2), 21–40. doi:10.4018/IJTD.2018040102

Naidoo, V. (2017). E-Learning and Management Education at African Universities. In N. Baporikar (Ed.), *Management Education for Global Leadership* (pp. 181–201). Hershey, PA: IGI Global. doi:10.4018/978-1-5225-1013-0.ch009

Naidoo, V., & Igbinakhase, I. (2018). Opportunities and Challenges of Knowledge Retention in SMEs. In N. Baporikar (Ed.), *Knowledge Integration Strategies for Entrepreneurship and Sustainability* (pp. 70–94). Hershey, PA: IGI Global. doi:10.4018/978-1-5225-5115-7.ch004

Nayak, S., & Prabhu, N. (2017). Paradigm Shift in Management Education: Need for a Cross Functional Perspective. In N. Baporikar (Ed.), *Management Education for Global Leadership* (pp. 241–255). Hershey, PA: IGI Global. doi:10.4018/978-1-5225-1013-0.ch012

Ndede-Amadi, A. A. (2016). Student Interest in the IS Specialization as Predictor of the Success Potential of New Information Systems Programmes within the Schools of Business in Kenyan Public Universities. *International Journal of Information Systems and Social Change*, 7(2), 63–79. doi:10.4018/IJISSC.2016040104

Nedelko, Z., & Potocan, V. (2016). Management Practices for Processes Optimization: Case of Slovenia. In G. Alor-Hernández, C. Sánchez-Ramírez, & J. García-Alcaraz (Eds.), *Handbook of Research on Managerial Strategies for Achieving Optimal Performance in Industrial Processes* (pp. 545–561). Hershey, PA: IGI Global. doi:10.4018/978-1-5225-0130-5.ch025

Nedelko, Z., & Potocan, V. (2017). Management Solutions in Non-Profit Organizations: Case of Slovenia. In V. Potocan, M. Üngan, & Z. Nedelko (Eds.), *Handbook of Research on Managerial Solutions in Non-Profit Organizations* (pp. 1–22). Hershey, PA: IGI Global. doi:10.4018/978-1-5225-0731-4.ch001

Nedelko, Z., & Potocan, V. (2017). Priority of Management Tools Utilization among Managers: International Comparison. In V. Wang (Ed.), *Encyclopedia of Strategic Leadership and Management* (pp. 1083–1094). Hershey, PA: IGI Global. doi:10.4018/978-1-5225-1049-9.ch075

Nedelko, Z., Raudeliūnienė, J., & Črešnar, R. (2018). Knowledge Dynamics in Supply Chain Management. In N. Baporikar (Ed.), *Knowledge Integration Strategies for Entrepreneurship and Sustainability* (pp. 150–166). Hershey, PA: IGI Global. doi:10.4018/978-1-5225-5115-7.ch008

Nguyen, H. T., & Hipsher, S. A. (2018). Innovation and Creativity Used by Private Sector Firms in a Resources-Constrained Environment. In S. Hipsher (Ed.), *Examining the Private Sector's Role in Wealth Creation and Poverty Reduction* (pp. 219–238). Hershey, PA: IGI Global. doi:10.4018/978-1-5225-3117-3.ch010

Nycz, M., & Pólkowski, Z. (2016). Business Intelligence as a Modern IT Supporting Management of Local Government Units in Poland. *International Journal of Knowledge and Systems Science, 7*(4), 1–18. doi:10.4018/IJKSS.2016100101

Obaji, N. O., Senin, A. A., & Olugu, M. U. (2016). Supportive Government Policy as a Mechanism for Business Incubation Performance in Nigeria. *International Journal of Information Systems and Social Change, 7*(4), 52–66. doi:10.4018/IJISSC.2016100103

Obicci, P. A. (2017). Risk Sharing in a Partnership. In *Risk Management Strategies in Public-Private Partnerships* (pp. 115–152). Hershey, PA: IGI Global. doi:10.4018/978-1-5225-2503-5.ch004

Obidallah, W. J., & Raahemi, B. (2017). Managing Changes in Service Oriented Virtual Organizations: A Structural and Procedural Framework to Facilitate the Process of Change. *Journal of Electronic Commerce in Organizations, 15*(1), 59–83. doi:10.4018/JECO.2017010104

Ojasalo, J., & Ojasalo, K. (2016). Service Logic Business Model Canvas for Lean Development of SMEs and Start-Ups. In N. Baporikar (Ed.), *Handbook of Research on Entrepreneurship in the Contemporary Knowledge-Based Global Economy* (pp. 217–243). Hershey, PA: IGI Global. doi:10.4018/978-1-4666-8798-1.ch010

Ojo, O. (2017). Impact of Innovation on the Entrepreneurial Success in Selected Business Enterprises in South-West Nigeria. *International Journal of Innovation in the Digital Economy, 8*(2), 29–38. doi:10.4018/IJIDE.2017040103

Okdinawati, L., Simatupang, T. M., & Sunitiyoso, Y. (2017). Multi-Agent Reinforcement Learning for Value Co-Creation of Collaborative Transportation Management (CTM). *International Journal of Information Systems and Supply Chain Management, 10*(3), 84–95. doi:10.4018/IJISSCM.2017070105

Ortner, E., Mevius, M., Wiedmann, P., & Kurz, F. (2016). Design of Interactional Decision Support Applications for E-Participation in Smart Cities. *International Journal of Electronic Government Research, 12*(2), 18–38. doi:10.4018/IJEGR.2016040102

Related References

Pal, K. (2018). Building High Quality Big Data-Based Applications in Supply Chains. In A. Kumar & S. Saurav (Eds.), *Supply Chain Management Strategies and Risk Assessment in Retail Environments* (pp. 1–24). Hershey, PA: IGI Global. doi:10.4018/978-1-5225-3056-5.ch001

Palos-Sanchez, P. R., & Correia, M. B. (2018). Perspectives of the Adoption of Cloud Computing in the Tourism Sector. In J. Rodrigues, C. Ramos, P. Cardoso, & C. Henriques (Eds.), *Handbook of Research on Technological Developments for Cultural Heritage and eTourism Applications* (pp. 377–400). Hershey, PA: IGI Global. doi:10.4018/978-1-5225-2927-9.ch018

Parry, V. K., & Lind, M. L. (2016). Alignment of Business Strategy and Information Technology Considering Information Technology Governance, Project Portfolio Control, and Risk Management. *International Journal of Information Technology Project Management, 7*(4), 21–37. doi:10.4018/IJITPM.2016100102

Pashkova, N., Trujillo-Barrera, A., Apostolakis, G., Van Dijk, G., Drakos, P. D., & Baourakis, G. (2016). Business Management Models of Microfinance Institutions (MFIs) in Africa: A Study into Their Enabling Environments. *International Journal of Food and Beverage Manufacturing and Business Models, 1*(2), 63–82. doi:10.4018/IJFBMBM.2016070105

Patiño, B. E. (2017). New Generation Management by Convergence and Individual Identity: A Systemic and Human-Oriented Approach. In N. Baporikar (Ed.), *Innovation and Shifting Perspectives in Management Education* (pp. 119–143). Hershey, PA: IGI Global. doi:10.4018/978-1-5225-1019-2.ch006

Pawliczek, A., & Rössler, M. (2017). Knowledge of Management Tools and Systems in SMEs: Knowledge Transfer in Management. In A. Bencsik (Ed.), *Knowledge Management Initiatives and Strategies in Small and Medium Enterprises* (pp. 180–203). Hershey, PA: IGI Global. doi:10.4018/978-1-5225-1642-2.ch009

Pejic-Bach, M., Omazic, M. A., Aleksic, A., & Zoroja, J. (2018). Knowledge-Based Decision Making: A Multi-Case Analysis. In R. Leon (Ed.), *Managerial Strategies for Business Sustainability During Turbulent Times* (pp. 160–184). Hershey, PA: IGI Global. doi:10.4018/978-1-5225-2716-9.ch009

Perano, M., Hysa, X., & Calabrese, M. (2018). Strategic Planning, Cultural Context, and Business Continuity Management: Business Cases in the City of Shkoder. In A. Presenza & L. Sheehan (Eds.), *Geopolitics and Strategic Management in the Global Economy* (pp. 57–77). Hershey, PA: IGI Global. doi:10.4018/978-1-5225-2673-5.ch004

Pereira, R., Mira da Silva, M., & Lapão, L. V. (2017). IT Governance Maturity Patterns in Portuguese Healthcare. In S. De Haes & W. Van Grembergen (Eds.), *Strategic IT Governance and Alignment in Business Settings* (pp. 24–52). Hershey, PA: IGI Global. doi:10.4018/978-1-5225-0861-8.ch002

Perez-Uribe, R., & Ocampo-Guzman, D. (2016). Conflict within Colombian Family Owned SMEs: An Explosive Blend between Feelings and Business. In J. Saiz-Álvarez (Ed.), *Handbook of Research on Social Entrepreneurship and Solidarity Economics* (pp. 329–354). Hershey, PA: IGI Global. doi:10.4018/978-1-5225-0097-1.ch017

Pérez-Uribe, R. I., Torres, D. A., Jurado, S. P., & Prada, D. M. (2018). Cloud Tools for the Development of Project Management in SMEs. In R. Perez-Uribe, C. Salcedo-Perez, & D. Ocampo-Guzman (Eds.), *Handbook of Research on Intrapreneurship and Organizational Sustainability in SMEs* (pp. 95–120). Hershey, PA: IGI Global. doi:10.4018/978-1-5225-3543-0.ch005

Petrisor, I., & Cozmiuc, D. (2017). Global Supply Chain Management Organization at Siemens in the Advent of Industry 4.0. In L. Saglietto & C. Cezanne (Eds.), *Global Intermediation and Logistics Service Providers* (pp. 123–142). Hershey, PA: IGI Global. doi:10.4018/978-1-5225-2133-4.ch007

Pierce, J. M., Velliaris, D. M., & Edwards, J. (2017). A Living Case Study: A Journey Not a Destination. In N. Silton (Ed.), *Exploring the Benefits of Creativity in Education, Media, and the Arts* (pp. 158–178). Hershey, PA: IGI Global. doi:10.4018/978-1-5225-0504-4.ch008

Radosavljevic, M., & Andjelkovic, A. (2017). Multi-Criteria Decision Making Approach for Choosing Business Process for the Improvement: Upgrading of the Six Sigma Methodology. In J. Stanković, P. Delias, S. Marinković, & S. Rochhia (Eds.), *Tools and Techniques for Economic Decision Analysis* (pp. 225–247). Hershey, PA: IGI Global. doi:10.4018/978-1-5225-0959-2.ch011

Radovic, V. M. (2017). Corporate Sustainability and Responsibility and Disaster Risk Reduction: A Serbian Overview. In M. Camilleri (Ed.), *CSR 2.0 and the New Era of Corporate Citizenship* (pp. 147–164). Hershey, PA: IGI Global. doi:10.4018/978-1-5225-1842-6.ch008

Raghunath, K. M., Devi, S. L., & Patro, C. S. (2018). Impact of Risk Assessment Models on Risk Factors: A Holistic Outlook. In K. Strang, M. Korstanje, & N. Vajjhala (Eds.), *Research, Practices, and Innovations in Global Risk and Contingency Management* (pp. 134–153). Hershey, PA: IGI Global. doi:10.4018/978-1-5225-4754-9.ch008

Related References

Raman, A., & Goyal, D. P. (2017). Extending IMPLEMENT Framework for Enterprise Information Systems Implementation to Information System Innovation. In M. Tavana (Ed.), *Enterprise Information Systems and the Digitalization of Business Functions* (pp. 137–177). Hershey, PA: IGI Global. doi:10.4018/978-1-5225-2382-6.ch007

Rao, Y., & Zhang, Y. (2017). The Construction and Development of Academic Library Digital Special Subject Databases. In L. Ruan, Q. Zhu, & Y. Ye (Eds.), *Academic Library Development and Administration in China* (pp. 163–183). Hershey, PA: IGI Global. doi:10.4018/978-1-5225-0550-1.ch010

Ravasan, A. Z., Mohammadi, M. M., & Hamidi, H. (2018). An Investigation Into the Critical Success Factors of Implementing Information Technology Service Management Frameworks. In K. Jakobs (Ed.), *Corporate and Global Standardization Initiatives in Contemporary Society* (pp. 200–218). Hershey, PA: IGI Global. doi:10.4018/978-1-5225-5320-5.ch009

Renna, P., Izzo, C., & Romaniello, T. (2016). The Business Process Management Systems to Support Continuous Improvements. In W. Nuninger & J. Châtelet (Eds.), *Handbook of Research on Quality Assurance and Value Management in Higher Education* (pp. 237–256). Hershey, PA: IGI Global. doi:10.4018/978-1-5225-0024-7.ch009

Rezaie, S., Mirabedini, S. J., & Abtahi, A. (2018). Designing a Model for Implementation of Business Intelligence in the Banking Industry. *International Journal of Enterprise Information Systems, 14*(1), 77–103. doi:10.4018/IJEIS.2018010105

Riccò, R. (2016). Diversity Management: Bringing Equality, Equity, and Inclusion in the Workplace. In J. Prescott (Ed.), *Handbook of Research on Race, Gender, and the Fight for Equality* (pp. 335–359). Hershey, PA: IGI Global. doi:10.4018/978-1-5225-0047-6.ch015

Romano, L., Grimaldi, R., & Colasuonno, F. S. (2017). Demand Management as a Success Factor in Project Portfolio Management. In L. Romano (Ed.), *Project Portfolio Management Strategies for Effective Organizational Operations* (pp. 202–219). Hershey, PA: IGI Global. doi:10.4018/978-1-5225-2151-8.ch008

Rostek, K. B. (2016). Risk Management: Role and Importance in Business Organization. In D. Jakóbczak (Ed.), *Analyzing Risk through Probabilistic Modeling in Operations Research* (pp. 149–178). Hershey, PA: IGI Global. doi:10.4018/978-1-4666-9458-3.ch007

Rouhani, S., & Savoji, S. R. (2016). A Success Assessment Model for BI Tools Implementation: An Empirical Study of Banking Industry. *International Journal of Business Intelligence Research, 7*(1), 25–44. doi:10.4018/IJBIR.2016010103

Ruan, Z. (2016). A Corpus-Based Functional Analysis of Complex Nominal Groups in Written Business Discourse: The Case of "Business". *International Journal of Computer-Assisted Language Learning and Teaching*, 6(2), 74–90. doi:10.4018/IJCALLT.2016040105

Ruhi, U. (2018). Towards an Interdisciplinary Socio-Technical Definition of Virtual Communities. In M. Khosrow-Pour, D.B.A. (Ed.), Encyclopedia of Information Science and Technology, Fourth Edition (pp. 4278-4295). Hershey, PA: IGI Global. doi:10.4018/978-1-5225-2255-3.ch371

Ryan, J., Doster, B., Daily, S., & Lewis, C. (2016). A Case Study Perspective for Balanced Perioperative Workflow Achievement through Data-Driven Process Improvement. *International Journal of Healthcare Information Systems and Informatics*, *11*(3), 19–41. doi:10.4018/IJHISI.2016070102

Safari, M. R., & Jiang, Q. (2018). The Theory and Practice of IT Governance Maturity and Strategies Alignment: Evidence From Banking Industry. *Journal of Global Information Management*, *26*(2), 127–146. doi:10.4018/JGIM.2018040106

Sahoo, J., Pati, B., & Mohanty, B. (2017). Knowledge Management as an Academic Discipline: An Assessment. In B. Gunjal (Ed.), *Managing Knowledge and Scholarly Assets in Academic Libraries* (pp. 99–126). Hershey, PA: IGI Global. doi:10.4018/978-1-5225-1741-2.ch005

Saini, D. (2017). Relevance of Teaching Values and Ethics in Management Education. In N. Baporikar (Ed.), *Management Education for Global Leadership* (pp. 90–111). Hershey, PA: IGI Global. doi:10.4018/978-1-5225-1013-0.ch005

Sambhanthan, A. (2017). Assessing and Benchmarking Sustainability in Organisations: An Integrated Conceptual Model. *International Journal of Systems and Service-Oriented Engineering*, 7(4), 22–43. doi:10.4018/IJSSOE.2017100102

Sambhanthan, A., & Potdar, V. (2017). A Study of the Parameters Impacting Sustainability in Information Technology Organizations. *International Journal of Knowledge-Based Organizations*, 7(3), 27–39. doi:10.4018/IJKBO.2017070103

Sánchez-Fernández, M. D., & Manríquez, M. R. (2018). The Entrepreneurial Spirit Based on Social Values: The Digital Generation. In P. Isaias & L. Carvalho (Eds.), *User Innovation and the Entrepreneurship Phenomenon in the Digital Economy* (pp. 173–193). Hershey, PA: IGI Global. doi:10.4018/978-1-5225-2826-5.ch009

Related References

Sanchez-Ruiz, L., & Blanco, B. (2017). Process Management for SMEs: Barriers, Enablers, and Benefits. In M. Vemić (Ed.), *Optimal Management Strategies in Small and Medium Enterprises* (pp. 293–319). Hershey, PA: IGI Global. doi:10.4018/978-1-5225-1949-2.ch014

Sanz, L. F., Gómez-Pérez, J., & Castillo-Martinez, A. (2018). Analysis of the European ICT Competence Frameworks. In V. Ahuja & S. Rathore (Eds.), *Multidisciplinary Perspectives on Human Capital and Information Technology Professionals* (pp. 225–245). Hershey, PA: IGI Global. doi:10.4018/978-1-5225-5297-0.ch012

Sarvepalli, A., & Godin, J. (2017). Business Process Management in the Classroom. *Journal of Cases on Information Technology*, *19*(2), 17–28. doi:10.4018/JCIT.2017040102

Satpathy, B., & Muniapan, B. (2016). Ancient Wisdom for Transformational Leadership and Its Insights from the Bhagavad-Gita. In U. Aung & P. Ordoñez de Pablos (Eds.), *Managerial Strategies and Practice in the Asian Business Sector* (pp. 1–10). Hershey, PA: IGI Global. doi:10.4018/978-1-4666-9758-4.ch001

Saygili, E. E., Ozturkoglu, Y., & Kocakulah, M. C. (2017). End Users' Perceptions of Critical Success Factors in ERP Applications. *International Journal of Enterprise Information Systems*, *13*(4), 58–75. doi:10.4018/IJEIS.2017100104

Saygili, E. E., & Saygili, A. T. (2017). Contemporary Issues in Enterprise Information Systems: A Critical Review of CSFs in ERP Implementations. In M. Tavana (Ed.), *Enterprise Information Systems and the Digitalization of Business Functions* (pp. 120–136). Hershey, PA: IGI Global. doi:10.4018/978-1-5225-2382-6.ch006

Seidenstricker, S., & Antonino, A. (2018). Business Model Innovation-Oriented Technology Management for Emergent Technologies. In M. Khosrow-Pour, D.B.A. (Ed.), Encyclopedia of Information Science and Technology, Fourth Edition (pp. 4560-4569). Hershey, PA: IGI Global. doi:10.4018/978-1-5225-2255-3.ch396

Senaratne, S., & Gunarathne, A. D. (2017). Excellence Perspective for Management Education from a Global Accountants' Hub in Asia. In N. Baporikar (Ed.), *Management Education for Global Leadership* (pp. 158–180). Hershey, PA: IGI Global. doi:10.4018/978-1-5225-1013-0.ch008

Sensuse, D. I., & Cahyaningsih, E. (2018). Knowledge Management Models: A Summative Review. *International Journal of Information Systems in the Service Sector*, *10*(1), 71–100. doi:10.4018/IJISSS.2018010105

Sensuse, D. I., Wibowo, W. C., & Cahyaningsih, E. (2016). Indonesian Government Knowledge Management Model: A Theoretical Model. *Information Resources Management Journal*, *29*(1), 91–108. doi:10.4018/irmj.2016010106

Seth, M., Goyal, D., & Kiran, R. (2017). Diminution of Impediments in Implementation of Supply Chain Management Information System for Enhancing its Effectiveness in Indian Automobile Industry. *Journal of Global Information Management*, *25*(3), 1–20. doi:10.4018/JGIM.2017070101

Seyal, A. H., & Rahman, M. N. (2017). Investigating Impact of Inter-Organizational Factors in Measuring ERP Systems Success: Bruneian Perspectives. In M. Tavana (Ed.), *Enterprise Information Systems and the Digitalization of Business Functions* (pp. 178–204). Hershey, PA: IGI Global. doi:10.4018/978-1-5225-2382-6.ch008

Shaikh, A. A., & Karjaluoto, H. (2016). On Some Misconceptions Concerning Digital Banking and Alternative Delivery Channels. *International Journal of E-Business Research*, *12*(3), 1–16. doi:10.4018/IJEBR.2016070101

Shams, S. M. (2016). Stakeholder Relationship Management in Online Business and Competitive Value Propositions: Evidence from the Sports Industry. *International Journal of Online Marketing*, *6*(2), 1–17. doi:10.4018/IJOM.2016040101

Shamsuzzoha, A. (2016). Management of Risk and Resilience within Collaborative Business Network. In R. Addo-Tenkorang, J. Kantola, P. Helo, & A. Shamsuzzoha (Eds.), *Supply Chain Strategies and the Engineer-to-Order Approach* (pp. 143–159). Hershey, PA: IGI Global. doi:10.4018/978-1-5225-0021-6.ch008

Shaqrah, A. A. (2018). Analyzing Business Intelligence Systems Based on 7s Model of McKinsey. *International Journal of Business Intelligence Research*, *9*(1), 53–63. doi:10.4018/IJBIR.2018010104

Sharma, A. J. (2017). Enhancing Sustainability through Experiential Learning in Management Education. In N. Baporikar (Ed.), *Management Education for Global Leadership* (pp. 256–274). Hershey, PA: IGI Global. doi:10.4018/978-1-5225-1013-0.ch013

Shetty, K. P. (2017). Responsible Global Leadership: Ethical Challenges in Management Education. In N. Baporikar (Ed.), *Innovation and Shifting Perspectives in Management Education* (pp. 194–223). Hershey, PA: IGI Global. doi:10.4018/978-1-5225-1019-2.ch009

Related References

Sinthupundaja, J., & Kohda, Y. (2017). Effects of Corporate Social Responsibility and Creating Shared Value on Sustainability. *International Journal of Sustainable Entrepreneurship and Corporate Social Responsibility, 2*(1), 27–38. doi:10.4018/IJSECSR.2017010103

Škarica, I., & Hrgović, A. V. (2018). Implementation of Total Quality Management Principles in Public Health Institutes in the Republic of Croatia. *International Journal of Productivity Management and Assessment Technologies, 6*(1), 1–16. doi:10.4018/IJPMAT.2018010101

Smuts, H., Kotzé, P., Van der Merwe, A., & Loock, M. (2017). Framework for Managing Shared Knowledge in an Information Systems Outsourcing Context. *International Journal of Knowledge Management, 13*(4), 1–30. doi:10.4018/IJKM.2017100101

Soares, E. R., & Zaidan, F. H. (2016). Information Architecture and Business Modeling in Modern Organizations of Information Technology: Professional Career Plan in Organizations IT. In G. Jamil, J. Poças Rascão, F. Ribeiro, & A. Malheiro da Silva (Eds.), *Handbook of Research on Information Architecture and Management in Modern Organizations* (pp. 439–457). Hershey, PA: IGI Global. doi:10.4018/978-1-4666-8637-3.ch020

Sousa, M. J., Cruz, R., Dias, I., & Caracol, C. (2017). Information Management Systems in the Supply Chain. In G. Jamil, A. Soares, & C. Pessoa (Eds.), *Handbook of Research on Information Management for Effective Logistics and Supply Chains* (pp. 469–485). Hershey, PA: IGI Global. doi:10.4018/978-1-5225-0973-8.ch025

Spremic, M., Turulja, L., & Bajgoric, N. (2018). Two Approaches in Assessing Business Continuity Management Attitudes in the Organizational Context. In N. Bajgoric (Ed.), *Always-On Enterprise Information Systems for Modern Organizations* (pp. 159–183). Hershey, PA: IGI Global. doi:10.4018/978-1-5225-3704-5.ch008

Steenkamp, A. L. (2018). Some Insights in Computer Science and Information Technology. In *Examining the Changing Role of Supervision in Doctoral Research Projects: Emerging Research and Opportunities* (pp. 113–133). Hershey, PA: IGI Global. doi:10.4018/978-1-5225-2610-0.ch005

Studdard, N., Dawson, M., Burton, S. L., Jackson, N., Leonard, B., Quisenberry, W., & Rahim, E. (2016). Nurturing Social Entrepreneurship and Building Social Entrepreneurial Self-Efficacy: Focusing on Primary and Secondary Schooling to Develop Future Social Entrepreneurs. In Z. Fields (Ed.), *Incorporating Business Models and Strategies into Social Entrepreneurship* (pp. 154–175). Hershey, PA: IGI Global. doi:10.4018/978-1-4666-8748-6.ch010

Related References

Sun, Z. (2016). A Framework for Developing Management Intelligent Systems. *International Journal of Systems and Service-Oriented Engineering, 6*(1), 37–53. doi:10.4018/IJSSOE.2016010103

Swami, B., & Mphele, G. T. (2016). Problems Preventing Growth of Small Entrepreneurs: A Case Study of a Few Small Entrepreneurs in Botswana Sub-Urban Areas. In N. Baporikar (Ed.), *Handbook of Research on Entrepreneurship in the Contemporary Knowledge-Based Global Economy* (pp. 479–508). Hershey, PA: IGI Global. doi:10.4018/978-1-4666-8798-1.ch020

Tabach, A., & Croteau, A. (2017). Configurations of Information Technology Governance Practices and Business Unit Performance. *International Journal of IT/Business Alignment and Governance, 8*(2), 1–27. doi:10.4018/IJITBAG.2017070101

Talaue, G. M., & Iqbal, T. (2017). Assessment of e-Business Mode of Selected Private Universities in the Philippines and Pakistan. *International Journal of Online Marketing, 7*(4), 63–77. doi:10.4018/IJOM.2017100105

Tam, G. C. (2017). Project Manager Sustainability Competence. In *Managerial Strategies and Green Solutions for Project Sustainability* (pp. 178–207). Hershey, PA: IGI Global. doi:10.4018/978-1-5225-2371-0.ch008

Tambo, T. (2018). Fashion Retail Innovation: About Context, Antecedents, and Outcome in Technological Change Projects. In I. Management Association (Ed.), Fashion and Textiles: Breakthroughs in Research and Practice (pp. 233-260). Hershey, PA: IGI Global. doi:10.4018/978-1-5225-3432-7.ch010

Tambo, T., & Mikkelsen, O. E. (2016). Fashion Supply Chain Optimization: Linking Make-to-Order Purchasing and B2B E-Commerce. In S. Joshi & R. Joshi (Eds.), *Designing and Implementing Global Supply Chain Management* (pp. 1–21). Hershey, PA: IGI Global. doi:10.4018/978-1-4666-9720-1.ch001

Tandon, K. (2016). Innovative Andragogy: The Paradigm Shift to Heutagogy. In S. Tiwari & L. Nafees (Eds.), *Innovative Management Education Pedagogies for Preparing Next-Generation Leaders* (pp. 238–257). Hershey, PA: IGI Global. doi:10.4018/978-1-4666-9691-4.ch014

Tantau, A. D., & Frățilă, L. C. (2018). Information and Management System for Renewable Energy Business. In *Entrepreneurship and Business Development in the Renewable Energy Sector* (pp. 200–244). Hershey, PA: IGI Global. doi:10.4018/978-1-5225-3625-3.ch006

Related References

Teixeira, N., Pardal, P. N., & Rafael, B. G. (2018). Internationalization, Financial Performance, and Organizational Challenges: A Success Case in Portugal. In L. Carvalho (Ed.), *Handbook of Research on Entrepreneurial Ecosystems and Social Dynamics in a Globalized World* (pp. 379–423). Hershey, PA: IGI Global. doi:10.4018/978-1-5225-3525-6.ch017

Trad, A., & Kalpić, D. (2016). The E-Business Transformation Framework for E-Commerce Architecture-Modeling Projects. In I. Lee (Ed.), *Encyclopedia of E-Commerce Development, Implementation, and Management* (pp. 733–753). Hershey, PA: IGI Global. doi:10.4018/978-1-4666-9787-4.ch052

Trad, A., & Kalpić, D. (2016). The E-Business Transformation Framework for E-Commerce Control and Monitoring Pattern. In I. Lee (Ed.), *Encyclopedia of E-Commerce Development, Implementation, and Management* (pp. 754–777). Hershey, PA: IGI Global. doi:10.4018/978-1-4666-9787-4.ch053

Trad, A., & Kalpić, D. (2018). The Business Transformation Framework, Agile Project and Change Management. In M. Khosrow-Pour, D.B.A. (Ed.), Encyclopedia of Information Science and Technology, Fourth Edition (pp. 620-635). Hershey, PA: IGI Global. doi:10.4018/978-1-5225-2255-3.ch054

Trad, A., & Kalpić, D. (2018). The Business Transformation and Enterprise Architecture Framework: The Financial Engineering E-Risk Management and E-Law Integration. In B. Sergi, F. Fidanoski, M. Ziolo, & V. Naumovski (Eds.), *Regaining Global Stability After the Financial Crisis* (pp. 46–65). Hershey, PA: IGI Global. doi:10.4018/978-1-5225-4026-7.ch003

Turulja, L., & Bajgoric, N. (2018). Business Continuity and Information Systems: A Systematic Literature Review. In N. Bajgoric (Ed.), *Always-On Enterprise Information Systems for Modern Organizations* (pp. 60–87). Hershey, PA: IGI Global. doi:10.4018/978-1-5225-3704-5.ch004

van Wessel, R. M., de Vries, H. J., & Ribbers, P. M. (2016). Business Benefits through Company IT Standardization. In K. Jakobs (Ed.), *Effective Standardization Management in Corporate Settings* (pp. 34–53). Hershey, PA: IGI Global. doi:10.4018/978-1-4666-9737-9.ch003

Vargas-Hernández, J. G. (2017). Professional Integrity in Business Management Education. In N. Baporikar (Ed.), *Management Education for Global Leadership* (pp. 70–89). Hershey, PA: IGI Global. doi:10.4018/978-1-5225-1013-0.ch004

Vasista, T. G., & AlAbdullatif, A. M. (2017). Role of Electronic Customer Relationship Management in Demand Chain Management: A Predictive Analytic Approach. *International Journal of Information Systems and Supply Chain Management, 10*(1), 53–67. doi:10.4018/IJISSCM.2017010104

Vergidis, K. (2016). Rediscovering Business Processes: Definitions, Patterns, and Modelling Approaches. In P. Papajorgji, F. Pinet, A. Guimarães, & J. Papathanasiou (Eds.), *Automated Enterprise Systems for Maximizing Business Performance* (pp. 97–122). Hershey, PA: IGI Global. doi:10.4018/978-1-4666-8841-4.ch007

Vieru, D., & Bourdeau, S. (2017). Survival in the Digital Era: A Digital Competence-Based Multi-Case Study in the Canadian SME Clothing Industry. *International Journal of Social and Organizational Dynamics in IT, 6*(1), 17–34. doi:10.4018/IJSODIT.2017010102

Vijayan, G., & Kamarulzaman, N. H. (2017). An Introduction to Sustainable Supply Chain Management and Business Implications. In M. Khan, M. Hussain, & M. Ajmal (Eds.), *Green Supply Chain Management for Sustainable Business Practice* (pp. 27–50). Hershey, PA: IGI Global. doi:10.4018/978-1-5225-0635-5.ch002

Vlachvei, A., & Notta, O. (2017). Firm Competitiveness: Theories, Evidence, and Measurement. In A. Vlachvei, O. Notta, K. Karantininis, & N. Tsounis (Eds.), *Factors Affecting Firm Competitiveness and Performance in the Modern Business World* (pp. 1–42). Hershey, PA: IGI Global. doi:10.4018/978-1-5225-0843-4.ch001

von Rosing, M., Fullington, N., & Walker, J. (2016). Using the Business Ontology and Enterprise Standards to Transform Three Leading Organizations. *International Journal of Conceptual Structures and Smart Applications, 4*(1), 71–99. doi:10.4018/IJCSSA.2016010104

von Rosing, M., & von Scheel, H. (2016). Using the Business Ontology to Develop Enterprise Standards. *International Journal of Conceptual Structures and Smart Applications, 4*(1), 48–70. doi:10.4018/IJCSSA.2016010103

Walczak, S. (2016). Artificial Neural Networks and other AI Applications for Business Management Decision Support. *International Journal of Sociotechnology and Knowledge Development, 8*(4), 1–20. doi:10.4018/IJSKD.2016100101

Wamba, S. F., Akter, S., Kang, H., Bhattacharya, M., & Upal, M. (2016). The Primer of Social Media Analytics. *Journal of Organizational and End User Computing, 28*(2), 1–12. doi:10.4018/JOEUC.2016040101

Related References

Wang, C., Schofield, M., Li, X., & Ou, X. (2017). Do Chinese Students in Public and Private Higher Education Institutes Perform at Different Level in One of the Leadership Skills: Critical Thinking?: An Exploratory Comparison. In V. Wang (Ed.), *Encyclopedia of Strategic Leadership and Management* (pp. 160–181). Hershey, PA: IGI Global. doi:10.4018/978-1-5225-1049-9.ch013

Wang, F., Raisinghani, M. S., Mora, M., & Wang, X. (2016). Strategic E-Business Management through a Balanced Scored Card Approach. In I. Lee (Ed.), *Encyclopedia of E-Commerce Development, Implementation, and Management* (pp. 361–386). Hershey, PA: IGI Global. doi:10.4018/978-1-4666-9787-4.ch027

Wang, J. (2017). Multi-Agent based Production Management Decision System Modelling for the Textile Enterprise. *Journal of Global Information Management*, *25*(4), 1–15. doi:10.4018/JGIM.2017100101

Wiedemann, A., & Gewald, H. (2017). Examining Cross-Domain Alignment: The Correlation of Business Strategy, IT Management, and IT Business Value. *International Journal of IT/Business Alignment and Governance*, *8*(1), 17–31. doi:10.4018/IJITBAG.2017010102

Wolf, R., & Thiel, M. (2018). Advancing Global Business Ethics in China: Reducing Poverty Through Human and Social Welfare. In S. Hipsher (Ed.), *Examining the Private Sector's Role in Wealth Creation and Poverty Reduction* (pp. 67–84). Hershey, PA: IGI Global. doi:10.4018/978-1-5225-3117-3.ch004

Wu, J., Ding, F., Xu, M., Mo, Z., & Jin, A. (2016). Investigating the Determinants of Decision-Making on Adoption of Public Cloud Computing in E-government. *Journal of Global Information Management*, *24*(3), 71–89. doi:10.4018/JGIM.2016070104

Xu, L., & de Vrieze, P. (2016). Building Situational Applications for Virtual Enterprises. In I. Lee (Ed.), *Encyclopedia of E-Commerce Development, Implementation, and Management* (pp. 715–724). Hershey, PA: IGI Global. doi:10.4018/978-1-4666-9787-4.ch050

Yablonsky, S. (2018). Innovation Platforms: Data and Analytics Platforms. In *Multi-Sided Platforms (MSPs) and Sharing Strategies in the Digital Economy: Emerging Research and Opportunities* (pp. 72–95). Hershey, PA: IGI Global. doi:10.4018/978-1-5225-5457-8.ch003

Yusoff, A., Ahmad, N. H., & Halim, H. A. (2017). Agropreneurship among Gen Y in Malaysia: The Role of Academic Institutions. In N. Ahmad, T. Ramayah, H. Halim, & S. Rahman (Eds.), *Handbook of Research on Small and Medium Enterprises in Developing Countries* (pp. 23–47). Hershey, PA: IGI Global. doi:10.4018/978-1-5225-2165-5.ch002

Zanin, F., Comuzzi, E., & Costantini, A. (2018). The Effect of Business Strategy and Stock Market Listing on the Use of Risk Assessment Tools. In *Management Control Systems in Complex Settings: Emerging Research and Opportunities* (pp. 145–168). Hershey, PA: IGI Global. doi:10.4018/978-1-5225-3987-2.ch007

Zgheib, P. W. (2017). Corporate Innovation and Intrapreneurship in the Middle East. In P. Zgheib (Ed.), *Entrepreneurship and Business Innovation in the Middle East* (pp. 37–56). Hershey, PA: IGI Global. doi:10.4018/978-1-5225-2066-5.ch003

About the Contributors

Bryan Christiansen is the Chief Executive Officer of Tactical Systems, LLC in Indiana, USA. A former business lecturer at universities in Russia, Turkey, and the USA, he has traveled to 41 countries where he has conducted international business since 1985 in multiple languages and various industries with Global 500 firms and smaller. Christiansen received his Bachelor of Science degree in Marketing at the University of the State of New York in 1996 and his MBA degree at Capella University in 2003. The author of 29 Scopus-indexed Reference books on business, cultural studies, economics, and psychology, he is fluent in Chinese, Japanese, Spanish, and Turkish. Christiansen is currently working with a Russian theoretical mathematician on a new economic model for developing nations.

* * *

Yakup Arı is an Assistant Professor in the Department of Economics and Finance at Alanya Alaaddin Keykubat University. Having graduated with a bachelor's degree in Mathematics, he pursued an MBA degree in Finance and a PhD degree in Financial Economics – all of which at Yeditepe University. He worked as a statistical consultant at several private consultancy firms in Istanbul. He teaches courses in time series analysis, mathematical economics, technical analysis, probability and statistics, biostatistics and econometrics. His primary research interest lies in the area of time series analysis, Lévy driven stochastic processes, the Bayesian approach in statistics and econometrics, in addition to statistical methods in Engineering and Social Sciences.

Asmat Abdul-Talib teaches international business and international marketing at the Universiti Utara Malaysia. He received his PhD in International Marketing from Aston Business School, Aston University, UK, his MBA in International Business from Cardiff University, UK, and a Bachelors Degree in Economics from Concordia University, Canada. At current, his academic research has received financial support or support in kind from various institutions. His research interests

About the Contributors

lie primarily in international marketing and strategic marketing, especially in export market intelligence, and the use of export market intelligence in the firm's export decision process.

Murat Atalay received his MBA and Ph.D. in Business Administration from Akdeniz University. Currently, he is an Assistant Professor in the Kemer Maritime Faculty at Akdeniz University in Antalya. His research interests include organizational behaviour, organization theory, sociology of professions and maritime management.

Cinzia Colapinto joined Ca' Foscari University in 2011 as Assistant Professor of Strategy and Innovation. In the past she held academic positions at Nazarbayev University, Free University of Bozen and Universita' della Svizzera Italiana. Cinzia's research interests lie in the area of strategy-innovation interface, and decision making. She published in international refereed journals (including European Journal of Operational Research, Annals of Operations Research, Energy Policy, and Media Culture and Society). Cinzia has been a visiting scholar at London School of Economics and Political Science (United Kingdom), University of Canberra (Australia), Laurentian University (Canada), and Queensland University of Technology (Australia).

Evangelina Cruz Barba, Ph.D. in Education, Master in Business and Economic Studies and BA in Tourism from the University of Guadalajara. Professor at the Department of Social and Legal Sciences of the University of Guadalajara. Research interest: Education in economical administrative science environments.

Onur Dirlik is an assistant professor of management at Eskişehir Osmangazi University Business School. His research focuses on institutional change, Turkish business systems and varieties of capitalism. Currently, he is interested in how context-specific institutions differentiate organizational forms; how global, regional, national, and local influences affect organizations; and the power of the state in shaping the market. Onur Dirlik received his Ph.D. in Economics and Administrative Sciences from Akdeniz University, and he served as a Visiting Research Scholar at the European University Viadrina Frankfurt (Oder), Business School and as a Visiting Scholar at the Buffett Institute for Global Affairs at Northwestern University.

Nadia Japeri is a post graduate student at Universiti Utara Malaysia and her research is in marketing management and cross-cultural consumer analysis.

Janset Özen-Aytemur is an associate professor on management at Akdeniz University, Department of Business Administration. She received her MBA and

238

About the Contributors

Ph.D in Management and Organization from Akdeniz University. Her research interests include varieties of capitalism, business systems and management history.

Gordana Pesakovic holds a Ph.D. in Economics from the University in Belgrade, Master of Science in International Economics, BS in Economics with concentrations in Marketing and International Trade. She holds a graduate certificate from the Institute Agronomique Mediterranneen de Montpellier, France. Dr. Pesakovic has an extensive experience in economics and international business. Her teaching experience includes both undergraduate and graduate teaching in the areas of economics, international business, international economics, and cross-cultural studies. She has developed curriculums for different courses and programs, with economics and international business focus. Dr. Pesakovic is teaching in USA, China, Russia, Thailand, Chile, Argentina, Mexico, Serbia, Taiwan and Kyrgyzstan. Dr. Pesakovic served as Program Chair for Graduate and Undergraduate Business. She has published in professional journals and was contributing author in few books. Dr. Pesakovic received the Best Professor award.

Duane Windsor (PhD, Harvard University) is the Lynette S. Autrey Professor of Management in Rice University's Jesse H. Jones Graduate School of Business. A Rice alumnus, his research and teaching emphasize corporate social responsibility, sustainability, and the stakeholder theory of the firm. He investigates corruption and anti-corruption reform.

Index

A

Afghanistan 39-40, 43, 46, 48-50, 55, 58, 94, 101, 155
Anti-Corruption Reform 39-40, 42, 44, 49, 51, 55-58, 69
ARDL Bounds Test 70, 77, 79
Authoritarianism 39, 43-44, 51, 57-58, 62, 69

B

Bibliometric 69, 151, 154
Bootstrap Panel Granger Causality 1, 15, 41
Borat Effect 98-99, 102, 105
Brand Consciousness 106, 108-111, 113-116, 119-120, 124, 126
Brand Loyalty 107-109, 111-113, 115-116, 118-121, 123-126, 142

C

Captialism, Varieties of 128-129, 144, 146-147, 149
Caucasus Economies 17
Central Asia 15, 37, 39-40, 42-44, 46-47, 49-53, 55-60, 62-73, 85-86, 90-91, 93, 95, 97, 100-105, 127, 130-131, 137-140, 144, 146, 148, 152-155, 163
Central Asia, Tourism in 146
China 3, 6-7, 11, 14, 40-41, 43-44, 46, 48-49, 55-56, 58, 62-63, 65, 68, 72, 93, 102-103, 108, 129, 131, 155, 157, 175
Climate Change 2, 17
Constitutional Polity 69

Corruption

Corruption 39-51, 55-69, 133-134, 138, 144-145, 147
Corruption, Culture of 57, 69
Corruption, Grand 69
Corruption, Petty 69
Corruption, Political or Systemic 69
Curriculum 154, 162-170, 172

E

Economic Growth 1-2, 4-7, 11-22, 27, 30, 33-35, 37, 41, 51, 57, 61, 65, 85-86, 92, 132, 151-154, 156-160, 163-164, 168-174
EGARCH 70, 75-76, 78-79, 89
Electricity 19, 22, 27, 32-33, 38, 86
Emission 25, 27, 32-33, 38
Entrepreneurship 18-20, 26, 33-37, 67
Error Correction Models (ECM) 70

G

Goal Programming 18-20, 22-23, 27, 33, 35-37
Gross Domestic Product (GDP) 1, 3-8, 11-14, 16-19, 22, 27, 37, 56, 131-132, 134, 153, 156-159

H

Human Capital 32-33, 37, 41, 59, 129, 151-159, 164-165, 168, 171-173

Index

I

Institutional Context 127, 129-130, 137
International Trade 8, 71, 73, 86, 103, 154, 172

K

Kazakhstan 1-4, 7, 12-14, 17-19, 24, 26-28, 30, 32-33, 35-38, 43, 46, 48-51, 54-55, 58, 60-62, 64, 69-71, 91, 93-105, 127, 130-142, 144-150, 152, 155, 163, 171, 175
Kazakhstan, Tourism in 127, 135, 137, 163, 175
Kyrgyzstan 3, 17, 46, 48-51, 54-55, 57-58, 60-64, 69-71, 90, 93-95, 97, 101-102, 136, 155

L

Labour 18-19, 24, 26-28, 33, 36, 132-133, 143
Long-Run Sustainability 36

M

Malaysia 6, 32, 36, 106-108, 111, 114, 119-122, 157, 173
Mongolia 44, 46, 48-49, 55, 58, 101
Multi-Criteria 19-22, 35, 37

N

Nation Branding 90-105
National Business Systems 127-129, 144-146
Natural Gas Consumption 1-2, 4-8, 11-16
Natural Gas Exporters 1, 3, 17
Natural Gas Importers 17

P

Pakistan 6, 40, 43, 46, 48-49, 55, 94, 101, 156, 170
Paris Climate Change Agreement (COP21) 2, 17

Perception 59-60, 94, 97, 99-102, 106, 108-109, 111-112, 142, 162, 169

R

Romer 151, 153, 156, 159, 165, 174
Russia 3, 7, 12, 17, 40-41, 43-44, 46, 49-50, 54, 56, 58, 61-65, 72-73, 86, 93, 102, 131, 136, 143, 162, 170

S

Solow 151, 155-157, 159, 174
Students 32, 101, 106, 109-110, 114, 118-121, 123, 161-165, 172
Sustainability 2, 21-22, 26, 32-37, 123, 149

T

Tajikistan 3, 17, 46, 48-51, 54-55, 61, 69, 71, 155
Transdisciplinarity 167, 170
Transparency International 40, 44-47, 50, 55-56, 59, 65-66, 69, 133
Triple Helix approach 18
Triple Helix Model 21, 30, 38
Turkey 1, 6-7, 12, 14-15, 70-73, 79, 84, 86, 127, 136, 147
Turkmenistan 1-4, 7, 12-14, 17, 43, 46, 48-49, 51, 55, 58, 60-61, 64, 69-71, 155

U

Uzbekistan 1-4, 7, 12-14, 17, 43, 46, 48-52, 54-56, 58, 61-62, 64, 66, 69-71, 73, 87, 90, 93, 95-98, 101-102, 105, 136, 152, 155

V

Volatility 70-72, 74-75, 78-82, 84, 86-87

W

Weighted Goal Programming 18, 27, 35
World Bank 26, 37, 45, 48-50, 55-56, 67, 132-133, 149

Purchase Print, E-Book, or Print + E-Book

IGI Global's reference books can now be purchased from three unique pricing formats:
Print Only, E-Book Only, or Print + E-Book.
Shipping fees may apply.
www.igi-global.com

Recommended Reference Books

ISBN: 978-1-5225-6201-6
© 2019; 341 pp.
List Price: $345

ISBN: 978-1-5225-7262-6
© 2019; 360 pp.
List Price: $215

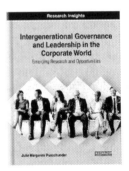

ISBN: 978-1-5225-8003-4
© 2019; 216 pp.
List Price: $205

ISBN: 978-1-5225-5763-0
© 2019; 304 pp.
List Price: $205

ISBN: 978-1-5225-6980-0
© 2019; 325 pp.
List Price: $235

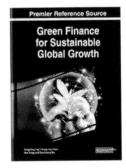

ISBN: 978-1-5225-7808-6
© 2019; 397 pp.
List Price: $215

Looking for free content, product updates, news, and special offers?
Join IGI Global's mailing list today and start enjoying exclusive perks sent only to IGI Global members.
Add your name to the list at **www.igi-global.com/newsletters**.

Publisher of Peer-Reviewed, Timely, and Innovative Academic Research

www.igi-global.com   Sign up at www.igi-global.com/newsletters   facebook.com/igiglobal   twitter.com/igiglobal

Ensure Quality Research is Introduced to the Academic Community

Become an IGI Global Reviewer for Authored Book Projects

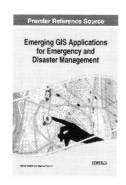   

The overall success of an authored book project is dependent on quality and timely reviews.

In this competitive age of scholarly publishing, constructive and timely feedback significantly expedites the turnaround time of manuscripts from submission to acceptance, allowing the publication and discovery of forward-thinking research at a much more expeditious rate. Several IGI Global authored book projects are currently seeking highly-qualified experts in the field to fill vacancies on their respective editorial review boards:

Applications and Inquiries may be sent to:
development@igi-global.com

Applicants must have a doctorate (or an equivalent degree) as well as publishing and reviewing experience. Reviewers are asked to complete the open-ended evaluation questions with as much detail as possible in a timely, collegial, and constructive manner. All reviewers' tenures run for one-year terms on the editorial review boards and are expected to complete at least three reviews per term. Upon successful completion of this term, reviewers can be considered for an additional term.

If you have a colleague that may be interested in this opportunity, we encourage you to share this information with them.

IGI Global Proudly Partners With eContent Pro International

Receive a 25% Discount on all Editorial Services

Editorial Services

IGI Global expects all final manuscripts submitted for publication to be in their final form. This means they must be reviewed, revised, and professionally copy edited prior to their final submission. Not only does this support with accelerating the publication process, but it also ensures that the highest quality scholarly work can be disseminated.

English Language Copy Editing

Let eContent Pro International's expert copy editors perform edits on your manuscript to resolve spelling, punctuaion, grammar, syntax, flow, formatting issues and more.

Scientific and Scholarly Editing

Allow colleagues in your research area to examine the content of your manuscript and provide you with valuable feedback and suggestions before submission.

Figure, Table, Chart & Equation Conversions

Do you have poor quality figures? Do you need visual elements in your manuscript created or converted? A design expert can help!

Translation

Need your documjent translated into English? eContent Pro International's expert translators are fluent in English and more than 40 different languages.

Hear What Your Colleagues are Saying About Editorial Services Supported by IGI Global

"The service was very fast, very thorough, and very helpful in ensuring our chapter meets the criteria and requirements of the book's editors. I was quite impressed and happy with your service."

– Prof. Tom Brinthaupt,
Middle Tennessee State University, USA

"I found the work actually spectacular. The editing, formatting, and other checks were very thorough. The turnaround time was great as well. I will definitely use eContent Pro in the future."

– Nickanor Amwata, Lecturer,
University of Kurdistan Hawler, Iraq

"I was impressed that it was done timely, and wherever the content was not clear for the reader, the paper was improved with better readability for the audience."

– Prof. James Chilembwe,
Mzuzu University, Malawi

Email: customerservice@econtentpro.com   www.igi-global.com/editorial-service-partners

Celebrating Over 30 Years of Scholarly Knowledge Creation & Dissemination

www.igi-global.com

InfoSci®-Books

A Database of Over 5,300+ Reference Books Containing Over 100,000+ Chapters Focusing on Emerging Research

GAIN ACCESS TO **THOUSANDS** OF REFERENCE BOOKS AT **A FRACTION** OF THEIR INDIVIDUAL LIST **PRICE.**

InfoSci®-Books Database

The **InfoSci®-Books** database is a collection of over 5,300+ IGI Global single and multi-volume reference books, handbooks of research, and encyclopedias, encompassing groundbreaking research from prominent experts worldwide that span over 350+ topics in 11 core subject areas including business, computer science, education, science and engineering, social sciences and more.

Open Access Fee Waiver (Offset Model) Initiative

For any library that invests in IGI Global's InfoSci-Journals and/or InfoSci-Books databases, IGI Global will match the library's investment with a fund of equal value to go toward **subsidizing the OA article processing charges (APCs) for their students, faculty, and staff** at that institution when their work is submitted and accepted under OA into an IGI Global journal.*

INFOSCI® PLATFORM FEATURES

- No DRM
- No Set-Up or Maintenance Fees
- A Guarantee of No More Than a 5% Annual Increase
- Full-Text HTML and PDF Viewing Options
- Downloadable MARC Records
- Unlimited Simultaneous Access
- COUNTER 5 Compliant Reports
- Formatted Citations With Ability to Export to RefWorks and EasyBib
- No Embargo of Content (Research is Available Months in Advance of the Print Release)

*The fund will be offered on an annual basis and expire at the end of the subscription period. The fund would renew as the subscription is renewed for each year thereafter. The open access fees will be waived after the student, faculty, or staff's paper has been vetted and accepted into an IGI Global journal and the fund can only be used toward publishing OA in an IGI Global journal. Libraries in developing countries will have the match on their investment doubled.

To Learn More or To Purchase This Database:
www.igi-global.com/infosci-books

eresources@igi-global.com • Toll Free: 1-866-342-6657 ext. 100 • Phone: 717-533-8845 x100

www.igi-global.com